PUBLICATIONS OF THE GERMAN HISTORICAL INSTITUTE
WASHINGTON, D.C.

Edited by Christof Mauch
with the assistance of David Lazar

The German Historical Institute is a center for advanced study and research whose purpose is to provide a permanent basis for scholarly cooperation among historians from the Federal Republic of Germany and the United States. The Institute conducts, promotes, and supports research into both American and German political, social, economic, and cultural history; into transatlantic migration, especially in the nineteenth and twentieth centuries; and into the history of international relations, with special emphasis on the roles played by the United States and Germany.

Recent books in the series:

Manfred Berg and Martin H. Geyer, editors, *Two Cultures of Rights: The Quest for Inclusion and Participation in Modern America and Germany*

Elizabeth Glaser and Hermann Wellenreuther, editors, *Bridging the Atlantic: The Question of American Exceptionalism in Perspective*

Jürgen Heideking and James A. Henretta, editors, *Republicanism and Liberalism in America and the German States, 1750–1850*

Hubert Zimmermann, *Money and Security: Troops, Monetary Policy, and West Germany's Relations with the United States and Britain, 1950–1971*

Roger Chickering and Stig Förster, editors, *The Shadows of Total War: Europe, East Asia, and the United States, 1919–1939*

Richard J. Bessel and Dirk Schumann, editors, *Life after Death: Approaches to a Cultural and Social History of Europe During the 1940s and 1950s*

Marc Flandreau, Carl-Ludwig Holtfrerich, and Harold James, editors, *International Financial History in the Twentieth Century: System and Anarchy*

Andreas W. Daum, Lloyd C. Gardner, and Wilfried Mausbach, editors, *The Vietnam War and the World: International and Comparative Perspectives*

Detlef Junker, editor, *The United States and Germany in the Era of the Cold War: A Handbook*, 2 volumes

A World at Total War

GLOBAL CONFLICT AND THE POLITICS OF DESTRUCTION, 1937–1945

Edited by

ROGER CHICKERING
Georgetown University

STIG FÖRSTER
University of Bern

BERND GREINER
Hamburg Institute for Social Research

GERMAN HISTORICAL INSTITUTE
Washington, D.C.
and

CAMBRIDGE
UNIVERSITY PRESS

CAMBRIDGE UNIVERSITY PRESS
Cambridge, New York, Melbourne, Madrid, Cape Town, Singapore,
São Paulo, Delhi, Dubai, Tokyo, Mexico City

Cambridge University Press
The Edinburgh Building, Cambridge CB2 8RU, UK

Published in the United States of America by Cambridge University Press, New York

www.cambridge.org
Information on this title: www.cambridge.org/9780521155137

First published 2005
First paperback edition 2010

A catalogue record for this publication is available from the British Library

Library of Congress Cataloguing in Publication Data
A world at total war : global conflict and the politics of destruction, 1937–1945 / edited by
Roger Chickering, Stig Förster, Bernd Greiner.
p. cm. – (Publications of the German Historical Institute)
Results of a fifth conference on the history of total war held in Aug. 2001, in Hamburg.
Includes bibliographical references and index.
ISBN 0-521-83432-5
1. World War, 1939–1945. 2. Total war. I. Chickering, Roger, 1942– II. Förster, Stig.
III. Greiner, Bernd. IV. German Historical Institute (Washington, D.C.) V. Series.
D743.W63 2005
940.53–dc22 2004046563

ISBN 978-0-521-83432-2 Hardback
ISBN 978-0-521-15513-7 Paperback

Contents

Contributors

John Barber
King's College, Cambridge University

Birgit Beck
University of Bern

Stephen Broadberry
University of Warwick

Roger Chickering
Georgetown University

Jürgen Förster
Militärgeschichtliches Forschungsamt (retired)
(Research Institute for Military History)

Stig Förster
University of Bern

Bernd Greiner
Hamburger Institut für Sozialforschung
(Hamburg Institute for Social Research)

Myriam Gessler
University of Bern

Mark Harrison
University of Warwick

Holger H. Herwig
University of Calgary

Michael Howard
Oxford University (retired)

Peter Howlett
London School of Economics

Martin Kutz
Führungsakademie der Bundeswehr, Hamburg
(Officers Academy of Bundeswehr)

Robert L. Messer
University of Illinois at Chicago

Hans Mommsen
Ruhr-Universität Bochum (retired)

Hans-Heinrich Nolte
University of Hannover

Richard Overy
King's College, London

Daniel Marc Segesser
University of Bern

Dennis Showalter
Colorado College

Jill Stephenson
University of Edinburgh

Hew Strachan
All Souls College, Oxford University

Gerhard L. Weinberg
University of North Carolina (retired)

Louise Young
University of Wisconsin

A World at Total War

GLOBAL CONFLICT AND THE POLITICS OF DESTRUCTION, 1937–1945

Are We There Yet?

World War II and the Theory of Total War

ROGER CHICKERING AND STIG FÖRSTER

In the vast library that now houses the historical literature on World War II, the volume that Gordon Wright published more than forty years ago occupies a special place.[1] It is one of the shortest books in the entire collection. It is also perhaps the most comprehensive survey ever published on the war in the European theater. It ranges over military operations, the diplomacy of war, the mobilization of economies and popular morale, occupation and resistance, psychological warfare, the harnessing of science and technology to destruction, and the war's revolutionary impact on society and culture. The volume is remarkable in an additional respect. Although it bears the title *The Ordeal of Total War*, it proffers neither a sustained discussion nor a definition of this pivotal term. Instead, it appears to argue by implication that World War II was paradigmatic, that the defining feature of total war was the very enormity of its scope and impact, and that such a degree of comprehensiveness made this conflict a singular phenomenon in military history.

This is a defensible argument that other historians of the Second World War have embraced in the same axiomatic spirit, which has had to work in lieu of analytical reflection.[2] However, at the conclusion of a series of volumes on total war, it seems appropriate to reexamine some of the premises of this argument. Defining the Second World War as the paradigmatic instance of total war has important methodological ramifications, which pertain above all to issues of narrative logic. The central analytical questions revolve around the degree to which this war resembled its predecessors – particularly,

1 Gordon Wright, *The Ordeal of Total War, 1939–1945* (New York, 1968).
2 See Peter Calvororessi and Guy Wint, *Total War: Causes and Courses of the Second World War* (New York, 1979); David Jablonsky, *Churchill, the Great Game, and Total War* (London and Portland, OR, 1991); Michael A. Barnhart, *Japan Prepares for Total War: The Search for Economic Security, 1919–1941* (Ithaca, 1987).

1

given the purview of this series of volumes, the American Civil War and the First World War.[3]

Four previous volumes have failed to produce a definition of total war that can command general assent. The most common and practical approach has been to treat total war as an "ideal type," a model that features a number of salient characteristics, elements, or ingredients.[4] Most of these indices pertain to the same expanding parameters of warfare that Gordon Wright's volume emphasized. Total war, in this rendering, assumes the commitment of massive armed forces to battle, the thoroughgoing mobilization of industrial economies in the war effort, and hence the disciplined organization of civilians no less than warriors. Other hallmarks of total war have proved more difficult to measure. Total war erodes not only the limits on the size and scope of the war effort: it also encourages the radicalization of warfare, the abandonment of the last restraints on combat, which were hitherto imposed by law, moral codes, or simple civility. Moreover, in order to sustain popular commitment to the war effort, governments pursue extravagant, uncompromising war aims; and they justify these goals through the systematic demonization of the enemy. Finally – and in the eyes of some authors, most characteristically – total war is marked by the systematic erasure of basic distinctions between soldiers and civilians. Because civilians, regardless of gender, are no less significant to the war effort than the soldiers, they themselves become legitimate if not preferred targets of military violence.

By all these hallmarks, the evidence speaks powerfully to the "totality" of the Second World War – to the unique degree to which this conflict approximated the ideal type. By a significant margin, this was the most immense and costly war ever fought. If coastal waters are counted, its theaters of combat extended to every continent save Antarctica. It involved most of the sovereign states on the planet, the bulk of the world's population, and the largest armed forces ever assembled. Well over seventy million human beings were mobilized for military service. This was the quintessential "deep war."[5] Economies were massively reoriented everywhere to war; in most of the belligerent countries, military production accounted for well over half of capital investment and GNP, while a majority of the civilian workforce,

---

3 Stig Förster and Jörg Nagler, eds., *On the Road to Total War: The American Civil War and the German Wars of Unification, 1861–1871* (Cambridge, 1997); Manfred Boemeke, Roger Chickering, and Stig Förster, eds., *Anticipating Total War: The German and American Experiences, 1871–1914* (Cambridge, 1999); Roger Chickering and Stig Förster, eds., *Great War, Total War: Combat and Mobilization on the Western Front, 1914–1918* (Cambridge, 2000); Roger Chickering and Stig Förster, eds., *The Shadows of Total War: Europe, East Asia, and the United States, 1919–1939* (Cambridge, 2003).

4 Chickering and Förster, "Introduction," *Shadows of Total War.*

5 Richard Overy, *Why the Allies Won* (New York and London, 1995), 190.

both male and female, was absorbed, along with millions of prisoners of war and deportees, into producing and delivering the tools of destruction to the warriors.[6]

The Second World War set other standards as well. Once announced at the Casablanca conference in early 1943, the doctrine of "unconditional surrender" symbolized the abandonment of compromise by all sides as they pursued the military defeat of their enemies.[7] The brutal handling of Soviet prisoners of war by the German army and the cruelties Japanese and American forces inflicted on one another signaled a savagery in combat that was – in the modern era at least – unprecedented in both its extent and routinization.[8] In the European and Pacific theaters alike, it fed on the same dehumanizing popular stereotypes that drove the mobilization of civilians on the home front.[9] These stereotypes also underlay perhaps the most telling statistics of the war, which speak to the ratio of civilian-to-military casualties. The numbers remain necessarily vague, for many of the casualties occurred in circumstances, particularly in China, Poland, and the Soviet Union, that were calculated to make the accounting difficult. J. David Singer and Melvin Small have estimated a total of fifteen million soldiers killed in all theaters, which is probably a conservative figure.[10] It pales, in any event, in the face of civilian deaths that doubtless exceeded forty-five million.[11] The preponderance of civilians was no accidental or peripheral feature of this war; it reflected the central significance of civilians in the conflict, the indispensable roles that they played in the war's outcome, as well as the vulnerabilities that they shared, as a direct consequence, with the soldiers.

Rehearsing these "total" features of the Second World War risks belaboring the obvious. The paradigmatic significance of the Second World War has become orthodox in the literature on this great ordeal, and Gordon Wright could surely plead that the proposition needed little justification or elaboration. Since 1945, the same proposition has also lent the Second World War a special place in the broader history of warfare in the modern era. The

6 Alan Milward, *War, Economy, and Society, 1939–1945* (Berkeley and Los Angeles, 1979); Mark Harrison, ed., *The Economics of World War II: Six Great Powers in International Comparison* (Cambridge, 1998).

7 Alfred Vagts, "Unconditional Surrender – vor und nach 1945," *Vierteljahrshefte für Zeitschichte* 7 (1959): 280–309.

8 Christian Streit, *Keine Kameraden: Die Wehrmacht und die sowjetischen Kriegsgefangenen 1941–1945* (2d ed., Bonn, 1997).

9 John W. Dower, *War without Mercy: Race and Power in the Pacific War* (New York, 1986).

10 J. David Singer and Melvin Small, *The Wages of War, 1816–1965: A Statistical Handbook* (New York, 1972), 67.

11 See Gerhard Weinberg, *A World at Arms: A Global History of World War II* (Cambridge, 1994), 894.

paradigmatic status of this war, its privileged proximity to the ideal type, has provided the structuring principle in what one might call the "master narrative" of modern military history.[12]

The narrative conventionally begins in the era of the French Revolution, which saw the first modern attempts to mobilize entire populaces in support of a war and ushered in an era of "peoples' wars." The technologies and productive capacities that were then liberated during the industrialization of the nineteenth century furnished the material wherewithal to equip, feed, and transport the mass armies whose ideological credentials had been defined during the revolutionary era. Industrialism also multiplied the difficulties of providing material support to the new field armies; and to this end, waging war required the efficient organization of modern economies and the mobilization of durable loyalties among the civilian workforce. Success in these efforts marked a major moment in the history of warfare. "Industrialized peoples' war" in the nineteenth century, the marriage of industrialization with popularly mandated and recruited armies, provided the material basis of total war in the twentieth.

The history of warfare since the middle of the nineteenth century can thus be portrayed as the halting yet inexorable march toward the practical realization of total war, the ever-closer approximation of the ideal type. The American Civil War revealed in inchoate form the institutions and practices that gauged the subsequent development of warfare, including huge armies, the industrial manufacture and transportation of their supplies, and the exhaustion and utter defeat of one of the belligerents. In this connection, precocious significance attaches to the names of Grant, Sheridan, and Sherman, who early understood the ramifications of industrial mobilization and the importance of civilian morale to the war's outcome. In this reading, the First World War differed from the Civil War less in its basic dynamics than in its scale, as well as in the sophistication with which industrial technologies and organization were marshaled to military ends. These developments resulted between 1914 and 1918 in a war of such immense proportions that it defied a decision-at-arms and remanded the outcome to the home front. The exertions of civilians were ultimately the deciding factor.

The Second World War stands at the end of the story, the goal of 150 years of military history. In its dynamics, this vast conflict resembled its two major predecessors, for it witnessed the perfection of features of modern warfare that had been earlier introduced and cultivated. Now, however, all

---

12 Chickering, "Total War: The Use and Abuse of a Concept," in Boemeke, Chickering, and Förster, *Anticipating Total War*, 13–28.

the elements of "totality" – the mobilization of belligerent societies, the exploitation of material and moral resources to military ends, and the systematic implication of civilians in war – were brought to their fulfillment.

The logic of this progression permeates textbooks that have been written since 1945 on modern military history. It has also provided the foundation for this series of volumes, which has mapped the "road to total war" from 1861 to 1945, from its putative beginnings in practice to its destination. To a large degree, the previous volumes thus prefigure the present one. These volumes have testified to the power and persistence of an analytical framework that arrays three great wars along a single narrative axis, whose culmination is situated in the Second World War. The preceding volumes have also offered cautions, however, about the analytical hazards that lurk within this framework; and some of these cautions deserve another hearing, for they pertain with special force to the historical place of the Second World War.

It bears emphasis in the first place that this grand narrative entails, like all historical narratives, an exercise in teleological thinking. If Hayden White is correct, historians must engage in this exercise if they hope to provide a structured or coherent account of the past.[13] They can, however, attend to the dangers of what the literary scholar Michael Andre Bernstein has recently called, in connection with the Holocaust, "backshadowing" or a "kind of retroactive foreshadowing" of past events.[14] Defining the Second World War as the telos of modern military history establishes the narrative perspective on preceding developments in compelling ways. It requires the framing of earlier conflicts as efforts in anticipation or approximation of institutions and practices that found subsequent fulfillment. The question "How total was the American Civil War (or the Great War)?" translates into "How much was the American Civil War (or the First World War) like the Second World War?" The question itself flirts with "retroactive foreshadowing" in two ways. For one thing, it is not a historical question. It judges the earlier conflicts by criteria that were defined only later in a different historical context. And by virtue of the very terms in which it is posed, the question privileges the similarities and continuities among these wars.

The earlier volumes have struggled with these problems, even as they have insisted on the importance of comparing the major wars of the modern era – an undertaking that requires some kind of analytical denominator. The

---

13 Hayden White, *Metahistory: The Historical Imagination in Nineteenth-Century Europe* (Baltimore and London, 1973).

14 Michael Andre Bernstein, *Foregone Conclusions: Against Apocalyptic History* (Berkeley and Los Angeles, 1994), 16.

essays in these volumes have provided compelling evidence that the "road to total war" was anything but straight and narrow. Contingency, accident, and inadvertence figured prominently between the way stations. Nothing inevitable or foreordained drove the progression to the monster war of the mid-twentieth century. The earlier contests differed from the last – and from one another – in essential ways. The first volume made clear that the American Civil War was in major respects a limited, primitive conflict. Many people on both sides remained untouched; and even the most notorious acts of war committed against noncombatants, the campaigns of Sheridan and Sherman, observed constraints that discouraged the loss of civilian life.[15] The second volume, which addressed the era between the Civil War and the Great War, documented the near-universal failure of observers, military as well as civilian, to recognize the portents of the latter conflict in the former.[16] The third volume, which dealt with the First World War, likewise laid bare the extent to which institutions conventionally associated with total war took shape eclectically, with no precedents or foresight whatsoever, while in other respects, such as the techniques used to finance it, the Great War resembled the Napoleonic Wars more than it did the war that followed.[17] The First World War was itself limited in basic respects. Its hallmark, strategic stalemate on the western front, rendered the combat a protracted siege, which confined the scope of operations and reduced the scope of violence that could be inflicted on civilians, at least in this part of Europe.[18]

Stressing the limitations, the unachieved "totality" of the American Civil War and the Great War, conforms to a master narrative that culminates in the Second World War. Insofar as it casts limitation in an aura of insufficiency or imperfection, however, this emphasis imputes characteristics to this last struggle that are hard to demonstrate. The rhetorical extravagance of the

15 Mark E. Neely, Jr., "Was the Civil War a Total War?" Förster and Nagler, in *On the Road to Total War*, 29–53; cf. James M. McPherson, "From Limited War to Total War in America," ibid., 295–310; Herman M. Hattaway, "The Civil War Armies: Creation, Mobilization, and Development," ibid., 173–98; Stanley L. Engermann and J. Matthew Gallman, "The Civil War Economy: A Modern View," ibid., 217–48.

16 Gerald D. Feldman, "Hugo Stinnes and the Prospect of War before 1914," in Chickering and Förster, *Anticipating Total War*, 77–96; John Whiteclay Chambers, "The American Debate over Modern War, 1871–1914," ibid., 241–80; Thomas Rohkrämer, "Heroes and Would-Be Heroes: Veterans' and Reservists' Associations in Imperial Germany," ibid., 189–216; cf. Stig Förster, "Dreams and Nightmares: German Military Leadership and the Images of Future Warfare, 1871–1914," ibid., 343–76.

17 Elizabeth Glaser, "Better Late than Never: The American War Effort, 1917–1918," in Chickering and Förster, *Great War, Total War*, 389–408; Niall Ferguson, "How (Not) to Pay for the War: Traditional Finance and 'Total' War," ibid., 409–34; Roger Chickering, "World War I and the Theory of Total War: Reflections on the British and German Cases, 1914–1915," ibid., 35–53.

18 Hew Strachan, "From Cabinet War to Total War: The Perspective of Military Doctrine, 1861–1918," ibid., 19–34.

word "total" is itself a major obstacle to a sober appreciation of the Second World War, for it tends to equate "totality" with fulfillment, which in the governing narrative logic implies the removal of every restraint in the conduct of war.

The Second World War resists this characterization. It, too, remained limited in significant respects. While the theaters of war sprawled around the globe, combat was concentrated overwhelmingly in Central and Eastern Europe and East Asia, while large parts of the planet's landmass, including sub-Saharan Africa and the entire Western Hemisphere, remained largely exempt. The destruction of civilian life and property observed the same geographical confinements. Economic mobilization was by no means uniformly "deep." Richard Overy's words are worth pondering in this connection. "Throughout the war," he writes, "the German economy produced far fewer weapons than its raw resources of materials, manpower, scientific skill and factory floorspace could have made possible."[19] The same proposition was true of all the other belligerents, save possibly the Soviet Union.[20] Although the American economy registered prodigious productive achievements, it was far less dislocated, regimented, or intensively committed to the war effort than were the economies of the other major belligerent countries. The mobilization of the American armed forces, which featured the "Ninety-Division Gamble," left vast reserves of manpower unexploited.[21] Civilian life was likewise far less disrupted in this country than elsewhere by shortages of food, resources, or labor. Consumer purchases rose, amid what David Kennedy has recently called "loosely supervised affluence," by 12 percent between 1939 and 1944.[22] In sum, to characterize as "total mobilization" the experience of war in the United States, the pivotal participant in this total war, is to indulge in hyperbole.

Other features of the Second World War likewise blemish easy generalizations about its "totality." Save again in the Soviet Union, the mobilization of armed forces deferred to limits dictated by traditional gender roles, for nowhere else were women allowed into combat roles. The reluctance of all sides to employ poison gas against one another in the European theater was

19 Overy, *Why the Allies Won*, 198; cf. Alan Milward, *The German Economy at War* (London, 1965); Ludolf Herbst, *Der totale Krieg und die Ordnung der Wirtschaft: Die Kriegswirtschaft im Spannungsfeld von Politik, Ideologie und Propaganda 1939–1945* (Stuttgart, 1982).
20 Mark Harrison, *The Soviet Home Front, 1941–1945: A Social and Economic History of the U.S.S.R. in World War II* (London, 1991); cf. Harrison, *The Economics of World War II*.
21 Maurice Matloff, "The Ninety-Division Gamble," in Kent Roberts Greenfield, *Command Decisions* (Washington, DC, 1960), 365–81.
22 David Kennedy, *Freedom from Fear: The American People in Depression and War, 1929–1945* (New York, 1999), 664; Milward, *War, Economy, and Society*, 63.

due to practical calculations of interest, but it also represented an apprecia-
ble act of restraint.[23] The treatment of prisoners of war was not universally
savage; and those who fell captive in Western Europe or North Africa could
expect, as a rule, to survive in reasonably humane conditions.[24] The doctrine of "unconditional surrender" was admittedly declared to exclude the
prospect of a compromise peace, but it was motivated in no small part by
British and American fears, which were not entirely groundless, that the
Soviet Union was prepared to accept just such a peace with the Axis.[25]

Finally, the master narrative of total war comports uneasily with the fact
that the Second World War was in significant ways "less total" than its
predecessors. Thanks to the ruthless exploitation of human and material
resources in occupied Europe, life on the German home front was, by a
wide margin, less disrupted or deprived during most of the Second World
War than it had been during the First.[26] The war aims of the Western Allies
involved far less violence to basic social institutions in the Axis states than
the Union forces had earlier imposed on the Confederacy in the Civil War.
Unlike slavery in the American South, the legal and institutional foundations
of German, Italian, and Japanese capitalism were not at issue. In this respect,
only the Soviet Union among the Allies fought for anything that might be
called "total war aims" – a characterization that is modeled largely on the
racial utopia that the Nazis sought to create in Eastern Europe.

All these conundrums address isolated aspects of the Second World War,
but they are numerous and central enough to enjoin caution about the
master narrative that has conventionally defined the significance of this war
in military history. They also lend support to an alternative of this narrative.
This one is less immediately dependent on an ideal type for its structure;
instead, it addresses total war as a narrower, more concrete phenomenon
whose meaning and contours emerged in a specific historical context.

The key to this reading lies in the fourth volume of the series, which
considered the period between the two world wars.[27] This volume was the
first to confront the problem of total war on its own historical terrain, for

23 Weinberg, *World at Arms*, 558–60.
24 See S. P. MacKenzie, "The Treatment of Prisoners of War in World War II," *Journal of Modern History*
   66 (1994): 487–520; Arnold Krammer, "German Prisoners of War in the United States," *Military
   Affairs* 40 (1976): 68–73.
25 Ingeborg Fleischhauer, *Die Chance des Sonderfriedens: Deutsch-sowjetische Geheimgespräche 1941–1945*
   (Berlin, 1986); H. W. Koch, "The Spectre of a Separate Peace in the East: Russo-German 'Peace
   Feelers,' 1942–44," *Journal of Contemporary History* 10 (1975): 531–49; Bernd Martin, *Friedensinitia-
   tiven und Machtpolitik im Zweiten Weltkrieg 1939–1942* (Düsseldorf, 1974).
26 Lothar Burchardt, "Die Auswirkungen der Kriegswirtschaft auf die deutsche Zivilbevölkerung im
   Ersten und im Zweiten Weltkrieg," *Militärgeschichtliche Mitteilungen*, No. 1 (1974): 65–97.
27 Chickering and Förster, *Shadows of Total War*.

only in the interwar period did the term surface in professional and popular discourse. Erich Ludendorff's pamphlet *Der totale Krieg*, which appeared in 1935, played the principal role in popularizing the term, but its author was by no means an original thinker.[28] The honor of paternity belonged instead to French civilian leaders who, during the late phase of the Great War, coined the terms *guerre totale* and *guerre intégrale* in announcing their ambitions to mobilize the country's every resource.

The vision of total war took on more specific contours and connotations after the war.[29] Central in this process were debates over strategic airpower. So was popular interest in the new regimes in the Soviet Union and Fascist Italy, both of which invoked the experience of the Great War as they attempted to establish the material and moral mobilization of society as a principle of rule. The propagandists of the latter regime coined the word "totalitarian" in the mid-1920s to describe the Italian designs. The word thereupon migrated northward, where it fed the ideas of several German neo-Hegelian scholars who were sketching out a "total" theory of state, which likewise invoked the mobilization of society for war as a normative principle. The most influential voice in this discourse was that of the writer Ernst Jünger, who in 1930 introduced the term "total mobilization." In 1934, the term modulated for the first time into "total war" in the German military literature.[30]

Several aspects of this story are significant here. In the first place, the term total war gestated historically amid ideological debate; and it was born with far-reaching political implications. Ludendorff's vision of total war featured the centralization of power over the entire war effort in the hands of soldiers. This proposition was bitterly contested before it was everywhere rejected. Many other figures, from Alfred Jodl to Joseph Goebbels, subsequently invoked the idea of total war to justify the ambitions of their own agencies in Nazi Germany's bureaucratic wars; and the term was similarly exploited in bureaucratic struggles elsewhere during the Second World War.[31] The

28 Hans-Ulrich Wehler, "'Absoluter' und 'totaler' Krieg: Von Clauseweitz zu Ludendorff," *Politische Vierteljahresschrift* 19 (1969): 220–48; cf. Roger Chickering, "Sore Loser: Ludendorff's Total War," in Chickering and Förster, *Shadows of Total War.*

29 See now the comprehensive analysis of the interwar discourse in Stig Förster, ed., *An der Schwelle zum Totalen Krieg: Die militärische Debatte über den Krieg der Zukunft* (Paderborn, 2002).

30 Markus Pöhlmann, "Von Versailles nach Armageddon: Totalisierungserfahrung und Kriegserwartung in deutschen Militärzeitschriften," ibid., 346–51.

31 Jost Dülffer, "Vom Bündnispartner zum Erfüllungsgehilfen im totalen Krieg: Militär und Gesellschaft in Deutschland," in Wolfgang Michalka, *Der Zweite Weltkrieg: Analysen, Grundzüge, Forschungsbilanz* (Munich, 1989), 297–98; Peter Longerich, "Joseph Goebbels und der totale Krieg: Eine unbekannte Denkschrift des Propagandaministers vom 18. Juli 1944," *Vierteljahrshefte für Zeitgeschichte* 35 (1987): 289–314; cf. Hans Wenke, "Zur Philosophie des totalen Krieges," in Wenke, ed., *Geistige Gestalten*

polemical overtones that have attached to the idea of total war since its birth serve as an additional caution against its uncritical deployment as a tool of historical analysis.[32]

The early history of total war also suggests, however, chronological markers narrower than the modern era for using the concept in historical analysis. Total war was born of one twentieth-century European war in anticipation of another. In all its variations, its reference point was the Great War and the critical place of civilian mobilization in this conflict. The concept served simultaneously as an analysis of one great war and a vision of the next. To this extent, the Second World War was in fact supposed to represent the fulfillment of trends marked out by the First, for in the German discourse at least, total war implied the redressing of mistakes committed by the country's military and civilian leadership during the Great War. The object of the whole enterprise was to ensure more coordination between the elements of the German leadership, to exert more ruthless control over morale on the home front, and to mobilize resources more effectively for use at the battlefront.

These features of the concept point finally to another truth. Total war was historically not in the first instance about soldiers. The vision rested instead on the insight that the claims of industrial war had become all-embracing, that they demanded the loyal participation of entire populations – men, women, and children – and that civilians had become more important than soldiers to the outcome of modern war. One might therefore mark the debut of total war in the second half of the Great War, at about the time that contemporary observers started employing the term to describe their own efforts to drive the mobilization of the home front to new extremes. The juncture found its symbols in the accession of Ludendorff, Lloyd George, and Clemenceau to power in 1916 and 1917, for all of these leaders recognized that stalemate on the battlefield had turned the home front into the decisive dimension of the war. The scope of military activity had broadened to require the ruthless reorganization of industrial production and civilian energies. Military victory demanded the regimented commitment of productive forces at home no less than of armed forces at the front. And the home front, no less than the fighting front, was logically a legitimate theater of direct military action.

und Probleme: Festschrift für Eduard Spranger (Leipzig, 1942), 266–89; John Burnham, *Total War: The Economic Theory of a War Economy* (Boston, 1943).

32 See Fabio Crivellari, "Der Wille zum totalen Krieg," Arbeitskreis Militärgeschichte, *Newsletter* 12 (2000): 10–14.

In this sense, in the playing out of this logic, the Second World War did in significant respects represent the consummation of the First. The war against civilians of all descriptions achieved a virtuosity in the second war that became conceivable only in the aftermath of the first, as retrospective analysis of the Great War riveted attention on the civilians' role in the outcome – particularly, however, on their deficiencies and vulnerabilities. The conclusion seemed inescapable. Civilians were critical to the supply of weapons, munitions, and the other essential materials of combat, and they provided the moral backing without which the war could not be sustained. However, civilians were also more vulnerable to both subversion and military attack, for they were less acclimated to the terrors, deprivations, and demoralization of war. The *Dolchstoss*, the "stab in the back," legend drew much of its force from this observation. The German military leadership genuinely believed that the moral collapse of the home front in 1918 had wrecked what would otherwise have been a victorious military campaign. They concluded that in a future war the civilian front would again constitute the weakest dimension of any belligerent's war effort, hence the most vulnerable and inviting target of an enemy's attentions.

The Germans were in good company in this reasoning. Their logic corresponded to the thinking of military planners elsewhere, above all to the calculations of strategic airpower's early enthusiasts, who likewise reasoned that attacking "soft" civilian targets offered the most feasible, if not the only way to break the frontline stalemate that inhered, they believed, in modern industrial warfare. "Future wars will be total in character and scope," wrote Guilio Douhet in 1921. From this premise, he reasoned that "merciless pounding from the air" held the key to victory. "A complete breakdown of the social structure cannot but take place in a country" subjected to this kind of attack. "The time will soon come when," he concluded, "to put an end to horror and suffering, the people themselves, driven by the instinct of self-preservation, would rise up and demand an end to the war."[33]

This confidence was not entirely vindicated in the war that followed, but the statistics of this conflict nevertheless revealed the extent to which military violence against noncombatants had become the hallmark of total war. Historically, the process had two central aspects. The first, which might be called the technological dimension, had to do with the weapons that could

---

33 Douhet, *The Command of the Air* (New York, 1942), 5–6, 57–8, cited in Edward Warner, "Douhet, Mitchell, Seversky: Theories of Air Warfare," in Edward Meade Earle, ed., *Makers of Modern Strategy: Military Thought from Machiavelli to Hitler* (New York, 1966), 491, 495; cf. Azar Gat, *Fascist and Liberal Visions of War: Fuller, Liddell Hart, Douhet, and Other Modernists* (Oxford, 1998), 43–79.

be directed against civilian targets. For the most part, civilians remained spared from direct attack during the Great War, but their good fortune was due only in part to the strategic circumstances that kept great land armies locked – on the western front at least – at some distance from areas that were heavily populated by civilians. The principal means of disrupting civilian activity remained a strategy with a hoary tradition, the blockade. Over time, it devastated the economies of the Central Powers, but it could not engage civilian areas directly. Strategic airpower could; and both sides employed it during the First World War. Some 740 Germans, almost of all of them civilians, perished in aerial bombing attacks in the course of this war.[34] Airpower was restrained only by its own infancy; and its impact grew apace with its technological advance and the determination of the belligerent powers to extend the purview of combat to civilian areas. More than half of the bombing tonnage and civilian deaths occurred during the war's last two years.

Airpower was a central element of total war, for its technologies mandated bombing strategies that did not discriminate between military and nonmilitary targets, soldiers and noncombatants. Theorists of airpower in the interwar period merely sought to make virtues of the necessities imposed by an inability to aim weapons of enormous explosive power from great heights. The technologies of airpower did not change enough to alter this dynamic much in the Second World War. Many leaders of the Allied air war against Germany, including Arthur Harris and Hap Arnold, found "city busting" a distasteful strategy, but they discovered that even the most scrupulous choice of targets and the most surgical execution of air attacks entailed the colossal destruction of civilian life and property, which they were prepared to accept as a collateral benefit in the name of demoralizing the enemy.[35]

Destructive technologies and the grudging acceptance of their unpleasant ramifications did not alone bring the apotheosis of war against the civilians. This frightful result owed as well to cultural and political factors, to ideological creeds that germinated during the First World War and culminated in the Second. These legitimated the destruction of entire groups of human beings, whose danger was thought to exceed that of enemy soldiers because it lay disguised in their civilian status itself. Genocide was the other face of total war.[36] Although its antecedents reached far into the past, the Holocaust had thick roots in the residual ideological animosities of the Great

---

34 Christian Geinitz, "The First Air War against Noncombatants: Strategic Bombing of German Cities in World War I," in Chickering and Förster, *Great War, Total War*, 207–26.
35 Overy, *Why the Allies Won*, 111–17; cf. Overy, *The Air War, 1939–1945* (New York, 1980).
36 Stig Förster and Gerhard Hirschfeld, eds., *Genozid in der modernen Geschichte* (Münster, 1999).

War, above all in the perception that the Jews had first systematically under-mined home front morale in Germany and then engineered the mutiny of the civilians in 1918. Long before it eventuated in the decision to annihilate them physically, Nazi racial policy entailed a "war against the Jews," which represented a primary theater in an all-embracing conflict.[37]

From this perspective, the era of total war commenced in the First World War and concluded at the end of the Second. The history of total war was driven by material and ideological forces that culminated respectively in Hiroshima and Auschwitz – in weapons that did not discriminate and policies that did so with a vengeance.[38] After 1945, the concept of total war lived on as an ideal type (or countertype), now as the nuclear nightmare that would succeed the Second World War, set the ultimate parameters of "totality," and capped the master narrative in apocalypse. Its realization has so far been confined to an imaginary realm invoked by Stanley Kubrick and others. In the meantime, however, a master narrative shaped in its image has ceased to provide much guidance to the military history of the twentieth century's second half.

This series of volumes has thus yielded two approaches to the problem of total war, both of which offer analytical advantages. The one, which treats the concept of total war as an ideal type, might be characterized as a "realist" approach to the problem, insofar as it insists that the elements of this ideal represent real historical phenomena that gestated over more than a century. Invoking total war as an ideal type has made possible an imposing body of scholarship, which can trace the distant antecedents of a form of warfare that reached its culmination in the middle of the twentieth century. This scholarship suggests that if critically employed, this approach need not fall prey to uncritical teleologies. In the other approach, which might be called a "nominalist" reading, the analytical purview is necessarily less ambitious. It treats total war instead as a discrete historical phenomenon that was confined to the first half of the twentieth century – an era that the Second World War brought to a close.[39] Whatever the differences in their methodological foundations, the two understandings of total war have much in common. Above all, both insist that total war was characterized principally by the

---

37 Lucy Davidowicz, *The War against the Jews, 1933–1945* (New York, 1975); Peter Longerich, *Politik der Vernichtung: Eine Gesamtdarstellung der nationalsozialistischen Judenverfolgung* (Munich and Zurich, 1998).

38 See Erich Markusen and David Kopf, *The Holocaust and Strategic Bombing: Genocide and Total War in the Twentieth Century* (Boulder, CO, 1995); cf. Hew Strachan, "Essay and Reflection on Total War and Modern War," *International History Review* 22 (2000): 342.

39 This distinction was suggested by Robert Tombs in the discussion during the final session of the conference.

calculated, systematic conflation of the military and civilian dimensions of industrial warfare.

As they have the previous four, several central problems dominate the present volume, which grows out of the proceedings of a conference on the Second World War held in Hamburg in August 2001. Disagreements persist over the definition of "total war," even as the authors confront a conflict that many of them instinctively regard as a paradigmatic case. The first section of the volume is devoted to general problems of interpretation. Gerhard Weinberg emphasizes the global dimensions of the conflict as its distinguishing feature. Hew Strachan then explores the radicalization in the conduct of military operations over the course of the war. The reasons for this development lay, he argues, above all in the salience of racism in the ideologies of both sides. Myriam Gessler and Stig Förster then emphasize the centrality of genocide as a potential element of total war. The Second World War represents the closest historical approximation of total war as an ideal type, they claim, for the Holocaust approximated "absolute genocide."

The second section of the volume explores the question whether specific modes of combat and operations distinguished total war. Holger Herwig underscores the elements of central command control, limitless aims, and rhetorical extravagance in the German conduct of the Battle of the Atlantic. Jürgen Förster's paper on the German land war likewise finds indices of "totality" in the unlimited and uncompromising objectives of the German forces, the lack of restraint with which they pursued these aims, and the central control exercised by Hitler. By contrast, in his broad analysis of the American war in two theaters, Dennis Showalter concludes that this country did not fight a total war, insofar as mobilization never reached the extremes that it did in other belligerent countries. Nonetheless, the American effort was not only geared from the outset to global dimensions, but was also conceived as a "mega-war," which, Showalter contends, "changed the world's paradigms" technologically and institutionally for the rest of the twentieth century.

The next section deals with economic aspects of the war, and it suggests some specific parameters for measuring the "totality" of war. Mark Harrison, Stephen Broadberry, and Peter Howlett argue that the economic dimension was in any case pivotal to the nature and outcome of this conflict. Harrison examines the plight of the Soviet economy during the war and concludes that the mobilization of resources was the single most important factor in deciding the war in favor of the USSR. The analysis of the British economy Broadberry and Howlett present likewise contends that in total war "victory is dependent on the scale of resources that can be mobilized." The two economists argue further that a national commitment of more than 40 percent of a country's resources to the war effort might well be taken as the threshold of "totality" – a standard by which all the belligerents, save Italy, met during the Second World War. Hans Mommsen's review of compulsory labor in German society makes clear another feature of the war's economic dimension, as it emphasizes the brutality under which laborers from the Soviet Union and Eastern Europe suffered in the service of the German war economy.

The mobilization of societies is the theme of the following section of the volume. Martin Kutz returns to the debates about total war in Germany during the interwar period, and he compares the ideological visions to the realities of German mobilization during the Second World War. Jill Stephenson then offers a comparative analysis of the war's impact on women in Germany and Great Britain. Her conclusions raise questions about totality of this war, insofar as they suggest that even in the wholesale mobilization of women, basic sectorial divisions of class, confession, gender, and region survived in both countries. John Barber's survey of the involvement of Soviet women in the war makes clear that in this, as well as other respects, the experience of the USSR represented an extreme, if not paradigmatic case, if the measure of totality is the "intensity of destruction and suffering." Bernd Greiner's survey of American society at war highlights the distinctions between the experience of war on the two sides of the Atlantic. The watchword in North America was "volunteerism," which mitigated sectorial tensions and turned mobilization into a "truly national effort."

The blurring of distinctions between combatants and noncombatants dominates the next section. Hans-Heinrich Nolte's essay on partisan war in Belorussia lends support to John Barber's view of the Soviet war effort as well as to the proposition that the war reached a pinnacle of brutality, if not "totality," in the Soviet Union. Nolte's analysis demonstrates how the German effort was directed indiscriminately not only against the indigenous populations of areas controlled by partisans, but also against the natural environment. The casualties of the partisan war included crops, trees, and the "scorched earth" itself. Two papers then take up the strategic air war. Richard Overy's survey of the war against German cities nods to the economists, as it argues that strategic bombing was based on materialist premises – the proposition that material destruction was the key to undermining enemy morale. Robert Messer's analysis of the American decision to drop atomic bombs on Japanese targets raises the issue of proportionality, the "morality of killing some innocent people in order to save the lives of others." Messer also makes it clear, though, that despite questions subsequently raised by historians, the American leaders who ordered the bombings were sufficiently committed to a doctrine of total war that they were not troubled by their decision.

Questions of morality, atrocity, and law are featured then in a section on "criminal war." Birgit Beck examines the problems of sexual violence and racism among German troops, noting that the proliferation of unreported cases makes conclusions difficult to document. She argues nonetheless that civilian women became primary targets of sexual violence during this total war, particularly on the eastern front, where incidents were at once racially motivated, far more numerous, and more leniently prosecuted than in France. Louise Young explores the cultural contexts of Japanese atrocities against the Chinese in occupied Asia. She argues that atrocities began amid counterinsurgency in 1931, but that they rested on long-held Japanese cultural perceptions, which portrayed the Chinese as a primitive people who stood outside the purview of the law. Daniel Segesser's survey of the development of international law represents an appropriate conclusion to this section. It underscores the impact of the Second World War in broadening the understanding of war crimes as well as the Allies' determination to establish legal and institutional foundations to punish them.

Michael Howard's reflections bring the volume to a close. They also dwell on the broader problems of analyzing total war, and hence represent a fitting coda to the entire series.

PART A

The Dimensions of War

1

Total War

The Global Dimensions of Conflict

GERHARD L. WEINBERG

When should we consider that World War II began? I will operate with the view that the Italian attack on Abyssinia was a resumption of the sort of colonial war that Italy and other Europeans had waged in prior times. Similarly, it seems to me that the war Japan started in China in 1937 belongs in the series of wars that Japan had initiated beginning with that against China in 1894 for the expansion of its empire in East Asia. The very traditional expansionist nature of these two conflicts in their initial stages helps explain why both Italy and Japan switched sides after World War I. They had snatched from the Central Powers all that could be taken from them, so further expansion of the traditional kind could come only at the expense of their allies in the Great War. They imagined that the opportunity to do so was provided for them by the war Germany began in September 1939, and it is therefore with the German invasion of Poland that World War II should be seen to begin.

In spite of some confusion on this subject among such authors as John Lukacs,[1] the conflict that Germany started in September 1939 was global from the very beginning. The participation of Canada, the Union of South Africa, Australia, and New Zealand guaranteed this. And the global character of warfare was real, not nominal. With Soviet assistance, the Germans moved an auxiliary cruiser into the Pacific Ocean in 1940; there it sank or captured some 64,000 tons of Allied shipping before returning to Germany.[2]

The heaviest loss of life in Australia's navy came in November 1941 when another German auxiliary cruiser, disguised as a neutral, sank the cruiser *Sydney* with all hands just off the coast of that continent.[3] It is too often forgotten that already in the first years of World War II Australian,

---

1 John Lukacs, *The Last European War, September 1939–December 1941* (New York, 1976).
2 Gerhard L. Weinberg, *Germany and the Soviet Union, 1939–1941* (Leyden, 1954), 83–84.
3 Tom Frame, *HMAS Sydney: Loss and Controversy* (Sydney, 1993).

New Zealand, Indian, and South African units were essential to the British war effort in North Africa, East Africa, Iraq, and Syria – and are these places not in Africa and Asia rather than in Europe?

If World War II was global from September 1939 on, did those who initiated it and those who joined them intend it to be total from the start? The word "total" here is used with a double aspect: first, that all sorts of weaponry would be utilized regardless of its potential for what has come to be called "collateral damage," and second, that civilians would be deliberately targeted. There are no doubt other definitions, but here this is the standard that will be applied. In this analysis, chronology will be followed: first Germany, then Italy, then Japan.

What were German intentions in the planning and first stage of the war? The evidence is quite clear. The attack on Poland was described by Hitler himself as aiming at the obliteration of that society by mass killing; he used a reference to the massacre of Armenians by Turks in World War I as a way of explaining things to his military commanders before operations actually started. Since all in the room had been adults when the events to which he referred had taken place – and many had no doubt either read or heard about the best-selling book *The Forty Days of Musa Dagh*[4] – one may be certain that he was understood. And it was not only the Einsatzgruppen that quickly began to slaughter civilians on a massive scale. As for the utilization of weapons, the situation of Warsaw is instructive. When the surrounded city's commander asked for terms, the Germans demanded unconditional surrender, a concept about which they were enthusiastic at that time. When that was not immediately forthcoming, the German air force immediately carried out massive raids designed to destroy as much of the city and kill as many of its inhabitants as possible.

One further aspect of the very earliest days of World War II is revealing about the nature of the conflict as the Germans understood the war and intended to wage it. Years before, Hitler had told those who urged the killing of people deemed "unworthy of life" that such a program could be carried out only under the cover of war. As he decided in the winter of 1938–39 that it had been a terrible mistake to shrink back from war in 1938 and that he would under no circumstances repeat such a mistake in 1939, he ordered the preparations for what came to be called the "euthanasia" program early in 1939. The first stages came in the summer of that year, and when he signed the authorization for the murder program in late October

---

4 Franz Werfel, *The Forty Days of Musa Dagh* (London, 1934), English translation of *Die Vierzig Tage des Musa Dagh*.

1939, he carefully backdated it to September 1. As with his repeated redating of his January 30, 1939, threat to kill the Jews of Europe in a future war to September 1, 1939, one can see here how intimately the racial reordering of the globe was linked to the war in the thinking of those in charge. But what is critical here is that the murder of patients in hospitals, mental institutions, and homes for the elderly was immediately extended into the newly occupied portions of Poland.[5] I will come back to the further steps along this route, but the prehostilities intentions of Italy and Japan have to be examined first.

In its preparations for the attack on Abyssinia, the Italian government planned to use poison gas on civilian targets, and it proceeded to do so once hostilities began.[6] There was also consideration of setting huge areas on fire deliberately; but unlike the Japanese, the Italians as far as we know did not even try to implement this concept in their fight to conquer Abyssinia. When Italy joined Germany in World War II, the assumption was that the war was almost over; Italy had to get into the war in order to participate in the distribution of the loot at the expected peace conference. There was no substantial planning and preparation for combat on the Italian-French border or in North Africa, so it is not possible to say that Italy expected to wage a total war; it really did not expect to fight seriously at all.

This absence of a prior conceptual framework for a long war is most likely related to Italian conduct in the fighting that actually developed. Poison gas was not used, presumably for fear of retaliation. Italian planes shared in the bombing of London in 1940, but without any clear purpose except to demonstrate to the Germans that Italy was doing something. Although vastly larger numbers of men were involved, the same thing must be said about Italian participation in the land fighting in North Africa and on the Eastern Front. There were a number of terrible incidents in the Italian occupation zones in Yugoslavia and Greece, but the most recent scholarship on that subject points to these incidents as just that, not as portions of a policy of systematic slaughter as was simultaneously characteristic of German occupation forces in adjacent zones.[7] This is also a likely explanation for the general refusal of the Italians to share in the German enthusiasm for

---

5 Michael Burleigh, *Death and Deliverance: "Euthanasia" in Germany, c. 1900–1945* (Cambridge, 1994), 130–33.

6 See the piece by Giulia Brogini, "Total Colonial Warfare: Ethiopia," in Roger Chickering and Stig Förster, eds., *The Shadows of Total War: Europe, East Asia, and the United States, 1919–1939* (New York, 2003).

7 Enzo Collotti, "Zur italienischen Repressionspolitik auf dem Balkan," in Loukia Droulia and Hagen Fleischer, eds., *Von Lidice bis Kalavryta: Widerstand und Besatzungsterror* (Berlin, 1999), 105–24.

the policy of murdering Jews and the high priority that the Third Reich accorded to that policy.[8]

All this is not to suggest that Italy's participation in World War II did not result in terrible suffering for many or that there were no instances of atrocities. The point should be made, however, that after the 1935–36 war against Abyssinia, there is no evidence of any systematic policy of extermination of conquered people or minorities. Mussolini wanted mustard gas used in Abyssinia against resistance there in March 1940, but even in that conquered country he seriously expected that, along with some settlement by Italians, a million local people would be recruited into Italy's armed forces.[9]

The situation of Japan was fundamentally different from that of Italy. The point is most dramatically illustrated by a comparison with the record of Japan in World War I. At that time, the Japanese had treated prisoners of war entirely properly.[10] It is hard to believe now, but in the interwar years the Japanese were held up as models of the correct treatment of prisoners of war. The horrible experiments with chemical and biological warfare agents the Japanese conducted in the 1930s point toward a new type of warfare. Massive use of such agents against the Chinese starting in 1937 continued all through the following years, though fear of reprisals restrained their use against the British, Dutch, and Americans. On both bombing policy and prisoner of war policy, however, the Japanese planned to act and did act differently from the first day of their joining the Germans.

From the first time that Japanese planes could reach Australian cities, the indiscriminate bombing previously visited on the Chinese was extended to them.[11] The sort of references to observance of international law that had been included in prior imperial rescripts when Japan went to war were conspicuously absent from the rescript Emperor Hirohito began to draft in October and issued in December 1941.[12] In a society careful about precedent, such an omission cannot be considered accidental. Practice followed intent. Having begun by slaughtering literally thousands of Chinese prisoners of war, the Japanese killed and generally mistreated British, American, Filipino, and Dutch POWs; and it needs to be stressed that this practice characterized Japanese conduct from the first days of the wider fighting.

---

8 Jonathan Steinberg, *All or Nothing: The Axis and the Holocaust* (London, 1990).
9 MacGregor Knox, *Mussolini Unleashed, 1939–1941: Politics and Strategy in Fascist Italy's Last War* (Cambridge, 1982), 150; Pompeo Aloisi, *Journal* (Paris, 1957), July 1936, 382.
10 Charles Burdick and Ursula Moessner, *The German Prisoners of War in Japan, 1914–1920* (Lanham, MD, 1984).
11 Douglas Lockwood, *Australia's Pearl Harbor: Darwin 1942* (Melbourne, 1966).
12 Herbert P. Bix, *Hirohito and the Making of Modern Japan* (New York, 2000), 433.

There has been much discussion about the fact that the Americans tried and executed General Yamashita Tomoyuki for his connection with the mass murder, rape, and pillage by his soldiers in Manila early in 1945, but it is not a coincidence that it was the troops under his command who slaughtered thousands of Chinese civilians in Malaya and tied British POWs to posts and used them for bayonet practice, all at the beginning of 1942.[13] Terrible incidents unfortunately occur in most wars and are committed by some soldiers of all armies; systematic murder by members of hierarchically structured forces are invariably the result of orders laid down or of a tone set at the top.

Let us now turn to the intentions of the Allies and their conduct in the first part of the war. The Poles hoped to defend themselves against attack; there was no planning beyond that. The French had a rather similar perspective: they hoped to have as much of the fighting done elsewhere than in France, which had been so terribly devastated and weakened by World War I. Whatever else might be said about the massive investment in the Maginot Line, building extensive fortifications on your own territory hardly demonstrates a desire to wreck another country and decimate its civilian population. The best recent study of French planning for war underlines the defensive and partial nature of the French effort.[14] This fits with the fact that the French vetoed every British project in the early months of World War II that could possibly be interpreted as moves toward total war, such as mining the Rhine River or bombing industrial installations in the Ruhr area.

Whatever unkindly things people might say about Neville Chamberlain, pushing for total war would surely not be one of them. Again, it is easy to make fun of the Royal Air Force dropping leaflets rather than bombs on German cities and being essentially restricted by instructions to trying – without success – to hit German warships; but there is here a very clear sign of an intent, one is tempted to say forlorn hope, that the war could be kept limited. There were all manner of efforts to persuade German military and civilian leaders who claimed or pretended to be against the Hitler regime to overthrow that government and make peace,[15] but it turned out that these very individuals had instead been busy preparing and then leading the invasions of five neutral countries. The dramatic actions of Germany in the spring of 1940 had two equally dramatic effects on the British government: they destroyed for the rest of the war any credibility that internal opponents

---

13 Louis Allen, *Singapore, 1941–1942* (London, 1977), 265–69.
14 Eugenia C. Kiesling, *Arming against Hitler: France and the Limits of Military Planning* (Lawrence, KS, 1996).
15 Gerhard L. Weinberg, *A World at Arms: A Global History of World War II* (Cambridge, 1994), 89–95.

of the Hitler regime had, and they led to the removal of the restrictions hitherto imposed on the bombing policy of the Royal Air Force. In the years after World War II, there would be much wailing about both of these effects but little attention to their cause.

The Chinese had been fighting to defend themselves against Japan for years. At no time did the Nationalist government have much in the way of options as to how to conduct their defense. Most of the time their major problem was obtaining modern weapons and training their soldiers to use them. In the last years of the war, there was a concerted attempt to provide the American air force with air fields from which to bomb the Japanese home islands, but this project and other factors prompted the Japanese Ichigo Offensive of 1944 that effectively ended the military role of China and prepared the way for the communist takeover in that country.

The Soviet Union had tried desperately to avoid war; had helped Germany extensively; and from all evidence was prepared to make even greater concessions in 1941 to buy off Germany. The only war that Stalin had even remotely been willing to enter was, ironically, against the United States. Repeated efforts by Moscow to get the Germans to respond to the Soviet offer to join the Tripartite Pact with its explicit potential for war with the United States never elicited a reply from Berlin, which was too busy planning to attack the Soviet Union to risk losing valuable Soviet supplies by engaging in difficult negotiations.[16] There has never been any evidence available on Soviet plans for the contingency of war together with Germany, Italy, and Japan against the United States and Great Britain. Against the United States, geographical factors alone would have restricted Soviet participation to the naval and supply fields other than a possible assault on Alaska in conjunction with the Japanese. Against Great Britain, the Soviets would presumably have moved in the Middle East or toward India. But of course all this is speculation; the Germans wanted war against, not in alliance with, the Soviet Union.

As the signs mounted that the Germans intended to invade the Soviet Union rather than ally with it, planning in the Soviet leadership moved in two opposite directions. Some of the military leaders, seeing the German military buildup as pointing toward what we know today was in fact intended, suggested that the Red Army not wait for an attack but instead launch a preventive strike against the German forces.[17] Stalin, who had

---

16 Ibid., 198–205.
17 The relevant documents have been published in Gerd R. Ueberschär and Lev A. Bezymenski, eds., *Der deutsche Überfall auf die Sowjetunion 1941: Die Kontroverse um die Präventivkriegsthese* (Darmstadt, 1998).

rejected all warnings and even summaries and copies of the German invasion plan as provocations, was certain that the German assembling of forces in the East was a means of pressure for concessions, not a prelude to invasion. In his eyes, the Germans who had hitherto carefully avoided a two-front war were not about to launch themselves into one. Blinded by his belief in the Marxist-Leninist doctrine that he spouted, he could not conceive of the possibility that Nazi ideology was for real, that the German leaders, far from being the tools of monopoly capitalism, actually believed the racial policies they spouted, and that they seriously intended to seize vast lands in the East (rather than investments in Latin America) to settle German farmers.

None of this, of course, should be read to suggest that Stalin would not order the defense of the Soviet Union against attack from the Germans and whatever allies they might have. Any conceivable doubts on this subject should be removed by the analogous reaction of the Soviet regime to aggression by Japan. As long as the Japanese had aimed their expansion at China, the Soviet Union had been prepared to appease Tokyo as it subsequently appeased Berlin. But when it came to border incidents, the Soviets had fought – and fought hard and victoriously, most recently in 1939 at Nomonhan (Chalkin-Gol).[18] The Germans, who as far as one can tell had failed to pay the slightest attention to these revealing events, would find out the hard way what the Japanese had learned earlier. In 1941, as before and after, German leaders forgot that the first half of the word *Weltkrieg* is *Welt*, world.

There could, therefore, be no doubt that a German attack would, after a brief interval in which Stalin worried that this might just be a provocation, be met by the Red Army's fighting back as best it could. The regime would muster the human and material resources of the state and throw them into battle, regardless of the cost. And if it could retain control of those portions of the country that the Germans had not conquered, those resources together with whatever the Soviet Union's new allies could provide would doom the invaders. Alexander I had maintained control over the portions of Russia Napoleon had not taken, but both the governments of Nicholas II and of Kerensky had lost effective control of whatever the Germans had failed to reach. The critical issue for Stalin was, therefore, internal, not external, and his regime would pass this crucial test.

The United States, like the Soviet Union, had gone to extraordinary lengths to avoid involvement in the war, though it had tried to accomplish this goal by a policy opposite to that of Stalin: helping Hitler's enemies defeat

18 Alvin D. Coox, *Nomonhan: Japan against Russia, 1939* (Stanford, 1985).

Germany rather than helping Hitler win. What sorts of plans did it have when forced into the war by the Japanese, Germans, and Italians? While the broader strategic concept pointed to a priority for defeating Germany before crushing Japan, the means to those ends were essentially traditional. Rearmament had begun in the 1930s with a naval construction program and continued with the beginnings of an air force buildup at the end of 1938, and the first-ever peacetime draft was introduced in 1940.

There was much discussion in air force circles about strategic bombing, and the first four-engine bombers to implement such ideas were coming off the assembly lines – but in very small numbers – in 1941. The American air force, however, expected to rely on carefully targeted bombing to disrupt the enemy's production of weapons in a manner designed to avoid or at least minimize civilian casualties. Again, it may be easy to make fun today of the notion that the navigation and bombsight technologies of the time would make it possible to drop a bomb into a barrel, as the saying went at the time. The point that must be stressed is that these concepts, however silly in retrospect, provide insight into the frame of reference within which the leaders of the time thought. And it is worth noting that the American air force adhered to these views at least nominally until the end of February, beginning of March 1945. It was only then that, for a complex of reasons, the Army Air Force turned to area bombing against Japan.

As Gerald Linderman pointed out in his *The World within War*, American soldiers fighting the Japanese in the first stages of the war in the Pacific expected that Japanese soldiers would fight according to the established conventions. They were quickly disabused of this as the Japanese systematically killed wounded soldiers who fell into their hands, tortured prisoners to death, and generally treated captured Filipino and U.S. soldiers horrendously.[19] As word of this behavior spread rapidly through the American military, and as the publicly reported killing of captured American airmen registered with the armed forces as a whole, the war in the Pacific took on a character in many ways different from that of the Americans against Germany and Italy. It should not, under these circumstances, surprise anyone that the Japanese mistreatment of prisoners combined with a constant refusal to acknowledge reality continues to cast a cloud over relations between the two countries.[20]

This reference to the remaining impact of wartime behavior takes us back from the discussion of initial plans and policies of the belligerents

19 Gerald F. Linderman, *The World within War: America's Combat Experience in World War II* (New York, 1994), chap. 4.
20 Linda Goetz Holmes, *Unjust Enrichment: How Japan's Companies Built Postwar Fortunes Using American POWs* (Mechanicsburg, PA, 2001).

to developments during the conflict. Once again we must first turn our attention to the Germans. Two aspects of the campaign in the West in 1940 need to be mentioned as harbingers of what followed. The racist nonsense with which young Germans had been indoctrinated began to manifest itself in horrible ways. French soldiers of African background were very badly mistreated when captured – a subject that unfortunately has not yet found its historian. The most fully ideologically indoctrinated German soldiers were those of the first Waffen SS units employed at the front. Is it a coincidence that the first significant atrocities, the killing of substantial numbers of prisoners of war, were carried out by the Leibstandarte Adolf Hitler and the Totenkopf Division on May 27 and 28, 1940?[21]

The second aspect of the campaign in the West that must be mentioned is the role of the German air force both in bombing cities and in machine-gunning civilians. The Germans would subsequently blame the British for the shift toward the indiscriminate bombing of urban areas; it is only appropriate that the example utilized by German propaganda on this subject was an air raid on the city of Freiburg that the German air force had itself carried out by mistake.[22] The German violation of the treaty and laws that prohibited Germany from building an air force would return to haunt those living in Germany's cities; curiously enough, this does not keep some historians from continuing to refer to German rearmament in the 1930s as one of the Third Reich's "successes."

The German campaign in the Balkans in the spring of 1941 ushered in a new phase in the escalation of horror. Both the mass killing of civilians in alleged retribution for real or imaginary resistance acts and the systematic killing of Jews were initiated by the German army in the spring of 1941; the former on Crete, the latter in Serbia.[23] But these can now be seen as preliminaries to the vastly greater scale of atrocities that were a planned and implemented, in fact central, characteristic of the German invasion of the Soviet Union. By its own reckoning in early 1942, the German army killed or let die ten thousand prisoners of war each day, seven days a week, for the first seven months of the campaign in the East.[24] At the same time, the program of killing all Jews that the Germans could reach began to be

---

21 A recent brief account in Peter Padfield, *Himmler: Reichsführer SS* (London, 2001), 300.

22 Anton Hoch, "Der Luftangriff auf Freiburg am 10. Mai 1940," *Vierteljahrshefte für Zeitgeschichte* 4 (1956), 115–44.

23 Walter Manoschek, *"Serbien ist Judenfrei": Militärische Besatzungspolitik und Judenvernichtung in Serbien 1941/42* (Munich, 1993); *Das Deutsche Reich und der Zweite Weltkrieg*, Vol. 3 (Stuttgart, 1984), 508; G. C. Kiriakopoulos, *The Nazi Occupation of Crete, 1941–45* (Westport, CT, 1995), chap. 2.

24 Christian Streit, *Keine Kameraden: Die Wehrmacht und die deutschen Kriegsgefangenen, 1941–1945* (Stuttgart, 1978).

implemented in a systematic manner. This is not the place for a review of what has come to be called the Holocaust; there is, however, one aspect of it that must be mentioned in any discussion of the connections between global and total war.

On November 28, 1941, Hitler had a long conversation with the Grand Mufti of Jerusalem. By this time, the mass killing of Jews in the newly occupied Soviet territories was well under way and was being extended to other portions of Europe under German control. The killing centers in German-occupied Poland were under construction. As Hitler now explained, the countries of Europe were being emptied of Jews one by one; at the appropriate time this would be extended to what Hitler called "non-European countries." In other words, a global concept. Since the Mufti was presumably not interested in the Jews of Australia or Argentina, Hitler became more explicit. Once the Germans arrived there, their only objective in the Middle East would be the killing of the Jews there.[25] Hitler did not explain to the Mufti that a museum of an "extinct race" was being developed in Prague; the point that belongs in the context of any understanding of World War II is the global dimension of German racial ambitions. When any non-Germans left on the globe were to be taken briefly to the world capital Germania, as Berlin was to be renamed, so that they might be properly impressed by its colossal buildings, there would be no Jews among them.[26]

What must be considered the most extreme form of warfare seriously contemplated and then implemented during World War II has to be credited to Japan. In September 1942, the Japanese government decided to develop and build large numbers of balloons that would be carried across the Pacific Ocean by the prevailing winds to come down in the western portions of Canada and the United States. The balloons would carry incendiaries in the expectation that they would set colossal fires in the forests of the North American West and destroy everything there in infernos too vast to contain – a scorched earth policy of hitherto unimagined dimensions. There were problems of both timing and production. The timing problem was that the winds were strongest in the winter – but the snow would make it harder to start fires – while the summer was best for starting fires – but the winds were not as strong. The production issue was simply one of material and labor resources. The timing issue could only be overcome by huge numbers; the resource problem by using cheap materials and drafting thousands of

25 *Documents on German Foreign Policy 1918–1945*, Series D, vol. 13, no. 515.
26 Jochen Thies, *Architekt der Weltherrschaft: Die "Endziele" Hitlers* (Düsseldorf, 1976), chap. 2.

schoolgirls to make the balloons.[27] By the time American B-29 bombers put an end to the project in the summer of 1945, some nine thousand balloons had been launched. In practice, the impact of the project was minimal, but the concept of setting fire to huge areas of two countries – as compared with setting fire to individual villages or cities – belongs in any study of total war.[28]

A recent work suggests that the Japanese also had plans for submarines that might have been designed for nuclear power and that would carry planes to drop atomic bombs on American West Coast cities while the Germans launched missiles with atomic warheads at New York and other East Coast cities from submarines in the Atlantic.[29] There is no doubt that the Japanese had airplane-carrying submarines – one such plane dropped bombs on a city in Oregon – and were working, like the Germans, on atomic bombs, but beyond that there is at this time too much uncertainty about these issues to convince at least this historian.

What is beyond doubt is that, in what they feared was a race with Germany, Britain and the United States were trying to build atomic bombs – as were the Soviets – and that work continued after it became clear that the Germans were behind, not ahead of, the Allies. By the end of 1944, President Roosevelt was informed that the first atomic bombs would be available in the summer of 1945; there is no evidence whatever that he would have followed a policy different from that of his successor as to their use. All of the evidence points to the conclusion that General George C. Marshall, the Army Chief of Staff, wanted them used in tactical support of the landing on Kyushu scheduled for November 1945 that was expected to be terribly difficult and costly. He agreed with President Truman that the first, and if necessary the second, would be dropped on Japanese cities in the hope of shocking the Tokyo government into surrender. If that did not work, those becoming available thereafter were to be saved up for use in support of operation "Olympic."

The first two achieved the purpose of forcing surrender in the face of the argument of those in the Japanese government who asserted that people killed by them were no more dead than those killed by what came to be called conventional raids. Since such raids had earlier caused both more casualties and more destruction than the atomic bombs, there was only the contrary

---

27 One such schoolgirl gives an account in Haruko Taya Cook and Theodore F. Cook, eds., *Japan at War: An Oral History* (New York, 1992), 187–92.
28 A summary with references in Weinberg, *A World at Arms*, 650–51.
29 Philip Henshall, *The Nuclear Axis: Germany, Japan, and the Atomic Bomb Race, 1939–1945* (Phoenix Hall, UK, 2001), esp. chap. 8 and 200–203.

argument that the Americans could simply drop more of the new devices until there was no one left alive in Japan and thus destroy people and country without ever having to land and provide the Japanese armed forces with the expected opportunity to defeat them. As is well known, the Emperor sided with the latter argument.

A further comment on the end of the war in Europe and in Asia is essential for comprehension of how and why the war took the form that it did. It had been a mere twenty-one years since World War I, a disaster that most people on earth outside of Germany considered more than adequate for the century. Once Germany insisted on trying again, those on the Allied side had as their most important objective beyond defending themselves that of making certain that there would not be a third world war. Two minor but instructive ways to gain insight into this: while a prisoner of war in December 1945, German Field Marshal Ritter von Leeb entered into his diary some detailed musings as to how Germany could improve on its performance so that it could defeat the Allies the next time.[30] In the United States during and in the years right after the war, there was an organization called "The Society for the Prevention of World War III." It is very easy to forget today how seriously this issue was thought about at the time.

There were several aspects to the determination to preclude a third world war and its implications for Allied postwar planning, but the most important one for the actual conduct of war was the demand for unconditional surrender. Although the terminology was not used in London at the time, the behavior of those allegedly opposed to Hitler inside Germany – on the one hand, no action against the regime but invasions of neutrals instead, on the other hand, territorial demands that outraged the British government – produced the conclusion in London that Germany had to be totally crushed, occupied, and then remade into a member of the civilized world. The unconditional surrender of Germany, but without use of the term, became the British objective.[31]

Roosevelt by all indications had thought that unconditional surrender should be imposed on Germany already in 1918 but had kept quiet about this as a loyal member of the Wilson administration. He had no doubts about the subject this time, and although the public proclamation of this demand was not issued until early 1943, that timing was the result of domestic and diplomatic considerations having nothing to do with the substance of the

30 Georg Meyer, ed., *Generalfeldmarschall Ritter von Leeb: Tagebuchaufzeichnungen und Lagebetrachtungen aus zwei Weltkriegen* (Stuttgart, 1976), 80, n. 195.
31 Albrecht Tyrell, *Grossbritannien und die Deutschlandplanung derAlliierten, 1941–1945* (Frankfurt am Main, 1987).

demand, which the president had approved long before. Like Churchill, he would almost certainly have been willing to confine the call to Germany and Japan; it was the British cabinet that insisted on the inclusion of Italy.[32] Whether or not one agrees with the analysis underlying the demand at the time, it is surely correct to point out that since their surrender, neither Germany nor Japan has shown much inclination to try again.

Almost nothing has been said about the domestic implications of global total war. In many ways, the experience of World War I on the home front was repeated: massive mobilization of human, material, and fiscal resources. There were, however, significant differences. German mobilization of women appears to have been both later and slightly more limited than in the prior conflict; this was offset by an enormously greater employment of prisoners of war and slave labor of various types. British and Soviet mobilization went substantially further than in World War I, while in the United States the length in time was, of course, very much greater. Because of the advances in technology, it can be argued that the involvement of what came to be called "Big Science" played a larger role in all belligerents. Japan, like Germany, drew in prisoners and forced labor on a large scale; like Italy, its domestic effort was hampered by the exertions imposed by immediately preceding military conflicts. Rationing universally accompanied hostilities – and so did black markets. The details differed from country to country, but the pattern was in many ways more similar than different across the world.

The final accounting on the war is a grim one. The material costs and destruction of the conflict were colossal. The majority of Allied prisoners taken by the Axis powers did not survive; the overwhelming majority of Axis prisoners taken by the Allies did. That can certainly be said without entering into the argument over precise statistics. But the majority of the casualties of the war were civilians, not soldiers. The efforts made, especially after the terrible impact of World War I, to contain the application of force in international affairs failed before the determination of Germany and Japan to escalate terror as deliberate means toward what they assumed would be easier and more complete conquests. Their people would learn that this was a grotesque miscalculation.

32 Weinberg, *A World at Arms*, 438–39.

2

Total War

The Conduct of War 1939–1945

HEW STRACHAN

I

To call the Second World War a total war is not anachronistic. It is the only war of which that can be said. The phrase "total war" was not current in the First World War, but it was by the 1930s, and it became a commonplace in the rhetoric of both sides in 1939–45. To that extent, the notion that the Second World War was a total war was a self-fulfilling prophecy: extrapolating from the experience of the First World War, commentators expected a future war in Europe to be "total," and so it became. In reality there was no such inevitability.

The First World War was, after all, more a warning than a model. It was "the war to end wars," not the war to act as a benchmark for future war. Two of the more influential military theorists of the interwar years, J. F. C. Fuller and Basil Liddell Hart, examined the conduct of war with a view to minimizing – not maximizing – its impact. And a succession of disarmament conferences aimed to buttress, not undermine, cardinal principles like noncombatant immunity. John Mueller has gone so far as to argue that the obsolescence of what he calls "major war" dates from 1918 and that only the ambition and personality of Hitler can explain what followed.[1] He oversimplifies, but the proposition that more people wanted to avoid total war in 1939 than sought it hardly seems controversial.

The observation is important rather than trite because there were phases and aspects of the Second World War that defy the description "total." Prewar expectations did not simply evaporate. Ultimately, what made the Second World War total war was – dare it be said – its totality: it was the

---

1 J. Mueller, *Retreat from Doomsday: The Obsolescence of Major War* (New York, 1990; first published 1989); on my own reactions to this line of thought, see Hew Strachan, "On Total War and Modern War," *International History Review* 22 (2000): 341–70.

bundling up of all its facets into a whole. But if the war is disaggregated, a more complex picture emerges.

In the 1960s and 1970s, it was common to divide the war in two. The only continuity, up until 1941, A. J. P. Taylor, John Lukacs, and others argued, was the antagonism between Britain and Germany: instead of fighting a world war, Germany waged a European war and, moreover, one divided into a series of short and distinct campaigns.[2] Not until the invasion of the Soviet Union in June 1941 and the entry of the United States in December of the same year did the war become a world war. These sorts of arguments were Eurocentric in that they ignored Japan, whose war in Asia began in China in 1937, but it remained true that the wars against Germany and against Japan continued, by and large, in separate compartments.

Thus, one obvious method of disaggregation is geographical. What follows will consider in turn Germany's war in Western Europe (including the Mediterranean and North Africa); the Russo-German War; and the war in the Pacific. Each has quite distinct characteristics and thus begs different definitions of totality.

There is also, however, a chronological dimension to what follows. The initial German conquests in the west were by and large the achievement of 1939–41; the Russo-German struggle dominated the years 1941–45; and the war only ended with the defeat of Japan in 1945. Chronology is important on two counts. First, within the war itself, its length bred its own intensity: successive waves of violence fed on and developed from what had gone before. Total war grew more from the war itself than from its prewar expectations. Second, what was meant by total war itself changed its emphasis as the Second World War unfolded.

Before 1939, total war referred as much to the enemy within as the enemy without. Total war was not defined; instead, it was a given to necessitate and justify a revolution in domestic government. Ludendorff's *Der totale Krieg* (1935) was not concerned with tactics or strategy. Instead he described the sort of government required to ensure full national mobilization: for "total" read totalitarian.[3] In France, the concept of *couverture* was designed to secure France's national resources and industrial infrastructure, and so create time for their conversion to war production. When political leaders harped on the idea of "total war" in wartime speeches, they used the phrase in this

---

2 John Lukacs, *The Last European War* (London, 1977).
3 Erich Ludendorff, *The Nation at War* (London, 1936; published in Germany in 1935). For a discussion, see Roger Chickering, "Sore Loser: Ludendorff's Total War," in Roger Chickering and Stig Förster, eds., *The Shadows of Total War: Europe, East Asia, and the United States, 1919–1939* (Cambridge and Washington, DC, 2003), 151–78.

prewar sense. Their words were addressed to their own populations and were a summons to a greater effort. Churchill's oratory, particularly in 1940–41, falls within this category. So too does Goebbels's famous "total war" speech, delivered in the Sportpalast in Berlin on February 18, 1943.

After the war, the phrase "total war" carried different connotations. It referred less to the efforts of one's own population and more to the death and destruction inflicted on the populations of others. The key idea was not national mobilization and its accompanying governmental structures, but the erosion of the principle of noncombatant immunity. This took three distinct forms, although each elided into the other. One was the shift from shooting enemy prisoners of war in the heat of battle to shooting them as an act of policy: the "barbarization" of warfare. Another was the readiness to use strategic bombing against civilians. And a third was genocide. The implementation of the "final solution" became possible in part through the impact of the first two, through the brutalization of the conduct of war.[4] But the ideas that underpinned genocide came less from military or strategic thought than from political and cultural assumptions. To this extent, they did of course feed on the prewar rhetoric of total – or rather totalitarian – war. Yet they were applied not only to the internal enemy but also to the external and so in turn reinforced the application of indiscriminate violence in the conduct of the war itself.

One way in which the Second World War confounded expectations of total war derived from the First World War was the restraint shown by all sides in the use of chemical weapons. Military necessity both favored gas when fighting defensively (and for this reason Britain intended to use it against a German invasion in 1940) and regretted its tendency to reduce tempo in the conduct of operations. Therefore, the decision not to use gas in the conduct of the war was at one level evidence of military opportunism. At another, it shows how such self-interest could be made virtuous, with all sides seemingly engaged in mutual self-restraint and in reducing opportunities for retaliation. But gas was of course used by Germany, and to massively lethal effect. Soldiers serving at the front may have become cavalier about carrying gas masks; Jews in extermination camps would not have been.[5]

The Holocaust – whether as concept or reality – now so bestrides thinking and writing not only on the Second World War but also on modern

4 Christopher Browning, *Ordinary Men: Reserve Police Battalion 101 and the Final Solution in Poland* (Harmondsworth, 2001; first published 1992), 161–3, 186.
5 Jeffrey Legro, *Cooperation Under Fire: Anglo-German Restraint during World War II* (Ithaca, 1995), 145–214; Peter Schrijvers, *The Crash of Ruin: American Combat Soldiers in Europe during World War II* (New York, 1998), 61–2.

European history as a whole that it permeates fin de siècle perceptions of the nature of war in the twentieth century. Ultimately, it is the vulnerability of women and children, and the destruction of so much of the infrastructure of European civilization, that gives the phrase "total war" its contemporary resonance. But that shift in definition was more a product of the war than a consequence of its design. What happened at Stalingrad or at Treblinka was far worse than prewar figurings: reality had outstripped imagination. It was also more awful than much of the fighting and killing that was going on at the same time in the rest of the world.

II

The so-called phoney war illustrates this point exactly. If the war had ended with the fall of France (an event which, arguably, could after all have concluded the First World War), Western Europeans would not have regarded the Second World War as a total war.

This does not mean that the leaders on both sides imagined that they were engaged in a limited war. They knew they were not, but their application of the ideas of total war was determined by rationality: the concepts of total war were guided by political considerations. A British member of parliament and former naval officer, Stephen King-Hall, made this very point in a book published in 1941. The object of war, even total war, was not war itself but victory. King-Hall's wartime reworking of what were essentially Clausewitzian concepts makes sense of James Turner Johnson's observation that ultimately even total war is limited. Total war, Johnson argues, must not be construed as "a sadistic bent to make the weak suffer," for total war embodies "the idea that there exist certain values, perceived as ultimate, in defense of which individuals and nations must be prepared to fight with no observance of restraints."[6]

Goering's Four-Year Plan organization, created in 1936, was committed to preparations for total war. But what Goering meant by that, as the Reichsmarschall made clear in a speech on October 24, 1939, was a proper division of resources between Germany's three fronts – the military front, ammunitions production, and the civilian population.[7] There may have been little fighting on land between September 1939 and May 1940, but all the belligerents were frenetically active – bending their efforts to the creation of

6 James Turner Johnson, *Just War Tradition and the Restraint of War: A Moral and Historical Enquiry* (Princeton, NJ, 1981), 229–77, esp. 276. See Stephen King-Hall, *Total Victory: Its Meaning and Its Achievement* (London, 1941).

7 Militärgeschichtliches Forschungsamt, ed., *Germany and the Second World War*, vol I– (Oxford, 1990–), II, 335.

war economies and to the development of government agencies to manage them.

Moreover, in harnessing their own resources, they were not unaware of the need to target those of their enemies. The principal British contribution to the continental war was not an expeditionary force but the reimposition of the blockade which it seemed had defeated Germany in 1918: by the beginning of November 1939, Germany's imports had fallen to 4 percent of their 1938 monthly average.[8] Raeder, in response, was anxious to use surface ships and the Luftwaffe both to break the British blockade and to disrupt Britain's own trade. But what Hitler would not let him do was resort to unrestricted U-boat warfare. The sinking of the passenger ship, SS *Athenia*, on September 3 was a mistake: German submarine commanders were under orders to obey prize rules in accordance with international law. These restrictions were gradually removed in the winter of 1939–40, but the impact was limited, at least for the time being, because of both the insufficiency of submarines and the lack of Atlantic bases.[9]

Political calculation was both essential to the implementation of economic warfare and a key to its restraint. Both powers were sensitive to neutral opinion, in particular that of the United States. Recognizing that cooperation had been central to the closing of Germany's trade with its border neutrals in 1914–18, Britain handled the Baltic states with such tact in 1939–40 that its submarines did not even engage as German troop transports closed on the Norwegian coast in April. And Hitler still harbored a hope that a deal could be brokered with Britain – a hope which he feared would be forfeited if Germany were the first to break international law. Therefore, although economic warfare included among its targets the supply of food, and thus at least indirectly infringed the principle of noncombatant immunity, it was still an instrument of total war conducted within a framework of rationality and restraint.

What made economic warfare both an instrument of total war and a factor in its limitation was that its conduct was maritime. It struck at the civilian populations of the enemy indirectly rather than directly. Therefore, the most significant aspect of all in this phase of the war was that bombers were not deliberately and continuously directed against civilian targets. Admittedly, this was in part, as with the submarine, a product of procurement. The German decision to go for Stukas and medium bombers left the Luftwaffe (in the words of an assessment of 1938) "not strong enough to seek a resolution

---

8 Ibid., IV, 463.
9 Ibid., II, 176–8; IV, 461; Legro, *Cooperation Under Fire*, 55–61.

by attacking the enemy's war economy."[10] Although the British created Bomber Command in 1936 and opted for the development of a four-engined bomber, they did not have the capability to mount a full strategic bombing offensive until 1943. Nevertheless, before 1939 both the Luftwaffe and the Royal Air Force contained within their ranks enthusiasts for the sort of total war that implied the erosion of the principles of noncombatant immunity and of proportionality. Major Erwin Gehrts combined Douhetism and Nazism in a 1937 essay in which he argued that the key aim of the war was "to break the will of the enemy 'home army of workers'"; rather than destroy munitions factories, the Luftwaffe should seek to "depopulate" them.[11] The Royal Air Force under Lord Trenchard had used the moral effects of bombing civilian targets as the principal strategic rationale both for its independence and for its funding.[12]

The primary reason why neither conception was put into immediate practice was – once again – rational calculation. In 1940, both the Germans and the British did begin bombing civilian targets, although neither air force was ready in terms of equipment to do so. In 1939, pragmatism was shaped both by these economic considerations and by sensitivity to international law. On September 3, all of Germany, Britain, and France responded positively to Roosevelt's urging that they refrain from attacking civilians from the air. Thereafter the fear of retaliation and the knowledge of each of its own weaknesses, both in air defense and in aircraft production if the other side were to retaliate, made restraint longer lasting in the air than at sea.

On land, Germany's consciousness of the economic difficulties in sustaining total war did much to determine both the direction and the tempo of its operations. The conquest of Norway and the overrunning of northern France were both pivotal in breaking the need for restraint in the conduct of economic war. First, Germany's domination of the iron ore and coal of Scandinavia and northwestern Europe – together of course with its overrunning of Poland and Czechoslovakia, and its pact with the Soviet Union – eliminated its vulnerability to maritime blockade. Second, its acquisition of naval bases as far apart as Trondheim and Brest enabled it to escape the North Sea in a way that it had not done in the First World War and so gain direct access to the Atlantic and to Britain's principal trade routes. And third, it had

---

10 *Germany and the Second World War*, II, 48.   11 Ibid., II, 37.
12 Frederick M. Sallager, *The Road to Total War* (New York, 1969), 9–13; Philip Meilinger, "Clipping the Bomber's Wings: The Geneva Disarmament Conference and the Royal Air Force, 1932–1934," *War in History* 6 (1999): 306–30; Meilinger, "Trenchard and 'Morale Bombing': The Evolution of R. A. F. Doctrine Before World War II," *Journal of Military History* 60 (1996): 243–70.

acquired airfields which enabled its aircraft to strike Britain directly despite their short range.

Although the ground campaigns of 1940 therefore laid the basis for the removal of restraint in the conduct of total war in the west, the actual fighting was, by the standards of soldiers with memories of battles in the same theater a quarter of a century earlier, remarkably limited. Casualties were light: Germany suffered a total of 92,807 dead in all theaters in the year ending August 31, 1940.[13] France's losses seemed heavy but were made up disproportionately of prisoners of war. Second, the campaigns were short: Denmark and Norway were defeated in two months, Holland in five days, Belgium in seventeen days, and France in six weeks. And finally, the conquests having been completed, both occupiers and occupied behaved in ways that were compatible with the expectations of international law. The verdict of the battlefield was accepted and resistance was exceptional.

This is not to say that there were not civilian casualties. The key operational characteristics of Germany's initial victories were mobility and tempo. One interacted with the other: "Where the fronts became rigid," Gehrts had written, "time starts to operate," and, given the expectations of Germany's economic vulnerability to a long war, time "would always work against Germany."[14] It was mobility that minimized both loss of life and munitions consumption, and it was mobility that enabled the Wehrmacht to get inside the enemy's command loop and decision-making cycle, and so shatter the cohesion of its armies. Blocked roads and fixed defenses were the Germans' principal enemy, and confronting either brought with it the risk of civilian casualties.

The speed of the Germans' advance produced panic, and in France especially families encumbered with their goods and chattels fled their homes. As the army of France lost its cohesion, its stragglers mixed with the refugees on the roads. The Luftwaffe killed both as they fought to clear the routes for their ground forces, but its justification was military necessity. Significantly, a 1938 study of the Wehrmacht on "warfare as an organizational problem" had declared that in the conduct of war "necessity knows no law."[15] In due course, such a readiness to flout the principle of noncombatant immunity would seem a pointer to the future, but in the context of 1940 it was more a reminder of 1914: the necessity was a narrowly defined military one dictated by the determination to achieve victory in short order.

---

13 *Germany and the Second World War*, V/1, 953.   14 Ibid., II, 37.
15 Ibid., II, 37; also 300.

Cities and towns were potentially even greater obstacles to mobile warfare. In the First World War, the armies of 1914 had contrived more often to bypass major conurbations than to enter them. Moltke the younger sidestepped Paris, and Conrad von Hötzendorff eschewed a direct attack on Belgrade. Thereafter, the static nature of much of the war kept civil and civic life comparatively free from the direct dangers of the fighting. Houses made natural defensive zones; streets were defiles easily blocked; the attacking forces were broken into small units as they cleared buildings; and their cohesion was further undermined by the invitations to plunder and loot. So, too, in 1939–40 armies maneuvered around towns rather than through them.

The major exception in the west was the bombing of Rotterdam, in which about eight hundred civilians were killed. In this case, tempo demanded totality. The Germans' justification was not dissimilar to that advanced by Liddell Hart in *Paris or the Future of War* (1925). The war was kept short and determined Dutch resistance outflanked. In reality, the Dutch had already begun to negotiate the city's surrender, but the order countermanding the air attack was too late. The destruction of Rotterdam, like that of Warsaw in September 1939, seemed to provide evidence of the utility of independent strategic bombing. It was easy to conclude that ruthlessness had been repaid by results: the linking of cause and effect became a precept for the future.[16]

Northwest Europe was the most urbanized and industrialized theater of war in the world. In 1940, it was simply impossible to conduct mobile war there without collateral damage, but this did not make civilians either active participants in the war or the deliberately selected targets of the uniformed services. Peacetime armies, too, easily saw terrain as a space for maneuver, where the landscape was strangely devoid of human occupation and where the only obstacles were those set by nature, such as mountains and rivers. The desert came closest to this ideal. In the North African campaign, both sides could focus on each other, with the result that – in the German title of *The Rommel Papers* – it was a "war without hate." The British more often expressed admiration than animosity for the Germans and particularly for Rommel himself. Private J. M. Butler, an Australian at Tobruk in 1941, wrote, "the German is a worthy opponent and in this campaign at least he is a clean and fair fighter – I have yet to see a German who is afraid: I have yet to see a German who resorts to low and mean subterfuge."[17] On the

16 Ibid., II, 283, 337; Nicola Lambourne, *War Damage in Western Europe: The Destruction of Historic Monuments During the Second World War* (Edinburgh, 2001), 43.
17 Mark Johnston, *Fighting the Enemy: Australian Soldiers and Their Adversaries in World War II* (Cambridge, 2000), 32.

other side of the line at about the same time, a German tank officer was "inclined to think of the romantic idea of a knight's tourney."[18] Chivalry was a word that both sides used at least occasionally, and it found reflection in the humane treatment both of the wounded and of prisoners of war.

Certainly prisoners were shot out of hand in the heat of battle. Certainly each side accused the other of acts of treachery and outrage. But underpinning these complaints was the recognition that atrocities should be seen for what they were rather than treated as the normal currency of war. When the commander of the 6th New Zealand Brigade, Brigadier G. H. Clifton, was captured, Rommel concluded that he was "a courageous and likeable man" and expressed admiration rather than fury when he attempted to escape. The German general did however complain to Clifton that the New Zealand division had repeatedly broken international law by massacring wounded and prisoners of war. Significantly, Clifton attributed these infractions to the large number of Maori in the division.[19] Similarly, when the Allies entered Italy, the misconduct of the French troops, including pillage and rape, was attributed to the Goums from Morocco.[20]

Racism within Europe had the ability to sustain the warriors' code of war. Lapses were attributed (perhaps rightly) to ethnic groups who came from outside Europe, with the obvious implication that those from within knew how to behave. The implication, however, was that the restraints observed when fighting related nationalities did not apply when the enemy was more visibly different. The conduct of war in Europe did not necessarily have the potential to become total war, but that of world war did.

It is easy to see the fighting in North Africa as peripheral – a throwback to an anglocentric view of the war, where the key issues are operational, where armies fought each other rather than partisans, where political ideology was less important than military honor, and where genocide and terror have been airbrushed out of the historical record. Although a major theater for Italy, it was – after all – a minor one for Germany.

Thus, its evidence that fighting in the Second World War was capable of being conducted along lines that accorded with convention can be marginalized. But what is interesting is that Rommel himself did not see the desert campaign in those terms. The talk of chivalry and its evocation of antiquity should not obscure the fact that for him, "of all theatres of operations, it was probably in North Africa that the war took on its most advanced form. The

18 Ibid., 44. See also Bruce Allen Watson, *Desert Battle: Comparative Perspectives* (Westport, CT, 1995), esp. 10–11; Correlli Barnett, *The Desert Generals* (London, 1960).
19 B. H. Liddell Hart, ed., *The Rommel Papers* (London, 1953), 281–2.
20 Schrijvers, *Crash of Ruin*, 47.

protagonists on both sides were fully motorised formations, for whose employment the flat and obstruction-free desert offered hitherto undreamed-of possibilities. It was the only theatre where the principles of motorised and tank warfare, as they had been taught theoretically before the war, could be applied to the full – and further developed."[21]

Rommel regarded the campaigns in Poland and France as inappropriate pointers to the future because in those theaters Germany's enemies had still "to take account of their non-motorised infantry divisions and had thus to suffer the disastrous limitation in their freedom of tactical decision which this imposes." By contrast, the British in North Africa were fully mobile, and "out of this pure motorised warfare, certain principles were established ... These principles will become the standard for the future, in which the fully-motorised formation will be dominant."[22]

For Rommel, therefore, the most modern form of war was not necessarily total war: the future of war was an operational matter, and its means was the maintenance of high tempo. But Rommel's analysis, even within his circumscribed perspective, was deficient. His summary of the technical and organizational aspects of desert warfare made no mention at all of air power despite his recognition of the dependence of tempo on up-to-date intelligence and on regular resupply. And, second, although he recognized that it was "the flat and good-driving terrain" that had enabled operational success, he made the mistake of assuming that methods evolved in one geographical environment could be applicable to another. Terrain could determine totality in war.

When the war extended to northwestern Europe in 1944, the principles governing the employment of armor were very different from those advocated by Rommel or that had been applied in 1940. In both the earlier campaigns, tanks were massed and were deployed where the going favored them. They were creatures of the open countryside. By 1944, they were integrated with infantry to provide direct fire support not only in the bocage of Normandy but also in towns and cities. The destruction of Rouen and especially Caen symbolized the value of a city as a defensive node, and its vulnerability to the fire of tanks and artillery as well as to close air support and interdiction bombing.

Thus modern war proved to be all-arms war in a way that Rommel had failed to grasp. Moreover, although street fighting carried the risk of civilian casualties, they were not its only consequence. People could flee the battle zone or take to the cellars. Many American soldiers were surprised

21 Liddell Hart, ed., *Rommel Papers*, 197.   22 Ibid., 198.

at how canny the populations of Europe proved to be, disappearing when fighting was imminent, only to pop up again when it was over.[23] Buildings were fixed, and therefore the destruction of Europe's cultural and architectural inheritance was one of the most searing indications of what total war meant.

This was not deliberate. It was not part of a policy to obliterate a specific culture in the way in which mosques and churches were targeted in the Balkans or Middle East in the 1990s. Eisenhower told the invading forces before D-Day that, "in the path of our advance will be found historical monuments and cultural centres which symbolize to the world all that we are fighting to preserve."[24] The idea that that inheritance was common to all Europeans was reciprocated in Germany. Hitler's plan to raze Paris was not implemented; Rome was declared an open city; the damage in Florence was restricted to the Arno bridges. The nearest either side came to a declared policy of cultural destruction was the Luftwaffe's "Baedeker" raids against English cathedral cities in April–June 1942, and these were presented as retaliation for the destruction by the Royal Air Force of Lübeck and Rostock, neither of them cities of obvious military utility.[25]

Sir Arthur Harris, following in Trenchard's footsteps, adopted a policy of destroying cities, which in 1942 could be defended as the only practicable strategy open to the Royal Air Force – and even to Britain. At that stage of the war, Bomber Command lacked the techniques and technology for precision bombing. The Casablanca conference in 1943 confirmed that the target of the bomber offensive was German morale. The destruction of cathedrals and medieval city centers was therefore presented as collateral and incidental rather than deliberate. But by 1945, the Royal Air Force was capable of greater precision in its targeting. It could reasonably aspire to hit the industries which lay not in the center of cities but on their outskirts. Harris's indifference to cultural damage was now less defensible, as the response to the bombing of Dresden in 1945 revealed, both at the time and thereafter. Civilian deaths have been computed at 35,000 as a minimum and perhaps 100,000 or more, but what generates feeling today is as much the destruction of a Baroque city, the Zwinger damaged, the Residenzschloss devastated, and the Frauenkirche flattened. The buildings of Dresden were part of a Christian and European patrimony. The justification for the bombing, however questionable, was not total war in the sense of the replacement

23 Schrijvers, *Crash of Ruin*, 106.
24 Lambourne, *War Damage in Western Europe*, 161.
25 Ibid., 52, 141–2.

of one set of ideas with another. The British press explained Dresden in terms of military necessity: the city was a center of communication whose destruction would ease the advance of the Soviet armies.[26]

The fighting in northwestern Europe in 1944–45 was intense and terrifying, but in the main it continued to conform to the laws of war. Gerald Linderman has called it "the war of rules."[27] Those rules were more regularly broken than in 1939–40 for two interlocking reasons. First, the intensity and length of the war had themselves served to dull sensitivities as to what constituted proper conduct. Second, the service of the German army on the eastern front had created a pattern of behavior that was now visited on the west. The two most notorious examples of where the rules were not obeyed both involved the SS. On June 10, 1944, the village of Oradour-sur-Glane was razed and 642 of its inhabitants killed. On December 17, eighty-six captured American soldiers were executed at Malmédy during the battle of the Ardennes. Relativizing atrocity is both fraught and morally suspect, but doing so leads to two conclusions about these incidents. First, they were small in comparison with what was happening on the eastern front. Second, they have been accorded so much attention precisely because they were deemed to be exceptional. Before them, the Americans had continued to believe that such things did not occur in war. Thereafter, they were less sure: "You don't fight a Kraut by Marquis of Queensbury rules," opined William Mauldin, an American soldier in Italy.[28] But some still did – including the Krauts themselves. In the hard-fought battle for the Arnhem bridge, the Germans appeared to warn the occupants of the white house on the defensive perimeter by firing tracer over its roof before opening fire on the British paratroops within.[29]

The business of fighting did therefore generate a hatred for the enemy, but it was not unequivocal. Of American units in training that went on to perform with average competence in action, only 6 percent really wanted to kill a German. By the war's end, 41 percent of American soldiers hated German soldiers, but 55 percent did not – and only 20 percent hated German civilians. GIs had a lower opinion of their nominal allies, the French, than they did of the Germans, and the distinction between the German people

---

26 Tami Davis Biddle, "Bombing by the Square Yard: Sir Arthur Harris at War, 1942–5," *International History Review* 21 (1999): 626–64.

27 Gerald F. Linderman, *The World Within War: America's Combat Experience in World War II* (Cambridge, MA, 1997; 1999 ed.), 90.

28 Schrijvers, *Crash of Ruin*, 77; S. A. Stouffer et al., *The American Soldier: Combat and Its Aftermath* (Princeton, NJ, 1949; 1965 ed.), vol. II, 159.

29 James Sims, *Arnhem Spearhead* (London, 1978), 74; I am grateful to Dr. William Buckingham for this reference.

and the Nazi leadership remained an important one.[30] The German soldier remained just that – a soldier, but one gulled by Hitler. The war in the west never totally lost touch with humane principles or with the notion that even total war is subject to rationality.

III

That point cannot be sustained for the war in the east. So much of the recent historiography has focused here that it would be redundant to catalogue all the ways in which it can be deemed total. Suffice it to say that, if total war moved from theory to abstraction anywhere in the twentieth century, it did so here.

Terrain played its part. In theory and in practice, the steppe was a maneuvering space for mechanical formations as uncluttered as that of the desert. But most of the German army was not mechanized, and what bore in upon the foot-sore infantryman was the sense that it was a land without a goal – an infinite space.[31] Ultimately, even the Panzer divisions were swallowed up, their logistical support unable to cope with the distances involved. The obstacles on which the army's planners had focused were those set by nature – the successive river lines of the Dniester, Dnieper, Donets, and Don. But the goals that Hitler set were cities – Leningrad, Moscow, and Kiev. Given the physical opportunities for maneuver on a massive scale, the political choke points became even more important. Leningrad, Stalingrad, and – in due course – Warsaw and Berlin were ready-made defensive battlefields and used as such. Where there were no such obstacles, the Soviets created them, as at Kursk.

Noncombatant immunity was forfeited, however, primarily for a second reason. In the west, the populations of the occupied territories did not turn to active resistance until late in the war. Partisan warfare characterized operations in the East much sooner. Although Engels, reflecting on the war in France in 1871, had defined the erosion of the distinction between soldier and civilian as total war, partisan war was not developed as a policy option by the Soviet Union in the 1930s. It had to be imposed in July 1941, and it was slow to gain a footing.[32] Partisan warfare both breached international law and

30 Stouffer, *The American Soldier*, II, 34, 158–9, 565–6; see also Schrijvers, *Crash of Ruin*, 64–77.

31 Hans Joachim Schroeder, "German Soldiers' Experiences During the Initial Phase of the Russian Campaign," in Bernd Wegner, ed., *From Peace to War: Germany, Soviet Russia, and the World 1939–1941* (Oxford, 1997), 313.

32 Joachim Hoffmann, *Stalin's War of Extermination 1941–1945: Planning, Realization and Documentation* (Theses and Dissertations Press, 2001); see also Hoffmann, "The Conduct of the War Through Soviet Eyes," in *Germany and the Second World War*, V, 833–940; and, for a more balanced approach, Amir

struck a nerve in a German army made sensitive by the experiences of 1871 and 1914. But those killed in antipartisan operations included many who were palpably not partisans – including women, children, and, of course, Jews.

Although civilian loss of life in urban combat or in antipartisan operations might be condoned under the heading of military necessity, what transpired in 1941–42 was qualitatively and quantitatively different. The turning point in the war from the viewpoint of totality was not the decision to launch Operation Barbarossa in June 1941, the war against the enemy without, but the decision to implement the Final Solution, the war against the enemy within. When the attack in the east did not defeat the Soviet Union in a single blow, as Hitler had intended, then the external war became even more fused with the idea of totalitarian war. The pursuit of racial and ideological goals usurped the conduct of war and in doing so breached the underlying rationality of total war developed in the 1930s.

When Nazi Germany overran Western Europe, it curbed the destructive effect of war in order to leave the region's infrastructure intact. But this sort of economic self-interest did not apply in the east: the opportunities for cooperation and therefore exploitation in, say, Ukraine were deliberately flouted as antipartisan operations became embroiled with genocide. Not least as a result of the irrationalities of its own reinterpretation of total war, the German army was not able to feed exclusively off the land, and by the spring of 1942 the production of all raw materials in the occupied Soviet Union had collapsed – with the exception of oil, which was running at 75 percent of its prewar output.[33]

In theory, the German army had reached the buffers of its ability to wage industrialized war. Its equipment levels were falling: it had 3,648 armored fighting vehicles and assault guns in June 1941 and 1,803 in January 1942.[34] Omer Bartov has talked of its "demodernisation."[35] By rights, it ought to have renounced total war as beyond its capabilities. In practice, it now cleaved to the notion with an increased commitment whose principal propellant was psychological rather than actual. War at an ideological level showed its ability to burst the bounds of economic calculation. Shorn of any quantitative edge over the Red Army, the Wehrmacht fell back on a qualitative superiority – but one expressed less in individually superior weapons and more in National Socialist ideology. What is significant about

---

Weiner, *Making Sense of War: The Second World War and the Fate of the Bolshevik Revolution* (Princeton, NJ, 2001), esp. 129–90.

33 *Germany and the Second World War*, IV, 1184.   34 Ibid., IV, 1129.

35 Omer Bartov, *Hitler's Army: Soldiers, Nazis, and War in the Third Reich* (Oxford, 1991), 16–18.

the bomb plot of July 1944 is less that a small group of conservative officers were ready to oppose Hitler and more that in its aftermath Guderian, as the new Chief of the General Staff, was committed to the full nazification of the army. Guderian was not only reflecting what others like Reichenau and Manstein had already advocated, but also striking a deep chord in an army all too mindful of the *Dolchstosslegende* and the belief that defeat was the consequence of a split between the army and civilian society. This was where the Nazis profited from the similarities between their own vocabulary and the calls to self-sacrifice of military service.[36]

What made the war in Russia total was the fact that this deep ideological commitment was common to both sides. In the 1930s, the Soviet Union had also employed the vocabulary as well as the threat of war in the pursuit of economic mobilization. And the NKVD used the war as the Nazis did – as an excuse to liquidate the enemy within. German prisoners of war in Soviet hands were no more likely to survive than were Soviet prisoners in German hands. As Stalin confessed to Djilas: "This war is not as in the past; whoever occupies a territory also imposes on it his own social system."[37]

James Turner Johnson's contention that even total war can be a rational activity renders the principal authors of what happened on the eastern front, Hitler and Stalin, rational actors. But some of the things done in their name suggest that Johnson's construction became increasingly inapplicable. It does not account for the motives of their subordinates, of the behavior of those who had to do the killing – of Christopher Browning's "ordinary men."

What the war in the east reveals is that many men can become used to killing. They may need the state to order it in the first place to get them over their initial revulsion, and they may still need the state's authority to rationalize their actions to themselves, but in the immediacy of execution other more basic impulses – including sadism – can come into play.[38] Most discourse about war works within Clausewitzian parameters. It distinguishes between individual acts of violence, such as murder or manslaughter, and war as a social activity waged for political ends. What was horrific about the link between the Russo-German War and the Final Solution is that for many soldiers on both sides it broke down their division between war and violence, and therefore robbed the conflict of reason.

---

36 Stephen G. Fritz, *Frontsoldaten: The German Soldier in World War II* (Lexington, KY, 1995), 199, 213; Klaus Latzel, *Deutsche Soldaten – nationalsozialistischer Krieg? Kriegserlebnis-Kriegserfahrung 1939–1945* (Paderborn, 1998), 219–29.
37 Milovan Djilas, *Conversations with Stalin* (London, 1963), 90.
38 Browning, *Ordinary Men*, 203–9; Dave Grossman, *On Killing: The Psychological Cost of Learning to Kill in War and Society* (Boston, 1995), 36, 161, 164–9, 234–6, 243–4, 250–60; Joanna Bourke, *An Intimate History of Killing: Face-to-Face Killing in Twentieth-Century Warfare* (London, 1999), 5, 31–42.

It did so in large part because of its ability to "distance" the enemy and so rob him of his humanity. The conduct of war itself had its part in this process. Killing in twentieth-century warfare was carried out at increasing ranges – in the case of air forces at heights so great that the enemy on the ground could not be seen. On the ground, the cult of the bayonet grew in almost inverse proportion to its effectiveness as artillery became the principal killer of modern war: but it was less the gunners than the infantry who had to witness the damage the shells inflicted on the human frame.

Distancing was also achieved by dehumanizing the enemy. In the era of so-called limited war in the eighteenth century, European armies respected each other even if they did not show similar respect to the civilians who lay in their path. That same respect between soldiers characterized much of the Second World War in the west. But it did not apply in the east. The Jews of Eastern Europe could be killed more easily once they had been degraded and dehumanized in the ghettos and concentration camps. Cognate methods were applied in combat. For the Germans, the Russians were uncivilized, barbaric, and Asiatic.[39] For the Russians, they were "Fascist carrion," "plague-carrying rats," and "cannibals."[40]

IV

Racism was the most effective of all creators of distance. In the eighteenth century, European armies fought with far greater ferocity against the Turks. Race was a factor in the barbarization of the war in Russia. But it was the dominant characteristic of the war against Japan. It is one tool at least by which to understand a paradox. On the Russian front, total war (if that was what it was) was waged by totalitarian powers; but in the Pacific, the conduct of war achieved at least one definition of totality in the hands of two states, Britain and the United States, that were liberal.

"Your enemy is a curious race," Thomas Blamey told his Australian troops in New Guinea in early 1943, "a cross between the human being and the ape. And like the ape, when he is cornered he knows how to die. But he is inferior to you, and you know it, and that knowledge will help you to victory."[41] Private Jo Gullett absorbed the words of his commanding

39 Latzel, *Deutsche Soldaten*, 219–29; see also the essays in Hannes Heer and Klaus Naumann, eds., *Vernichtungskrieg. Verbrechen der Wermacht 1941–1944* (Hamburg, 1995), esp. Heer, "Killing Fields: Die Wehrmacht und der Holocaust."
40 *Germany and the Second World War*, IV, 912.
41 John W. Dower, *War Without Mercy: Race and Power in the Pacific War* (London, 1986), 70.

officer: "They were like clever animals with certain human characteristics, but by no mean the full range, and this is how we thought of them – as animals."[42]

Apes were not the only analogy used by Australian and American troops: baboons and monkeys entered the repertoire. The atrocities committed by the Japanese confirmed the belief that they were subhuman: prisoners were tortured to death, their bodies mutilated, and in some cases their livers and other parts of their anatomy eaten. At the outset of the war, the Americans had believed that the Japanese would respect the laws of war. But medical officers came to realize that the red crosses on their helmets and their lack of arms drew enemy fire rather than deterred it. Japanese soldiers feigned surrender and then killed their captors; their sick and wounded clutched hand grenades under their bed clothes so as to kill their enemy as well as themselves. One U.S. Marine officer who was particularly shocked by this sort of behavior concluded that the Japanese conduct of war displayed a "complete lack of inhibiting battle ethics, as defined by modern civilization and the precepts of the Geneva convention."[43]

The decision on the part of the Allied armies also to disregard the laws of war was condoned from on high. The chief of naval operations, Admiral William D. Leahy, who became Roosevelt's chief of staff, declared in January 1942 that "in fighting with Japanese savages all previously accepted rules of warfare must be abandoned."[44] Blamey went on to tell his Australians at Port Moresby in 1942 that, "Beneath the thin veneer of a few generations of civilisation [the Japanese] is a subhuman beast, who has brought warfare back to the primeval, who fights by the jungle rule of tooth and claw."[45]

The upshot was the dehumanization of both sides. American soldiers pulled the golden teeth of Japanese dead and took their ears and skulls as souvenirs. They became as ready not to take prisoners as the Japanese themselves. Forty-two percent of American soldiers responded when seeing Japanese prisoners in 1944 that they felt all the more like killing them: in Europe, only 18 percent of GIs felt that way about German prisoners. Only 20 percent felt that the Japanese were men just like them, but 54 percent responded in that way to the Germans.[46]

The fanaticism of the Japanese soldier rationalized the imperative to kill. Courage and the refusal to surrender ceased to be admirable soldierly qualities symptomatic of a shared code of military honor and became instead evidence of an alien and incomprehensible culture. Because the Japanese did

42 Johnston, *Fighting the Enemy*, 86.
44 Dower, *War Without Mercy*, 141.
46 Stouffer, *The American Soldier*, II, 161.

43 Linderman, *The World Within War*, 160.
45 Ibid., 53.

not retreat when they were defeated, it seemed that the only way to win was to kill them – and go on doing so regardless of convention.[47]

Nor was this a false conclusion. In the 1930s, the Japanese were led to believe that war itself was a form of spiritual purification. An army pamphlet of 1934 described war as the father of creation and the mother of culture. Japanese philosophers borrowed from Shintoism to suggest that the self-denial fostered by war would enable the world to be purged of individualism, capitalism, and Marxism. The "cabinet institute for the study of total war" – in itself a revealing title – produced a massive report on protracted war designed to show that war was constructive.[48]

What is significant about the report is the date of its completion: March 1945. To all rational observers, Japan was already defeated. Japan justified the continuing struggle in terms that saw virtue in death and honor in the fighting itself, rather than in the political objectives for which the war was being fought. In this, its presentation of the war as an end in itself was little different from the propaganda of Nazi Germany: the struggle had its own validity. Germany, like Japan, carried on with the war for roughly a year after it was self-evidently lost. The killing mounted as the purpose declined. Germany suffered 64 percent of its total deaths in the war after January 1944, including 1.5 million dead between December 1944 and April 1945.[49] Over half of all U.S. losses in the Pacific occurred between July 1944 and July 1945.[50] Thus, from the perspective of Turner's morality, total war was robbed of its implicit restraints because its rationality was increasingly far-fetched. In this respect, the Second World War was radically different from the First. Then the outcome was not fully clear until the summer of 1918, and when it was, negotiation followed: Clausewitzian imperatives were – ultimately – reasserted.

Fanaticism distanced the enemy, but the nature of the fighting did not necessarily do so. Terrain, once more, had a determining role in shaping concepts of totality. When Slim took over the 14th Army, he found an army frightened of the jungle, too ready to see it as an obstacle rather than as "a welcome means of concealed maneuver."[51] At Guadalcanal, James Jones, a prewar regular in the U.S. army, thought "it looked more like a massive wall than anything else. Dense, solid."[52] The "jungle was Jap," the open spaces were American.

47 Johnston, *Fighting the Enemy*, 90; Linderman, *The World Within War*, 174.
48 Dower, *War Without Mercy*, 215–16, 225–6.
49 Rüdiger Overmans, *Deutsche militärische Verluste im Zweiten Weltkrieg* (Munich, 1999), 239, 270.
50 Dower, *War Without Mercy*, 295, 300.
51 Anthony Kellett, *Combat Motivation: The Behaviour of Soldiers in Battle* (Boston, 1982), 243–4.
52 Linderman, *The World Within War*, 170.

By becoming an obstacle rather than a medium for small group infiltration, and by making the Japanese invisible, the jungle could – like racism and fanaticism – distance the enemy. But it also meant that, when combat occurred, it was close-range. It highlighted the field skills of the individual and should therefore have humanized rather than dehumanized the war.[53] In the southwest Pacific, small arms fire accounted for 32 percent of American deaths (as opposed to 19.7 percent in the war as a whole), and artillery fire for only 17 percent (as opposed to 57.5 percent).[54]

In practice, however, the more personal the combat the more brutal it seemed to become. The "demodernization" of the Japanese army highlighted their backwardness: infantry still charged to bugle calls, relying on their bayonets, and egged on by officers who not only carried swords but used them. The confidence both Americans and Australians felt in the superiority of their weapons gave them greater confidence not only in their eventual victory but also in their capacity to achieve it by inflicting casualties. Banzai assaults and Kamikaze pilots were evidence more of primitiveness than of courage.[55]

The readiness of the United States and British imperial forces to abandon restraint in the conduct of war finds its moral justification in reciprocity. But it had its roots in the experience of colonial warfare. Here, too, the possession of modernity by one side, the colonial power, had not resulted in restraint in the application of new technology. Moreover, colonial wars were conducted against the entire native population and their means of livelihood. The connections were determined partly by geography. The British in Burma were operating out of India, building on an army whose combat experience was derived from the lessons of the northwest frontier of India as much as those of the trenches of France.[56] The American penchant for calling the Japanese "Gooks" derived from the slang applied to the Filipinos in 1898. Although the U.S. Army's experience of colonial warfare was much more limited than that of the British, the Americans drew on its equivalent – the Indian wars – when seeking an analogy for the war with Japan.[57]

Thus, it was the United States that dropped the atomic bomb, and it was two Japanese cities that were the targets. Before the war, the United States had denounced the bombing of civilians and had advocated precision bombing as more compatible with the principles of proportionality and military utility. During the war, area bombing of Japanese cities deliberately

---

53 Paul W. Thompson et al., *How the Jap Army Fights* (Harmondsworth, 1942), 88.
54 Johnston, *Fighting the Enemy*, 77.
55 Ibid., 109, 115; Stouffer, *American Soldier*, II, 158–60.
56 Thompson, *How the Jap Army Fights*, 73.   57 Dower, *War Without Mercy*, 33, 148, 152, 162.

abandoned those tenets and did so to popular acclaim. The distinction between bureaucrats and perpetrators in the implementation of genocide seemed to be eroded in the hands of democracy. Of those American infantrymen who saw Japanese prisoners in 1944, 58 percent said that they would like to "wipe out the whole Japanese nation."[58] Admiral William Halsey, commanding in the South Pacific, announced in the same year, "When we get through with them, the Japanese language will be spoken only in hell."[59] Vice Admiral Arthur Redford, anticipating the invasion of Japan in 1945, said "Japan will eventually be a nation without cities – a nomadic people." The dropping of the atomic bomb was not only popular at the time but remained so: in December 1945, 22.7 percent of respondents to an American poll expressed disappointment that more bombs had not been dropped before the Japanese surrendered.[60]

If total war is to be defined in terms of the technologies deployed – a definition by and large eschewed in this essay – then the atomic bomb was its confirmation. But it also exposed two important ideological points. First, it helps explain why totality in the conduct of war is a concept with which the liberal powers have been comfortable. Their industrial and economic superiority has enabled them to use the technology of total war while themselves escaping its consequences. It is legitimate to ask whether such a one-sided use can reasonably be accorded the epithet total. Second, nuclear weapons removed the baggage of totalitarianism from total war. They gave democratic powers the ability to wage total war without the sort of economic and social mobilization anticipated by the 1930s commentators.

Whatever the hatreds and cultural assumptions at the time of Hiroshima and Nagasaki, the rationalizations that followed the dropping of the atomic bomb – which we now call nuclear deterrence – gave back to total war the sort of logic in which it has been clothed by Johnson. But the point remains that during the Second World War the conduct of war exceeded the worst prefigurings and imaginings of the interwar theorists. It did so because theirs were rational constructs that did not allow for the possibility of violence usurping war for its own ends. The philosophical difficulty when that occurs is whether that is still war, and therefore evidence of total war, or whether it needs a new and different vocabulary – like murder, rape, and pillage. The trouble with such a distinction is that it was the Second World War's intensity and length which themselves gave rise to the dehumanization of the conduct of war.

58 Stouffer, *American Soldier*, II, 160.   59 Linderman, *The World Within War*, 178.
60 Dower, *War Without Mercy*, 54–5.

3

The Ultimate Horror

Reflections on Total War and Genocide

STIG FÖRSTER AND MYRIAM GESSLER

The radicalization of warfare appears to have reached a climax during the Second World War. Not only did the belligerent powers come closer than ever before to putting total war into practice, but this war also witnessed the most shocking genocide in history. The Second World War is thus rightly regarded as the ultimate horror of the modern age. It resulted in the deaths of some 60 million people worldwide, at least 10 percent of whom fell victim to some form of genocidal action.

The moral dimensions of this catastrophe were enormous, but they must not obscure the effort to explain. This essay accordingly examines analytically the relationship between total war and genocide in the Second World War. It also offers some general reflections on the relationship between the two phenomena, particularly about the extent to which genocide represents a constituent element of total war.

Total war and genocide share the characteristic of being difficult to define. While several attempts have been made to study genocide comparatively, a model has only recently been proposed to overcome the many theoretical difficulties.[1] In the first part of this essay, we shall therefore offer a theoretical model that is intended to address both genocide and total war.

The second part of the essay will provide reflections on the empirical relationship between total war and genocide. The fact that the two phenomena converged in the Second World War raises the question whether the connection was due to more than coincidence. Was it due uniquely to the policies of Adolf Hitler and the National Socialists, or were genocide and total war linked more fundamentally? Did they share a common history? Did genocide represent the logical culmination of total war? Do the policies

---

1 Myriam Gessler, "Die Singularität des Holocaust und die vergleichende Genozidforschung: Empirische und theoretische Untersuchung zu einem aktuellen Thema der Geschichtswissenschaft" (Lizentiatsarbeit, Bern 2000).

of the other belligerent powers during the Second World War also point to the convergence between total war and genocide?

TOTAL WAR AND GENOCIDE: CONCEPTUAL DIFFERENCES

While scholars have been able to agree on the features of total war, they have yet to settle on a general definition of the concept.[2] Authors who prefer an analytical approach understand total war to be a unique form of warfare. But opinions about its historical significance differ widely. According to Roger Chickering, the elements of total war were not historically confined to the nineteenth and twentieth centuries.[3] If this argument is correct, it undermines the proposition that total war was a distinctly modern phenomenon, that it was a product of developments such as industrialization, mass communications, and modern forms of social control.[4] The variety of views about total war is bewildering. There is little agreement over which wars deserve the label "total" or, for that matter, whether a "genuinely" total war could ever have been fought.[5] In these circumstances, a Weberian ideal type appears to offer the most practical solution. We, in any event, will employ one here.

Comparative research on genocide has raised similar problems. Scholars are still trying to define it. Their ideas differ widely despite the fact that they agree on the elements. The differences reflect important disagreements over emphasis. A generally accepted definition of genocide does not exist. The definition set out in the United Nations Convention on Genocide[6] has

---

2 Stig Förster, "Das Zeitalter des totalen Krieges 1861–1945: Konzeptionelle Überlegungen für einen historischen Strukturvergleich," *Mittelweg 36* (1999/2000): 20–8. See also the four essay collections that, like the present volume, had their origins in a series of conferences on the concept of total war: Stig Förster and Jörg Nagler, eds., *On the Road to Total War: The American Civil War and the German Wars of Unification, 1861–1871* (Cambridge, 1997); Manfred F. Boemeke, Roger Chickering, and Stig Förster, eds., *Anticipating Total War: The German and American Experiences, 1871–1914* (Cambridge, 1999); Roger Chickering and Stig Förster, eds., *Great War, Total War: Combat and Mobilization on the Western Front, 1914–1918* (Cambridge, 2000); Roger Chickering and Stig Förster, "Introduction," Chickering and Förster, eds., *In the Shadows of Total War: Europe, East Asia, and the United States, 1919–1939* (Cambridge, 2003).

3 Roger Chickering, "Total War: The Use and Abuse of a Concept," Manfred F. Boemeke, Roger Chickering, and Stig Förster, eds., *Anticipating Total War: The German and American Experiences, 1871–1914* (Cambridge, 1999), 13–28.

4 Stig Förster and Jörg Nagler, "Introduction," Förster and Nagler, eds., *On the Road to Total War*, 4–15; Stig Förster, "Introduction," Chickering and Förster, eds., *Great War, Total War*, 1–15.

5 See James M. McPherson, "From Limited War to Total War in America," Förster and Nagler, *On the Road to Total War*, 295–309; Chickering, "Total War," 23–5.

6 Most important in this context is Article 2, which reads as follows:

In the present Convention, genocide means any of the following acts committed with intent to destroy, in whole or in part, a national, ethnical, racial or religious group, as such:
(a) Killing members of the group;
(b) Causing serious bodily or mental harm to members of the group;

primarily served legal purposes, and several scholars have criticized it as an inadequate basis for scholarly research.[7] A variety of overly narrow or overly broad definitions are now in competition.[8] Some authors have emphasized the importance of the intentions of the perpetrators to destroy a specific group of people.[9] This intentionalism has come under criticism from authors who argue that it distracts attention from the development of genocidal structures. According to these critics, the intentionalist position also ignores cases in which premeditated planning cannot be demonstrated.[10] Another problem is the role of the state. Some authors emphasize the significance of state authorities in planning and executing genocide. Others, however, point out that nongovernmental groups, such as settlers, have also participated in genocide.[11] The confusing variety of definitions has now reached the point where new terms have been introduced, such as *cultural genocide* and *democide*.[12]

Insofar as the terms total war and genocide are not unambiguous, there is little common basis for discussion of the two. Rather than extending the search for definitions, we propose here to characterize total war and genocide within their respective historical contexts. Individual cases have provided empirical data that can be compared. Empirical comparison can then support theoretical generalizations to distinguish total war and genocide from other related phenomena such as "limited war" or "massacre." In this way, individual cases can be used to suggest common denominators.

(c) Deliberately inflicting on the group conditions of life calculated to bring about its physical destruction in whole or in part;

(d) Imposing measures intended to prevent births within the group;

(e) Forcibly transferring children of the group to another group.

Yearbook of the United Nations, Special Edition UN Fiftieth Anniversary 1945–1995, ed. Department of Public Information United Nations (The Hague, 1995), 288.

7 Gessler, "Singularität," 19–29.

8 Israel W. Charny, *Encyclopedia of Genocide*, 2 vols. (Santa Barbara, 1999); Gessler, "Singularität," 18–32.

9 Leo Kuper, *Genocide: Its Political Use in the Twentieth Century* (New York, 1981), 86; Frank Chalk and Kurt Jonassohn, *The History and Sociology of Genocide: Analyses and Case Studies* (New Haven, 1990), 23, 26; Robert Melson, "Problems in the Comparison of the Armenian Genocide and the Holocaust: Definitions, Typologies, Theories, and Fallacies," *Jahrbuch für Historische Friedensforschung* 7 (1999): 28.

10 See George J. Andreopoulos, "Introduction: The Calculus of Genocide," *Genocide: Conceptual and Historical Dimensions* (Philadelphia, 1994), 7–13; Isidor Wallimann and Michael N. Dobkowski, "Introduction," *Genocide and the Modern Age: Etiology and Case Studies of Mass Death* (New York, 1987), xvi; Israel W. Charny, "Toward a Generic Definition of Genocide," in Andreopoulos, *Dimensions*, 74–5, 78.

11 Irving Louis Horowitz, *Taking Lives: Genocide and State Power* (New Brunswick, NJ, 1997); Chalk and Jonassohn, *History and Sociology*, 16, 23, 26.

12 Charny, "Generic Definition," 84–5; Rudolph J. Rummel, *Death by Government* (New Brunswick, NJ, 1994), 31–42.

The comparative method assumes that specific historical events are not only to be analyzed according to their unique features, but that they can be regarded as examples of more general phenomena.[13] The difficulty of this method is that common characteristics are not always equally salient. In World War II, for instance, the war aims of the National Socialists and the Western Allies did not display the same degree of radicalization. The aims of both contained elements of total warfare, but in different ways, to different extents, and to different ends. But the elements of total warfare did, in one way or another, provide a common denominator between the two sides. For purposes of comparative generalization, it is thus necessary to determine the common elements in total warfare.

The ideal type of total war lies at the core of this comparative exercise. Four elements of total war have been identified:[14]

1. Total war aims: unconditional surrender, subjugation of the enemy state or nation, the principle of destruction.
2. Total methods: disregard for international law and common moral principles, reckless use of all military means against the enemy.
3. Total mobilization: the employment of all resources of state, society, and economy for the single purpose of warfare.
4. Total control: centralized organization and purposeful guidance of all aspects of public and private life within the context of warfare.

Implicit in all four elements is the erosion of the boundary between soldiers and civilians; civilians become the backbone of the war effort as well as targets of military violence.

The combination of these elements distinguishes total war from other forms of warfare. However, this model is only theoretical, for neither the individual elements nor their combination has materialized fully in practice. Total war therefore is an ideal type; it does not exist in empirical reality, but derives from comparative study of historical phenomena, whose main characteristics or tendencies are taken to the extreme. History provides only individual instances in which one or another element, or a combination of them, is put into practice to a certain degree. Empirical research can only detect developments and events that display tendencies toward total war. Any given war might approach the ideal type but will never realize it in full.

---

13 Hartmut Kaelble, *Der historische Vergleich: Eine Einführung zum 19. und 20. Jahrhundert* (Frankfurt am Main, 1999).
14 Förster, "Zeitalter," 20–8.

One can in turn identify three typical elements of "genocide":

1. Intention of the perpetrators: aiming at the systematic physical destruction of a given group on the basis of political, economic, religious, racial, or social criteria.[15]
2. Dehumanization of the victims: specifically defined groups are expelled from society according to the ideologies of the perpetrators. These groups are defined as useless, dangerous to civilization, and therefore unentitled to human rights. They are accordingly vulnerable to acts of violence.[16]
3. Execution: centrally planned administrative measures. These are carried out by governmental institutions, the armed forces, or civilian collaborators. Execution relies on bureaucracy, communications, and logistics.[17]

These elements distinguish genocide from other forms of organized mass killings, such as massacres. In contrast to total war, however, genocide has occurred in reality. All its elements and their combination taken to their extremes would constitute "absolute genocide," in other words an ideal type.

The Ideal-Typical Models of Total War and Genocide

These reflections on the heuristic use of the ideal type are based on Max Weber's understanding of the term as well as Clausewitz's distinction between real and absolute war.[18] Our approach employs an abstract model as a measurement of reality. Empirical cases do not display all elements in the extreme measure that defines the ideal type. How closely these cases approximate one another and their ideal type is determined by empirical limitations, such as logistics, terrain, climate, and political, social, and economic circumstances that impede planning and execution. In this context,

15 It should be noted that decision-making within a given leadership is not the only area where such intention can be demonstrated. The aim of genocide can also be traced in memoranda, orders, and actions of the bureaucratic and military apparatus. Likewise, ideology and political programs provide information on destructive intentions. See Gessler, "Singularität," 54.

16 Kuper, *Genocide*, 85–91; Helen Fein, "Genocide, Terror, Life Integrity, and War Crimes: The Case for Discrimination," Andreopoulos, *Dimensions*, 101–3; Yves Ternon, *Der verbrecherische Staat: Völkermord im 20. Jahrhundert* (Hamburg, 1996), 79–80.

17 Roger W. Smith, "Human Destructiveness and Politics: The Twentieth Century as an Age of Genocide," Wallimann and Dobkowski, *Modern Age*, 32.

18 Carl von Clausewitz, *Vom Kriege*, ed. Werner Hahlweg (Bonn, 1980), 192–200, 954–6; Max Weber, "Die 'Objektivität' sozialwissenschaftlicher und sozialpolitischer Erkenntnis," *Gesammelte Aufsätze zur Wissenschaftslehre*, ed. Johannes Winckelmann (Tübingen, 1985), 190–5, 199. See also Chickering, "Total War," 23–5; Chickering, "Militärgeschichte als Totalgeschichte im Zeitalter des totalen Krieges," Thomas Kühne and Benjamin Ziemann, eds., *Was ist Militärgeschichte?* (Paderborn, 2000), 307; Stig Förster, "'Vom Kriege': Überlegungen zu einer modernen Militärgeschichte," ibid., 269–73. It should be noted here that "total war" and Clausewitz's "absolute war" are two different concepts: the former applies only to a specific kind of warfare, the latter deals with war in general.

Clausewitz wrote of "frictions."[19] These restricting factors have prevented belligerents from realizing the ideal type of total war. Likewise, perpetrators have not put absolute genocide into practice.

Ideal types are general descriptions. It is necessary to take into account the uniqueness of every empirical case. This proposition applies to its historical individuality as well its context and the dynamic political, economic, social, and cultural factors that shape this context. Historical developments, as well as the degree to which elements in a given case approach the ideal type of total war or the ideal type of genocide, must be investigated. Moreover, each case must be analyzed in its global, regional, and local contexts. These research imperatives imply an enormous empirical and methodological effort. In other words, "Total war requires total history."[20] The effort now exceeds the capacities of any single scholar and places a premium on collaborative efforts, such as the present volume, that pool the energies of scholars from several disciplines. But in their empirical research, scholars must attend to the ideal type.

What are the implications of these observations for the relationship between total war and genocide? Not every element of total war tends toward genocide. However, on a theoretical level at least, total war implies the elimination of the boundaries between the military and civilian spheres. If the destruction of the enemy entails not only the destruction of its armed forces but also of its society, physical extermination of whole peoples lies within the logic of total war. Here the ideal types of total war and genocide meet in theory.

Total War and Genocide in Modern History

The ideal type provides a theoretical platform to facilitate an understanding of empirical reality. But this reality has proved to be different from theory. Leaders who have tried to achieve total war and perpetrators of genocide have been forced to compromise under the pressures of restricting circumstances. Political, social, economic, cultural, organizational, and military considerations have made it impossible to realize the ideal type in historical practice. Hence neither total war nor absolute genocide has ever occurred or could have occurred. The Second World War nonetheless came close in both respects.

Tendencies toward total war and absolute genocide have constituted two distinct phenomena in modern history. They were not necessarily related.

---

19 Clausewitz, *Vom Kriege*, 262, 954–5.   20 Chickering, "Total War," 27.

The war between Iran and Iraq displayed several elements of total warfare, but apart from Saddam Hussein's massacre of the Iraqi Kurds, this war showed little tendency toward genocide.[21] The genocide in Rwanda, on the other hand, one of the most ruthless crimes of this sort in the twentieth century, was carried out in the context of a civil war; the conflict was of low intensity and did not remotely approximate total war.[22] Genocide has often accompanied war. In the case of "foreign genocide," military invasion provided the basis for exterminating a foreign people. "Domestic genocide," too, has often occurred within the context of war, particularly during civil wars such as the one in Rwanda. However, genocide has also taken place in the absence of war. The deliberate mass starvation of Ukrainian farmers in 1932–33 was arguably such a case.[23]

In any event, during "the age of total war" tendencies toward total war and genocide appear to have been distinct developments. The American Civil War and the Franco-Prussian War were fought largely along traditional lines. Industrialized warfare had only just begun. Yet some indications showed that Americans and Europeans had indeed embarked "on the road to total war" by the middle of the nineteenth century. The demand for unconditional surrender during the Civil War, calls for the complete subjugation of the French, the readiness of the belligerents in both wars to employ terror to win, the astonishing degree of mobilization and control on the home front in both cases all demonstrated that the character of modern warfare was changing.[24] Nevertheless, there were no significant tendencies toward genocide. Neither Sherman during his march to the sea nor Moltke in his drive on Paris contemplated the physical extermination of enemy populations. In other words, tendencies toward total war and genocide were not at this time linked.

The reason was not that genocide was unthinkable. The same Union generals who had shied away from this option when fighting the Confederacy showed less restraint when fighting others. Grant, Sherman, and Sheridan did engage in genocide against the indigenous populations of the Great Plains, who, it was alleged, stood in the way of "progress."[25] Three decades later, American forces again came close to committing genocide during the

21 Anthony H. Cordesman, *Iran and Iraq: The Threat from the Northern Gulf* (Boulder, CO, 1994); W. Thom Workman, *The Social Origins of the Iran-Iraq War* (Boulder, CO, 1994), 161–3.
22 Ternon, *Staat*, 181–95.   23 See Ternon, *Staat*, 204–7.
24 Förster and Nagler, *Road*.
25 Michael Fellman, *Citizen Sherman: A Life of William Tecumseh Sherman* (New York, 1995), 259–77; cf. Robert M. Utley, "Total War on the American Indian Frontier," Boemeke, Chickering, and Förster, *Anticipating*, 399–414.

campaign against Philippine guerrillas.[26] Europeans were also capable of genocidal tendencies when they confronted dark-skinned enemies. The German-led expedition to China at the turn of the century revealed terrifying fantasies that pointed in this direction.[27] Most significant in this respect, however, was German rule in Africa. Ruthless suppression and exploitation, which was a common feature of European colonialism generally, reached a climax in the German wars of extermination. The destruction of the Nama and Herero peoples in Southwest Africa constituted the first genocide of the twentieth century.[28] Large-scale massacres, which implied the threat of exterminating whole peoples – hence genocide – were not alien to European and American soldiers and their political sponsors. Colonial wars and other such military expeditions differed, though, from the American Civil War and the Franco-German War. One did not massacre a "civilized" foe.

The modern histories of total war and genocide thus originated in different military contexts. The tendency toward total war gestated in large-scale military conflicts between antagonists of more or less similar strength and cultural backgrounds. This tendency accompanied the emergence of the industrialized nation-state and the increasing participation of citizens in politics. By contrast, the tendency toward genocide grew and moved along with the frontiers of American and European imperial expansion. It occurred in wars that were at least in one sense total as well, insofar as indigenous people were fighting for their very survival, had mobilized all their resources, and did not shy from committing atrocities themselves. To the "civilized" aggressors, however, these wars were limited affairs. Full mobilization was not required. The war aims of the colonizers, however, did tend toward totality, and the means they employed to achieve these ends were often ruthless – to the point of genocide.[29] Above all, disregard for the cultural achievements of the "natives," which often took the form of naked racism, opened the way to genocide. In turn, the introduction of racism into the concept of total war provided the linkage to genocide.

Prior to 1914, colonial wars took place in an intellectual environment in which few could imagine total warfare among the great European powers.

26 Glenn Anthony May, "Was the Philippine-American War a 'Total War'?" Boemeke, Chickering, and Förster, *Anticipating*, 437–58.
27 Sabine Dabringhaus, "An Army on Vacation? The German War in China, 1900–1901," ibid., 459–76.
28 Trutz von Trotha, "'The Fellows Can Just Starve': On Wars of 'Pacification' in the African Colonies of Imperial Germany and the Concept of 'Total War,'" ibid., 415–36; Jürgen Zimmerer, *Deutsche Herrschaft über Afrikaner. Staatlicher Machtanspruch und Wirklichkeit im kolonialen Namibia* (Hamburg, 2001), 32–41.
29 Michael Howard, "Colonial Wars and European Wars," J. A. de Moor and H. L. Wesselink, eds., *Imperialism and War: Essays on Colonial Wars in Asia and Africa* (Leiden, 1989), 218–23.

Some observers, like the elder Hellmuth von Moltke, did warn of the disastrous consequences of long "people's wars." Nonetheless, the full mobilization of society and economy, war aims that entailed complete subjugation of an enemy, the abandonment of all restraints in warfare, and the establishment of complete control over society were still beyond imagination.[30] Nor did anyone of consequence envisage genocide as a feature of a major war in the future, despite the spread of racism and Social Darwinism in Europe.[31]

When the Great War arrived in 1914, it proved to be a disaster that few had predicted. Not until 1916, however, did tendencies toward total war gain significant momentum. Leaders in Britain, Germany, and elsewhere tried now to institute full mobilization and tighter controls; war aims radicalized, and the fighting became more brutal. All sides became less willing to spare the lives of civilians. Never before in modern history had belligerents come so close to waging total war, but because of the many "frictions" they encountered, they could not go all the way. The same belligerents would show a quarter century later just how far the Great War fell short of the ideal type of total war. Nonetheless, it did represent a major step in that direction.[32]

The carnage of this war was horrible. The hatreds that it engendered were fearsome. Racism became the common coin of war propaganda. Yet in the European theater of war, the notion of genocide played little part. The bonds of "civilization" among Europeans, North Americans, Australians, and New Zealanders were still strong enough to withstand pressures toward this end. The tendencies toward total war and genocide remained distinct, although massacres of "civilized" people did take place several times.[33]

But the Great War was not just a European war. Genocide did take place on its fringes. Under the pressures of war and military defeat, and fearing the breakup of their empire, the Ottoman leadership decided in 1915 to settle old scores with Christian minorities and to "deport" almost all its Armenian population. As many as a million and a half people perished in the process. This was genocide, although not in an absolute sense, as "frictions" allowed many would-be victims to escape. War nevertheless provided the context, as well as the pretext, to realize Turkish nationalist dreams of ethnic homogeneity.[34] Still, the relationship between the total war and genocide

30 Boemeke, Chickering, and Förster, *Anticipating*.
31 Stig Förster, "Im Reich des Absurden: Die Ursachen des Ersten Weltkrieges," Bernd Wegner, ed., *Wie Kriege entstehen: Zum historischen Hintergrund von Staatenkonflikten* (Paderborn, 2000), 211–52.
32 See Chickering and Förster, *Great War, Total War*.
33 John Horne and Alan Kramer, *German Atrocities 1914: A History of Denial* (New Haven, 2001).
34 Jean-Marie Carzou, *Arménie 1915, un génocide exemplair* (Paris, 1975); Yves Ternon, *Tabu Armenien: Geschichte eines Völkermords* (Frankfurt am Main, 1981); Richard G. Hovannisian, *The Armenian Genocide in Perspective* (New Brunswick, NJ, 1986).

in this case was problematic. The Ottoman Empire maintained its war effort for four years. Some 3 million men were conscripted, and many of them kept up a stubborn fight against the allies. Economic and administrative deficiencies, however, made full mobilization of the home front impossible. The Ottoman Empire was in no position to wage total war.[35] The genocide of the Armenians also had as much to do with an Ottoman tradition of massacring rebellious minorities as with the more modern concept of exterminating ethnic or political groups. The modern aspects of this genocide should nevertheless not be underestimated. World War I encouraged the transformation of the Ottoman Empire into a Turkish nation-state. Ottoman leaders believed that this process would be served by creating an ethnically purified nation. The genocide of the Armenians thus represented the dark side of nation-building in Turkey. Because, however, these events took place on the peripheries of the continent, few in Europe took notice of them, and fewer still understood their meaning. The genocide of the Armenians was not, in any event, a blueprint for World War II.[36]

World War II: Another German Sonderweg?

Two decades ago, historians engaged in a heated debate about Germany's presumed special path, or *Sonderweg*, into the modern world. Hans-Ulrich Wehler and others argued that German authoritarianism and militarism deviated from a Western model of modernization. In response, Geoff Eley and David Blackbourn argued that developments in Germany were less unique than their German colleagues had assumed.[37] By now, the notion of the German *Sonderweg* is, in most respects, all but dead.

World War II, however, appears to offer an exception. The German approach to total war and genocide was in fact unique. The Nazi leadership had an idiosyncratic idea of total war. The Germans tightened controls on the home front almost to the extremes realized in the Soviet Union. Hitler and his minions pursued limitless war aims.[38] Above all, except for the

---

35 M. E. Yapp, *The Making of the Modern Near East, 1792–1923* (London, 1987), 266–300; Alan Palmer, *The Decline and Fall of the Ottoman Empire* (London, 1992), 221–43; Fikret Adanir, *Geschichte der Republik Türkei* (Mannheim, 1995), 9–21.

36 See Taner Akçam, *Armenien und der Völkermord: Die Instanbuler Prozesse und die türkische Nationalbewegung* (Hamburg, 1996).

37 David Blackbourn and Geoff Eley, *The Peculiarities of German History* (New York, 1984); Hans-Ulrich Wehler, "'Deutscher Sonderweg' oder allgemeine Probleme des westlichen Kapitalismus? Zur Kritik einiger 'Mythen deutscher Geschichtsschreibung,'" *Merkur* 35 (1981): 478–87; Volker R. Berghahn, "Militär, industrialisierte Kriegführung und Nationalismus," *Neue Politische Literatur* 26 (1981): 20–41.

38 Ian Kershaw, *Hitler*, 2 vols. (London, 1998–2000), 2: 231–747.

decision not to use chemical and biological weapons, the Germans adopted a new kind of warfare of unbounded brutality. But in one crucial respect the German war effort did not correspond to the ideal type of total war. At least until 1943 and the defeat at Stalingrad, the German leadership did not consider total mobilization. Even after Goebbels's famous "total war" speech in February 1943, it took the Germans a year to institute anything like total mobilization. The reason was that Hitler feared a repetition of the collapse of the home front as at the end of World War I. The Nazis thus hoped to win total victory without having to pay the price for it. This strategy could not work.[39]

Even more distinct was the Nazi attitude toward genocide. Nazi Germany was the only power in World War II that resorted to genocide as a strategic program, as a means as well as an end. The Western Allies were prepared to go to great lengths to win the war. Strategic bombing of civilian targets, including the use of atomic bombs, and the demand for unconditional surrender signaled their commitment to fighting total war. Nor was the Allied war effort free of racism in the war against Japan, but the Allies never contemplated the physical extermination of entire enemy peoples, as their treatment of defeated enemies after the war demonstrated.[40]

To a certain extent, the same also holds true for the Soviet Union. Stalin had not shrunk from genocide during collectivization. During the war, the Soviet authorities deported entire peoples to remote places in Asia in order to satisfy their leader's paranoia about traitors and collaborators. Volga Germans, Crimean Tartars, Chechens, Ingushi, and others were violently removed from their homes and sent east, many to their deaths. In addition, thousands of suspected enemies were deported from occupied territories in Poland and the Baltic states, or they were summarily shot. These measures approached genocidal dimensions, but they did not represent genocide in a strict sense, since the aim was not the extermination of these groups.[41] Nor did Stalin intend to exterminate the German people. In this respect at least, he agreed with the Western Allies. Despite the manifold cruelties, massacres, and rapes committed by the Red Army in Germany, the German people were to survive, albeit under a new regime.[42]

---

39 See Richard Overy, *Why the Allies Won* (London, 1995) and the essay by Martin Kutz in the present volume.

40 Gerhard L. Weinberg, *A World at Arms: A Global History of World War II* (Cambridge, 1994).

41 John Barber and Mark Harrison, *The Soviet Home Front, 1941–1945: A Social and Economic History of the USSR in World War II* (London, 1991), 112–16; Ternon, *Staat*, 210–13.

42 Andreas Hillgruber, *Der 2. Weltkrieg: Kriegsziele und Strategie der grossen Mächte*, ed. Bernd Martin (Stuttgart, 1996).

The Allies did resort at the end of the war to what can be called, in today's parlance, ethnic cleansing when they allowed the deportation of millions of Germans from the eastern provinces of the Reich and other areas. This was a cruel and arbitrary measure, and it was brutally executed and often attended by massacres. But it was not genocide. The Allies never intended to murder these people; however, they accepted the deaths of a few thousand of them as an incidental part of the process.[43]

Nor did most of Germany's allies go to the same extremes as the Nazis. Fascist Italy had waged a cruel colonial war in Ethiopia, where the methods used verged on genocide.[44] During World War II, however, Mussolini and his henchmen did not resort to genocide, and they gave the SS only unenthusiastic support in rounding up Jews. Bulgaria and, until the last phase of the war, Hungary followed the Italian example.[45] By contrast, the Romanian authorities undertook pogroms in the territories that they occupied, but they were slow to deliver Romanian Jews to the gas chambers.[46] The Ustasha regime in Croatia carried out its own genocide against ethnic Serbs, and it assisted its German allies in exterminating Jews. Croatia was the only power to follow the Nazi example during World War II.[47]

Japan is a difficult case. It was prepared to wage total war. In 1937, when World War II started in the Pacific theater, both Japanese mobilization at home and warfare abroad headed in this direction. The Japanese army fought ruthlessly. The rape of Nanking in 1937–38 brought this kind of warfare to an early culmination. This huge massacre, which was matched by Japanese atrocities elsewhere, tended toward genocide. Nevertheless, it would be wrong to state that Japanese leaders aimed at the complete destruction of the Chinese people.[48]

The Nazis nonetheless outdid all their rivals. Genocide was their trade. Nazi aims and methods in the east were genocidal. Their object was the

---

43 Wolfgang Benz, ed., *Die Vertreibung der Deutschen aus dem Osten: Ursachen, Ereignisse, Folgen* (Frankfurt am Main, 1995).

44 Guilia Brogini, "Italien und der Abessinienkrieg, 1935/36. Ein Kolonialkrieg oder ein totaler Krieg?" Ph.D. diss. (University of Bern, 2002).

45 Gabriele Nissim, *L'uomo che fermò Hitler: La storia di Dimitar Pesev che salvo gli ebrei di una nazione intera* (Milan, 1998). Toward the end of the war, however, Hungarian authorities took an active part in the Holocaust. See Christian Gerlach and Götz Aly, *Das letzte Kapitel. Realpolitik, Ideologie und der Mord an den ungarischen Juden 1944/45* (Stuttgart, 2002).

46 I. C. Butnaru, *The Silent Holocaust: Romania and its Jews* (New York, 1992), 89–159.

47 *Europa unterm Hakenkreuz: Die Okkupationspolitik des deutschen Faschismus 1938–1945*, 8 vols. (Berlin, 1988–96), 6: 42–53.

48 Akira Iriye, *The Origins of the Second World War in Asia and the Pacific* (London, 1987); Yuji Ishida, "Der 'totale Krieg' und die Verbrechen des japanischen Militärs, 1931–1945," *Zeitschrift für Geschichtswissenschaft* 5 (1999): 430–44; Uwe Makino, "Terrorgenozid Nanking 1937/38: Zum systematischen Charakter der japanischen Verbrechen," *Zeitschrift für Geschichtswissenschaft* 6 (2000): 525–40.

deportation and destruction of millions of Slavs. The survivors were to be kept as slaves in the new Germanic empire; they were to be deprived of their culture and their human rights. Had the Germans won the war, they would have undertaken the largest genocide in history. Before their defeat, they nearly managed to annihilate the Jews of Europe. This genocide was unique not only because of its size, but also because of the industrial means with which it was carried out. Nothing has come as close as the Holocaust to absolute genocide.

Total war was not, however, necessarily connected to genocide. In World War II, the Allies pursued the one and not the other. Only Nazi Germany joined the two, thanks to the special character of this regime and the policies it sought to implement. Did the combination of one kind of total war with nearly absolute genocide represent therefore a Nazi *Sonderweg*?

The Logic of Nazi Germany's Policy of Genocide

With the German invasion of the Soviet Union on June 22, 1941, outright genocide became a matter of policy. A policy of murder and ethnic cleansing had already been introduced in occupied Poland. The Jewish population had been rounded up while the Nazi leadership, Himmler and Heydrich in particular, pondered programs, such as the Madagascar plan, for a "final solution of the Jewish question" in Europe. At home, the euthanasia program rehearsed mass murder on a smaller scale.[49] Genocide was looming. But only when the Wehrmacht invaded the Soviet lands did the floodgates open.

Even in the planning stages, it became clear that operation Barbarossa was to be a "racial" war. Hitler had long wished to fight such a war in the east. His henchmen hastened to anticipate his intentions or, as the process has been described, to "work toward the Führer" in this matter; and the generals did not object. The army leadership provided detailed plans for the military operation, but planning for the new racial order in Eastern Europe proved far more difficult. Administrative chaos within the Nazi regime itself did not make things any easier. The envisaged resettlement of entire populations represented a gigantic task that posed enormous problems. It was not clear what to do with the millions of Jews and Slavs who were to be evacuated in order to make room for German settlers. In his roles as Reichskommissar für die Festigung deutschen Volkstums and Reichsführer SS, Himmler failed to find practical solutions to these problems. An enlarged version of *Generalplan*

---

49 Götz Aly, "*Endlösung*": *Völkerverschiebung und der Mord an den europäischen Juden* (Frankfurt am Main, 1995), 29–227; Kershaw, *Hitler*, 2: 234–61.

Ost emerged well after the invasion of the Soviet Union, but it too was impractical. When Barbarossa began, Nazi leaders and administrators thus had only vague ideas about how to change the demographic face of the east. But it was clear that the effort would involve murder. The campaign in the Soviet Union was a war of annihilation; it linked the concepts of total war and genocide. Göring had already calculated that 30 million inhabitants of the northern half of Russia would die. Heydrich considered plans to remove all Jews from Central and Eastern Europe and to march them to certain death in Arctic Russia. The formation of *Einsatzgruppen* under the command of the SS was another step in the same direction, as was Himmler's agreement with the army about a division of labor. The army leadership collaborated with the SS, issuing orders to kill Soviet political commissars and removing legal protection from enemy civilians in the eastern war zone.[50]

The lack of consistent planning created chaos, however. Although it was well under way by 1942, the extermination of Eastern European Jews was marked by a lack of coordination. The "final solution," which led to Auschwitz and other death camps, took shape in a slow and complicated process. The treatment of Slavic populations within the conquered territories was likewise badly organized and full of contradictions. Administrative chaos, lack of coherent planning, and the military failure of Barbarossa combined to create an untenable situation.

It has been claimed that the Nazi policy of genocide was basically the product of circumstances. Götz Aly has argued that the Holocaust resulted from problems inherent in German resettlement policy and from the requirements of feeding both the Wehrmacht and German civilians at home. "Superfluous eaters" thus had to be exterminated. The same logic was extended to Slavs and particularly to Jews.[51] However, as Christian Gerlach has shown with respect to the Slavic populations, as the war dragged on, mass starvation and extermination flew in the face of ever-increasing German requirements for forced labor. A "final solution of the Slav problem" therefore did not take shape, although millions were killed.[52]

Situational determinants provide a compelling explanation for the emergence of a German policy of genocide. But emphasizing them obscures important questions. Why did the Nazi leadership set these developments

---

50 Ibid., 341–89; Rolf-Dieter Müller, *Hitlers Ostkrieg und die deutsche Siedlungspolitik* (Frankfurt am Main, 1991), 83–114; Helmut Krausnick and Hans-Heinrich Wilhelm, *Die Truppe des Weltanschauungskrieges: Die Einsatzgruppen der Sicherheitspolizei und des SD 1938–1942* (Stuttgart, 1981).
51 Aly, "Endlösung."
52 Christian Gerlach, *Kalkulierte Morde: Die deutsche Wirtschafts- und Vernichtungspolitik in Weissrussland 1941 bis 1944* (Hamburg, 1999).

in motion in the first place? Why did they themselves create the circumstances that forced their hands? Why did they react to every new challenge in the most radical way possible? The answers must be sought in ideology. The Nazi Weltanschauung provided the strange logic that underlay the policy of genocide.

"Hitler's Weltanschauung" needs little discussion here.[53] It suffices to note that ideology substantially shaped the perceptions of many leading Nazis. Hitler and Himmler were driven by ideology.[54] Ideology made these leaders believe that the Jews were not only dispensable as "superfluous eaters," but that their annihilation was also desirable. Ideology also convinced them of the need to embark on a war of annihilation against the Slavs and "Jewish bolshevism."

Nazi ideology was also a critical element in relating total war and genocide. The Nazis' understanding of history prepared them to contemplate genocide. Hitler and many of his followers genuinely believed that a Jewish conspiracy had led to the "stab in the back" and Imperial Germany's defeat in World War I. The disaster of 1918 had been traumatic for many of those who led the Third Reich. Hitler in particular was determined to avenge this shame. But he also drew another lesson from the First World War. He concluded that this war had been waged for the wrong purposes and in inadequate ways. In his eyes, war should not be waged to conquer a few provinces or colonies; the sacrifice of millions of German lives for such modest war aims was, in his eyes, a crime. By his logic, war was only worth the sacrifice if it were waged for the destruction of the Jews and for the sake of *Lebensraum* on a grand scale in the east. When Hitler first committed this terrible vision to paper in *Mein Kampf*, it represented but a dream. But he spoke of it several times after he came to power. The vision offered the basic guidelines for Nazi policy, particularly after 1939, as the radicalization of the war removed all restraints. The details of making this vision a reality Hitler left to his henchmen, who encountered enormous practical problems. But the policy of genocide could not have emerged without the vision, which was in turn rooted in racism and Social Darwinism as well as in an analysis of World War I. Social Darwinism and a racist view of history lay at the core of Nazi ideology, but so did a perverse analysis of World War I.

Total war presupposes the systematic involvement of civilians in the war effort. Civilians provided essential support for the armed forces, hence they themselves became targets of enemy action. Sherman's march through the

---

53 Eberhard Jäckel, *Hitlers Weltanschauung: Entwurf einer Herrschaft* (Stuttgart, 1981).
54 Kershaw, *Hitler*; Richard Breitman, *The Architect of Genocide. Himmler and the Final Solution* (New York, 1991).

South signaled the importance of breaking the will of the entire enemy population in order to achieve victory. This goal shaped the strategies of all the powers in World War I. From there, it was no great step to contemplate the annihilation of the enemy's civilian population not only to bring total victory, but also to remove all fears that a defeated enemy could rise again. Hitler took this step. He combined the idea of total war with a policy of genocide. That meant, in other words, a war of annihilation against soldiers and civilians alike. Jews and Slavs, the most dangerous enemies from Hitler's point of view, could be fought only in this fashion. The fact that millions of others were prepared to execute Hitler's vision indicated the power of its logic.

Total war and genocide are distinct phenomena in modern history, but they are linked nonetheless in theory. The Nazi policy of genocide remained unique within the context of World War II. Both of these propositions need qualification, however. Genocide was inherent in the logic of total war in practice as well as theory; it represented one potential outcome of the quest for total war. This outcome required a specific, extreme set of circumstances to overcome the threshold to barbarity. These circumstances remained historically unique to Nazi Germany, and the outcome was not inevitable. Other powers approached total war in different ways and shied away from genocide. Still, the Nazi *Sonderweg* was the logical, albeit extreme consequence of the logic of total war.

PART B

Combat

4

Germany and the Battle of the Atlantic

HOLGER H. HERWIG

> And harbingers of victory soft descend; the battle's
> Ours! Endure on high, O Fatherland,
> Count not the dead! For Thee
> Beloved! not *one* too many has fallen.
>
> Friedrich Hölderlin, *Tod fürs Vaterland*, 1796[1]

The Second World War was global, intense, and frightfully devastating. It ranged from conventional warfare to the dropping of the first atomic bomb, from terror bombing to genocide. Many scholars have assumed, like the historian Gordon Wright, that the "ordeal of total war" from 1939 to 1945 hardly requires definition.[2] Still, as the essays collected in this volume demonstrate, scholars continue to debate whether the Second World War was, in fact, a "total" war.

It seems to me most profitable to regard what Carl von Clausewitz called "absolute" war as a logical abstraction, as a mental construct against which all "real" wars can be measured. In chapter two of Book Eight of *On War*, Clausewitz laid this out clearly and cogently. "Theory . . . has the duty to give priority to the absolute form of war and to make that form a general point of reference, so that he who wants to learn from theory becomes accustomed to . . . measuring all his hopes and fears by it, and to approximating it *when*

---

1 Michael L. Hadley used this verse to great effect in his brilliant book, *Count Not the Dead: The Popular Image of the German Submarine* (Montreal and Kingston, 1995). The original German is:

> Und Siegesboten kommen herab: die Schlacht
> Ist unser! Lebe droben, o Vaterland,
> Und zähle nicht die Toten! Dir ist,
> Liebes! nicht *einer* zu viel gefallen.

2 Gordon Wright, *The Ordeal of Total War, 1939–1945* (New York, 1968).

he can or *when he must.*"[3] To further drive home this point, Clausewitz introduced no fewer than fifteen "modifications in practice" to his mental construct. Military action, he argued, is never continuous. Rather, it is punctuated by pauses, both short and lengthy, in which one or both sides seeks allies, mobilizes resources, trains forces, and gathers intelligence. If war were "a complete, untrammeled, absolute manifestation of violence (as the pure concept would require)," it would "of its own independent will usurp the place of policy" and "rule by the laws of its own nature."[4] That, obviously, would have made mockery of Clausewitz's entire book. A century later, the sociologist Max Weber may well have had Clausewitz and his notion of "absolute" war in mind when he developed his ideal type: an analytical accentuation of aspects of one or more attributes of a phenomenon to create a mental construct that will never be encountered in practice, but against which "real" world approximations can be measured.[5]

I have taken the definitions offered by Clausewitz and Weber as guidelines in measuring the "total" war of the Battle of the Atlantic. It was, as Clausewitz put it in chapter one of Book One regarding every war in practice, "a pulsation of violence, variable in strength and therefore variable in the speed with which it explodes and discharges its energy."[6] Even the "total" war state of Grand Admiral Karl Dönitz had a maximum level beyond which its military forces could not expand and come into play. The limits are obvious: size of population; industrial configuration; access to raw materials, wealth, or the ability to borrow; access to surplus labor; competing commitments; and the willingness of its citizens to make sacrifices for the war effort.

This was certainly the case with regard to the U-boat war between 1939 and 1945. Steel production and skilled labor distribution had to be balanced out among army, navy, and air force. Shipyards had a finite building capacity. Hard choices had to be made: whether to concentrate on large or small surface units and whether to build multipurpose or task-specific U-boats. Repair and outfitting stations for all manner of naval craft likewise were constrained by size and resources. Moreover, all the services competed for skilled workers. Aircraft and tank production competed with the U-boats for professional crews and for steel. It was within the confines of this "real"

3 Carl von Clausewitz, *On War*, ed. and tr. Michael Howard and Peter Paret (Princeton, NJ, 1976), 581.
4 Ibid., 87.
5 Max Weber, *The Methodology of the Social Sciences*, ed. and tr. Edward S. Shils and Henry A. Finch (Glencoe, IL, 1949), 90–5. I am indebted to Professor Ned Lebow of the Mershon Center at The Ohio State University for this insight.
6 Clausewitz, *On War*, 87.

war that Dönitz fought the Battle of the Atlantic. It was against the theory of "absolute" or "total" war that he shaped his policies. This dichotomy should not be ignored. One was the ideal; the other, the reality.

METHOD OF WARFARE

In the volume of this series dealing with *Great War, Total War*, I entitled my contribution on the Imperial German Navy's submarine effort "Total Rhetoric, Limited War." This was to suggest that rhetoric had raced ahead of capability.[7] Still, the Kaiserliche Marine destroyed more than 5,000 Allied ships of about 12 million tons during the First World War; it lost 199 U-boats and 5,249 officers and ratings. A quarter of a century later, the design would be for total war, and this time around the effort also would be total. Furthermore, the losses would be commensurate with the new standard for waging total war. On a ring of bronze tablets at the U-boat Memorial at Möltenort near Kiel are inscribed the names of 30,003 submariners who died on board 739 U-boats destroyed or lost at sea between 1939 and 1945. That number represents approximately 70 percent of all the men who served in Grand Admiral Dönitz's so-called "gray sharks."[8]

In fact, the Battle of the Atlantic was the longest campaign of the Second World War. It ran from the first to the last day of that violent struggle. It was costly not only to the Germans: the British merchant marine alone lost 30,248 seamen on board 2,603 freighters and tankers of more than 13.5 million tons; the Royal Navy lost 73,642, and the Royal Canadian Navy 1,065 men on 175 naval vessels sunk by the U-boats.[9]

One of the many ironies of the Second World War is that the campaign in the Atlantic was never intended to take the shape that it ultimately did. The German Navy under Grand Admiral Erich Raeder planned to fight a Mahanian "blue-water" war for sea control with a traditional symmetrical battle fleet centered on battleships, battle cruisers, heavy cruisers, and aircraft carriers. On January 27, 1939, Adolf Hitler approved the construction within six years of a mighty armada of 684 ships, to be manned by 201,000

---

7 Holger H. Herwig, "Total Rhetoric, Limited War: Germany's U-Boat Campaign, 1917–1918," Roger Chickering and Stig Förster, eds., *Great War, Total War: Combat and Mobilization on the Western Front, 1914–1918* (New York, 2000), 189–206.

8 A recent revisionist work suggests that about 48,000 to 50,000 men served in the U-boats, and that of these 68% were killed or captured. Timothy P. Mulligan, *Neither Sharks Nor Wolves: The Men of Nazi Germany's U-boat Arm, 1939–1945* (Annapolis, 1999), 251–6.

9 Terry Hughes and John Costello, *The Battle of the Atlantic* (New York, 1977), 303–5. A detailed breakdown of ships sunk and men lost in the Battle of the Atlantic is provided by Clay Blair, *Hitler's U-Boat War*, 2 vols. (New York, 1996, 1998).

officers and sailors, at the staggering cost of 33 billion Reichsmark.[10] But the so-called "Z Plan" never reached fruition; instead, a general European war broke out on September 3, 1939.

There was little for the fleet to do but to "die gallantly," as Admiral Raeder put it.[11] There was to be no repeat of the sailors' revolt of 1917, the revolution of 1918, and the scuttling of the interned High Sea Fleet at Scapa Flow in 1919. From 1939 to 1941, German surface raiders such as the battleships *Scharnhorst*, *Gneisenau*, and *Bismarck* as well as the pocket battleships *Deutschland* and *Graf Spee* along with the heavy cruisers *Admiral Hipper* and *Admiral Scheer* conducted commerce warfare on the high seas. The loss especially of the *Bismarck* in May 1941 ended this phase of Raeder's surface strategy. There remained the U-boats.

On September 1, 1939, the very day that Germany attacked Poland, then-Commodore Dönitz, Leader U-Boats, had submitted to Raeder a different vision of a future war at sea: 300 U-boats could bring Britain to her knees by way of a total war against that island nation's vital overseas commerce.[12] Unfortunately, Germany had but 57 submarines, of which only 27 (instead of Dönitz's requested 90) were fit for service on the broad reaches of the Atlantic Ocean. On the evening of the first day of the war, disaster struck. *U-30*, formally operating under the Hague Convention Prize Rules that demanded the skipper place passengers and crew in safety before dispatching a vessel, torpedoed the 13,581-ton ocean liner *Athenia* northwest of Ireland.[13] The incident, which was reminiscent of the sinking of the *Lusitania* in 1915, cost 118 people their lives. The German reaction was threefold: to lie about the sinking, to falsify the U-boat's war log, and to order U-boat commanders to observe the Prize Rules – at least until December when Dönitz instructed his skippers, "Rescue no one and take no one with you. Have no care for the ships' boats."[14]

Still, for the next two years of what came to be known as the Battle of the Atlantic, the U-boats, in the words of the naval historian Michael Salewski, fought a "romantic war."[15] The German public was fed a steady stream of tales of daring-do by a host of Knight's-Cross bedecked U-boat

10 Michael Salewski, *Die deutsche Seekriegsleitung 1935–1945*, 3 vols. (Frankfurt, 1970–73), vol. 1, 57ff.; Siegfried Breyer, *Der Z-Plan. Streben zur Weltmachtflotte* (Wölfersheim-Berstadt, 1996), 8–10.
11 Raeder's notes of September 3, 1939. Bundesarchiv-Militärarchiv (hereafter BA-MA), Freiburg, Germany. Case GE 539, "Besprechungspunkte für Vorträge beim Führer 3.9.39–27.12.40."
12 "Gedanken über den Aufbau der U-Bootswaffe, 1. September 1939." BA-MA, Case 378, PG 32419a. Seekrieg 1939.
13 See Blair, *Hitler's U-Boat War: The Hunters 1939–1942*, 66–8.
14 Cited in Peter Padfield, *Dönitz: The Last Führer. Portrait of a Nazi War Leader* (London, 1984), 206.
15 Michael Salewski, "The Submarine War: A Historical Essay," in Lothar-Günther Buchheim, *U-Boat War* (New York, 1978), n.p.

"aces" – Günther Prien, Joachim Schepke, Otto Schuhart, Herbert Schultze – who had ravaged the pride of the Royal Navy, including the aircraft carrier *Courageous* and the battleship *Ark Royal*. This was the first "happy time" of the U-boats, which, despite the unmitigated technical disaster of the G 7a torpedo, sank 421,156 tons of Allied shipping in the first four months of the war, and about 2.1 million in each of the next two years. A second "happy time" came in the first half of 1942, after the United States had entered the war in December 1941, when the "wolf packs" massacred about 2.34 million tons of shipping mainly along the eastern and Gulf coasts of the United States.

But the decisive campaigns of the war were being fought elsewhere. Late in 1942, the Southern German Army Group failed to knock the Soviet Union out of the war; early in 1943, the Sixth Army capitulated at Stalingrad. Concurrently, vast quantities of American aid arrived in the Soviet Union via sea to Murmansk and Archangel, and through the Persian Gulf. According to the postwar recollections of General Alfred Jodl, Hitler admitted at the end of 1942 that he had lost his last chance to "alter destiny" and that "victory could no longer be realized" in the continental land war.[16] Admiral Raeder spoke darkly of Germany's "encirclement" by a hostile coalition. All that remained was the Battle of the Atlantic – "To sink [merchant ships], regardless of where or whether loaded or empty."[17] It was to be a desperate race against the clock to at least slow down the daily shipments of war material from America to Britain in anticipation of a future cross-Channel invasion of "Fortress Europe." Increasingly, Hitler turned to the last weapon remaining in his shrinking arsenal – the submarine – and to its dynamic and dedicated leader – Karl Dönitz – for a last-minute "miracle."

CONTROL

"Distance," the military historian John Keegan has percipiently observed, "is a negative dimension."[18] To overcome that "negative," Dönitz decided to direct the actions of each and every U-boat from a central command post on land – first from a small château at Kernevel outside Lorient, then from an apartment block on the Avenue Maréchal Maunoury in Paris, later

16 Cited in Andreas Hillgruber, "Der Faktor Amerika in Hitlers Strategie 1938–1941," *Aus Politik und Zeitgeschichte. Beilage zur Wochenzeitung "Das Parlament*," B19/66, 21. Jodl made his comments immediately after the German capitulation.
17 "Lagebetrachtung der Seekriegsleitung 20. Oktober 1942." BA-MA, Case 536, PG 32621.
18 John Keegan, *The Mask of Command* (New York, 1988), 316–17.

from the Hotel Steinstrasse at Berlin-Charlottenburg, and finally from the
Koralle at Bernau near Berlin. U-boat skippers had to report in a prompt
and timely fashion not only position and heading point, but also fuel oil and
torpedo status, sinkings and damage, food and weather, and even evaluations
of new equipment.[19] The number of messages emanating daily from U-Boat
Headquarters grew from about 300 in 1940 to roughly 2,500 by 1941. And
since the U-boats could not all be expected to be on the surface at the same
time to receive Dönitz's instructions from Kernevel, the "Great Lion," as
he was called by his submariners, had them repeated every two, six, twelve,
and twenty hours from the powerful French Colonial Office transmitter at
Sainte Assise, southeast of Paris.

   This highly centralized control and command process began in a
bombproof bunker at Kernevel. There, Commander Hans Meckel and his
staff received Dönitz's instructions for encipherment and transmission. Fifteen to twenty radiomen per shift enciphered the messages on the top-secret
Enigma machine. The two inner settings of the naval cipher were made by
"officers only" every forty-eight hours; cipher clerks then changed the
Enigma's two external settings every twenty-four hours. Operators could
choose to activate three of the machine's eight rotors; each rotor's revolv-
ing ring had twenty-six positions. Finally, the operators at Kernevel set
each active rotor to one of twenty-six different positions. By multiplying all
these possible combinations, Dönitz and Meckel estimated that in theory
there were 160 trillion possible settings for a complete shortwave (high-
frequency) transmission! All messages carried a date-time number as well
as a serial number. Each was then checked by another radioman for proper
encipherment. Every U-boat in a patrol line operating against a convoy used
one of two nets ("Diana" or "Hubertus"), and each of these had up to six
frequencies of its own. The system, in short, seemed foolproof.

   Dönitz's role in the Battle of the Atlantic defies conventional description.
He was the strategist, operations officer, battlefield commander, intelligence
chief, and quartermaster-general of that war. He decided where, when, and
how his "gray sharks" would operate. He directed their attacks on convoys.
He evaluated each and every one of their after-action reports. He promoted
and dismissed officers accordingly. He made the rounds of his boats and their
captains. He was their cheerleader. No one dared challenge his system of
total command and control. To assist him, the "Great Lion" selected a small,
homogeneous staff of about twenty men. All had prior U-boat experience,

---

19 See David Kahn, *Seizing the Enigma: The Race to Break the German U-Boat Codes, 1939–1943* (Boston,
    1991).

and almost all had operated against convoys out in the Atlantic. Headed by Captain Eberhard Godt, chief of staff, and Commander Günter Hessler, first operations officer, the staff supervised the day-to-day, even hour-by-hour actions of up to 100 U-boats out at sea. They instilled morale and élan in the "Volunteer Corps Dönitz," oversaw its constant training, enhanced its tactical proficiency, and evaluated its operational efficiency.

But the system carried within it the seeds of its own destruction. By concentrating almost exclusively on operations, Dönitz's staff failed to see the larger side of what Winston Churchill called the "Wizard War." They constantly searched for a quick-fix tactical solution for their new "killer" boats – acoustic torpedoes such as the Zaunkönig, radar search receivers such as the Hagenuk, Metox, and Naxos, or radar decoys such as the Aphrodite and Thetis buoys – without understanding that what the Americans called "operations research" was the key. Unlike the British, who employed an army of top-notch scientists and academics (including two Nobel Prize winners) in their anti-submarine effort, Dönitz failed to recruit the Reich's best scientists and engineers for ongoing analyses of the U-boat war.[20] Germany never undertook research sharing with its allies, in the manner of the British Tizard commission that brought the cavity magnetron (centimetric radar) to the United States in the fall of 1940. Again, unlike the Allies, who recruited barristers and academics to their intelligence services, German intelligence rarely, if ever, solicited new people or new ideas.

The system bred arrogance and hubris. Time and again, Dönitz's calculations erred. In March 1942, for example, his staff claimed 1.1 million tons of Allied shipping sunk; in reality, 645,000 tons had been dispatched. For 1943, they claimed that the enemy had 10.3 million tons of new construction; in reality, the figure was 14.4 million.[21] And, until his death in 1980, Dönitz never understood that his allegedly secure Enigma traffic was being read, albeit with varying delays, by the Government Code and Cypher School at Bletchley Park near London (Ultra). The naval historian Jürgen Rohwer has calculated that Ultra reduced losses at sea by 65 percent by the second half of 1941.[22] Over and over, when his skippers suspected that the enemy was reading the Enigma traffic, Dönitz rejected such claims and instead suggested treason as the possible reason why so many convoys avoided his patrol

20 Kathleen Broome Williams, *Secret Weapon: U.S. High-Frequency Direction Finding in the Battle of the Atlantic* (Annapolis, 1996), 15, 19.
21 Werner Rahn, "Der Seekrieg im Atlantik und Nordmeer," in *Das Deutsche Reich und der Zweite Weltkrieg*, vol. 6, *Der Globale Krieg. Die Ausweitung zum Weltkrieg und der Wechsel der Initiative 1941–1943* (Stuttgart, 1990), 301, 307–9.
22 *Die Funkaufklärung und ihre Rolle im Zweiten Weltkrieg*, ed. Jürgen Rohwer and Eberhard Jäkel (Stuttgart, 1979), 386ff.

lines. Germany could not read all Allied radio traffic; therefore, the Allies could not read his! In the end, Dönitz lost the Battle of the Atlantic not only to convoying, escort carrier groups, and air coverage, but especially to operations research into radar, sonar, high-frequency direction finding (HD/DF), Ultra, and to American industrial output.

The German failure to integrate scientific thinking into all levels of the command structure in the Battle of the Atlantic – that is, its downright distrust of "outside" consultants – limited its "totality" and is reflected in the development of the so-called Walter boat. For years, Dönitz insisted that the Type VII boat (see below) was the world's premier submarine; and for years, his construction staff rejected experimentation, arguing that "every special design disrupts the smooth operation of series production."[23] And yet, already in the 1930s the Hamburg engineer Hellmuth Walter had developed a hydrogen peroxide gas turbine that theoretically could drive a U-boat at 30 knots submerged. At the same time, the Dutch were perfecting a "Schnorchel" that would allow a submarine to take in air while submerged at minimal depths. Germany did not meld the two designs until February 1942. It did not order the Walter boats until December. Series production did not begin before May 1943, with the result that the first Type XVIII boats did not go into service until April–May 1945.[24] It was a dismal performance for innovation in total war.

MOBILIZATION

Dönitz pressed for total war against any and all shipping on the North Atlantic. He gave perhaps the clearest statement of his aims on April 15, 1942: "The enemy's shipping constitutes one single, great entity. It is therefore immaterial where a ship is sunk – for in the final analysis, it has to be replaced by a new ship." For him, the Battle of the Atlantic came down to a "race between sinkings and new construction."[25] The following month Dönitz assured Hitler that, given Allied shipbuilding of 8.2 million tons in 1942, monthly sinkings of 400,000 to 500,000 tons would keep pace with new construction; at the current rate of dispatching 700,000 tons per month, victory could be guaranteed.[26] Commander U-boats never deviated from the belief – already current in 1917–18 under Grand Admiral Henning von

23 Eberhard Rössler, *Geschichte des deutschen Ubootbaus*, 2 vols. (Munich, 1986–87), vol. 2, 290.
24 Werner Rahn, "Die Entstehung neuer deutscher U-Boot-Typen im Zweiten Weltkrieg. Erprobung und erste operative Erfahrungen," *Militärgeschichte* 2 (1993), 13–20.
25 Entry of April 15, 1942. BA-MA, 1/SKL Teil C IV KTB U-Boot-Kriegführung 1942.
26 Discussion of May 14, 1942. *Lagevorträge des Oberbefehlshabers der Kriegsmarine vor Hitler 1939–1945*, ed. Gerhard Wagner (Munich, 1972), 394.

Holtzendorff – that victory was a matter of slide-rule calculation. "Tonnage war," or *Tonnagekrieg*, became an obsession. He rejected all suggestions from the Naval High Command to concentrate on sinking loaded convoys and tankers. The problem throughout the war was finding enemy convoys: even during the period of peak U-boat successes, January to August 1942, the U-boats sank only 30 of 3,283 convoyed ships.

The Type VII submarine was the workhorse of the Battle of the Atlantic.[27] With a displacement of roughly 750 tons, it was manned by a crew of about fifty officers. Type VIIC boats carried fourteen torpedoes, and were armed with an 8.8 cm deck gun and two 20 mm antiaircraft guns. Their two diesels (1,400 hp each) allowed a surface best speed of 18 knots, while their two electric motors (750 hp each) permitted a top submerged speed of 7.4 knots (for about 30 minutes). Dönitz had more than 660 Type VII boats built during the war, and as late as April 1943 he maintained that they were "today still the best type for fighting convoys."[28] At just 200 feet long and 20 feet wide, the Type VII U-boat was an incredibly small craft. But it was robust and reliant, basically a First World War prototype (the *U-70* series) that really was a torpedo boat that could dive for brief periods of time. Its major asset was stealth.

Total war requires total mobilization. In September 1939, Dönitz had requested a fleet of 300 U-boats, with 90 to operate in the Atlantic. He surpassed that figure by July 1942 with a total of 330 (of which 138 were at the front). But with the ever-expanding theaters of war, the U-boat force was hopelessly scattered. On January 1, 1941, to take a representative point in the war, Germany had 249 U-boats at its disposal. Of these, only 91 were with the various fronts: 33 were undergoing repair and refit, 23 were in the Mediterranean, 6 off Gibraltar, 4 in Norway, and 3 en route to the Mediterranean – leaving a mere 22 boats out in the North Atlantic, the "decisive theater of the war."[29] In the spring of 1941, "wolf pack" tactics became standard, as Dönitz from Kernevel positioned his U-boats in lines of twenty to forty vessels across anticipated Allied convoy routes.

For five years, Dönitz moved heaven and earth to try to get as many boats as possible to the front as quickly as possible and for as long as possible. This, in turn, required vast quantities of steel and copper as well as crews and technicians. The admiral's ideal was a ratio of 40 days in port for every sixty days at sea. After every patrol, each boat received a minor overhaul of

---

27 The following is from Robert C. Stern, *Type VII U-boats* (Annapolis, 1991).
28 Entry for April 30, 1943. *Kriegstagebuch der Seekriegsleitung 1939–1945*, eds. Werner Rahn and Gerhard Schreiber, 68 vols. (Herford and Bonn, 1988–97), vol. 44, 575.
29 Karl Dönitz, *Zehn Jahre und zwanzig Tage. Erinnerungen 1935–1945* (Frankfurt, 1958), 192.

twenty-eight days; after every third patrol a modest overhaul of forty-two days; and after fifteen months in service a major overhaul of ninety days. This does not include the added weeks and months required to repair the damage from the pounding the boats were taking out in the Atlantic from enemy bombs, depth charges, hedgehogs, air-to-surface missiles, and ramming. The submarine pens at Lorient, for example, estimated that 175 workers (including 50 French forced laborers) were required for each boat just for routine repairs. By the summer of 1942, the navy was 2,200 technicians short for just the maintenance of U-boats.[30]

As for new boats, Hitler had decreed on June 30, 1941, that twenty-five U-boats were to be be built every month. Before Munitions Minister Albert Speer introduced the American method of prefabricating U-boats in sections, it took almost two years to complete a craft. Each monthly batch of twenty-five boats required 20,000 tons of steel and 450 tons of copper as well as 60,000 expert workers to build; the 238 U-boats produced in 1942 absorbed 77 million work-hours.[31] With regard to new construction, the navy was short 25,000 workers already by 1941. At the same time, U.S. shipyards were building 7,000-ton Liberty ships in less than two months; three were launched each day by October 1942; and in 1943 American yards produced 19 million tons of merchant shipping.[32] Dönitz was drawing the shorter straw in an ever-escalating "tonnage war" – by 500,000 tons per month in 1942 and by 1 million tons in the U-boats' second most productive month of April 1943.[33]

The months of January and February 1943 were extraordinary, even by the standards of the Second World War. On January 31, the German Sixth Army surrendered at Stalingrad. In July, the Wehrmacht lost the Battle of Kursk, thereby ending the offensive phase of Hitler's war. Dönitz succeeded Raeder as commander-in-chief of the Kriegsmarine on January 31, 1943. Even though Dönitz warded off Hitler's demand that all surface ships be paid off, the appointment of the former Commander U-Boats nevertheless was a clear signal that the submarines were to be the primary weapon of the Battle of the Atlantic. Moreover, Dönitz introduced a much harsher, more brutal tone to the war effort. In his first general order to senior naval commanders on February 5, 1943, the grand admiral announced that the Kriegsmarine would conduct the war at sea "with uncompromising decisiveness [and]

30 Guntram Schulze-Wegener, *Die deutsche Kriegsmarine-Rüstung 1942–1945* (Hamburg, 1997), 56.
31 Ibid., 45, 49.
32 George W. Baer, *One Hundred Years of Sea Power: The U.S. Navy, 1890–1990* (Stanford, 1994), 199–200.
33 Rahn, "Der Seekrieg im Atlantik und Nordmeer," 311.

according to the orders of the Führer." He demanded total dedication, total effort, and total commitment from his men. "Our lives belong totally to the state. Our honor lies in our commitment to duty and to service. None of us has the right to a private life." The goal was total victory. "We must pursue this goal with fanatical dedication and the most severe will to victory."[34] There was no doubt in Dönitz's mind in February 1943 that he was conducting "total war."

Partly to overcome the depression caused by Stalingrad, Joseph Goebbels decided to stage a monster rally in Berlin to show Hitler that the German people stood squarely behind him in what would now be a defensive struggle for survival.[35] On February 18, the propaganda minister worked a packed throng at the Sportpalast into frenzied hysteria. "The mood of the Volk is like wild mayhem." Ten times, Goebbels demanded to know whether they wished "total war." Ten times, he demanded that they rise against "Bolshevist-capitalist tyranny," "anarchy," "terror," and "the Jewish world revolution." Ten times, the audience screamed its readiness to sacrifice and persevere. "Total war," Goebbels concluded, was the "catchword of the hour." And when the throng was at a fever pitch, Goebbels, resorting to Theodor Körner's famous appeal from the Wars of Liberation against Napoleon I, gave them their marching orders: "Now, Volk, rise up; and storm, break loose!"[36]

The spectacle did not fail to impress Dönitz. Within forty-eight hours, he came to pay his respects. The propaganda minister found the new head of the navy ready to revitalize the offensive spirit of that branch of the armed forces, to rejuvenate its ranks, and to press on with the war at sea on the basis of his general order of February 5. "He [Dönitz] desires the closest cooperation with me and my office," Goebbels wrote in his diary, "and is especially anxious that the Kriegsmarine from now is seen by the public as a National-Socialist and not as an atrophied Imperial force."[37] All that remained, Goebbels stated, was for Dönitz to forge a link to another power figure, Heinrich Himmler, Reichsführer SS.

---

34 The full speech is reproduced in Michael Salewski, "Von Raeder zu Dönitz. Der Wechsel im Oberbefehl der Kriegsmarine 1943," *Militärgeschichtliche Mitteilungen* 14 (1973), 145–6.
35 See the "Lagebetrachtung der Seekriegsleitung, 20. August 1943." BA-MA, Case 537, PG 32629.
36 "Nun Volk, steh auf und Sturm brich los!" in Willi A. Boelcke, ed., *"Wollt Ihr den Totalen Krieg?" Die Geheimen Goebbels-Konferenzen 1939–1943* (Munich, 1969), 23–4. See also Bernhard R. Kroener, "'Nun, Volk, steh auf...!' Stalingrad und der 'totale' Krieg," in Jürgen Förster, ed., *Stalingard. Ereignis – Wirkung – Symbol* (Munich and Zurich, 1992), 166; and Iring Fetscher, *Joseph Goebbels im Berliner Sportpalast 1943: "Wollt ihr den totalen Krieg?"* (Hamburg, 1998).
37 Entry for February 20, 1943. Elke Frölich, ed., *Die Tagebücher von Joseph Goebbels*, Part 2, Dictates 1941–1945, vol. 7, January–March 1943 (Munich, 1993), 380.

Out in the Atlantic, Dönitz's "tonnage war" reached its climax. In March, in what would constitute the greatest convoy battles of the Second World War, the U-boat packs *Raubgraf, Stürmer,* and *Dränger* sank 21 ships of 142,465 tons out of convoys HX229 and SC122. Overall, the "gray sharks" that month dispatched 108 ships of 627,377 tons. They lost only 14 boats to enemy action.[38] A third "happy time" appeared to be at hand. But then the tide turned: in the period from April 10 to May 23, in twelve major convoy battles the U-boats sank only 29 ships while losing 22 of their own. For all of May, Dönitz lost 35 boats and 1,026 dead – for a return of but 96,000 tons. The "exchange rate" was down to one U-boat for every 10,000 tons of Allied shipping.[39] A combination of radar, Ultra, HD/DF, land and sea air, and U.S. Navy "hunter-killer" groups had reclaimed the North Atlantic. On May 24, 1943, the "Great Lion" recalled his U-boats from the North Atlantic and shifted them to the Azores. After a brief return to the northern latitudes on September 18, Dönitz realized by November 7 that he had lost the Battle of the Atlantic: only eight merchant ships had been destroyed at a cost of twenty U-boats sunk.[40]

Unknown to Dönitz, the two Western alliance leaders, Winston Churchill and Franklin D. Roosevelt, had secretly met at Casablanca in January 1943 and agreed to give top priority in the war effort to defeating the U-boats and to securing the sea lanes across the Atlantic.[41] From "cracked" Japanese diplomatic ciphers (Magic) emanating from "Hitler's Japanese confidant," General Oshima Hiroshi at Berlin, the Allies knew the precise scope and direction of the German U-boat war campaign.[42] Thus, the Allied anti-submarine effort fully came into play at the very moment that Dönitz believed he was within reach of victory in the Battle of the Atlantic.

RADICALIZATION

But defeat did not translate into an end to the U-boat campaign. Quite the reverse: Dönitz immediately announced a "new U-boat war" and promised Hitler that he would mount a last-ditch defensive war against the Allies – that is, to delay losing the war for as long as possible. In short, he launched a

---

38 David Syrett, *The Defeat of the German U-Boats: The Battle of the Atlantic* (Columbia, SC, 1994), 25.
39 Ibid., 141.   40 Ibid., 227.
41 Proceedings of the conference are in *Foreign Relations of the United States. The Conferences at Washington,*
   1941–1942, and Casablanca, 1943 (Washington, DC, 1968), 487ff.; see also David Stafford, *Roosevelt*
   and Churchill: Men of Secrets (New York, 2000), 196–203.
42 Stafford, *Roosevelt and Churchill,* pp. 136–7. See also Carl Boyd, *Hitler's Japanese Confidant: General*
   Oshima Hiroshi and MAGIC Intelligence, 1941–1945 (Lawrence, KS, 1993), 162ff.

process of radicalization of the U-boat war. "The year 43 was a hard nut to crack," the grand admiral informed his senior commanders in June 1943, "but the years 44, 45, 46, 47 will be better."[43] In language that is reminiscent of General Erich von Falkenhayn's decision at Christmas 1915 to "bleed the French white" at Verdun, Dönitz now assured his Führer that he would "bleed the enemy to death" with regard to its available merchant tonnage.[44] This was the new language of total war.

Hitler at once agreed to accelerate U-boat production from twenty-five to forty boats per month. Dönitz, however, had more in mind than simply targeting enemy resources with existing U-boats in a race of attrition. Rather, he decided to mobilize all remaining German resources as well. In June 1943, he convinced Hitler to sign off on what constituted the largest naval building program in German history: 11,134 new warships, including 2,400 U-boats and 40 destroyers, all to be built by 1948! Dönitz immediately demanded 141,800 new shipyard and construction workers, including 86,300 forced laborers. He threatened to "rot out" the old hide-bound naval bureaucracy if it did not accede to his demands.[45] He later raised the figure to 262,000 workers and, with the assistance of Reichsführer-SS Himmler, hoped to get at least 12,000 of these from the concentration camps.

Yet, not even a direct order from the Führer could overcome the increasing constraints on war materials production. There was only so much steel and so many workers to go around. Army, Navy, Air Force, and now SS all had to share available resources. All had their pet projects – new tanks, new U-boats, new rockets. Ruefully, Dönitz had to admit that the navy was short 62,000 tons of steel for the second quarter of 1943 alone.[46] Moreover, in 1943 his U-boat force was in danger of running short of torpedoes: the front received only 440 of the requested 600 G 7a and but 730 of the 1,400 G 7e "eels."[47]

Still, total war demanded total death. The U-boats were sent out into the Atlantic against all odds. The average life expectancy of crews was down to ninety days by 1943; then to a single patrol. They died by the thousands, sent to a watery grave by their "Great Lion." For Dönitz was resolved to fight

43 Speech to senior naval commanders, June 8, 1943. BA-MA, III M 1005/7. Cited in Salewski, *Die deutsche Seekriegsleitung*, vol. 2, 294.
44 Discussion of April 11, 1943. *Lagevorträge*, p. 475. Also, Schulze-Wegener, *Die deutsche Kriegsmarine-Rüstung*, 113–14.
45 Schulze-Wegener, *Die deutsche Kriegsmarine-Rüstung*, 127–8.
46 See Dönitz's "steel memorandum" of March 1943 in *Das Deutsche Reich und der Zweite Weltkrieg*, vol. 5/2, *Organisation und Mobilisierung des deutschen Machtbereichs: Kriegsverwaltung, Wirtschaft und personelle Ressourcen 1942–1944/45* (Stuttgart, 1999), 601–2.
47 Salewski, *Die deutsche Seekriegsleitung*, vol. 2, 273.

on until the very last moment. He demanded that the "new U-boat war" be unleashed in early 1945. He pressed Speer for additional construction workers and for more steel. The gaping chasm between wish and reality apparently never entered his utopian world – not even as late as November 17, 1944, when he was informed by Speer that Allied air raids had ravaged the Ruhr, the German industrial heartland. Five main train stations lay in ruin; coal production for October was off 100,000 tons; steel output was down to 800,000 tons; and 80 percent of all steel plants had been badly damaged.[48]

Still undaunted, the grand admiral assured his Führer throughout February 1945 that he was about to launch the "new U-boat war." On February 18, Dönitz informed Hitler that the new Type XXI "electro" boats could travel from Germany to Japan under water! Five days later, he rosily told Hitler that the navy now possessed no fewer than 551 U-boats, of which 350 could operate at the front. This was a figure almost double what Dönitz in 1939 had predicted would be necessary to defeat the "Anglo-Saxon powers" in the Atlantic. On February 28, 1945, came the final piece of good news: "The U-boat once more can operate successfully even in areas of the strongest escorts."[49] Hitler was delighted. Dönitz pressed his case. The "rebirth of the U-boat war," he crowed in the eerie atmosphere of the bunker in Berlin, could be "significant for the overall war situation."[50] But the "new U-boat war" was a mirage. The first Type XXI boat left Bergen, Norway, on patrol on April 30, 1945. The Type XXI craft never sank a ton of enemy shipping. The U-boat war, in the words of naval historian Salewski, "dragged on like a ghostly, senseless, and murderous charade."[51]

In a final, incredible turn in the process of radicalization, Dönitz wrapped himself up in the National Socialist rhetoric of total war. His U-boat crews had long been peppered with slogans such as "attack-forward-sink," "destroy," "at them," "be hard," and "beat them to death." In September 1943, he issued a "Decree Against Criticism and Complaints" in which he threatened courts-martial for any and all "complainers" and "deprecators."[52] Three months later, Dönitz demolished one of the most sacred myths of the German military, the myth of the "apolitical" soldier. "And it really is nonsense, for example, to say that the soldier or the officer must be apolitical," he lectured his commanders. "The soldier personifies the state in which

---

48 Entry for November 17, 1944. *Kriegstagebuch der Seekriegsleitung 1939–1945*, vol. 63/II, 367.
49 Entry of February 28, 1945. *Kriegstagebuch der Seekriegsleitung*, vol. 66, 342.
50 Entry for February 17, 1945. *Lagevorträge*, 656. See also Salewski, *Die deutsche Seekriegsleitung*, vol. 2, 496, 526–7.
51 Salewski, "The Submarine War," n.p.   52 Padfield, *Dönitz*, 321.

he lives; he is the representative, the visible exponent of this state. Thus he has to stand behind the state with all his combined might."[53] In February 1944, breaking the sacred Prusso-German tradition of officers being above politics, he joined the NSDAP as member No. 9,664,999. After the Allied invasion at Normandy in June 1944, he demanded of his men "the harshest will to win" and vowed to "destroy with contempt and disgrace anyone who does not commit himself to the very last."[54] In contrast to senior Allied commanders, who usually reduced sentences meted out by courts-martial, the "Great Lion" routinely reviewed courts-martial rulings and appealed them repeatedly until he received what he desired – the maximum sentence allowed. His underlings followed his instructions so eagerly that even after Hitler's suicide they demanded that British soldiers in Norway execute sentences involving capital punishment handed down by Nazi courts-martial against sailors who had spoken ill of the Führer.[55]

After the failed attempt on Hitler's life on June 20, 1944, Dönitz broke all bonds of decency in the ever-escalating spiral of radicalization. In an address to senior commanders, the grand admiral railed against the conspiratorial "clique" of army officers who had undertaken this "childish" act. He demanded "fanatical adhesion" to Hitler; even the slightest doubting of the Führer constituted "a crime." He expected from his men a "fanatical ability to die." He informed his commanders that the concentration camps were "99% full of common criminals, who on average have 5-year sentences." And he swung fully in line with the state's diabolical anti-Jewish policy: "I would rather eat dirt," he crowed, "than have my grandchild raised and poisoned in Jewish spirit and filth."[56] He certainly knew of the monstrous nature of the Holocaust – at the latest by October 4, 1943, when he attended a special meeting in Posen at which Himmler spoke openly of "the extermination of the Jewish race."[57] And as late as April 11, 1945, as Germany lay under more than 520 million cubic yards of "total war" rubble, Dönitz could still speak of Adolf Hitler as "the single statesman of stature in Europe."[58] Finally, for Dönitz the war ended as it had begun – with a lie.

---

53 Speech to senior naval commanders, December 17, 1943. Cited in Salewski, *Die deutsche Seekriegsleitung*, 446.
54 Cited in Hadley, *Count Not the Dead*, 103.
55 See Chris Madsen, *The Royal Navy and German Naval Disarmament, 1942–1947* (London, 1998), 88–9. Also, Manfred Messerschmidt and Fritz Wüllner, *Die Wehrmachtjustiz im Dienste des Nationalsozialismus* (Baden-Baden, 1987).
56 The talk is fully reproduced in Salewski, *Die deutsche Seekriegsleitung*, vol. 2, 640–8.
57 Martin Gilbert, *The Holocaust: A History of the Jews of Europe during the Second World War* (New York, 1985), 615; Padfield, *Dönitz*, 322.
58 Padfield, *Dönitz*, 395.

On May 1, 1945, in his new capacity as "the last Führer," he announced: "Adolf Hitler has fallen. . . . a hero's death."[59]

CONCLUSION

Total war does not automatically translate into victory. Germany lost the Battle of the Atlantic. The U-boats failed to cut Britain off from overseas supplies; they failed to prevent American forces from landing in Europe; and they failed to protect German cities by interdicting American bomber deliveries to Great Britain. In fact, at no time did the U-boats come close to cutting the vital North American lifeline to Britain. During the decisive phase of the Battle of the Atlantic, September 1942 to May 1945, the Allies mounted 953 convoys of 43,526 merchant ships on the North and Middle Atlantic runs; of these, a mere 272 ships were sunk. Put differently, 99.4 percent of merchant ships reached their destinations intact.[60] Dönitz's "gray sharks" were only moderately more successful in either the nonrescue or the killing of merchant marine sailors: British sources reveal that even at the height of the slaughter in the Atlantic, in March–April 1943, 87 percent of merchant crews were rescued from ships sunk by U-boats.[61] Time and again, the grand admiral had admonished his U-boat commanders not to rescue survivors of torpedoed ships, most infamously in his radio order of September 17, 1942: "No attempt of any kind must be made at rescuing the crews of ships sunk. . . . Rescue remains contrary to the primary demands of warfare for the destruction of enemy ships and their crews."[62]

But Dönitz had succeeded beyond even his wildest dreams in one vital area: total control. Month after month, year after year, his crews headed out to certain death. There was no naval rebellion as in 1917, no mutiny as in 1918. And when the grand admiral ordered his "lions" in May 1945 to surrender their boats, 218 captains either scuttled or destroyed them in a last defiant expression of loyalty to the navy and to the state.[63] In both combat and sacrifice, the U-Boat service had come as close to Carl von Clausewitz's theoretical abstract of "absolute war" as was possible in a pre-atomic age.

With regard to the more general issue, whether the Battle of the Atlantic constituted a "total" war, the first point to be made is that there never was the slightest doubt in Karl Dönitz's mind that he was conducting a total war

59 Ibid., 412.
60 Blair, *Hitler's U-Boat War: The Hunted, 1942–1945*, 707.
61 Padfield, *Dönitz*, 288.
62 This so-called *Laconia* order is discussed in Mulligan, *Neither Sharks Nor Wolves*, 205–8.
63 Ibid., 239.

with total effort and mobilization for total victory. Thus, he saw no need to define the term. Second, there took place a general process of radicalization of the war over time. The "totality" of the war was incremental, and it developed over four years of escalating warfare. There existed no complete and finalized theoretical construct of total war to be pulled out of a bureaucrat's desk drawer and implemented at a designated point in time. Rather, the process of radicalization prompted Dönitz to devote ever-greater amounts of manpower and material to the Battle of the Atlantic and finally to adopt the language and practice of Nazism for that campaign. By demonizing the "Anglo-Saxon" enemy and reducing the war to a simple "them or us" struggle for survival, he accorded the Battle of the Atlantic all the trappings of total war.

5

From "Blitzkrieg" to "Total War"

Germany's War in Europe

JÜRGEN FÖRSTER

The Second World War has commonly been portrayed as the foremost example of total warfare, while Blitzkrieg has been seen as the form of warfare that Germany waged between 1939 and 1941. This essay examines both of these assumptions. Both terms originated between the wars and have since been used imprecisely by journalists, popular writers, politicians, soldiers, and historians. In Nazi Germany, neither Blitzkrieg nor total war represented a unified concept or a body of coherent doctrine before 1939.[1] When Hitler and German military leaders spoke of "quick knock-out blows," "lightning action," "surprise assaults," or of "Blitzkrieg" itself, as General Ludwig Beck did in his oft-cited memorandum of July 16, 1938, they were referring to speedy operations against Czechoslovakia and Poland.[2] "It was victory," Hew Strachan has written in connection with the campaign in France, "that gave Blitzkrieg the status of doctrine."[3] Michael Geyer, on the other hand, has argued that Blitzkrieg lived off "operational management," which had devoured "professional strategy."[4] Some historians have even claimed that Blitzkrieg was not only an operational, but also a strategic and economic concept.[5] Others have concluded that Germany

---

1 See Wilhelm Deist, "'Blitzkrieg' or Total War? War Preparations in Nazi Germany," in Roger Chickering and Stig Förster, eds., *The Shadows of Total War: Europe, East Asia, and the United States, 1919–1939* (Cambridge, 2003); J. Harris, "The Myth of Blitzkrieg," *War in History* 2 (1995): 335–52; Karl-Heinz Frieser, *Blitzkrieg-Legende: Der Westfeldzug 1940* (Munich, 1995), 5–14.

2 Printed in Klaus-Jürgen Müller, *General Ludwig Beck* (Boppard, 1980), 551–4; see also Klaus-Jürgen Müller, *Armee und Drittes Reich 1933–1939: Darstellung und Dokumentation* (Paderborn, 1987), 349–50.

3 Hew Strachan, *European Armies and the Conduct of War* (London, 1983), 163.

4 Michael Geyer, "German Strategy, 1914–1945," in Peter Paret, ed., *Makers of Modern Strategy from Machiavelli to the Nuclear Age* (Princeton, NJ, 1986), 572, 585.

5 See Alan S. Milward, *The German Economy at War* (London, 1965); cf. Bernhard R. Kroener's critique in his chapter on "The Manpower Resources of the Third Reich in the Area of Conflict between Wehrmacht, Bureaucracy, and War Economy, 1939–1942," in Militärgeschichtliches Forschungsamt, ed., *Germany and the Second World War*, 6 vols. (Oxford, 2000), 5/1, 789–93,

never embraced a comprehensive Blitzkrieg strategy.[6] Although the term has
been attributed to Hitler himself, he distanced himself from it in November
1941. "I have never used the word Blitzkrieg," he told his old comrades in
speaking of Operation Barbarossa, "because it is a very stupid word. If it has
any meaning in regard to one of the campaigns at all, then it would have to
be this one."[7]

Similar confusion surrounds the term "total war." Those who formulated the Third Reich's military plans and organized its war effort rarely
employed the phrase total war in official documents. The one exception
to this generalization was a statement by Lieutenant General Wilhelm
Keitel, head of the Wehrmachtamt, at the fourteenth meeting of the Reich
Defense Committee on April 21, 1937: "Total war demands the marching
in step of the Wehrmacht and the civil administration in preparing for
Reich defense [i.e., war] in depth, width, and pace."[8] Otherwise, political and military leaders usually spoke of the "fighting nation" in the
"war of the future," for which "total armament," "total mobilization,"
"total administration," "total control," and "total command of operations"
would be essential. The coming war "in its absolute form" (Carl von
Clausewitz) or totality would be fought for the existence of the nation.
"This high moral end gives war its total character and its ethical justification,
elevates it above a purely political act or a military duel for an economic
advantage," as Wilhelm Keitel and Alfred Jodl explained in April 1938.[9]
Hitler and his close military advisers did not need to read Ludendorff's

---

1140–54; Kroener, "The 'Frozen Blitzkrieg': German Strategic Planning against the Soviet Union
and the Causes of Its Failure," Bernd Wegner, ed., *From Peace to War: Germany, Soviet Russia and the
World, 1939–1941* (Providence, 1997), 135–9.

6 Deist, "'Blitzkrieg' or Total War?"

7 Max Domarus, *Hitler: Reden und Proklamationen 1932–1945*, 2 vols. (Wiesbaden, 1973), 2: 1776; cf.
Edward Mead Earle, "The Nazi Concept of War," *Makers of Modern Strategy: Military Thought from
Machiavelli to Hitler*, 2d ed. (Princeton, NJ, 1971), 505.

8 Bundesarchiv-Militärarchiv, Freiburg (hereafter BA-MA), Wi/IF 5.560, vol. 2. The term "total
war" was used and discussed in German military journals: see, e.g., *Militär-Wochenblatt*, October 18,
1934, 572–5; *Militärwissenschaftliche Rundschau* 1 (1936): 309–23, 733; and *Jahrbuch für Wehrpolitik und
Wehrwissenschaften* (1937–38): 228–30. See also the Austrian journal *Militärwissenschaftliche Mitteilungen*
68 (1937): 952–74. Interestingly, a German commander was reprimanded for using the term total war
in a lecture in the spring of 1937: BA-MA, RW 6/v. 56, 253. See also the critical discussion of the
Third Reich's military ideology by the exile Albert Schreiner, *Vom totalen Krieg zur totalen Niederlage
Hitlers* (Paris, 1939).

9 "Command in War as a Problem of Organization," OKW Memorandum, April 19, 1938, in *Trial
of the Major War Criminals Before the International Military Tribunal, Nuremberg, 14 November 1945–1
October 1946* (hereafter IMT), 42 vols. (Nuremberg, 1947–49), vol. 38, Annex 48. For the context of
this document see Wilhelm Diest, "The Rearmament of the Wehrmacht," in *Germany and the Second
World War*, vol. 1, 517 and Geoffrey Megargee, *Inside Hitler's High Command* (Lawrence, KS, 2000),
48–9.

book, *Der totale Krieg*, although Beck subscribed to every word of it.[10] These men had drawn their own lessons from the Great War. They believed that the next war would also be a great undertaking that would again encompass civilians as well as soldiers, home and abroad, that the conduct of operations could not be separated from economic and psychological warfare, nor from the organization of the nation's war effort, and that the moral solidarity of the home front was no less important than were armaments. While the army still hoped to force a quick decision on the battlefield by means of mobile operations, the general staff (Oberkommando der Wehrmacht, OKW) was convinced that the war of the future required more than a military strategy.[11]

The war that Hitler unleashed in September 1939 was total from the beginning, insofar as he pursued unlimited ideological objectives without restraint and these objectives determined the conception and execution of military action. The war was also total in the sense that Hitler ruled out the kind of German capitulation that had brought the Great War to an end in November 1918. Hitler's uncompromising will to wage war was met by Churchill's unequivocal reply after the fall of France: "Victory at all costs, victory in spite of all terror, victory however long and hard the road may be; for without victory there is no survival."[12]

The remarks that follow address the problem of total war in connection with the German case. They focus on the elements that are commonly thought to characterize the phenomenon. These elements include the ideas of total control, total war aims, total mobilization, and total methods of warfare.

Nazi Germany was a unitary state, but its administrative structure was chaotic. The dynamism of the Third Reich was determined by three principles – leadership, loyalty, and character. The leadership principle was opposed to government by cooperation or shared responsibility. In pursuing its racial goals, Germany was to be led, not administered. After 1938, the German state became the personal and absolute fiefdom of Hitler, who

---

10 The influence Erich Ludendorff's theory of "total war" had on German strategic thinking in the Inter-War Period has been overestimated. See Jehuda L. Wallach, *The Dogma of the Battle of Annihilation: The Theories of Clausewitz and Schlieffen and Their Impact on the German Conduct of Two World Wars* (Westport, CT, 1986), 241. See now Roger Chickering, "Sore Loser: Ludendorff's Total War," in Chickering and Förster, *The Shadows of Total War*; Müller, *General Ludwig Beck*, 579.
11 See Stig Förster, "The Age of Total War," in Roger Chickering and Stig Förster, eds., *Great War, Total War: Combat and Mobilization on the Western Front, 1914–1918* (Cambridge, 2000).
12 Hugo Bicheno, "Total War," *Oxford Companion to Military History* (Oxford, 1995), 916.

played much more than just another functional role within a polycratic system of rule. As Führer, he was leader of the nation, the people, and the Nazi movement. In this capacity, he acted as chief executive, chief legislator, supreme judge, ideological leader, commander of the armed forces, and – after December 1941 – commander-in-chief of the army. After February 1938, when he reduced the officer corps to a technical elite, Hitler allowed the military no influence in policy-making. Two factors abetted this design. The German military was unaccustomed to thinking in terms of grand strategy. The officer corps tended instead to equate strategy with operations, and it considered the command of operations to be an art. Second, in their desire to preserve their influence over matters of war and peace, the army's leaders, Werner von Fritsch, Ludwig Beck, and Franz Halder, had opposed the creation of an agency to oversee all the German armed forces – a project that Werner von Blomberg, the minister of defense, had favored. As a result, no institution such as a war cabinet, joint chiefs of staff, or a combined-services committee system existed in Nazi Germany; the threads came together only in the hands of Hitler. Given the peculiarities of the Führer state, the power of key officials below Hitler varied according to their personal ambitions, ability, and their relationship to Hitler himself.

Hitler was personally served by five different chancelleries or secretariats. The principal ones were led by Hans-Heinrich Lammers for administration, by Martin Bormann for the party (after 1941), and by Wilhelm Keitel for military affairs. These agencies were not concerned with policy-making, but they operated under Hitler's direct authority to draft laws, decrees, and directives. Hitler also issued directives to his principal lieutenants. These included Heinrich Himmler for domestic security and racial matters, Josef Goebbels for propaganda, Joachim von Ribbentrop for foreign affairs, and Hermann Göring, then Fritz Todt and Albert Speer, for the economy. Moreover, whether by design or necessity, Hitler set up special agencies or envoys for various tasks. Whether they were called plenipotentiaries, Reich commissioners, or inspectors-general, such officials ruled over matters of administration, economics, housing, labor, racial policy, total war, crude oil, water, and energy.

The Council of Ministers for Reich Defense, which was formed on August 30, 1939, might have played a useful role in coordinating civilian, industrial, and military requirements, but it disbanded after only six meetings because its chairman, Göring, did not want to challenge the Führer's political prerogatives. On September 5, 1939, the Council issued the decree against enemies of the people (*Verordnung gegen Volksschädlinge*), which served the same purpose in the civilian realm as the military's anti-sedition decree of

August 26, 1939 (*Kriegssonderstrafrechtsverordnung*). The death penalty was prescribed as punishment for attempting to undermine the war effort.

For much of the war, Germany had no central administrative authority to control the war effort. Hitler's personal directives (*Führerweisungen*) or orders (*Führerbefehle*) prescribed levels of arms production, allocated labor between industry and the military, and initiated operational planning. In 1943, with Hitler's support, Speer took control over the whole war economy as minister for armaments and munitions. To allocate manpower, a new authority was created in January 1943, during the Stalingrad crisis, after Goebbels and Speer had attempted without success to reactivate the Council of Ministers. The members of the new so-called "Committee of Three" were Bormann, Keitel, and Lammers, the heads of the chancelleries for administration, party affairs, and the armed forces. This committee met eleven times, but it failed to mobilize the German people for the kind of total war that Goebbels had advocated in his speech on February 18, 1943.[13] Only in mid-1944 did the regime introduce a series of measures that extended food rationing, froze prices and wages, and further regulated working conditions.

The summer of 1944 marked a turning point in Germany's conduct of the war. The catalyst was the abortive attempt on Hitler's life on July 20, after which Hitler himself ordered full mobilization for total war and appointed Goebbels as his plenipotentiary. This appointment paralleled Himmler's reform of the Wehrmacht's structure, his taking command of the Replacement Army and the newly formed *Volksgrenadier* divisions. At the same time, the SS and the judiciary increased their brutal grip on the German population in support of the total war effort. Yet, even in the last stages of the war, this grip was never complete. The Gestapo kept a watchful eye over the Germans and the foreign workers, but it remained a small agency, staffed more by career policemen than fanatical Nazis. With the aid of denunciations, the Gestapo effectively policed the Third Reich with techniques that included intimidation, preventive detention, "protective custody" in concentration camps, and summary executions.[14] In December 1944, nearly 198,000 men and women were in prison, including 15,774 Poles held in detention camps. Although the statistics of the criminal courts are incomplete, almost 15,500 death sentences were pronounced between 1933 and 1944,

13 See Bernhard R. Kroener, "'Nun Volk steh auf . . . !' Stalingrad und der 'totale' Krieg 1942–1943," in Jürgen Förster, ed., *Stalingrad: Ereignis, Wirkung, Symbol* (Munich, 1992), 151–70; Martin Kutz, "Fantasy, Reality, and Modes of Perception in Ludendorff's and Goebbels's Concepts of 'Total War'" in the present volume.

14 See Gerhard Paul and Klaus-Michael Mallmann, *Die Gestapo im Zweiten Weltkrieg: "Heimatfront" und besetztes Europa* (Darmstadt, 2000).

and more than three-quarters of them were carried out. The Wehrmacht's
statistics revealed that 9,732 persons had been executed by the end of 1944.
Military courts, notably the new mobile "flying courts-martial" (*fliegende
Standgerichte*), were in operation until May 1945; and by the end of the war,
at least 21,000 military executions had been carried out. Between 1939
and 1944, SS courts executed 1,001 of their men.[15] Never certain of the
cohesion of the *Volksgemeinschaft* that they had been forging since 1933,
the Nazis relied on a carrot-and-stick approach, which combined bribes
and threats, savage penalties and calls for decency, to keep German society
under control.

Germany controlled great expanses of Europe between 1939 and 1945.
To what extent was German rule coherent and policy-driven? Hitler was
pragmatic, and he admired the effectiveness of British colonial rule, particularly in India. He was more interested in winning the war and exploiting
the conquered territories than he was in prematurely establishing a "New
Order" in Europe and arousing resistance among the occupied or dependent countries. He was thus not interested in a unified system, but favored
practical arrangements until final victory would give him the freedom to
decide the concrete dimensions of a "New Order" in Europe.

The pattern of control in Europe was, accordingly, to extend German
administration with attention to several special circumstances. Some territories, including Danzig-West Prussia, the Warthegau, southeast Prussia,
and eastern Upper Silesia, were formally annexed to Germany. Others were
not formally incorporated in the Reich but were effectively treated as parts
of it. These included Alsace-Lorraine, Luxemburg, parts of Slovenia, and
Bialystok. Still others, such as Denmark after August 1943 and Hungary after
March 1944, were placed under German civilian administrators. Countries
whose populations were deemed to be Germanic, such as Norway, Holland,
and, after July 1944, the Flemish parts of Belgium, were also placed under
civilian administration but were slated for future incorporation into the
Greater German Empire. Finally, parts of Europe under civilian control
were designated areas of German colonization. These included the Protectorate of Bohemia and Moravia, the General Government of Poland, and
the Reich commissariats for *Ostland* and the Ukraine. Occupied areas that
were held to be of continuing military significance were placed, by contrast,
under military administration. These included Belgium before July 1944,

---

15 For an overview of the German court system under the Nazis and of the imprisonment and death
sentence statistics, see Jürgen Förster, "Germany" in *The Oxford Companion to the Second World War*
(Oxford, 1995), 460–6.

France and the British Channel Islands, and southeast Europe, as well as areas immediately to the rear of zones of operations in the Soviet Union.[16]

If total control be defined as an element of total war, the German record was thus mixed at best. The German pursuit of total war aims was less ambiguous. Hitler was a racist who saw himself as the executor of a historical mission. He believed that racial struggle would continue until the Germans had realized their claims to world mastery in a *Pax Germanica*. In this ideological context, war took on a special meaning for Hitler. It was the "highest expression of the life force" of the German people as well as a legitimate tool in his own hands for acquiring *Lebensraum*, the space for colonization that would secure the nation's future racially, economically, and militarily.[17] Because national survival was contingent on military victory, politics and strategy became indistinguishable. Policy was the conduct of war by other means, and strategic planning was the captive of militant policy. This new kind of war knew no distinction between the combat zone and the home front. Under Hitler's command, the full might of the German people would strike without restraint against all national and racial enemies within and outside the Reich.

Before 1939, no one talked more about peace than Hitler. He did so to conceal the military revitalization and rearmament of Germany, which were the foundations for a long-range policy of aggression. When Hitler decided to achieve his aims by force, he ordered the propaganda apparatus to prepare the nation psychologically for war. While Hitler's program was not a detailed blueprint for action, *Lebensraum* did have practical implications. It meant war, conquest, autarky, annihilation, and world power. All the measures that the Germans undertook behind the front lines thus represented a part of both the war effort and a wider scheme to reorganize Europe demographically and economically. The Nazis ranked peoples and countries racially and according to their behavior toward Germany. Nazi genocide was guided by more than anti-Semitism. The racial victims included Jews, Slavs, gypsies, blacks, homosexuals, and the mentally handicapped, as war, ideology, genocide, and social policy all merged. The link between grand strategy and racial and social policy made it impossible to separate any institution or any stratum of German society from the goals of the regime. The war radicalized the concept of *Lebensraum*. Nevertheless, Hitler thought it important to keep

---

16 See Hans Umbreit, "Towards Continental Dominion," in *Germany and the Second World War*, 5/1: 126–7 and Hans Umbreit, "German Rule in the Occupied Territories, 1942–1945, in ibid., vol. 5/2, 8–137.

17 See Gerhard Weinberg, *Germany, Hitler, and World War II: Essays in Modern German and World History* (Cambridge, 1995), 34–8.

his objectives hidden from world opinion. Even in mid-July 1941, after key steps had been taken to translate his horrendous vision of *Lebensraum* into reality, he stipulated, "it should not be recognizable that a final settlement [in the east] is beginning."[18]

The axioms of German policy, the alternatives of total victory or total destruction, were expounded not only in abstract terms in *Mein Kampf* and *Hitler's Secret Book*. Again and again, Hitler hammered home the message that space and race were critical. Germany must expand or die. In a little-noted address to the commanding officers of the army in February 1939, Hitler stated that he was determined to solve the problem of living space, to adjust *Lebensraum* to Germany's growing population, and that this effort dominated his life. He left his commanders in no doubt about the character of the impending war. Because racial considerations now drove peoples to war, the next conflict would be "a purely ideological war, i.e. consciously a people's and racial war." Hitler demanded from his Wehrmacht "that even if, in my struggle for this ideology, I am abandoned by the rest of the nation in its entirety, then, more than ever, every German soldier, the entire officers' corps, man by man, must stand beside me and by me."[19] Hitler's address to the commanders took on additional significance in light of the speech that he had delivered a fortnight earlier to the Reichstag. He announced that "if international financial Jewry within and outside Europe were to succeed in once more hurling the nations into a world war, then the result will be not the Bolshevization of the earth and thus the victory of Jewry, but the annihilation of the Jewish race in Europe."[20]

Military preparations for the invasion of Poland began at the end of March 1939. In another address to his military commanders on August 22, 1939, Hitler justified his decision to go to war. He declared that Germany had only a temporary advantage in military equipment, organization, tactics, and leadership. Time was working against the Reich, militarily and economically; but Poland was now isolated, and the Western Powers were deterred by Germany's might and the impending pact with the Soviet Union. Not Danzig, but the expansion of Germany's *Lebensraum*, was the issue in

---

18 IMT vol. 38, 87. Note also Joseph Goebbels's remark to select representatives of the press on April 5, 1940: "Today we say Lebensraum. Everyone can imagine what he wants. What we want we will know when the time is right."

19 Hans-Adolf Jacobsen, *Der Zweite Weltkrieg: Grundzüge der Politik und Strategie in Dokumenten* (Frankfurt am Main, 1965), 181; Müller, *Armee und Drittes Reich 1933–1939: Darstellung und Dokumentation* (Paderborn, 1987), 365–75.

20 Domarus, *Hitler*, vol. 2: 1058, and Jeremy Noakes and Geoffrey Pridham, eds., *Nazism 1919–1945: A Documentary Reader*, vol. 3 (Exeter, 1988), 1049; OKW, *Schulungshefte für den Unterricht über nationalsozialistische Weltanschauung und national politische Zielsetzung* 5 (1939).

the summer of 1939.[21] The immediate goal was the destruction of Poland in order to gain territory for the resettlement of Germans. In an address to the troops on September 1, 1939, the Commander-in-Chief of the Army pointed out that Nazi Germany's cause was clear and just. It was to achieve "the lasting security of the German *Volk* and German living space against foreign infringements and claims."[22]

By mid-October 1939, the top army leaders had clear knowledge of the Nazis' destructive designs in Poland. These leaders neither objected on principle nor shared this information with the officer corps at large, as they washed their hands of responsibility for the administration of Poland. When Himmler made it clear to the army's commanders in March 1940 that SS actions in Poland had been ordered by Hitler himself, all opposition among these officers came to an end. The dazzling victory over France in 1940 further encouraged the military's acceptance of the SS's "unparalleled radical measures for the final solution of the racial struggle [*Volkstumskampf*], which has been waged for centuries along the eastern frontier."[23]

The Führer announced his intention to attack in the west even before Prime Minister Chamberlain rejected the vague German peace offer of October 6, 1939. Visions of bloody stalemate on the western front briefly revived professional opposition to Hitler among leading soldiers, but it faded once a more promising offensive plan, which avoided a frontal assault on enemy lines, emerged in early 1940. The ensuing campaign in the west has been characterized as the classic example of Blitzkrieg. In reality, the German army's leadership had not thought of a Blitzkrieg as a strategic concept. It had assumed instead a much longer period of fighting, for which it had prepared a "second wave" of personnel and matériel. The unexpectedly rapid victory over France convinced Hitler and his generals that the aerial bombing of soldiers and civilians, breakthroughs by armored formations, and deep envelopments by motorized units offered a formula for success in a lightning war. They overlooked the basic question whether tank divisions that lacked absolute air superiority could succeed against a well-equipped, well-led enemy in a modern system of defensive positions.[24]

---

21 So Hitler explained to the leaders of the Wehrmacht on May 23, 1939; see Noakes and Pridam, *Nazism*, vol. 3, 737.

22 BA-MA, RH 53-7/v. 1069.

23 Helmut Krausnick and Hans-Heinrich Wilhelm, *Die Truppe des Weltanschauungskrieges: Die Einsatz-gruppen der Sicherheitspolizei und des SD 1938–1942* (Stuttgart 1981), 112. See also Alex B. Rossino, *Hitler Strikes at Poland: Blitzkrieg, Ideology, and Atrocity* (Lawrence, KS, 2003).

24 BA-MA, RH 35/88, Panzer-Regiment 3, Erfahrungen aus dem polnischen Feldzug, 20 January 1940; BA-MA, RH 19 III/157, Report of 6th Panzerdivision of 18 July 1940.

The period between the campaigns against France and the Soviet Union was too short to upgrade tactical training to meet operational demands.[25] The manpower transfers between the army and war industry, the shortage of fully trained reservists, the creation of new tank divisions through a cadre system, the special training of officers at the service schools (which hindered divisional training) all prevented the adjustment of Blitzkrieg tactics to the invasion of the Soviet Union in June 1941. So did inadequate attention to the staggering logistical problems of war in the great spaces of the east. Given these spaces, the seventeen armored divisions that were deployed in the east in 1941 represented a less massive force than the one that had been deployed in the west in 1940. The logical consequence of fighting a Blitzkrieg with inadequate equipment was a system of improvisations.

Operation Barbarossa was the greatest single campaign of the European war. It was designed to achieve a strategic objective within a single theater of war and within a set time frame. The object of its initial phase was to destroy the bulk of the Red Army in a series of envelopments west of the Dnepr and Dvina rivers as well as to prevent the withdrawal of Soviet combat units eastward. Then, by means of rapid pursuit, the final defeat of the Red Army was to be accomplished and a line established within three months between Archangel and the Volga. All the strategic, operational, tactical, and production decisions that were made before the invasion rested on the assumption that Germany could win a Blitzkrieg over the Soviet Union in the summer of 1941. Accordingly, no preparations had been made for a winter campaign. The gaze of the Führer and his generals was fixed upon victory even before the campaign had begun.

The decision to attack the Soviet Union represented a response to Germany's strategic dilemma in the summer of 1940, when Hitler's war aims exceeded those of his generals, who had persuaded themselves that German domination in Europe could be secured by negotiating peace with Britain. When Churchill refused to cooperate, the "Russian problem" became Hitler's strategic obsession. With the Soviet Union smashed, he reasoned, "Britain's last hope would be shattered. Germany then will be master of Europe and the Balkans."[26] In December 1940, Hitler laid out his grand strategy. All continental problems were to be solved in 1941, before

---

25 See Jürgen Förster, "The Dynamics of Volksgemeinschaft," in Williamson Murray and Allan R. Millett, eds., *Military Effectiveness*, 3 vols. (Boston, 1988), 3: 199–201, 209; Jürgen Förster, "Hitler's Decision in Favour of War Against the Soviet Union," in *Germany and the Second World War*, vol. 4; Kroener, "The Manpower Resources of the Third Reich," *Germany and the Second World War* vol. 5/1.

26 Charles Burdick and Hans-Adolf Jacobsen, eds., *The Halder War Diary 1939–1942* (Novato, CA, 1988), 244.

the United States could interfere in Europe.[27] After the defeat of Russia, Germany would be unassailable, Britain would be forced to sue for peace, and the United States would become a *quantité négligeable.*

The transformation and fusion of Germany's long-range goals of *Lebensraum, Volksgemeinschaft,* and *Entfernung der Juden* began, however, before Barbarossa. "Nazi racial policy was," as Christopher Browning has observed, "radicalized in quantum jumps" between 1939 and 1941.[28] The momentum of war further shaped all these objectives. Ideological aims provided the reason for going to war in 1939, but success in war opened favorable conditions to achieve these aims. The racial end justified the radical means. The symbiosis of ideology and strategy, ends and means, culminated in the *Vernichtungskrieg,* the war of annihilation, against the Soviet Union. In this war, Hitler began to use the Wehrmacht as an instrument of racial struggle. Between 1939 and 1941, the military moved, as Browning has written, from "abdication of responsibility to outright complicity."[29]

The Shoah, the most total of the German war aims, must be analyzed against the background of the war in the east. The road to Auschwitz was both a twisted road and a straight path. In the euphoria of initial success over "Jewish Bolshevism" in July 1941, Hitler combined his two most cherished goals – the acquisition of living space and the elimination of the Jews. The vision of a racially pure Germanic empire that stretched from the Atlantic to the Urals led first to the decisions to decimate the Slavic peoples and to prepare for the "Final Solution" of the Jewish problem in Europe. Then, a month after the invasion of the Soviet Union, when Hitler began to realize that the Blitzkrieg had failed, the extermination of the Russian and European Jews assumed priority. Both euphoria and frustration led to the rationalization and industrialization of mass murder. In this process, the Wehrmacht acted as perpetrator, collaborator, and bystander – seldom as resister.

Rearmament, autarky, and preparation for war had been Germany's policies since 1933. They were merely accelerated after 1936. Nonetheless, judged by the state of German armaments in 1939, the war began three to four years prematurely. Even as the war began, there was no total economic mobilization in anticipation of a long war of attrition. The peacetime

---

27 Percy Ernst Schramm, ed., *Kriegstagebuch des Oberkommandos der Wehrmacht (Wehrmachtführungsstab) 1940–1945,* 4 vols. in 7 (Frankfurt, 1961), 1: 996.

28 Christopher R. Browning, "Nazi Resettlement Policy and the Search for a Solution to the Jewish Question," *German Studies Review* 9 (1986): 519.

29 See Christopher Browning, *The Origins of the Final Solution* (Jerusalem, 2003) and Rossaino, *Hitler Strikes Poland.*

war economy, which was launched in the Four-Year Plan in 1936, was followed by a peacelike wartime economy. Business continued as usual. The regime produced consumer goods and kept food rations substantially higher than during the First World War. The immense material booty captured in Austria, Czechoslovakia, and France, as well as access to armaments factories in these lands, masked deep weaknesses in Germany's war economy, while the easy military victories belied the organizational deficiencies in the war effort. The competition among the Wehrmacht, war industries, and political agencies for manpower after 1939 emphasized Germany's unpreparedness for total war. The Wehrmacht and the armaments factories required the same young, physically fit, and technically trained men. Formally, the Wehrmacht had prior claims on them, but there were no regulations to guide the deferment of militarily trained personnel to industry. Moreover, despite the pleas of Göring, the Nazi state had established no "people's roster" before 1939, when only 58 percent of a labor force of 38 million was officially registered and possessed the necessary work book.[30]

The Wehrmacht comprised 4,556,000 men on September 1, 1939, and Germany had mobilized about 6 million men by the end of the year. Exempted personnel numbered 1,870,000. The outbreak of war did not bring the recruitment of women into the factories. On the contrary, for reasons of ideology, the Nazis resisted demands from the armed forces that women be enlisted into compulsory labor service; and the regime paid married soldiers generous allowances, which discouraged women from seeking work. In May 1941, there were nearly 440,000 fewer women in the workforce than in May 1939. Fears of lowering morale at home and on the front persuaded the regime to make one concession after another.[31]

While the Wehrmacht had increased its strength by over 1 million men by mid-June 1940, exemptions had also risen to 3.1 million. During the next six months, the Wehrmacht recruited only 936,000 men, while deferments rose to 4.8 million.[32] The regime believed that the "practice of granting fixed periods of temporary leave for soldiers to serve in the armaments industry had enabled it to solve the problem of mobilizing the population for the war effort."[33] In December 1940, Hitler himself resolved the conflict over manpower between the army and the war industries to the benefit of the

---

30 See Kroener, "The Manpower Resources of the Third Reich," 862.
31 Ibid., 882.   32 Ibid., 1089.
33 Bernhard R. Kroener, Rolf-Dieter Müller, and Hans Umbreit, "Conclusion," in *Germany and the Second World War*, 5/1, 1169.

latter. This *Führerbefehl* emphasized the priority of armaments production for the air force and navy "for the continuation of war against Britain."[34] In the summer of 1941, deferments outnumbered soldiers in the field army by 400,000 men. The number of exemptions peaked at nearly 7 million men by the end of May 1944 after changes to the conscription law had provided for the drafting of older men into the army.

Only in the winter of 1941 did the direction of the war economy enter a new phase. The assumption that the war would be short evaporated. The problem was now to mobilize personnel to handle available equipment, to produce the necessary weaponry for the soldiers, and to replace the immense losses among the combat units. In January 1943, a steering committee was established to allocate men and women to the various phases of the Reich's defense, including the armed forces. In November of the same year, the Wehrmacht was ordered to mobilize at least 1 million additional "fighters" from within its own ranks. Both measures failed to meet their objectives. In August 1943, the Wehrmacht received only 650,000 additional men, instead of the projected 800,000; and by June 1944, it had raised only about 583,000 additional men for combat duty. An accelerated influx of foreign workers replaced Germans who were called up for military service, and it reduced the demand for German female workers.

Thus, the composition of the German workforce was different in May 1944 from what it had been at the beginning of war. It totaled 28.6 million Germans – 14.1 million men (including 6.2 million deferred) and 14.5 million women. In addition, 7.1 million foreign workers (5.3 forced laborers and 1.8 prisoners of war) and about half a million slave-laborers from concentration camps were at work.[35] Almost without exception, Germans became foremen or supervisors of foreign workers in sectors of the armaments industry that still relied primarily on manual labor. Here, the proportion of foreign workers amounted to over 70 percent. The ruthless exploitation of the human and material resources in occupied Europe enabled the regime to relieve the burdens of war on the Germans. At the end of 1943, their food rations were nearly as generous as they had been in 1939.

The SS, too, registered a "success" in exploiting manpower reserves in Germany and elsewhere in Europe. Between December 1938 and May 1940, it increased its own armed forces, the Waffen-SS, almost fourfold to

---

34 BA-MA, Wi/IA 13. See also Kroener, "The Manpower Resources of the Third Reich," 975–6.
35 See Hans Mommsen, "The Impact of Compulsory Labor on German Society at War," in the present volume.

93,000.[36] The expansion of Nazi Germany in Europe, the growing realization of the SS's vision of the "Greater Germanic Empire," presented the
means to replace most of its manpower losses. The Waffen-SS changed into
a heterogeneous multinational army, incorporating "Germanic," "ethnic
German," and foreign volunteers into its ranks. By the end of 1943, the
Waffen-SS comprised over half a million men and was a major factor in the
German war effort. By the end of the war, more than 800,000 men had
served in its thirty-eight divisions; only 40 percent of them were German
nationals, and some 25 percent of the total had been killed in action.[37]
Altogether, some 18.3 million soldiers were mobilized in the Wehrmacht
and Waffen-SS. The losses amounted to about 5.3 million – which, at
28 percent, doubled the death rate of the First World War.[38]

The "ruthless, incontrovertible laws of attrition" did not lead to fundamental revision of Germany's approach to mobilization until the summer of
1944.[39] The catalyst for the change came in the heavy blows delivered by
the Western Allies in Normandy and by the Soviets on the eastern front,
as well as in the abortive attempt on Hitler's life in July. Resolved to continue the struggle until the enemy alliance broke up, Hitler himself now
ordered mobilization for total war and on July 25 appointed Goebbels as his
plenipotentiary. The establishment of the *Volkssturm*, a civil defense force
made up of boys and old men, made clear the desperation of the effort. All
German males between the ages of sixteen and sixty were declared liable for
military service. Industrial labor and air defense had priority, but training
in antitank and infantry combat was undertaken for four hours on Sundays.
By the time the Red Army reached German soil in 1944, the *Volkssturm*
was deployed in the front line.

The term "total mobilization" extended after 1942 to the battle for the
soldiers' minds, the effort to provide the troops "with that very belief in
victory which the realities of the battlefield seemed to contradict."[40] Ten

36 See Jürgen Förster, "Die weltanschauliche Erziehung in der Waffen-SS," in Jürgen Matthäus et al.,
    *Ausbildung zum Judenmord? "Weltanschauliche Erziehung" von SS. Polezei und Waffen SS im Rahmen der
    "Endlösung"* (Frankfurt am Main, 2003), 95.
37 See Bernd Wegner, "Waffen-SS," in *The Oxford Companion to the Second World War*, 1046–9; Bernd
    Wegner, *The Waffen-SS: Organization, Ideology and Function* (Oxford, 1982), 291–331; Bernhard
    R. Kroener, "Management of Human Resources," *Germany and the Second World War*, vol. 5/2,
    1059–64.
38 See Rüdiger Overmans, *Deutsche militärische Verluste im Zweiten Weltkrieg* (Munich, 1999), 316–9.
39 Williamson Murray, *Luftwaffe* (Baltimore, 1985), 293.
40 Omer Bartov, "The Barbarisation of Warfare: German Officers and Soldiers in Combat on the East-
    ern Front, 1941–1945" (Ph.D. thesis, St. Antony's College, Oxford, 1983), 171; cf. Jürgen Förster,
    "Ludendorff and Hitler in Perspective: The Battle for the German Soldier's Mind, 1917–1945,"
    War in History 10 (2003): 312–34, and Jürgen Förster, "Geistige Kriegsführung in Deutschland
    1919–1945," *Das Deutsche Reich und der Zweite Weltkrieg*, vol. 9/1 (in press).

years earlier, neither Hitler nor his generals had been much interested in an educational program for the army, beyond promoting an instinct for the needs of the *Volksgemeinschaft* and an unshakeable belief in the Führer. The pertinent paragraph on "spiritual guidance" (*geistige Betreuung*) in the general staff's manual of 1939 had correctly asserted that military success would best promote the morale of the troops, but that education would acquire greater significance should the war become prolonged. This became the case in the winter of 1943–44. The army met the new demands on its powers of resistance by strengthening traditional military values, tightening discipline, and promoting ideological uniformity. Strong doses of the Nazi *Weltanschauung* were calculated to bolster morale in the "battles of destiny" against "Jewish Bolshevism" and Western plutocracy. The idea of a war of extermination, which had earlier sustained the German offensive, now took on defensive connotations, as the basis of a campaign to save the German *Volksgemeinschaft* from extinction. This combination of professional initiatives and old party ideals culminated in a series of orders from Hitler in the winter of 1943–44 and a booklet that the army's personnel office published with the telling title *Wofür kämpfen wir?* ("What Are We Fighting For?"). It contained an order from Hitler that emphasized the officer's role in leading by personal example, both tactically and politically: "He who fights with the purest will, the staunchest belief and the most fanatical determination will be victorious in the end."[41] There was no room for nonpolitical officers. In December 1943, National Socialist Leadership Officers (NSFO) were assigned down to the divisional level, in order to aid commanders in instructing the soldiers in the principles of what Himmler called the true "National Socialist people's army."[42] The concept of "political soldiery" was invoked to sustain morale. These measures represented signs of military weakness as well as a paradox. They brought a reversal of trends then prevalent in the Red Army, where the influence of the political commissars yielded to that of the military commanders, while the Nazi Party took over increasing control of political indoctrination of the Wehrmacht as defeat became imminent.

Pursuing total aims, Hitler's war was an ideological crusade from the start. After the Wehrmacht crushed the Polish forces in a conventional campaign, the SS immediately began its racial war in the occupied territories. The Wehrmacht's attitude to the indigenous population in Poland rested on

---

41 Personal-Amt des Heeres, ed., *Wofür kämpfen wir?* (Berlin, 1944), 2–4.
42 Theodor Eschenberg, "Die Rede Himmlers von den Gauleitern am 3. August 1944," *Vierteljahreshefte für Zeitgeschichte* 1 (1953): 392.

racial arrogance, insecurity, and a naive faith in the efficacy of force. Fears among the army leadership were well founded that soldiers might become as brutal and bloodthirsty as the SS. Yet the army's reaction was limited to an attempt to maintain morale and discipline among the troops by withdrawing while the SS committed brutal acts of violence against the Polish and Jewish populations.

The occupation of Poland was a test case for Nazi racial policy. Although this occupation marked an escalation in the persecution of the Jews, the Final Solution was not yet a specific aim. "Jewish policy" still implied deportation and ghettoization. The Wehrmacht recognized that there was a "Jewish problem" in Poland, but it did not consider the solution of this problem to be its business. The Wehrmacht dealt ruthlessly, however, with insurgents; and individual soldiers looted, raped, and indiscriminately shot prisoners of war and Polish civilians, among them many Jews. The commanders worried about the resulting threat to military discipline and forbade "wild," unauthorized, or spontaneous measures against Poles and Jews as well as the participation of soldiers in executions carried out by the SS. The army also increased the numbers of courts-martial. On October 4, 1939, however, Hitler pardoned all military and police personnel who had overstepped military law. He justified this decision by declaring that these crimes had been natural responses to hostile Polish behavior toward Germans. The amnesty and, several weeks later, the granting of a separate military code to the SS encouraged further acts of terror.[43]

The campaign in the west differed from that against Poland. No SS-Einsatzgruppen crossed the border with the troops. At least during the first months of the occupation, the policy of the German military administration forbade "special measures" against the Jews.[44] Only in March 1942 did the OKW admit a Higher SS and Police Leader into France, as it had earlier in Serbia. This step came in response to increasing acts of sabotage and assassination by the French resistance, for the military administration was uncomfortable ordering mandatory reprisals.[45]

When preparations for Operation Barbarossa were fully advanced, Hitler declared that the war in the east would be more than a conflict between two enemy states. It would be a clash of antagonistic ideologies and races. The concept of racial extermination thereupon became a component of

43 Cf. Rossino, *Hitler Strikes Poland.*

44 Ulrich Herbet, "The German Military Command in Paris and the Deportation of the French Jews," in Herbert, ed., *National Socialist Extermination Policies: Contemporary German Perspectives and Controversies* (New York, 2000), 135.

45 Umbreit, "German Rule in the Occupied Territories, 1942–1945," *Germany and the Second World War,* vol. 5/2, 30.

both military operations and German policy behind the lines, as warfare and ideology joined in dynamic interplay. The military leaders did not object to the ideologization of the war, for they, too, believed that the threat of Russian Bolshevism should be eliminated forever. The difference between operations in Poland and the Soviet Union was that Hitler erased the line between military and political warfare in 1941. Before the first shot was fired, he issued a preemptive amnesty to permit the shooting of Soviet political commissars, prisoners of war, and suspected guerrillas. The concept of *ius in bello* had become an irksome obstacle to destruction of the Soviet Union. Barbarossa was to become a *Vernichtungskampf* against "Jewish Bolshevism," whether it was embodied in the Red Army or civilians. Illegal measures were authorized, and the "elimination of all active and passive resistance" proceeded according to the prescriptions of ideology.[46] The goal of the army and the SS alike was the speedy breakup of the Soviet system of rule and the pacification of the conquered territories. Responsibility for liquidating enemy cadres was to be shared. The SS was to eliminate civilian representatives of the inimical *Weltanschauung*, while the Wehrmacht liquidated the political commissars, the "Jewish-Bolshevik intelligentsia" within the Red Army, as well as real or suspected resisters. The German army's embrace of ideological goals in the name of military necessity, its linking of punitive and preventative measures, was the prelude to joining the SS in striking a fatal blow against the phantom of "Jewish Bolshevism." In this way, what Michael Geyer has called "escalatory warfare" grew out of Hitler's commitment to *Lebensraum*. German expansion to the east, the extermination of Bolshevism, and the annihilation of the Jews were inextricably intertwined. Hopes of achieving a more rapid and less costly military advance provided the officer corps with a clear conscience, as the army crushed active and passive resistance and created "chaos in Russia," forcing the population of the cities to flee eastward.[47]

Soviet atrocities and partisan activities fanned the flames. Hitler used them to portray extermination as a necessity of war. The brutalization of German soldiers had begun in Poland. The barbarization of warfare began in the Soviet Union. In mid-September 1941, the methods of total warfare, now implemented in the east, were exported to all occupied areas. Military commanders were ordered everywhere to use "the harshest methods . . . within

46 See Jürgen Förster, "Operation Barbarossa as a War of Conquest and Annihilation." *Germany and the Second World War*, vol. 4, 481–521.
47 BA-MA, RH 2/1327, Hitler's order, October 12, 1941. Cf. Johannes Hürter, "Die Wehrmacht vor Leningrad, Kreig und Besatzungspolitik im Herbst und Winter 1941/42," *Vierteljahreshefte für Zeitgeschichte* 49 (2001): 377–440.

the shortest possible time."[48] The guiding principle was the use of terror to crush the will to resist among the subject populations.

Both the discrepancy between German casualties and the number of partisans killed and the minor difference between the numbers of partisans arrested and executed pointed to the dialectical dimension of Wehrmacht's reprisal policy. The ravaging of the Soviet Union was ideological in its inspiration but rational in its implementation. Ordinary men performed extraordinary tasks. Military necessity provided the bridge. As long as destruction could be construed as reprisal against Germany's enemies, "it did not require nazified zealots (though surely such were not lacking), merely conscientious and politically obtuse soldiers to carry them out."[49]

The troops that invaded Poland in 1939 carried the everyday racism and xenophobia that transcended all the age cohorts and social groups that made up the German army. The duration of the fighting led many soldiers to adapt to a war environment. Because some commanders remained reluctant to order total warfare, Hitler decreed in December 1942 that the troops were obliged to use every means against partisans without restraint, even against women and children. "No German was to be disciplined or court-martialed because of his behavior in fighting bands or their sympathizers."[50] However ambivalent the military might once have been about "ideological terrorism," its pursuit of ideological warfare changed from a means for achieving rational ends to a means of extermination.[51] The obligation to prosecute military crimes by German troops was lifted, and no legal action was undertaken against soldiers who had violated international law. The highest legal standard was the welfare of the race.

When signs of demoralization became visible, Hitler ordered a "hard and merciless fight" not only against the outside enemy, but also against anyone at home who "should fail in this decisive hour."[52] Commanders, troops on the spot, and officials of the regime now joined in draconian measures to ensure that soldiers and civilians would continue to fight despite the prospect of

---

48 U.S. Department of State, ed., *Documents on German Foreign Policy*, Series D, vol. 12 (Washington, DC, 1962), 542.
49 Christopher R. Browning, "Wehrmacht Reprisal Policy and the Mass Murder of Jews in Serbia," *Militärgeschichtliche Mitteilungen* 33 (1983): 39.
50 War Archive, Prague, KdoStab RFSS, file 4, folder 21, OKW order December 16, 1942; cf. Helmut Heiber ed., *Hitlers Lagebesprechungen: Die Protokollfragmente seiner militärischen Konferenzen 1942–1945* (Stuttgart, 1962), 65.
51 See Geyer, "German Strategy," 592.
52 See Jürgen Förster, "Die Wehrmacht und das Ende des Dritten Reiches," in Arnd Bauernkämper et al., eds., *Der 8. Mai 1945 als historische Zäsur: Strukturen Erfahrungen, Deutungen* (Potsdam, 1995), 50–65; Andreas Kunz, "Die Wehrmacht in der Agonie der nationalsozialistischen Herrschaf 1944/45: Eine Gedankenskizze," in Jörg Hillmann and John Zimmermann, eds., *Kriegsende in Deutschland 1945* (Munich, 2002), 97–114.

total defeat. Military police were given special powers, and mobile courts-martial were created. A Berlin joke reflected the attitude of the German public in the last year of the war, as endurance dissolved into apathy and personal survival became the prime consideration. "I'd rather believe in final victory than run around with my head cut off."[53]

If total war is defined by the character of its methods, mobilization, aims, and control, Germany represented a mixed case. The war aims of the Nazi regime, like the methods with which it pursued them, were devoid of restraint and devoted to the total destruction of the enemy. The system of control, by contrast, was much more eclectic, as was the development of a Blitzkrieg strategy. Finally, the regime shied from total mobilization until the end of the war. Hitler's war was total in its design if not in all phases of its implementation.

How do we evaluate the impact of ideological salvoes fired? The transfer from public speech and writing into public thought is measured not just by the nature of the message, but also by the degree of receptivity to the message and the endurance of its readers and listeners in hard times. The historian of the Second World War is hesitant to credit Hitler with the success of this undertaking. Yet all the generals Sir Basil Liddell Hart asked after VE day unanimously declared that National Socialism had fortified the morale of their men, whether one liked it or not.[54] The dynamics of *Volksgemeinschaft*, faith in the righteousness of Germany's cause, and the Wehrmacht's tremendous confidence in its Supreme Commander, all contributed more to the troops' morale and the people's resilience than even Hitler was willing to acknowledge at the end of his life.[55] The *Führer* had won the battle for the hearts and minds of the German people, but he had lost the war anyway. The high level of endurance and sacrifice displayed by the Germans had a reverse side. It increased the destruction and ensured that the consequences for Germany were far more significant than they had been in 1918.

53 Förster, "Die Wehrmacht und das Ende des Dritten Reichs," 58–60.
54 B. H. Liddell Hart, *The Other Side of the Hill: Germany's Generals, Their Rise and Fall. With Their Own Account of Military Events, 1939–1945* (London, 1945), 265–7.
55 Cf. Francois Genould, ed., *The Testament of Adolf Hitler: The Hitler-Bormann Documents, February–April 1945* (London, 1961), 58–9.

6

Global Yet Not Total

The U.S. War Effort and Its Consequences

DENNIS SHOWALTER

Between 1941 and 1945 America waged a war of paradoxes. It was the only combatant to wage a global war in the literal sense, yet its mobilization fell far short of the "total" standards established by its allies and enemies. Fighting the war took precedence over focusing on it – and as a consequence the United States developed a "worldview" whose direct and indirect results far exceeded contemporary expectations.

I

The United States did not wage war in a mere two theaters. It deployed significant forces everywhere in the world, in every theater except the Russian. There it was excluded as a matter of Soviet policy, and being shut out of the theater where total war came closest to being realized might well have nurtured America's detachment from total war's consequences in terms of casualties and destruction.[1] Yet even on the eastern front, lend-lease aid was vital to stabilizing the Soviet economy in 1942–43 and sustaining the Red Army's offensives in 1944–45.[2]

The process of globalization began well before Pearl Harbor. U.S. strategists increasingly considered American security in hemispheric terms, directly incorporating Latin America in contingency planning. The United States not only sustained a significant military presence in the Aleutian Islands – as far away from anywhere as it is possible to get; it also drove a highway from Alaska to the lower forty-eight states. The United States not

1 Mark Conversino, *Fighting with the Soviets: The Failure of Operation FRANTIC, 1944–1945* (Lawrence, KS, 1997).
2 Hubert P. Van Tuyll, *Feeding the Bear: American Aid to the Soviet Union, 1941–1945* (New York, 1989); and Roger Munting, "Lend Lease and the Soviet War Effort," *Journal of Contemporary History*, 19 (1984): 495–510; cf. Boris V. Sokolov, "The Role of Lend-Lease in Soviet Military Efforts, 1941–1945," tr. D. Glantz, *Journal of Slavic Military Studies*, 7 (1994): 567–86.

only committed entire divisions to South Pacific islands barely on the map in 1941; it built an infrastructure to support them and carry their operations forward. The United States flew supplies across the Himalayas from India into China and committed a division-strength task force to the Burma campaign. U.S. aircraft flew regular routes across Africa. U.S. infantry stormed a half-dozen European beaches. U.S. merchant ships and merchant seamen supplied the Hawaiian Islands and fought through to Murmansk and Archangel.

Other combatants did some, or many, of these same things. No one did all of them. Germany's war was ultimately defined by the Russian front and the air battle over the Reich. Russia fought in a single theater. Japan played an exclusively Asian role. Britain came closest to the U.S. model, but its global role was generally defined by prewar imperial commitments – frequently reduced as far as possible, as in the case of Australia.[3] Britain's war was for the British Isles, and it was not without cause that its soldiers in Burma called themselves "the forgotten army." In America, by contrast, global war did not involve diffusion of effort. Europe and the Pacific vied for headlines throughout the war, and "Germany First" was a strategic principle rather than a public mood.[4]

The United States was unique in creating nearly from scratch two entirely different armed services – one for Europe, one for the Pacific theater. Europe was an army and Army Air Force project, with the navy playing secondary roles. The forces deployed there were essentially optimized, respectively, for large-scale ground combat and for the conduct of strategic bombardment. Their original doctrines and structures were modified to these ends. The AAF, for example, developed a far larger and more sophisticated ground-support element than had been projected in prewar thinking.[5] The army modified everything from its divisional organizations to its basic standard tank in order to deal more effectively with a German opposition that itself during the war's second stage made a major doctrinal shift from mobile offensives to active defense, and modified its equipment accordingly.[6]

---

3 On this issue, see most recently Christopher Waters, "Australia, the British Empire, and the Second World War," *War & Society*, 19 (2001): 93–107.

4 The tensions this brought to the Anglo–U.S. relationship are considered in Warren W. Kimball, *Forged in War: Roosevelt, Churchill, and the Second World War* (New York, 1997).

5 Thomas A. Hughes, *Over Lord: General Pete Quesada and the Triumph of Tactical Air Power in World War II* (New York, 1995) is a biographically based case study.

6 Russell Hart, *Clash of Arms: How the Allies Won in Normandy* (Boulder, CO, 2001) presents the comparative evolution of the U.S. and German armies, throwing in Britain and Canada as a bonus.

The Pacific, by contrast, was a navy show, with army and marine ground forces depending on the fleet for deployment and sustainability during the long drive toward Japan's home islands. The AAF played a tactical and operational role, engaging in strategic operations only at the war's end during the B-29 raids on Japan.[7] One might say that by 1945 the U.S. Navy was itself "triphibious"; in addition to its ships, it possessed one of the world's largest air forces and, in the U.S. Marine Corps, a ground component of over a half-million of the war's most formidable fighting men.

The limited degree of direct contact and exchange between the main theaters is noteworthy. Even in a technical process like amphibious landings, U.S. forces in Europe and the Pacific developed significantly different doctrines and methods – which did not blend particularly well when the attempt was made prior to the Normandy landings.[8] The number of senior army officers with operational experience in both theaters can be counted on the fingers of one hand: Alexander Patch, Charles Corlett, "Lightning Joe" Collins. And exchange ceased as soon as the European theater of operation developed even a shallow pool of experienced generals. Navy admirals as well tended to specialize, with those who began with Operation Torch remaining in the European theater as long as the fighting lasted. No marine units were deployed at Normandy. Nor did a U.S. Army with extensive experience under Asian conditions seek to institutionalize that experience after 1945. Instead it emphasized preparing for a rerun of its "real" war: a mechanized campaign in Europe.[9]

To a degree, this impermeability reflected interservice rivalries. Since their respective inceptions, the U.S. Army and Navy have stood on essentially equal institutional, political, and social footings, neither one deferring, or expected to defer, to the other.[10] This was a sharp contrast to Britain, where the army remained a bullet fired by the Senior Service, with the RAF a bit of a Brylcreemed outsider, and to Germany, where the Kriegsmarine and Luftwaffe alike remained psychologically subordinate to the army. In the Soviet Union, the Red Army was so dominant that the navy and air force acquired status only to the extent they acculturated to ground-war

---

7 On this, see particularly Thomas E. Griffith, Jr., *MacArthur's Airman: General George E. Kenney and the War in the Southwest Pacific* (Lawrence, KS, 1998).

8 Adrian Lewis, *Omaha Beach: A Flawed Victory* (Chapel Hill, NC, 2001).

9 The long-term consequences of the army's persistent European regional orientation are considered in Andrew Krepinevich, Jr., *The Army and Vietnam* (Baltimore, 1986).

10 The issue is important enough to merit an entry in the standard reference: James Kurth, "Rivalry, Interservice," in *The Oxford Dictionary of American Military History*, ed. John W. Chambers (New York, 1999), 619–20. Its impact was best expressed by Admiral William Halsey, who at one point in the South Pacific campaign hyperbolically threatened to make athletic supporters the uniform of the day, and brand everyone's rump with a star to remind them they were fighting the same war.

norms: the naval infantry and the Stormovik crews were their respective services' Heroes of the Soviet Union.

The potential disadvantages of equal balance are highlighted by the experience of the only other power whose armed forces had that relationship. The Japanese army and navy were so reluctant to cooperate that they wound up running autonomous maritime transport services as U.S. submarines sank the merchant ships from under the squabblers.[11] The United States was arguably fortunate – particularly given the personalities of Chief of Staff George Marshall and Chief of Naval Operations Ernest King – that each service had a theater and an enemy of its own.

Yet for all of the differences between and among operational theaters, five factors support the argument that the United States waged a homogenous global war effort, creating systems that proved successfully applicable everywhere in the world. First, America applied common procedures for organizing and training armed forces on large scales. The U.S. Army developed a mass-production system for organizing divisions from nothing, beginning with small cadres from previously organized units, then providing "fillers" in the form of draftees deliberately drawn from all quarters of the country.[12] This was a sharp contrast both to the British "artisanal" system that gave extensive freedom to unit commanders, and to the German practice of recruiting and reinforcing divisions from the same region. Senior army officers overtly favored this assembly-line approach over working with the country's existing and organized reserve, the National Guard. Initial experience reinforced prewar opinions that National Guard formations were excessively subject to local influences – the same pattern generally regarded as a strength of Britain's Territorial Army. Senior Guard officers were generally dismissed as poorly trained – lacking in particular the experience of advanced service schools like Leavenworth – over-age, and physically unfit.

While the criticisms may to an extent have been self-fulfilling, they were frequently shared by junior Guard officers and by the "outsiders" subsequently assigned to Guard units. Most National Guard regiments and battalions retained something of a hometown aura throughout the war, but a good part of the U.S. Army's internal history from 1940 to 1942 involved processes of homogenization. As the war progressed, Guard officers who remained in command above company level grew increasingly acculturated in professional terms to the regular army, however vehemently they might defend the Guard against its critics. Major General Robert Beightler led

---

11 Mark P. Parillo, *The Japanese Merchant Marine in World War II* (Annapolis, 1993).
12 John Sloan Brown, *Draftee Division: The 88th Infantry Division in World War II* (Lexington, KY, 1986) is a case study of the process at its best.

the 37th Division, originally the Ohio National Guard, throughout World War II, surviving the hostility of superiors the entire time. But he had studied at both the Command and General Staff College and the Army War College. He had served a peacetime appointment on the General Staff. And his driving ambition was to prove National Guardsmen could be as good as the regulars – but on terms the regulars set.[13]

The National Guard represented the major institutional challenge to homogenization. The Army Air Force and its naval counterpart expanded in roughly the same way as the ground forces, with units recently formed giving birth to even newer ones. Noteworthy in both services were an approach to pilot and air crew training that sought to produce effectiveness rather than excellence, and the rapid introduction of a rotation policy that ensured new units a steady supply of experienced flight and squadron commanders.[14]

Often overlooked is the success of the U.S. Navy in producing ships' crews and shore personnel by processes of mass training on shore unmatched since Rome built a fleet from scratch to confront Carthage. The navy had practice in the required techniques during 1917–18.[15] During the interwar period, it accepted the concept that a future conflict would demand more than just building on peacetime cadres – the essential practice of the Royal Navy between 1939 and 1945. In contrast to the army, the navy's relatively high peacetime strength compared to its mobilization numbers did make it possible to provide cadres of enlisted and commissioned regulars for most combat ships throughout most of the war. As a result, by the time wartime officer and petty officer reservists began taking over in the smaller combatants, the support ships, and the amphibious vessels, they in turn had gained enough experience to minimize their mistakes. American sailors took their lumps in both oceans, during the Battle of the Atlantic, around Guadalcanal, and in other locations. Unlike the Royal Canadian Navy, however, no significant elements of the U.S. Navy had to be withdrawn from operations for comprehensive retraining.[16]

The essential homogeneity of each service in turn meant that a U.S. soldier, sailor, or airman could find a "home" in any formation, station, ship,

13 John Kennedy Ohl, *Minuteman: The Career of General Robert S. Beightler* (Boulder, CO, 2000), incorporates a balanced general analysis of a Guard-regular controversy that continues to generate more heat than light. For the weeding process in practice, see Christopher Gabel, *The U.S. Army GHQ Maneuvers of 1941* (Washington, DC, 1991).

14 Dominick A. Paisano, *To Fill the Skies with Pilots: The Civilian Pilot Training Program, 1939–1946* (Washington, DC, 2000).

15 Michael Dennis Besch, *A Navy Second to None: The History of US Naval Training in World War I* (Greenwood, CT, 2002), presents the origins of the policy of training sailors on dry land.

16 Cf. David Syrett, *The Defeat of the German U Boats: The Battle of the Atlantic* (Columbia, SC, 1994); and Marc Milner, *North Atlantic Run: The Battle for the Convoys* (Toronto, 1985).

or squadron. His new unit did things in essentially the same ways as his old one. Even the U.S. Army's often-indicted system of individual replacement worked better than might have been expected, primarily on the grounds that standard operating procedures were developed, even in forward areas, to integrate new men into their new units.[17] Homogenization thus helped provide for economy of force, compensating for the casualness about human resources that characterized higher policy levels.

The second characteristic of U.S. armed forces in World War II was flexibility. American servicemen at all levels in all theaters adapted effectively to the conditions they faced. The process was neither automatic nor uniform, but U.S. combat and support formations alike had high learning curves. The U.S. Army began adjusting to the specific conditions of the Normandy bocage within days of landing and continued to match every German tactical or technical riposte until V-E Day.[18] The ground war in the Pacific witnessed a similar pattern – or rather, two of them. The army-dominated ground campaigns in New Guinea and the Philippines produced not merely formidably effective jungle-fighting divisions, but what might be called jungle/mechanized formations that combined motorized mobility and armored punch with the ability to operate away from road nets.[19] The marines who carried the burden of the Central Pacific campaign adjusted from a light infantry mentality to the shock troop demands of atoll fighting, and then to the demands of extended ground campaigns in the Marianas and on Okinawa. No one who surveys the complex order of battle of Fleet Marine Force, Pacific, in September 1945 would make the mistake of calling the marines "beach runners"![20]

Arguably the most flexible service was the one that began the war with the most rigid doctrinal principles. The Army Air Forces were committed to the concept of unescorted daylight strategic bombardment as their major institutional priority. Yet during the war the AAF not only established a massive tactical component, but created from nothing a short- and long-haul transport force as well. And the bomber generals proved increasingly flexible relative to their principal shibboleth, recalibrating the nature of their

---

17 Peter R. Mansoor, *The GI Offensive in Europe: The Triumph of American Infantry Divisions, 1941–1945* (Lawrence, KS, 1991), 254ff.; and Robert Sterling Rush, *Hell in Huertgen Forest* (Lawrence, KS, 2001), 304ff.

18 See particularly Michael Doubler, *Closing With the Enemy: How GIs Fought the War in Europe, 1944–1945* (Lawrence, KS, 1994).

19 This was particularly characteristic of a Luzon campaign still ignored by historians of ground war. The official history by Robert Ross Smith, *Triumph in the Philippines* (Washington, DC, 1963), remains the best overall analysis.

20 Joseph Alexander, *Storm Landings: Epic Amphibious Battles in the Central Pacific* (Annapolis, MD, 1997) is a good brief overview of this evolution.

daylight missions, reconsidering the concept of the escort fighter, and finally shifting to low-level incendiary raids against a Japan that continued to defy high-level precision strikes.[21]

The U.S. Navy also adjusted at operational levels, albeit less spectacularly. The conversion from a battle-line mentality to a carrier orientation in the months between Pearl Harbor and Midway was remarkably smooth despite the absence of alternatives.[22] The Battle of the Atlantic and the surface operations around Guadalcanal were noteworthy because no other navy could have mounted both operations simultaneously at any time during the war. By 1944, the navy had become not merely a two-ocean fleet, but two ocean fleets, one optimized for sea control and the other for littoral and antisubmarine operations, both with major amphibious capabilities.[23] Internally, moreover, each reflects a high learning curve relative to the professional competence of the respective opponent. A good internal reason for the navy's successive early defeats in the area of Iron Bottom Sound was the high loss/damage rate, which retarded the transmission of experience at substaff levels.[24] But by mid-1943, it was the U.S. Navy that was regularly forcing the Japanese to make mistakes by doing things its system could not sustain.

U.S. practice regarding senior officers also facilitated flexibility and responsiveness. The U.S. armed forces were, with the arguable exception of the Soviet Union, the most ruthless in relieving or reassigning admirals and generals "for cause" in World War II. It began with Husband Kimmel and Walter Short, the coauthors of Pearl Harbor. It continued in all theaters, with division-level commanders and their air and naval equivalents particularly vulnerable to the axe. A man might get two chances to repeat a mistake – seldom a third.

The policy was facilitated by the relatively small number of divisions and equivalent large formations the United States fielded. In contrast to Germany, where senior officer slots at times exceeded the available generals,

---

21 Conrad Crane, *Bombs, Cities, and Civilians: American Airpower Strategy in World War II* (Lawrence, KS, 1993), is perceptive. Cf. Kenneth P. Werrell, *Blankets of Fire: U.S. Bombers Over Japan during World War II* (Washington, DC, 1996).

22 For details see John B. Lundstrom, *The First Team: Pacific Naval Air Combat from Pearl Harbor to Midway* (Annapolis, MD, 1984); and from an unusual perspective, David C. Fuquea, "Task Force One: The Wasted Assets of The United States Pacific Battleship Fleet, 1942," *The Journal of Military History*, 61 (1997), 701–34.

23 Joel R. Davidson, *The Unsinkable Fleet: The Politics of U. S. Navy Construction in World War II* (Annapolis, 1996).

24 See the discussion in Richard B. Frank, *Guadalcanal* (New York, 1990), 603ff. Russell S. Crenshaw, *The Battle of Tassafaronga* (Baltimore, 1995) and James W. Grace, The *Naval Battle of Guadalcanal: Night Action, 13 November 1942* (Annapolis, MD, 1999) are good case studies of the learning process and its pains.

the United States always had new candidates and fresh blood. Part of the "no-defects" mentality was a heritage of World War I, when Black Jack Pershing ruthlessly and repeatedly weeded out the American Expeditionary Force's turkey flock.[25] A more general case might be made for the impact of the Social Darwinist, free-enterprise capitalist ethic that still dominated American society and was particularly influential in the armed forces. More directly, patterns of appointment and removal, especially from mid-level and senior command positions, tended to replicate those of civilian management: produce or else.[26]

Flexibility was finally influenced by technology. The United States stood head and shoulders above all other combatants in developing and producing general-purpose tools of war. U.S. electronics were unsurpassed, in particular the elaborate communications network that provided nervous systems to America's far-flung armed forces. The C-47 transport, the $2\frac{1}{2}$-ton truck, and the jeep were almost as central to the Russian and British armed forces as to the Americans. Some nations excelled in weapons systems tailored to particular environments: the Spitfire fighter or the Panther tank. None came near to matching the U.S. spectrum of universally deployable warships, combat aircraft, and weapons: the Fletcher class destroyers and the Essex class carriers, the B-24 and the P-51.

Each of those designs, and most of their stablemates, could go anywhere. The Liberator, in U.S. and RAF colors, served as a bomber, an antisubmarine aircraft, and a transport from Iceland to Burma. The Mustang excelled as an air superiority fighter over Germany and as a ground-support aircraft with the Chindits in Burma. But the best example of global flexibility is an armored fighting vehicle. The often-criticized M-4 Sherman was no match individually for its Panther and Tiger rivals in the specific conditions of northwest Europe. But in its upgunned versions, particularly the British Firefly, it was competitive. And neither of the German designs could have matched the Sherman under the conditions of Saipan, Okinawa, or Burma, where tanks played increasingly important roles.[27]

---

25 James J. Cooke, *Pershing and His Generals: Command and Staff in the AEF* (Westport, CT, 1997).

26 Wade Marker, "The Organization Man at War: Promotion Policies and Military Leadership, 1929–1992," Ph.D. diss., Harvard University, 2000. Patterns of course varied. In the ETO, Omar Bradley was regarded as an ax-swinger, while George Patton was more inclined to give a man a chance to find his feet. Douglas MacArthur had a quicker hook earlier in his Southwest Pacific campaign than in the later stages. The airborne divisions under Ridgeway were hard on regimental commanders. A good case study of high-end relief practices is Daniel Bolger, "Zero Defects: Command Climate in the First US Army, 1944–1945," *Military Review* (May 1991): 61–73. Cf. Martin Blumenson, "Relieved of Command," *Army* (August 1971): 30–37.

27 There is, surprisingly, no operational history of the world's first real universal tank. B. P. Hunnicutt, *Sherman: A History of the American Medium Tank* (San Rafael, CA, 1978), is a design history with

The third general quality of U.S. armed forces in two wars was sustainability. This depended first on management skill. So much is written these days about "warrior spirit" that it becomes easy to forget that modern war's bedrock is management: getting from here to there without tripping over one's administrative feet, and then staying there. That was uniquely true for the United States, a geostrategic island whose first considerations were correspondingly in the areas of policy, just as Germany's geographic location made tactical and operational issues the Third Reich's crucial priority.

The United States was well served by the lack of an "officer class" like those in Britain, Japan, and Germany. Its officers were drawn from the same groups and strata as the country's executives and administrators. One of the major conclusions emerging from World War I was that any future major war involving the United States would involve major management elements. The Industrial College of the Armed Forces was created in order to bring together mid-level military and civilian experts to consider issues of national security and national mobilization. Its direct achievements were marginal, but it established enduring precedents.[28] Richard Overy is only the most familiar of the scholars who have demonstrated the integration of management with warfighting in the U.S. armed forces of 1940–45.[29]

In war, nothing succeeds like excess, and management applied the excess. Although the U.S. effort is usually defined in terms of a sheer abundance of material resources, sustainability involved more than the proverbial "beans, bullets, and black oil." The U.S. Navy transformed central Pacific atolls into major maintenance centers, and established a fleet train that enabled warships to remain operational up to the limit of crew endurance. In the South Pacific, American logistical abundance contributed to the rise of religious sects, the "cargo cults," among the islanders.[30] American medical services were far and away the best of the combatants; they stood in particular contrast to both the "grenade therapy" that was frequently an early recourse of Japanese doctors and the medical practices of the Wehrmacht in Russia, which increasingly harked back to the mid-nineteenth century. The army's replacement system kept fighting units up to strength, requiring

operational overtones. Oscar Gilbert, *Marine Tank Battles in the Pacific* (Consohocken, PA, 2001), provides narrative on the Sherman's Pacific role.

28 Paul A. C. Koistinnen, *Planning War, Pursuing Peace: The Political Economy of American Warfare, 1920–1939* (Lawrence, KS, 1998).

29 Richard Overy, *Why the Allies Won* (London, 1995). Gerald D. Nash, *The Great Depression and World War II: Organizing America* (New York, 1979), offers a less positive affirmation of the same point. Char Roone Miller, *Taylored Citizenship: State Institutions and Subjectivity* (Westport, CT, 2002), stresses the military's wartime efforts at "managing" Americans for effectiveness.

30 For background, see *Cargo Cults and Millenarian Movements*, ed. G. Tromps (New York, 1990).

neither reduction and disbandment on the late-war British pattern nor the grouping of clusters of survivors into ad hoc battle groups that was the Wehrmacht's preferred emergency solution, nor the erosion of divisions to cadres of survivors that was the Red Army's norm.[31]

Sustainability was also a function of firepower. This again has become a cliché, with both former enemies and former allies quick to make the point that the U.S. armed forces won their war by what John Ellis calls "brute force."[32] In a general sense, it may be argued that saving blood by the sophisticated application of steel indicates virtuosity rather than awkwardness. Certainly, the heroic vitalism of Nazi Germany did nothing more than underwrite an ongoing process of demodernization exemplified by the *Panzerfaust*. This disposable rocket launcher accounted for hundreds of allied armored fighting vehicles – but its short range made the user's life a highly probable tradeoff. In Hitler's Wehrmacht, the exchange was considered acceptable. Soviet marshal Georgy Zhukov explained to a stunned Dwight Eisenhower that when Russian infantry encountered a minefield, they attacked through it, regarding the resulting casualties as equivalent to those suffered if the Germans had defended the ground tactically.[33] A U.S. officer giving such an order would have been relieved on the spot – assuming he survived long enough for the process to be implemented.

Instead, the U.S. armed forces integrated naval gunfire, close air support, artillery, armor, and small arms to produce tactical environments that extended battle zones beyond defenders' capacities to respond. They used naval, air, and ground transport, communications, maintenance, and traffic control systems to sustain offensives whose successes did not depend on obliging enemies like the ones Germany faced from 1939 to 1942. In both Europe and the Pacific, U.S. armed forces were willing to employ what British Field Marshal Montgomery called "colossal cracks": concentrations of firepower complemented by a willingness to take, and continue taking, heavy casualties in pursuit of specific tactical objectives like Aachen or Iwo Jima.[34]

The Americans were also consistently – though not always – able to fix and bypass German and Japanese forces, to keep campaigns moving when other military systems were slowed because of administrative reasons:

31 Mansoor, *GT Offensive*, 254–56.

32 John Ellis, *Brute Force: Allied Strategy and Tactics in the Second World War* (London, 1990).

33 Dwight Eisenhower, *Crusade in Europe* (New York, 1948), 467–68. Soviet records made available post–Cold War indicate Zhukov was talking a bit for effect, but was not merely shooting a line.

34 This represented a counterpoint to an overall policy of sparing casualties as far as possible. See Evan A. Huelfer, "Sacred Treasures: How the Casualty Issue Shaped the American Military Establishment, 1919–1941," Ph.D. Diss., University of North Carolina, 2000.

running out of gas or men.[35] In a wider total-war context, sustainability diminished the need and the temptation to exploit conquered or occupied peoples systematically. If anything, the reverse tended to be true, with GIs proverbially able to exchange the abundant personal resources available to them for anything they wanted, from souvenirs to companionship.

A fourth general element in the U.S. way of war was realism. American planners and commanders seldom fell into the trap of "making pictures," of exaggerating what their essentially improvised, essentially civilian, forces were able to do relative to a particular situation. The principal exception to that generalization involves army support for a cross-channel invasion in 1942/early 1943. And in that context, Kasserine Pass was all the wake-up call the generals needed. Henceforth the question became not "how quickly can we land in northwest Europe?" but rather "how quickly can we land, consolidate, and advance?"[36] Similarly in the Pacific, facing an enemy whose increasing withdrawal into vitalist illusion offered corresponding opportunities for ripostes, the Americans took a balanced approach to planning and operations. Admiral Spruance sacrificed an opportunity to finish off the Combined Fleet in the Battle of the Philippine Sea because he considered his primary mission to be the security of the Marianas landings.[37] The navy abandoned its Formosa option largely on grounds of unnecessarily high risk compared to the alternative of landing in the Philippines.[38]

Each of the previous factors is linked with a fifth, even more basic one: morale. Never in history has so relatively and absolutely large an armed force, citizen or professional, fought so far from its own borders in a war that was not obviously its fight. The ordinary GI, gyrene, or swabbie had no visceral reason to stay with it. Neither did his home folk. American territory was not under direct attack. To the extent that the U.S. serviceman had a "worldview" of the war, it was as a job to be done, as quickly and completely as possible.[39] Gerald Linderman provocatively links this mind-set

---

35 Steve Waddell, *United States Army Logistics: The Normandy Campaign* (Greenwood, CT, 1994), is an excellent case study, highlighting the roots of the autumn supply problems.

36 Kent Roberts Greenfield, *American Strategy in World War II* (Baltimore, 1963); and the relevant case studies in *Command Decisions*, ed. K. R. Greenfield (Washington, DC, 1960), combine for a still-useful illustration of American realism in action. See as well from a policy perspective Mark A. Stoler, *The Politics of the Second Front: American Military Planning and Diplomacy in Coalition Warfare* (Westport, CT, 1977).

37 The most complete account, critical of Spruance's decision, is William T. Y'Blood, *Red Sun Setting: The Battle of the Philippine Sea* (Annapolis, MD, 1980).

38 Robert Ross Smith, "Luzon versus Formosa," in *Command Decisions*, ed. K. R. Greenfield (Washington, DC, 1960), 461–77.

39 Still basic for its subject is the two-volume study *The American Soldier*, 2 vols., ed. Samuel Stouffer et al. (Princeton, NJ, 1949). All other works build more or less on its findings and conclusions. Among later studies, Lee Kennett, *GI: The American Soldier in World War II* (New York, 1987), stands

with the Great Depression, which put so many men out of work – and out
of an identity – that the concept of "the job" gave meaning to the war
at a personal level.[40] When the government thought of ways to thank and
motivate its men and women in uniform, it developed economic rewards –
like a Veterans' Administration program that provided low-cost home loans,
or professional ones – like a GI Bill that offered what amounted to free
vocational training and higher education to all veterans.[41]

By democratizing the ranks of homeowners and professionals, those programs and their counterparts laid the foundation of the United States' definition of itself as a middle-class society. Yet there was something more. U.S.
battle casualties overall may have been low – risibly low by German or Soviet standards. But American rifle companies in the ETO consistently took
casualties of 200, 300 percent, and kept coming. The Army Air Forces never
aborted a bombardment mission because of risk or loss. Marines climbed
the cliffs of Pelelieu when it was clear that the operation's purpose had
evaporated. The records show desertion, straggling, hanging back. But with
the possible exception of elements of a racially segregated infantry division
virtually programmed from its creation to fail, there were no significant
collective refusals of duty.[42] Even the much-abused 5307th Composite Unit
(Provisional), better known as Merrill's Marauders, as jerked around and
as far from home a formation as any the United States fielded, staggered
forward as long as its survivors could stand up.[43]

As many as 21,000 Germans were executed for "military" offenses by
the Wehrmacht during World War II.[44] The Red Army shot 10,000 of
its soldiers at Stalingrad alone. Throughout the war, one – one – U.S.
serviceman was executed for desertion – not because desertion did not exist,
and certainly not because of any principled hostility to capital punishment,
but because the ultimate deterrent was considered unneeded. The typical
American serviceman quit only when he broke and wound up in a hospital
or a psychiatric ward.[45]

out for perception and common sense; John C. McManus, *The American Combat Soldier in World War II* (Novato, CA, 1998), is also first-rate.

40 Gerald F. Linderman, *The World Within War: America's Combat Experience in World War II* (New York, 1997), 48ff.

41 Keith Olson, *The GI Bill, the Veterans, and the Colleges* (Lexington, KY, 1974).

42 Dale O. Wilson, "Recipe for Failure: Major General Edward M. Almond and the Preparation of the U.S. 92nd Infantry Division for Combat in World War II," *The Journal of Military History*, 56 (1992): 473–88.

43 James E. T. Hopkins and J. M. Jones, *Spearhead* (Baltimore, 1999).

44 See Manfred Messerschmidt and F. Wuellner, *Die Wehrmachtjustiz im Dienst des Nationalsozialismus. Zerstoerung einer Legende* (Baden-Baden, 1997).

45 Josephine C. Bresnahan, "Dangers in Paradise: The Battle against Combat Fatigue in the Pacific War, Ph.D. Diss., Harvard University, 2000, is a perceptive case study from a neglected perspective.

Morale was in turn the linchpin of effectiveness. By 1945, America had the world's largest navy – so exponentially superior to all comers that admirals wondered how in future to apply the Mahanian concepts of a decisive fleet action that had dominated their thinking for a half-century.[46] Its high average level of seamanship was indicated by the Third Fleet's performance during the great typhoons of autumn 1945. The U.S. Army Air Force was the strongest, best-balanced in the world – and a case can be made that tactically, at least, the Navy/Marine air arm stood second in effectiveness. The army had survived the "ninety division gamble," sacrificing mass for sustainability, and had developed some outstanding combat formations. Then and now, the Americans are usually described as standing somewhat behind the Germans at tactical and operational levels "when the odds were even."[47] But odds are never even in war, and the U.S. Army had shown increasing expertise in stacking tactical and operational decks in the ETO, pitting its strengths against opponents' shortcomings. The army, moreover, had demonstrated an ability to fight effectively under a far broader spectrum of conditions than any of its counterparts. The *Grossdeutschland* Division or Chuikov's Red Army guardsmen might have adapted perfectly to Leyte or Iwo Jima – but they never faced that test. The U.S. Army did. It passed.

II

America's war was global. It was not total. It was not a war for the direct survival of the country, its institutions, and its people. The concept of "free security" that had shaped U.S. policy and strategy since the early national period, though challenged in the 1920s and 1930s by strategic airpower advocates like Billy Mitchell and Hap Arnold, persisted through 1945. Whatever its desires, Japan had little prospect and no intention of seriously threatening, much less invading, the American mainland. The threat incorporated in Nazi Germany's "Z Plan" and its ramifications could only be manifested in a later conflict.[48] Air raid wardens may have been appointed as far inland as Minnesota, but air raids remained the stuff of newsreels. The U-boat campaign in U.S. waters during the "Happy Time" of 1942 did not

---

46 Vincent Davis, *Postwar Defense Policy and the US Navy, 1943–1946* (Chapel Hill, NC, 1962).
47 Keith Bonn, *When the Odds Were Even: The Vosges Mountain Campaign, October 1944–January 1945* (Novato, CA, 1994), is the best of a number of works arguing, never quite convincingly, for a rough equivalence at unit level between U.S. and Wehrmacht fighting power in the war's later years.
48 See most recently Norman Goda, *Tomorrow the World: Hitler, Northwest Africa, and the Path towards America* (College Station, TX, 1998).

arouse enough public concern to secure a comprehensive blackout of the coastline cities.[49]

The limited nature of America's war also manifested itself on the home front. All combatants sought to limit the conflict's stress on their own people. Even in Great Britain, the actual disruption of ordinary life was a good deal less than wartime and postwar mythologies admit.[50] Nazi Germany sought to export war's burdens, shifting them as far as possible to conquered peoples, and moved to official total mobilization only in the aftermath of Stalingrad.[51] The United States materialized its conflict. Seeking from the beginning to fight a high-tech war, it concentrated on building air and naval forces. Its approach to ground war was predicated on avoiding mass and minimizing casualties, instead taking a "ninety-division gamble" with an army that based its fighting power on firepower and logistical sustainability.

In no major combatant was the difference between efficiency and effectiveness more pronounced. National mobilization began with the fall of France, but not until the end of 1942 did the government hammer out a series of regulatory and administrative improvisations that moved the economy onto a war footing.[52] Students of modern war tend to privilege centralized control as part of a "Whig" progress toward total war. By contrast – and in sharp contrast to World War I – American mobilization relied heavily on voluntarism as opposed to executive authority. The improvised nature of mobilization left loopholes.[53] Roosevelt might in principle have preferred a "managed capitalism" along the lines of the NRA.[54] In practice, Secretary of War Henry L. Stimson put it bluntly and accurately: waging war in a capitalist economy was impossible unless business made money.

As the war progressed, the Roosevelt administration increasingly came to regard slack in the system as positive. Time and again, private initiative from a business community that was no longer the rhetorical enemy of the New Deal's heyday proved ultimately more productive than centralized fine-tuning. The war's best single-engine fighter emerged from the serendipitous linking of a British engine with the air frame of a second-rate attack plane. Civil engineer Henry Kaiser took another British design and developed it

---

49 Michael Gannon, *Operation Drumbeat: The Dramatic True Story of Germany's First U-Boat Attacks along the American Coast in World War II* (New York, 1990).

50 See particularly Angus Calder, *The People's War: Britain 1939–1945* (London, 1971).

51 See Gerhard Hirschfeld's contribution to this volume.

52 Keith E. Eiler, *Mobilizing America: Robert P. Patterson and the War Effort, 1940–1945* (Ithaca, 1997).

53 A major subtext, for example, of David Kennedy's now-standard *Freedom from Fear: The American People in Depression and War, 1929–1945* (New York, 1999), especially 619ff.

54 See Richard P. Adelstein, "The Nation as Economic Unit: Keynes, Roosevelt, and the Managerial Ideal," *Journal of American History*, 78 (1991): 160–87.

into a fleet of mass-produced merchant ships, "built by the mile and sawed off by the yard," that set at naught the best efforts of the U-boats. Design entrepreneur Andrew Jackson Higgins designed the landing craft that made amphibious operations possible in the face of comprehensive resistance by the Navy establishment.[55]

The American system could afford what seemed to outside observers like wasted motion. The Great Depression had cleared the decks. The United States began its mobilization with vast amounts of financial and material resources, managerial and administrative talent, even factory space and open land for more factories. Private investment was one-fifth lower in 1940 than in 1929. Calculations of lost output in the 1930s spoke in terms of thirty-five million homes unbuilt, nearly two hundred million cars unmanufactured. Yet the resources idled by crisis were ready at hand. The business and financial communities might have opposed U.S. entry into the war, but capitalists were also citizens, and capitalism played a constructive role in their country's mobilization – albeit in a framework of cost-plus contracts minimizing specific risks.[56]

Stimson might have expanded his point to say that war-waging in a democracy was impossible unless everyone made money. Taking up the Depression's slack was just a beginning. With Congress in some cases appropriating more funds than could be spent, American productivity doubled in some armaments sectors and increased 25 percent across the board after Pearl Harbor. The rapid expansion of defense-related industries, fostered by the administration's initial extravagant production predictions, created a cornucopia of increasingly well-paying jobs. Financial gain was accompanied by opportunities for training and promotion, even among previously excluded groups like blacks and women.

America in 1941 possessed a large surplus labor pool: as much as half of the nation's workforce. Millions of people, hundreds of thousands of them already socialized to industrial conditions, other hundreds of thousands already skilled workers, were available for the war effort. Their engagement was motivated by a high-test mixture of patriotism and self-interest: getting back to work in a righteous cause. Their productivity was voluntary, depending

---

55 And if Higgins eventually lost out to larger firms, able to produce more boats at lower cost, that too was part of the system's logic. Cf. Ray Wagner, *Mustang Designer: Edgar Schmued and the P-51* (Washington, DC, 2000); Peter Elphich, *Liberty: The Ships That Won the War* (London, 2001); and Jerry E. Strahan, *Andrew Jackson Higgins and the Boats That Won World War II* (Baton Rouge, LA, 1994).

56 Harold G. Vatter, *The U.S. Economy in World War II* (New York, 1985), remains a good overview. Cf. *The Rise of the Gunbelt: The Military Remapping of Industrial America*, ed. A. Markusen et al. (New York, 1991); and Bernd Greiner's contribution to this volume.

on benefits rather than compulsion. Men of suitable age and health for military service did risk induction if not working in a government-recognized defense industry, but that prospect did little to keep anyone in a particular job in an economy characterized until the end of the war by labor shortages high enough to encourage mobility that verged at times on labor piracy. Foreign workers, mostly Mexican and West Indian, were overwhelmingly introduced for agriculture and on short-term contracts. Their employment conditions seldom compared to their American counterparts. The programs nevertheless had no lack of applicants and were certainly a benign counterpoint to the forced labor policies of the Germans, the Soviets, and the Japanese.[57]

That money put pressure on an economy that until 1943 still produced almost a prewar spectrum of civilian goods and for the rest of the war still satisfied a civilian market whose recovery was deemed a near-miracle by businesses with a decade's experience of depression.[58] To a degree the consumption recovery was the product of smoke and mirrors. The levels of selective deprivation during the Depression had been high enough that a little during the war seemed like a lot. The wartime United States, however, experienced nothing like the regimentation of consumption characteristic of the prewar Soviet Union, with its five-year plans, or of wartime Britain, where bananas were a forgotten luxury and some children believed the natural form of eggs was powdered. As much to the point, Britain and the USSR both developed a public ethic that consumer sacrifice was morally good in itself. In Britain, consumer equality was also credited – legitimately – with helping the lower classes to eat better during the war than before it.[59] Their American counterparts ate well because they could afford to pay for it.

Shortage rather than deprivation was the dominant consumer reality in the United States between 1942 and 1945. Brands and firms encouraged that mind-set by stressing the temporary nature of their absence. Lucky Strike cigarettes had gone to war. Coca-Cola was helping defeat the Axis. Automobile and clothing manufacturers concentrated on describing a postwar *Schlaraffenland*, a consumer paradise at the outer edge of imagination

---

57 Nelson Lichtenstein, *Labor's War at Home: The CIO in World War II* (New York, 1982), stresses the success of government and business of sidestepping organized labor. See as well Casey P. Milligan, "Pecuniary Incentives to Work in the United States during World War II, *The Journal of Political Economy*, 106 (1998): 1033–87.

58 Alan Clive, *State of War: Michigan in World War II* (Ann Arbor, MI, 1979), is a good case study of these processes. See as well Marilynn Johnson, *The Second Gold Rush: Oakland and the East Bay in World War II* (Berkeley, 1993).

59 Ina Zweininger-Bargielowska, *Austerity in Britain: Rationing, Controls, and Consumption, 1939–1955* (Oxford, 2000).

even for Americans – who could imagine a lot.[60] The contributors to Studs Terkel's paradigmatic "*The Good War*," for all their dominant left-liberal orientation, refer as much to purely material aspirations as to any dreams of new social and political orders.[61]

Those aspirations came close to reality for millions in the first postwar decade, through purchases fueled by wartime savings often generated by multiple-income families. That was a shock to the expectations of dirigistes everywhere, who expected the U.S. economy to collapse into a new depression that would finally convince Americans of the virtues of management by elites. Even the Soviet Union thought it was doing its rival a favor by offering in 1945 to borrow what then was a huge sum to help stave off – albeit temporarily and for Stalin's own reasons – the collapse for which leftists around the world are still waiting.[62]

The availability of large amounts of cash in large numbers of pockets significantly affected a rationing system that, like the rest of America's war effort, was essentially locally administered. The result was a situation in which little groups of friends and neighbors enabled each other to get around what seemed unreasonable restrictions on commodities deemed officially scarce by the government. Hoarding and small-scale profiteering, fairly common in the war's early days, were frowned upon but tended to fade away because they were unnecessary. While inequalities based on money and "connections" persisted, America's wartime distribution system incorporated flexibility and informality enough for reasonable people – especially given the culture's enduring high level of tolerance for unequal results in an overall context of fair play.[63] That was in sharp contrast to a centralized Soviet system characterized throughout the war by large-scale unauthorized privatization of human resources, goods, and land titles – behaviors described by the state as "theft" and subject to a draconic spectrum of penalties.[64] That America's was not a total war is indicated even more clearly by its approach to human resources. Even in contrast to Britain and the USSR, who did

---

60 Mark H. Leff, "The Politics of Sacrifice in the American Home Front in World War II, *Journal of American History*, 77 (1990–91): 1296–1318. Surprisingly, there is no general history of American advertising in World War II. A good case study is F. L. Coldwell, *Selling the All-American Wonder: The World War II Consumer Advertising of Willys-Overland Motors, Inc.* (Lakeville, MN, 1996).

61 Studs Terkel, "*The Good War*" (New York, 1984).

62 George C. Herring, "Lend Lease to Russia and the Origins of the Cold War, 1944–1945," *Journal of American History*, 56 (1968): 93–104.

63 The most perceptive overview of home-front mentalities in general is Geoffrey Perrett's refreshingly unprofessorial *Days of Sadness, Years of Triumph: The American People at War, 1939–1945*. See as well the essays in *Produce and Conserve: Share and Play Square: The Grocer and the Consumer on the Home-Front Battlefield during World War II*, ed. Barbara McLean Ward (Hanover, NH, 1994).

64 John Barber and Mark Harrison, *The Soviet Home Front, 1941–1945: A Social and Economic History of the USSR in World War II* (New York, 1991).

less than is often believed, the United States made only marginal use of its women. Whether in uniform or in war work, their participation was voluntary and hedged around by a broad spectrum of conventional positions about women's nature, women's place, and women's roles. In the services, women were phased out in favor of men whenever possible. No significant public policy of encouraging women to remain in the workforce was developed or implemented during the war, with a resulting general exodus after 1945. It seems fair to mention, however, that the majority of women who participated directly in the war effort for its own sake, as opposed to being economically motivated, were like the majority of their male counterparts. However positively they may have processed their experience, women viewed their time in uniform or defense plant as temporary and were pleased enough to respond to society's enhanced postwar emphasis on home and family.[65]

A further 10 percent of American human power was not merely underutilized but squandered. The government's failure to utilize its black citizens in anything resembling their numbers or capacities is again comprehensively documented. Black sailors on fighting ships were restricted to waiting tables for the officers until the war's final months. Black soldiers were disproportionately assigned to stoop-labor organizations – which a high-tech military system could not employ profitably. Such policies reflected conscious decisions on the part of the armed forces and the administration that however serious the country's situation might be, it did not warrant assuming the perceived social risks of challenging a comprehensive system of segregation based on an assumption of comprehensive black inferiority.[66]

Prewar racism, like prewar sexism, did not face an external challenge sufficiently strong to modify any but the grosser shibboleths and stereotypes. Incomplete mobilization shows most clearly, however, in U.S. treatment of its core human resource: white males between the ages of seventeen and forty-five. The United States throughout the war maintained the most rigid qualifications of all the combatants – not for exclusion from service, but for induction into the armed forces. Physical unfitness, the famous

---

65 For general works, see, for example, D'Ann Campbell, *Women at War with America: Private Lives in a Patriotic Era* (Cambridge, MA, 1984); and Susan M. Hartmann, *The Home Front and Beyond: American Women in the 1940s* (Boston, 1982). Case studies include Molly Merryman, *Clipped Wings: The Rise and Fall of the Women Airforce Service Pilots: WASPs of World War II* (New York, 1998); and Lorry Fenner, "Ideology and Amnesia: The Public Debate on Women in the Military, 1940–1973," Ph.D. Diss., University of Michigan, 1995.

66 The most detailed analysis of America's military use of black manpower remains Ulysses Grant Lee's official history, *The Employment of Negro Troops* (Washington, DC, 1966). Michael Cooper, *The Double V Campaign: African Americans and World War II* (New York, 1998), is a recent general work.

IV-F classification, was allocated so generously that a good number of professional athletes were able to continue their careers throughout the war. Rejection – and post-induction discharge – for alleged psychological shortcomings was also widespread. Until late 1944, fatherhood, especially if antedating Pearl Harbor, was also grounds for deferment. And even healthy men could frequently sidestep the draft by finding government-approved war work.

The Selective Service System implementing these general policies was administered not by federal officials but by local boards of civilians. These "little groups of friends and neighbors" ultimately decided who went and who did not. Draft boards were seldom as representative socially as their epitaph suggests. Their membership was white, male, and "establishment": businessmen, professional men, educators, clergy. But on the whole they performed in ways their communities – at least the Caucasian elements – considered fair. Seldom were the sons of the privileged entirely exempted. When rules were bent, evidence suggests it was more likely to be for reasons perceived compassionate than for the benefit of local elites who, when all was said and done, had no wish to sacrifice authority by being considered overt slackers. Investing one's sons in the war was both patriotic and good business.[67]

Critics of the "inefficiencies and inequities" of selective service overlook the advantages of a system of personnel procurement that until the war's end incorporated a significant element of voluntarism. Eleven of the ninety-five ground divisions raised during the war – five airborne and six marine – were sustained essentially on a volunteer basis. A white male of any social class had a spectrum of possibilities, from parlaying a football knee into IV-F status to joining the marines. Special training programs even offered the chance to attend college while in uniform. Perceptions of choice and system flexibility helped keep enthusiasm high among the high school classes that kept ranks filled in 1944–45 and provided the fresh wave of junior officers that took Eisenhower's Americans into the Third Reich's heart.[68]

Characteristic of the limited global war waged by the United States was its absence of ideology. Nazi Germany had race and the Soviet Union, class. Great Britain, the weary titan, had fear; and Japan had nationalism. America had – the Four Freedoms? Few knew what they were. The

67 On the workings of the draft, see particularly George Q. Flynn, *Lewis B. Hershey: Mr. Selective Service* (Chapel Hill, NC, 1985); and *America and the Draft* (Chapel Hill, NC, 1993); and John O'Sullivan, *From Voluntarism to Conscription: Congress and Selective Service, 1940–1945* (New York, 1982).

68 The quotation at the paragraph's opening is from Kennedy, *Freedom from Fear*, p. 635; the observation at its end belongs to Stephen Ambrose, *Citizen Soldiers: The US Army from the Normandy Beaches to the Bulge to the Surrender of Germany, June 7, 1944–May 7, 1945* (New York, 1997).

Holocaust? A story on the back pages of a *New York Times* even fewer read. Government developed nothing like the "triumph or disaster" mentality of Nazi Germany, nothing like the "Great Fatherland Patriotic War" and "Soviet motherland" images of the USSR. The closest it came was a series of inspirational Hollywood documentaries on "Why We Fight." Nor did the United States generate a counterpart to the bloody-minded groundswell sentiment of "see it through and then vote Labor" in a Britain whose wartime "community" was arguably more apparent than real.[69] Americans' collective indifference to high causes was the bane of the Office of War Information and the burden of German POW interrogators.[70]

This lack of public enthusiasm both reflected and reinforced President Roosevelt's decision not to resurrect the Wilsonian crusading matrix of 1917–18. While not himself embarrassed by the nature of U.S. participation in the Great War, Roosevelt was sufficiently a scholar of public opinion polls to calibrate a general impatience with platitudes that long antedated Pearl Harbor.[71] Relevant as well was Roosevelt's concern that if he proposed to give the war a domestic social dimension, along the lines of the *Pittsburgh Courier*'s "Double V" campaign equating the Axis and racism, risked revitalizing the forces that had opposed the New Deal to such telling effect. "Doctor Win-the-War" seemed a more prudent prescriber. Underlying these pragmatic factors was Roosevelt's principled commitment to the virtues of a free society: openness to the world, self-help, voluntarism – and his accompanying belief that a free people could neither be compelled nor coerced by their betters along even the most desirable paths, but had to be convinced.[72]

Likewise, mobilizing hostility had limited effect at best. To most Americans, even those in uniform, the Germans remained throughout the war an abstract enemy.[73] That reflected in good part the fact that Germans fighting Americans as a rule did not behave like Nazis were supposed to.

---

69 See Paul Addison, *The Road to 1945* (London, 1977) and the essays in *War and Social Change: British Society in the Second World War*, ed. H. Smith (Manchester, 1986).

70 Allan M. Winkler, *The Politics of Propaganda: The Office of War Information* (New Haven, CT, 1978); and Gregory Black, *Hollywood Goes to War* (New York, 1987).

71 On this subject see particularly Michael D. Pearlman, *Warmaking and American Democracy* (Lawrence, KS, 1999), 221ff.

72 Thomas Fleming, *The War within World War II: Franklin Delano Roosevelt and the Struggle for Supremacy* (Reading, MA, 2001) is virulently critical of Roosevelt's approach from a liberal perspective. Frank Friedel, *Franklin D. Roosevelt: A Rendezvous with Destiny* (New York, 1990) and James Macgregor Burns, *Roosevelt: The Soldier of Freedom* (New York, 1970) are more sympathetic. Positions on the issue tend to be influenced strongly by authors' perceptions of the relative effort needed to win the war.

73 Cf. Richard W. Steele, "American Popular Opinion and the War against Germany: The Issue of a Negotiated Peace, 1942," *Journal of American History*, 65 (1978): 704–23.

They followed most of the conventional rules on such crucial issues as respecting the Red Cross and treatment of POWs enough of the time that violations could be seen as part of the "filth of war." In contrast to most conflicts, the levels of antagonism toward the German enemy in U.S. front-line units seemed to increase as the war progressed. That phenomenon was primarily ascribable to the behavior of German troops, both army and Waffen-SS, in the Battle of the Bulge, but found primary expression toward the Waffen-SS, whose men found surrender increasingly difficult between January and May 1945.[74] Looting in conquered Germany, however, was mostly small-scale, or involved artifacts perceived, however questionably, as "Nazi," and therefore "free goods."

Raw hatred for the Japanese, which began with the atrocity reports from China in the 1930s and metastasized following Pearl Harbor and Bataan, became instrumental and behavioral as the war progressed. What has been described as the dehumanization of the Japanese, paralleling an ideolo-gized Wehrmacht's approach to Slavs and Jews, is better understood as ahumanization: a sense of fighting aliens with whom no meaningful contact was possible. By 1945, U.S. soldiers and marines approached their battlefield missions with the mentality of insect exterminators.[75]

That mind-set was by no means an unreasonable response to front-line Japanese behavior that included cannibalism.[76] Its situational nature is strongly supported by wartime U.S. policies that emphasized the recon-struction of postwar Japan, not its annihilation as a society. It is supported as well by the behavior of U.S. servicemen in the immediate postwar oc-cupation of Japan. This was, it must be noted, an occupation and not an invasion. Actual veterans of the island campaigns, moreover, were rapidly rotated home. Criminal behavior and initiatives were nevertheless at low echelons and low levels. Arguably the occupation's relative benignity re-flected a victory so complete that no significant resistance or opposition emerged. Nevertheless, far from indulging in the expected orgy of rapine and pillage that led the Japanese government to create brothels staffed by

---

74 Linderman, 90ff. Linderman makes the point that both sides were willing to process battlefield atrocities as part of the "filth of war" as long as they appeared limited and unsystematic.

75 Ibid., 143ff.; and from a somewhat different perspective, Craig Cameron, *American Samurai: Myth, Imagination, and the Conduct of Battle in the First Marine Division, 1941–1945* (Cambridge, 1994). John W. Dower, *War without Mercy: Race and Power in the Pacific War* (New York, 1986), stresses the racist basis of American behavior. Allison B. Gilmore, *You Can't Fight Tanks with Bayonets: Psychological Warfare against the Japanese in the Southwest Pacific* (Lincoln, NE, 1998), demonstrates the extreme difficulty in eroding the fundamental beliefs whose application in turn made the Japanese seem an alien species.

76 For an overview see Yuki Tanaka, *Hidden Horrors: Japanese War Crimes in World War II* (Boulder, CO, 1996).

volunteers as a kind of frontline defense of Japanese virtue, the Americans were more fascinated than repelled by what they found. And with the exception of confiscated swords, they paid for most of what they took – women included.[77]

III

The United States waged a global war whose degree of extension made it different in kind from all the other combatants. The United States did not fight a total war: a war of comprehensive participation, comprehensively regulated by government authority. America nevertheless did develop a purpose, incorporating and reflecting four factors. At the base was the concept of a "stakeholder society." This owed something to the war, something to the New Deal, and arguably most to Thomas Jefferson. The United States produced no counterpart to a British Beveridge Report that, at bottom, was a proposal for providing equitable distribution of a static economy's declining fruits.[78] Stakeholding instead was based on the premise of baking a bigger pie by applying the lessons of production and distribution learned during the war to a society that had grown more conscious of itself as a single entity. It incorporated a conscious affirmation of and participation in a system preferable to the alternatives, realistically able to provide not merely sufficiency, but satisfaction, for all its members.[79]

A stakeholder society depended heavily on a concept of "fair play." U.S. war propaganda was most successful when it stressed enemy underhandedness – from the sneak attack on Pearl Harbor to the treachery of the Nazi U-boat captain in Alfred Hitchcock's *Lifeboat*.[80] Even before the war, Roosevelt's policies reflected his growing sense that the Axis powers were not merely changing the rules, but ignoring them.[81] The lightning offensive that overran Western Europe in 1940 was processed in some circles as a kind of military cheating: a product of fascist brutality principles and

---

77 John Dower, *Embracing Defeat: Japan in the Wake of World War II* (New York, 1999).
78 See Steven Fielding, "What Did 'the People' Want? The Meaning of the 1945 General Election," *Historical Journal*, 35 (1992): 623–39.
79 Compare this to Bernd Greiner's concept of a "shareholder society" in his contribution to this anthology – a development that came later in the century, as increasing numbers of Americans directly bought into the system. William L. O'Neill, *A Democracy at War: America's Fight at Home and Abroad in World War II* (New York, 1993), was the general inspiration for the "stakeholder" alternate.
80 See the overview by J. Michael Sproule, *Propaganda and Democracy: The American Experience of Media and Mass Persuasion* (New York, 1997).
81 See Waldo Heinrichs, *Threshold of War: Franklin D. Roosevelt and American Entry into World War II* (New York, 1988).

correspondingly alien to the values of a democracy.[82] On the other hand, Japan in 1945 could be given terms because it was obviously whipped and acknowledged the fact – again, an application of "fair play."

Related to fair play was a concept of "finishing the job": destroying the Axis systems. Unconditional surrender was not a public-relations afterthought. Roosevelt, though a consummate pragmatist, perceived the challenge to his country as morally based.[83] The binary division of "good against evil" frequently described as characterizing America's wartime policy is better understood as a sense of betrayal than a sense of righteousness. "We didn't have this coming" was the subtext of the indignation that fueled and structured the country's voluntarism until final victory. The indignation was negative, focusing on destroying America's enemies and punishing their crimes. It did not incorporate a need to demonize enemies – just crush them. Nor did finishing the job imply a return to some kind of status quo. Instead it nurtured the concept of "never again."[84]

"Never again," enduring freedom from external threat, was the final element of America's "general war." The concept was as important as it was ill-defined. The postwar dimensions of American security, while not ignored, were never fully developed.[85] That reflected in part a significant dissonance between Roosevelt's attitude toward the Soviet Union and that of the U.S. embassy in Moscow.[86] It reflected as well a tectonic shift in the military establishment's perception during the war of the locus of the greatest postwar danger: from Britain to the USSR.[87] "Never again" could emphasize involvement in, or withdrawal from, international affairs. It could involve reliance on a nuclear deterrent, or on conventional forces – the postwar American demobilization was neither as complete nor as head-over-heels as popular myths describe.[88] It was not a policy, but a state of mind firm in intention and equally ephemeral in method.

---

82 As in S.L.A. Marshall, *Blitzkrieg: Its History, Strategy, Economics, and the Challenge to America* (New York, 1940).
83 Cf. Warren F. Kimball, *The Juggler: Franklin Roosevelt as Wartime Statesman* (Princeton, NJ, 1991); and Raymond O'Connor, *Diplomacy for Victory: FDR and Unconditional Surrender* (New York, 1971).
84 Eliot Cohen, "The Strategy of Innocence? The United States, 1920–1945," in *Making of Modern Strategy*, ed. W. Murray, M. Knox, and A. Bernstein (New York, 1994), 428–65, is the best overview of American strategic culture at this period.
85 See Elliot V. Converse III, "United States Plans for a Postwar Overseas Military Base System," Ph.D. Diss., Princeton University, 1984.
86 Mary Glantz, "'Good Neighbors and Sincere Friends': United States Policy towards the Soviet Union under Franklin D. Roosevelt," Ph.D. Diss., Temple University, 2002.
87 Mark A. Stoler, *Allies and Adversaries: The Joint Chiefs of Staff, the Grand Alliance, and U.S. Strategy in World War II* (Chapel Hill, NC, 2000).
88 This is the particular theme of Michael Sherry, *In the Shadow of War: The United States since the 1930s* (New Haven, 1995).

"General war" was first institutionalized when research was completed for an atomic bomb whose target was indeterminate. Here again, as so often was the case in America's war, the initial primary issues involved divertible resources. The United States, in contrast to Britain, Russia, and Germany, had enough scientists, enough money and raw material, and enough system slack to pursue a line of research whose immediate prospects were questionable. The bomb's cost, indeed, was less than the country's annual advertising budget. The bomb itself might have been widely viewed during the war as just another weapon, more destructive and therefore potentially more decisive than its predecessors. Its designers, however, knew better. So, in the aftermath of the first nuclear strikes, did the generals and the politicians. After Hiroshima, to borrow from Yeats, concepts of power and strategy were changed utterly – though few would say that a terrible beauty was thereby born.[89]

The second institutional consequence of America's general war was its support for the creation of the United Nations. Roosevelt's initial postulate was simple: human civilization could not risk a third go-round of general war, especially with nuclear weapons added to the mix. The UN was intended less as a world government than a clearinghouse for grievances, with an eventually reconstructed consortium of regional powers acting through the Security Council as enforcers.[90] The UN, moreover, would be only one-half of a general approach to world peace. Roosevelt and his advisers supported, albeit generally and often ephemerally, the concept of global free trade: a system of open, voluntary movement of goods, services, and skills that was expected to generate a non-zero-sum situation of continued development in free-market contexts.[91]

Neither the atomic bomb nor the United Nations achieved the direct results variously hoped for, predicted, and feared at the end of World War II. Yet sixty years later, transnational institutions both formal and ad hoc are assuming an increasing number of roles previously reserved to the nation-state. Economic relations are steadily globalizing, with free movement of goods, ideas, and people successfully challenging boundaries of all kinds: political, commercial, and ethnic. Choice, individualism, self-definition, are becoming worldwide touchstones. And the United States is the inspiration and the driving force behind these processes.

89 See Richard Rhodes, *The Making of the Atomic Bomb* (New York, 1986) and Philip Henshall, *The Nuclear Axis: Germany, Japan, and the Atomic Bomb Race, 1939–1945* (Phoenix Hall, UK, 2001).
90 Robert C. Hilderbrand, *Dumbarton Oaks: The Origins of the United Nations and the Search for Postwar Security* (Chapel Hill, NC, 1990), contextualizes the U.S. perspective.
91 See the survey by Edward S. Kaplan, *American Trade Policy: 1923–1995* (Westport, CT, 1996).

Real alternatives have been limited.[92] Britain in 1945 was morally and materially exhausted, its brand of benevolent imperialism a spent force even to its defenders. Fascism, especially its Nazi variant, left nationalism and patriotism discredited, but as yet unreplaced in Europe as foci of identity. Marxism provided a worldview and a world vision. But its post-1945 versions developed into squalid tyrannies that alienated even true believers. "Islamism" has a limited appeal within its theological borders, none outside them. But if "civis Romanus sum" is on the way to becoming "civis Americanus sum" – with extra fries – the genie emerged from its bottle during America's World War II.

92 James Kurth, "America and the West: Global Triumph or Western Twilight," *Orbis*, 45 (2001), 333–41, is suggestive.

PART C

Mobilizing Economies

7

The USSR and Total War

Why Didn't the Soviet Economy Collapse in 1942?

MARK HARRISON

The aim of this chapter is to reconsider the importance of economic factors in the outcome of World War II and especially on the eastern front. In a recent essay on the war, I asserted that "Ultimately, economics determined the outcome."[1] Production was decisive: the Allies outgunned the Axis because they outproduced them. Economic factors carried more weight in the Allied victory than military or political factors. For example, the Allies did not make better soldiers or provide better weapons. Nor were they better led. It is true that some of the Allies were more democratic, but being a democracy did not save the Czechs, Poles, or French, and being a dictatorship did not defeat the Soviets. The Allies won the war because their economies supported a greater volume of war production and military personnel in larger numbers. The Allied preponderance in this dimension appears so decisive that, once one has grasped it, it hardly seems necessary to pay attention to anything else.

The historian Richard Overy has objected that this leaves no room for "a whole series of contingent factors – moral, political, technical, and organizational – [that] worked to a greater or lesser degree on national war efforts."[2] I agree that it was very important for each country to solve its moral, political, technical, and organizational problems of the war, and that

I thank the participants in the Total War V conference, Hamburg, August 29–September 1, 2001, and in the Department of History and Civilization seminar "Inquiries into the Age of Extremes" at the European University Institute, Florence, November 23, 2001. I would also like to thank John Barber, Louis Capdeboscq, Michael Ellman, Peter Howlett, Valery Lazarev, and Arfon Rees for advice and comments.

1 Mark Harrison, "The Economics of World War II: An Overview" in Harrison, ed., *The Economics of World War II: Six Great Powers in International Comparison* (Cambridge, 1998), 2. This view is directly descended from Raymond Goldsmith, "The Power of Victory: Munitions Output in World War II," *Military Affairs*, 10 (1946): 69–80.
2 R. J. Overy, "Who Really Won the Arms Race?" *The Times Literary Supplement*, November 13, 1998, 4–5.

Table 7.1. *Wartime GDP of the Great Powers, 1938–1945,*
in International Dollars and 1990 Prices (billions)

	1938	1939	1940	1941	1942	1943	1944	1945
Allied Powers								
USA	800	869	943	1,094	1,235	1,399	1,499	1,474
UK	284	287	316	344	353	361	346	331
France	186	199	82	–	–	–	–	101
Italy	–	–	–	–	–	–	117	92
USSR	359	366	417	359	274	305	362	343
Allied subtotal	1,629	1,721	1,757	1,798	1,862	2,064	2,325	2,342
Axis Powers								
Germany	351	384	387	412	417	426	437	310
France	–	–	82	130	116	110	93	–
Austria	24	27	27	29	27	28	29	12
Italy	141	151	147	144	145	137	–	–
Japan	169	184	192	196	197	194	189	144
Axis subtotal	686	747	835	911	903	895	748	466
Allies-to-Axis								
Overall	2.4	2.3	2.1	2.0	2.1	2.3	3.1	5.0
USSR to Germany	1.0	1.0	1.1	0.9	0.7	0.7	0.8	1.1

Note: French GDP in 1940 is allocated half to the Allies, half to the Axis. This table corrects a spreadsheet error in the source that affected figures for Soviet GDP.
Source: Mark Harrison, "The Economics of World War II: An Overview," in Harrison, ed., *The Economics of World War II: Six Great Powers in International Comparison* (Cambridge, 1998), 10.

finding solutions was always costly, sometimes prohibitively so. But on my reading of the history of the war, it was always easier to solve these problems if resources were favorable. On the other hand, moral, political, technical, or organizational defects could prove fatal only if resources were also lacking.

For the sake of argument, however, I will accept Overy's criticism as valid in two senses. First, he is right that economic determinism makes bad history. In fact, determinism also makes bad economics, for economics is about nothing if not choices. I agree that it is desirable to understand the role of economic factors in the war in a way that does not predetermine the role of the other factors. Second, I agree with Overy that if we pay no attention to moral, political, technical, and organizational factors we will not understand the eastern front. Specifically, we will fail to grasp the reasons why the Soviet economy, no larger than Germany's before the war, industrially less developed, and seriously weakened by invasion, did not collapse and instead succeeded in supplying more soldiers and weapons to the front than Germany.

This chapter proceeds as follows. Part I describes the global context of the Soviet war effort. Part II surveys the scale and purposes of Soviet war preparations and the wartime availability and uses of resources in the Soviet Union. It is suggested that the failure of the Soviet economy to collapse in 1942 is remarkable. Part III presents definitions of "economic collapse" and "the point of collapse," as when it is claimed that the Soviet Union in 1942 was at or near the point of collapse, and proposes a framework for understanding the choices behind the outcomes: how did individuals decide to work with or against the national war effort? Part IV places the strategies of the players in the Soviet economy in 1942 within this framework. Part V concludes.

I

The Allied economic superiority was never less than overwhelming. A few figures illustrate this point. Table 7.1 shows that, when the gross domestic products of the great powers are compared in each year of the war, the superiority of the Allied coalition over the Axis powers was never less than 2:1. It is true that a focus on the great powers alone might mislead, since one purpose of the building of empires and influence was to expand the extraterritorial resources available to each side. Therefore Table 7.2 aims to

Table 7.2. *World Population and GDP within 1942 Frontiers (figures for 1938)*

	Allies	Axis	Allies-to-Axis
Population (millions)			
Great Powers	345	191	1.8
Colonies	850	444	1.9
Neutral trading blocs	130	71	1.8
World	1,325	705	1.9
GDP ($ billion and 1990 prices)			
Great Powers	1,444	686	2.1
Colonies	626	866	0.7
Neutral trading blocs	259	151	1.7
World	2,329	1,703	1.4

Note: Allied powers are UK, USA, and USSR; Axis powers are Germany, Italy, and Japan. Allied colonies are mainly British dominions and colonies not occupied by the enemy, plus unoccupied China; Axis colonies are occupied Europe, Africa, and Asia (including occupied China). The Allied trading bloc is Ireland plus Central and South America; the Axis trading bloc is neutral Europe and its colonies.
Source: Calculated from Mark Harrison, "The Economics of World War II: An Overview," in Harrison, ed., *The Economics of World War II: Six Great Powers in International Comparison* (Cambridge, 1998), 7, 8, and 13.

Table 7.3. *Armed Forces of the Great Powers, 1939–1945 (thousands)*

	1939	1940	1941	1942	1943	1944	1945
Allied Powers							
USA	–	–	1,620	3,970	9,020	11,410	11,430
UK	480	2,273	3,383	4,091	4,761	4,967	5,090
France	5,000	5,000	–	–	–	–	–
USSR	–	5,000	7,100	11,340	11,858	12,225	12,100
Allied subtotal	5,480	12,273	12,103	19,401	25,639	28,602	28,620
Axis Powers							
Germany	4,522	5,762	7,309	8,410	9,480	9,420	7,830
Italy	1,740	2,340	3,227	3,810	3,815	–	–
Japan	–	1,630	2,420	2,840	3,700	5,380	7,730
Axis subtotal	6,262	9,732	12,956	15,060	16,995	14,800	15,560
Allies-to-Axis							
Eastern Front	–	–	1.1	1.5	1.4	1.9	2.3
Western and Pacific Fronts	1.2	0.7	0.9	1.1	1.9	1.9	1.6

Notes: The Allied-to-Axis ratio on the Western and Pacific Fronts for 1939 takes UK and France versus Germany; for 1940, the French and Italian forces are included, each with a 50 percent weight since Italy joined the war in midyear at the same time as the French surrendered; for 1942–43, USA and UK versus one-tenth of the German armed forces, plus Italy, plus Japan, but in 1943 the Italian forces are given a weight of two-thirds corresponding to the eight months of fighting before the Italian surrender; for 1944–45, USA and UK versus one-third of the German armed forces, plus Japan. On the Eastern Front, USSR versus 90 percent of the German armed forces in 1941–43, but only two-thirds in 1944–45.

Source: Mark Harrison, "The Economics of World War II: An Overview," in Harrison, ed., *The Economics of World War II: Six Great Powers in International Comparison* (Cambridge, 1998), 14, except that numbers in the French armed forces in 1940 are shown as held at 5 million rather than rising to 7 million on the advice of Louis Capdeboscq (personal communication, January 7, 2002) and based on figures from Jean-Louis Crémieux-Brilhac, *Les Français de l'an 40*, vol. 2, *Ouvriers et soldats* (Paris, 1990).

show the balance of resources on each side including those of their respective colonial empires and trading blocs in 1942, the year most favorable to the Axis. Since the world was in turmoil in 1942, we do not know exactly how many people and dollars of GDP that meant, but the estimates for 1938 get us as close as possible. Table 7.2 shows that even in 1942 the Allied share of the global economy dominated that of the Axis by nearly 1.9:1 in population and 1.4:1 in GDP; in resource terms, the main Allied weakness lay in the British Empire's vast, low-income African and Asian colonies. Correspondingly, France was the unexpected jewel in Germany's imperial crown.

Of course wars are fought with soldiers and weapons, not GDPs. The trail of Axis victories from 1937 to 1942 is to be explained only by the qualitative superiority of the Japanese and German armies and the strategic advantages

Table 7.4. *War Production of the Great Powers, 1942*

	Rifles and carbines (thousands)	Machine pistols (thousands)	Machine guns (thousands)	Guns (thousands)	Mortars (thousands)	Tanks (thousands)	Combat aircraft (thousands)	Major naval vessels
Allied Powers								
USA	1,542	651	662	188	11.0	27.0	24.9	1,854
UK	595	1,438	284	106	29.2	8.6	17.7	239
USSR	4,049	1,506	356	127	230.0	24.4	21.7	19
Allied subtotal	6,186	3,596	1,302	421	270.2	60.0	64.3	2,112
Axis Powers								
Germany	1,370	232	117	41	9.8	6.2	11.6	244
Italy	–	–	63	5	8.5	1.5	6.7	164
Japan	440	0	71	13	1.5	1.2	6.3	68
Axis subtotal	1,810	232	251	59	19.8	8.9	24.6	476
Allies-to-Axis								
Overall	3.4	15.5	5.2	7.1	13.6	6.7	2.6	4.4
Eastern Front	4.4	9.7	4.6	4.7	35.2	5.9	2.8	–
Western and Pacific Fronts	2.4	27.0	5.5	9.2	3.0	7.5	2.5	–

Notes: Half of Italian production between mid-1940 and mid-1943 is assumed to have taken place within 1942. Two-thirds of German army and air munitions produced in 1942 are assigned to the Eastern Front. No account is taken of the contribution of the Western Allies or of Italy to the munitions supply of the Eastern Front.

Source: Calculated from Mark Harrison, "The Economics of World War II: An Overview," in Harrison, ed., *The Economics of World War II: Six Great Powers in International Comparison* (Cambridge, 1998), 15–16.

of their leaders. Eventually, however, the Allies translated their economic superiority into overwhelming advantage on the battlefield. Table 7.3 shows that after a temporary disadvantage in 1939 and 1941 occasioned by their own late start and the fall of France, the Allies continually maintained larger armed forces than the Axis powers and that this advantage reached almost 2:1 in 1943 and 1944 before the final, desperate Japanese mobilization. But nothing conveys the crushing character of the Allied advantage better than Table 7.4, which shows the balance of weapons available to the two sides in 1942. It is true that in 1942 the war industries of both sides retained considerable untapped reserves. The indexes of British and Soviet war production were already close to their respective wartime peaks, but the rates of munitions output of the United States, Germany, and Japan were still accelerating. Still, 1942 was the decisive year of the war; if the Axis powers could not win in 1942 they would never get a better chance. Table 7.4 shows with dazzling clarity why the decision of that year was against them.

In each category, they were overwhelmed by Allied superiority measured at better than 2:1 (aircraft), 3:1 (rifles), 4:1 (warships), 5:1 (machine guns), 6:1 (tanks), 7:1 (guns), 13:1 (mortars), and 15:1 (machine pistols). Once we know this, what else is there to know?

Do we really need nothing else to understand the outcome of the war? This question becomes sharper when we narrow our focus from the global balance of resources to that on the eastern front. Tables 7.3 and 7.4 show that Germany was numerically just as disadvantaged in the east by the Soviet armed forces and war production as were the Axis powers facing Britain and America in the West European and Pacific theaters. Yet Table 7.1 showed that the Soviet Union was not superior to Germany in overall resources. Although Soviet GDP exceeded Germany's in 1940, German wartime mobilization and the deep invasion of Soviet territory shifted the balance strongly in Germany's favor. In the most critical years of the war, overall Soviet resources were only 70 percent of Germany's, and the increment arising from Allied aid compensated only to a small extent. It is true that Germany was engaged on two fronts. Taking this into account, the Soviet Union still maintained a bigger army in the field than Germany and outproduced German industry systematically in weapons other than warships.

The history of other wars and other countries suggests that the Soviet economy should have collapsed in 1942. In World War I, confronted by a small proportion of Germany's military might, Russia had struggled to mobilize itself and eventually disintegrated. The disintegration was just as much economic as military and political; indeed, it could be argued that Russia's economic disintegration had been the primary factor in both Russia's military defeat and the Russian revolution. Later in the same war the preponderance of the Western Allies eventually brought about the economic collapse of both Austria-Hungary and Germany. Similarly, in World War II the weaker economies of Italy and Japan collapsed when these countries were seriously attacked by stronger opponents.[3] Among the poorer countries that were invaded, only the Soviet Union did not undergo a complete economic disintegration. Instead, the Soviet economy mobilized its resources and the German army was overwhelmed by the scale and scope of Soviet resistance.

---

3 On Russia in World War I, see Peter Gatrell and Mark Harrison, "The Russian and Soviet Economy in Two World Wars," *Economic History Review*, 46(3) (1993): 425–52; on Italy and Japan in World War II, see Vera Zamagni, "Italy: How to Lose the War and Win the Peace," and Akira Hara, "Japan: Guns Before Rice," both in Harrison, ed., *Economics of World War II*, 177–223 and 224–67, respectively.

II

When war broke out, the Soviet Union had already engaged in substantial rearmament. In 1940, the last year of less than total war (the Soviet Union had used military force only in Finland and the Baltic region), the Red Army comprised between four and five million soldiers; the military budget consumed one-third of government outlays and 15 percent of the net material product at prevailing prices. One-third of the military budget was allocated to procurement of weapons, and Soviet industry produced thousands of tanks and combat aircraft, tens of thousands of guns and mortars, and millions of infantry weapons.[4]

The strategic purposes of prewar rearmament have been much debated. According to Lennart Samuelson's archival study of chief of Red Army armament Marshal M. N. Tukhachevskii, Soviet plans to build a military-industrial complex were laid down before the so-called war scare of 1927.[5] These plans were not aimed at immediate armament to counter any particular military threat, since at the time none existed. They involved huge forward-looking investments in heavy industry and defense industry. Samuelson does not rule on their precise motivation. Nikolai Simonov has set these plans in the context of the Stalinist regime's basic insecurity: the Soviet leadership feared a repetition of World War I, when the industrial mobilization of a poorly integrated agrarian economy in the face of an external threat resulted in economic collapse and civil war. Simonov concludes that although the 1927 war scare was just a scare, with no real threat of immediate war, it was also a trigger for change. It reminded Soviet leaders that the government of a poor country could be undermined by events at any moment; external difficulties would immediately give rise to internal tensions between the government and the peasantry that supplied both food and conscripts. The possibility of such an outcome could only be eliminated by countering internal and external threats simultaneously, in other words by executing the Stalin package of industrialization and farm collectivization as preconditions for sustained

4 Mark Harrison, *Accounting for War: Soviet Production, Employment, and the Defence Burden, 1940–1945* (Cambridge, 1996), 68 and 284; R. W. Davies and Mark Harrison, "The Soviet Military-Economic Effort Under the Second Five-Year Plan (1933–1937)," *Europe-Asia Studies*, 49(3) (1997): 372 and 394.

5 Lennart Samuelson, *Soviet Defence Industry Planning: Tukhachevskii and Military-Industrial Mobilization* (Stockholm, 1996); Lennart Samuelson, *Plans for Stalin's War Machine: Tukhachevskii and Military-Economic Planning, 1925–1941* (London and Basingstoke, 2000); Lennart Samuelson, "The Red Army's Economic Objectives and Involvement in Economic Planning, 1925–1940," in John Barber and Mark Harrison, eds., *The Soviet Defence-Industry Complex from Stalin to Khrushchev* (London and Basingstoke, 2000), 47–69.

rearmament.[6] This has important implications for our understanding of Soviet history. It is often suggested that the Russian Civil War was an important learning experience for the Bolsheviks. It is less often grasped that World War I also contributed something essential to the makeup of the communist economic development strategy.

Both Samuelson and Simonov confirm that in the mid-1930s Soviet military-economic planning was reoriented away from abstract threats to real ones emanating from Germany and Japan. As a result, the pace of war production was accelerated far beyond that envisaged earlier in the decade while contingency plans for a war of the future became increasingly ambitious. In Samuelson's view, the military archives leave open the question of whether these plans were designed to support an aggressive war against Germany, rather than to counter a German attack. However, the documentation assembled by Gabriel Gorodetsky in the central political, diplomatic, and military archives has surely settled this issue: Stalin was trying to head off Hitler's colonial ambitions and had no plans to conquer Europe, although it is true that his generals sometimes entertained the idea of a preemptive strike, and attack as the best means of defense was the official military doctrine of the time.[7]

It should not be forgotten that the Soviet Union remained relatively poor. The burden of prewar rearmament on Soviet resources and incomes was much greater than that of equivalent efforts in Germany, Britain, or the United States. Moreover, the cost of what was achieved by 1940 was only a small fraction of the fresh burdens encountered when war broke out.

The outlines of the Soviet wartime mobilization of resources can be depicted briefly. Under the pressure of a deep invasion, Soviet GNP fell by one-third, while the resources allocated to defense increased both relatively and absolutely. The pressure on resources was somewhat alleviated by foreign aid, which added approximately 5 percent to Soviet resources in 1942 and 10 percent in 1943 and 1944. Figure 7.1 compares Soviet military and civilian uses of resources with production possibilities through the war years. The bold line that wanders to the southeast before turning north marks the actual combinations of military and civilian uses of resources, or total final demand, in each year. In each year, the Soviet Union's real gross national product is used to mark a boundary with a −45-degree slope that shows the

6 N. S. Simonov, *Voenno-promyshlennyi kompleks SSSR v 1920–1950-e gody: tempy ekonomicheskogo rosta, struktura, organizatsiia proizvodstva i upravlenie* (Moscow, 1996); N. S. Simonov, " 'Strengthen the Defence of the Land of the Soviets': The 1927 'War Alarm' and its Consequences," *Europe-Asia Studies*, 48(8) (1996): 1355–64; N. S. Simonov, "The 'War Scare' of 1927 and the Birth of the Soviet Defence-Industry Complex," in Barber and Harrison, eds., *The Soviet Defence-Industry Complex*, 33–46.
7 Gabriel Gorodetsky, *Grand Delusion: Stalin and the German Invasion of Russia* (New Haven, 1999).

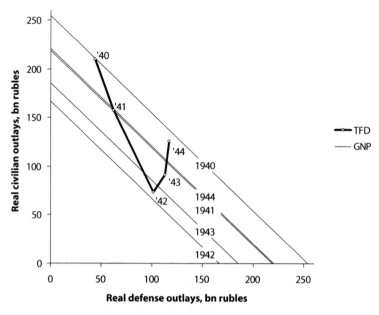

Figure 7.1. Soviet Production Possibilities and Uses of Resources, 1940–1944 (billion rubles at 1937 factor costs). Source: Mark Harrison, *Accounting for War: Soviet Production, Employment, and the Defence Burden, 1940–1945* (Cambridge, 1996), 104. Total final demand (TFD) is the sum of civilian and defense outlays on domestically produced and imported goods and services available for household and government consumption and investment and equals the gross national product (GNP) plus net imports.

alternative uses that were possible within the limits of its own production. The net import of Allied resources allowed the Soviet Union to use more resources than it produced in 1942, 1943, and 1944. The distance from the GNP line to the point representing total final demand in each year shows the difference that Allied resources made.

Wartime changes in the uses of output were accompanied by changes in both employment and productivity. Total employment fell by more than one-third, while numbers engaged in military service and war production rose. The biggest shift was out of agriculture; there were smaller movements out of civilian industry, transport, construction, and services. A considerable efficiency gain in defense industry pushed output per worker far above peacetime levels. A similar process was noted in Germany and accounts for much of the belated surge of German war production between 1941 and 1944.[8] There was no efficiency gain in other sectors, and labor productivity

8 R. J. Overy, *War and Economy in the Third Reich* (Oxford, 1994), 346; Werner Abelshauser, "Germany: Guns, Butter, and Economic Miracles," in Harrison, ed., *The Economics of World War II*, 155.

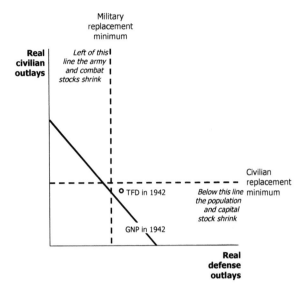

Figure 7.2. Soviet Production Possibilities and Uses of Resources in 1942: A Conjecture.

in the civilian economy declined. This raised the resource requirements of civilian output and made it more difficult to divert resources to military use.

When the war was at its most intense, the resources available to civilian producers and consumers were reduced below the minimum required to replace stocks of physical and human capital. Household consumption was already being squeezed a little by rearmament in 1940; it was squeezed ferociously in 1941–42 by the cut in overall resources and the ballooning defense budget, and squeezed even further in 1943 by the recovery of capital formation. At the low point, living standards were roughly 40 percent below the prewar level. Millions were overworked and malnourished, and there was substantial excess mortality among the civilian population.

Figure 7.2 illustrates a conjecture concerning the position of the Soviet economy in 1942. Again, the figure compares Soviet military and civilian uses of resources with production possibilities. Think of the vertical dashed line as showing the military replacement minimum, the minimum level of defense outlays that would maintain the Soviet armed forces and combat stocks of 1942 at a constant level while replacing their losses on and off the battlefield. The horizontal dashed line shows the civilian replacement minimum, the minimum level of civilian outlays that would maintain the Soviet population and capital stock of 1942 at a constant level while meeting subsistence and replacing wartime losses and depreciation. It is plausible that

Soviet production possibilities in that year were insufficient to meet both minima at the same time, so the −45-degree GNP boundary falls inside the point where the dashed lines intersect. Soviet production possibilities were augmented by Allied aid, so total final demand is shown outside the GNP boundary. In 1942, the Soviet armed forces and combat stocks were rising while the population and capital stock were shrinking, so the TFD point fell to the right of the military replacement minimum although below the civilian replacement minimum.[9]

What is remarkable about the Soviet economy is that the tendency of shrinkage did *not* end in economic collapse. Despite negative net investment and millions of hunger deaths, the war effort was maintained and economic recovery followed.

III

War production was a decisive element of the Soviet war effort. But in 1941 and 1942, its foundations were crumbling. Soviet factories could not operate without metals, machinery, power, and transportation. Their workers needed to be fed and clothed, and they competed for the same means of subsistence as the soldiers on the frontline and the farmers in the rear. As war production climbed, this civilian infrastructure fell away. While Soviet factories turned out columns of combat-ready vehicles and aircraft, guns and shells, civilians were starving and freezing to death. The tribulations of the other Allied economies, even Britain under submarine blockade and aerial bombardment, seem almost frivolous in comparison. Why the Soviet economy stopped short of outright collapse is therefore a proper and serious question.

How might such economies collapse? A country's war effort will collapse when citizens choose to invest effort elsewhere. In wartime, the citizen may choose to allocate effort to patriotic service of the country's interest and to service of self-interest. I define self-interest broadly: it includes service of anything to the exclusion of the interest of the country. Between the country and the self are many layers of association, for example the family, the village, or ethnic group. If the latter are served in ways that conduce to the country's interest, I define it as patriotic service. Otherwise self-interest is being served.

9 It should not be concluded that Allied aid was used only to augment Soviet defense outlays. In its absence, both defense and civilian uses of resources would probably have been reduced, but it is possible that civilian uses would have been cut by more. For discussion, see Harrison, *Accounting for War*, 128–54.

A patriotic citizen serves in whatever capacity the state directs, does his or her duty, obeys orders, accepts rations, and respects state property; call this person a mouse. Specifically, mice serve their country to prevent it from being defeated and in the hope of victory. A self-serving citizen behaves opportunistically and ignores orders or gets around regulations, goes absent without leave, jumps queues, and steals government property and the property of others; call this person a rat. Specifically, rats allocate effort between two kinds of theft. They steal nondurable goods, for example food or civilian or military materials, in the hope of surviving until victory. They also steal capital assets, for example durable goods, productive equipment, and even land titles, in anticipation of defeat and in the hope of being permitted by the enemy to establish postwar ownership rights. Thus, where mice have a strategy only for victory, rats have strategies for both victory and defeat.

Citizens may choose to be rats or mice, their choice depending on the relative payoffs. In other words, mice are not better people than rats; it is not a moral choice, just a choice between payoffs. This choice is forward-looking, being based on the probability of defeat. Within the framework that I propose, the probability of defeat depends exclusively on the balance of production available to the war effort on each side. But the probability of defeat is endogenous since the level of production available to the war effort depends on people's choices.

Some possible implications are illustrated in Figure 7.3. Being a mouse brings a payoff. The expected return to patriotic behavior is the citizen's

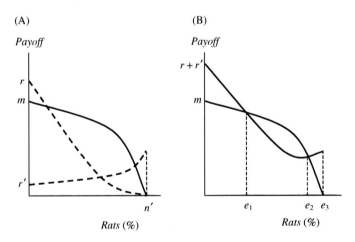

Figure 7.3. The Wartime Payoffs to Serving One's Country and Serving Oneself.

share in the utility that results from defending one's country (including one's community, one's family, and oneself). This return, labeled *m*, will fall as the number choosing to be mice falls. At the vertical axis there are only mice, and the payoff to mice has the value *m*. To the right, the proportion of rats to mice increases, and with the community's impoverishment the payoff to mice falls away. First, with fewer mice less output is produced. Second, the growing population of rats diverts a rising share of output away from the war effort. Both raise the probability of defeat and cut the payoff to patriotism. Third, as the probability of defeat increases, rats steal a rising share of productive assets, which additionally cuts output. Eventually, the payoff to mice falls to zero at a point labeled n' where defeat is certain because everyone has become a rat and output is zero.

Being a rat also brings returns. Consider panel (A). The return from stealing output is labeled *r*. When everyone else is being patriotic the payoff to the first rat will be substantial. The first to steal supplies will always be able to pick something of a value higher than the payoff to patriotic activity: why else do governments find it necessary to enforce wartime controls? So at the vertical axis $r > m$. But this return will fall as the number choosing to be rats increases. First, there are fewer mice producing less output for the rising population of rats to share. Second, as rats crowd in, the risk of confiscation rises at first. Wartime controls are enforced by threats: crime incurs a certain probability of punishment, which confiscates the rat's payoff and reduces it to zero. Let the probability of punishment depend on the proportion of rats to mice, so that it is low when rats are few and there is little threat for mice to guard against; it rises as rats multiply, then peaks and falls again as mice become few and are overwhelmed by rats.[10] These considerations make the rats' payoff decline more rapidly at first than the returns to mice. As rats begins to outnumber mice, the rats' risk of confiscation falls again, but the few remaining mice provide little output for rats to steal, so the two payoffs converge on zero at n', the point of certain defeat.

In addition to output, rats also steal durable assets. The return from stealing assets is labeled r' in panel (A). Under home rule, illegally held assets are always at risk of confiscation. However, rats may calculate that under enemy rule, the previous legal owner being unrepresented, possession of stolen assets will be nine-tenths of the law.[11] As an extension, the enemy

---

10 In this respect, the position of rats is different from that usually attributed to rent-seekers: up to a point at least, for rats there is no safety in numbers. On rent-seeking, see Kevin M. Murphy, Andrei Shleifer, and Robert W. Vyshny, "Why Is Rent-Seeking so Costly to Growth?" *American Economic Review Papers & Proceedings*, 83(2) (1993): 409–14.

11 In English law, possession implies ownership unless someone with a better claim comes forward. Recently the appeal court ruled that someone who had bought a car knowing it to be stolen was

may encourage rats by offering to protect their stolen assets after victory. Then the probability that property rights over grabbed assets will become enforceable, and the incentive to grab, will rise with the probability of defeat. And the probability of defeat will rise, the more output and assets are grabbed. Of course while the country is undefeated rats still face the threat of confiscation, and this rises at first when mice are still many, but eventually the danger of confiscation will fade as rats multiply and defeat becomes more likely.

Combine the rats' expected payoff under home rule with their payoff from the enemy. In Figure 7.3, these are shown in panel (B). The rats' combined payoff $r + r'$ is U-shaped; it has one maximum when rats are few and pickings are plentiful, and another when rats are so many that the country's defeat is ensured. In between, there is a zone of disputed territory and unresolved conflict where the incentive to grab is weakened by impoverishment and the risks of punishment: there is less to grab, and what is grabbed cannot be held securely. But as defeat becomes more predictable, the incentive to grab what's left rises again while the rats anticipate the enemy's arrival.

A result is a stable equilibrium at e_1. A few rats have invaded the community but, with the return to self-serving activity dropping away, grabbing stops at the point where the payoffs to rats and mice are equalized. Thus in any society at war, a degree of rule-breaking and self-serving activity might be normal without necessarily threatening the state's survival. Further to the right, there is an unstable equilibrium at e_2 that I define as the "point of collapse." At the point of collapse the payoffs to rats and mice are equal again. To the right of this point the higher reward goes to rats and the war effort collapses unstoppably, taking the country straight to the other stable equilibrium at e_3 where the war is lost. But the existence of the "bad" equilibrium at e_3 is not a problem as long as the "good" equilibrium at e_1 is self-sustaining.

The problem presented by the point of collapse can be translated into the terms of a dictatorship of the stationary-bandit type.[12] The dictator administers his assets through agents. Each agent will remain loyal to the dictator's interests as long as his share in the dictator's expected rents from the assets he administers exceeds the expected value of the asset if the agent

---

entitled to keep it since the previous owner was no longer identifiable: there could be no one with a better claim. In short, "even a thief is entitled to the protection of the criminal law against the theft from him of that which he has stolen" (*The Guardian*, London, March 23, 2001).

12 Mancur Olson, "Dictatorship, Democracy, and Development," *American Political Science Review*, 87(3) (1993): 567–76.

stole it. If the agent were allowed to gain by stealing from the dictator, he would become a roving bandit. This would reduce the expected value to all agents of serving the dictator loyally and increase the others' incentives to rove too. However, unregulated or roving banditry would also reduce the value of assets to all agents, so a rational dictator like Stalin could be expected to enforce cooperation and self-interested agents could be expected to comply. However, their incentives would change if a neighboring bandit such as Hitler were to offer to settle on the territory, expropriate the dictator, and share the rents on his new assets with the first few agents to defect, threatening the rest with wholesale destruction.

IV

When citizens chose between serving their country and serving themselves, their calculations were driven by the probability of defeat. In the framework that I propose, the probability of defeat depended exclusively on production. Thus, controlling for rats, greater initial wealth always raised the payoff per mouse relative to the payoff per rat and reduced the likelihood of a wartime collapse. A wealthier community would offer a greater private return to its defense. A poorer enemy was less likely to win and less likely in the event of victory to honor rats' postwar claims to assets. When Japan attacked the United States, the rewards to American mice from defending American prosperity were obviously substantial, and the Japanese ability to offer significant rewards to American rats was self-evidently limited. The size disparity of the U.S. and Japanese GDPs ensured that the zone of stability for the U.S. war effort was very large: even if the good equilibrium allowed for significant numbers of cheats and thieves, it remained far to the left of the point of collapse.[13] There was not the slightest chance that the U.S. war effort would collapse into a bad equilibrium, even if a more faint-hearted or more isolationist administration might have willfully chosen a less belligerent response to attack in the first place. This suggests that initial resource disparities can be decisive.

Think of two economies closer to each other in size, for example Germany and the USSR, engaged in a military struggle that had become too close to call. Consider the Soviet war effort in the winter of 1942. Huge Soviet wealth had already been destroyed or lost to the invader. In Figure 7.4, panel (A) illustrates this case. Controlling for rats, the payoff

---

13 On food rationing violations in the United States in World War II, see Geofrey Mills and Hugh Rockoff, "Compliance with Price Controls in the United States and the United Kingdom During World War II," *Journal of Economic History*, 47(1) (1987): 191–213.

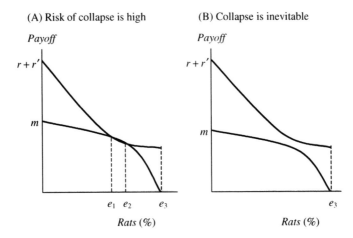

Figure 7.4. Two More Cases.

per mouse had been depressed by capital losses. Controlling for mice, the anarchy in the civilian economy and the dangers of outright defeat had raised the payoff per rat. The net effect was to shift the good equilibrium dangerously close to the point of collapse. Stalin could rationally fear that with only a small additional capital loss, the good equilibrium and the point of collapse would converge and then disappear, making a disintegration of the Soviet war effort inevitable. This case is illustrated in panel (B): there is only one equilibrium where collapse has already occurred.

Under the circumstances shown in panel (A) of Figure 7.4, the exact positions and slopes of the various schedules became critically important, and the contingent "moral, political, technical, and organizational" factors came fully into play. Fearing destabilization, and with few means available to raise the payoff to mice, the Soviet regime did everything it could to depress the payoff to rats. It is true that the latter was fixed in part by the expected policies of a victorious enemy, and Stalin was helped by the fact that Hitler promised little or nothing to ethnic Russians. The Soviet authorities also downshifted the expected payoff from German occupation by threatening potential collaboration with death: even if the enemy prevailed, collaborators would not live to receive any benefit.

Various experiences of 1941–42 testify both to the risks of destabilization and to the importance of the Soviet countermeasures taken to strengthen the stable equilibrium.[14] For example, in 1941 expectations were widespread

14 Unless otherwise noted, all cases are taken from John Barber and Mark Harrison, *The Soviet Home Front: A Social and Economic History of the USSR in World War II* (London, 1991).

that Soviet resistance to German invasion would follow the same course of unraveling and collapse as that already followed by Poland, Netherlands, Belgium, France, Norway, Greece, and Yugoslavia. These forecasts were reinforced by the ease with which the Wehrmacht moved into the Baltic and the western Ukraine and the warmth of its reception there. Such expectations raised the expected value to individuals of pursuing a strategy for defeat and threatened the existence of the "good" equilibrium. No single episode illustrates this more clearly than the Moscow "panic" of mid-October 1941: with the enemy a few kilometers distant, wrongly believing Stalin had left the city, crowds rioted and looted public property. The authorities took determined steps to counter such perceptions of likely defeat. Stalin suppressed information about Red Army setbacks and casualties. Many were executed for spreading defeatist rumors about events on the frontline that might simply have been the truth. Moscow and Leningrad were closed to refugees from the occupied areas in the autumn of 1941 to prevent the spread of information about Soviet defeats. Evacuation of civilians from both Leningrad and Stalingrad was delayed by the authorities' desire to conceal the real military situation.

Despite this, millions implemented or contemplated strategies for defeat. Huge numbers of Red Army soldiers rejected orders that prohibited surrender or retreat. Against orders, millions of encircled soldiers surrendered to the invader in the autumn and winter of 1941 and the spring of 1942. Some prisoners who survived the winter of 1942 subsequently went over to the German side and fought alongside the Wehrmacht, for example General A. A. Vlasov's "Russian Liberation Army," and the Germans also recruited national "legions" from ethnic groups in the occupied areas. At the end of July 1942, when the Germans' summer offensive reached Rostov on Don, significant numbers of Red Army troops ran away from the frontline. The risks arising from such behaviors led Stalin to impose the most severe penalties. His Order no. 270 of August 16, 1941, stigmatized the behavior of Soviet soldiers who allowed themselves to fall into captivity as "betrayal of the Motherland" and inflicted social and financial penalties on the families of the prisoners of war. His Order no. 227 of July 28, 1942 ("Not a step back") combated defeatism in the retreating Red Army by deploying military police behind the lines to shoot stragglers and men retreating without orders and officers who allowed their units to disintegrate. While the war continued, Stalin singled out several national minorities suspected of collaboration, for example the Chechens, for mass deportation to Siberia. After the war the *Vlasovtsy* were mercilessly pursued, and Vlasov himself was horribly executed.

Against the same background, civilians made similar calculations; this led them to withdraw their human capital from the war effort and steal or conspire to steal productive assets including land titles. In the countryside in the summer of 1941, defeatism stimulated speculative talk about sharing out state grain stocks and collective livestock. In 1941–42, there were widespread reports of collective farmers secretly agreeing to the redivision of the collective-farm fields into private property in anticipation of the arrival of German troops. They did not know that Hitler was determined to offer no concessions to Russian peasants, but the Germans permitted some decollectivization in the north Caucasus and this stimulated local collaborationism. Some of the trains evacuating the plant and equipment of the Soviet defense industries from the southern and western regions to the remote interior in the autumn and winter of 1941 were looted as they moved eastward. In the urban economy, although labor discipline became highly militarized, lateness, absenteeism, and illegal quitting remained widespread. Wartime "deserters" from war work on the industrial front were doggedly pursued and hundreds of thousands were sentenced to terms in prisons and labor camps while the war continued.[15]

Regardless of the prospects of defeat or victory, food crimes became widespread. People stole food from the state and stole from each other. Military and civilian food administrators stole rations for their own consumption and for sideline trade. Civilians forged and traded ration cards. In the winter of 1942, Red Army units in the Caucasus began helping themselves to local food supplies.[16] Food crimes reached the extreme of cannibalism in Leningrad in the winter of 1941.[17] But when millions lived on the edge, even quite trivial violations of food regulations could have lethal consequences for individuals who suffered losses as a result, and food crimes in general were harshly punished, not infrequently by shooting.

In short, it is apparent that the stability of the Soviet war effort was seriously at risk in 1941 and 1942. Millions of Soviet citizens faced desperately hard choices between serving the state and serving their own interests and the interests of those around them with whom they identified. Strategies for

15 Don Filtzer, "Labour Discipline and Criminal Law in Soviet Industry, 1945–1953," PERSA Working Papers no. 8, University of Warwick, Department of Economics (2000).

16 V. A. Zolotarev, ed., "Velikaia Otechestvennaia. Tyl Krasnoi Armii v Velikoi Otechestvennoi voiny 1941–1945 gg. Dokumenty i materialy," *Russkii Arkhiv*, 25(14) (1998): 304–5.

17 In addition to Barber and Harrison, *The Soviet Home Front*, see William Moskoff, *The Bread of Affliction: the Food Supply in the USSR During World War II* (Cambridge, 1990); and, on Leningrad, A. R. Dzeniskevich, "Banditizm (osobaia kategoriia) v blokirovannom Leningrade," *Istoriia Peterburga*, no. 1 (2001): 47–51, and John Barber, ed., *Zhizn' i smert' v blokadnom Leningrade. Istoriko-meditsinskii aspekt* (St. Petersburg, 2001).

victory and defeat diverged. However, beyond a certain point the danger that citizens might choose defeat in ever-increasing numbers was not realized. Both Stalin and Hitler played their part in stabilizing the Soviet war effort by closing off the options of honorable surrender and the restoration of private property under German occupation.

Roosevelt also contributed to Soviet stabilization. The first installment of wartime Allied aid that reached the Soviet Union in 1942, although small by later standards, amounted to some 5 percent of Soviet GNP in that year. Although Allied aid was used directly to supply the armed forces with both durable goods and consumables, indirectly it probably released resources to households. By improving the balance of overall resources, it brought about a ceteris paribus increase in the payoff to patriotic citizens. In other words, lend-lease was stabilizing. We cannot measure the distance of the Soviet economy from the point of collapse in 1942, but it seems beyond doubt that collapse was near. Without Lend-Lease, it would have been nearer.

Stalin himself recognized this, although he expressed himself more directly. He told Khrushchev several times that the Soviet Union had suffered such heavy losses that without Allied aid it would have lost the war.[18]

V

The outcome of the war was decided by production, and production rested on overall resources and their mobilization into the war effort. Taking a global view we can see that Allied superiority measured by overall resources was never in question. Moreover, once the Axis powers had exhausted their purely military advantages, it was not particularly difficult for the Allies to translate economic superiority into overwhelming superiority on the battlefield.

But every generalization has its limits. The limits of this one are to be found on the eastern front, where the war was most bitterly contested. On the eastern front, the Red Army soon outnumbered and outgunned the Wehrmacht. Yet the Soviet Union did not have an overall economic advantage over Germany. It should be considered surprising that under the pressure of deep invasion and devastating military setbacks, the Soviet war effort did not completely unravel in 1942.

The failure of the Soviet economy to collapse in 1942 demands explanation. In that year, the Soviet war effort rested on a knife-edge. A battle of

18 N. S. Khrushchev, *Vremia, liudi, vlast'* (Moscow, 1999), vol. 1, 598–99 and 638. I thank Michael Ellman for this reference.

motivations took place in which a hundred million people made individual choices based on the information and incentives available. The decisions that individuals made were aimed either at victory or at defeat. The battle of motivations took place in the context of a balance of resources between the two sides that was indecisive. Within this context, policy interventions by Stalin, Hitler, and Roosevelt could make a difference. Thus, where the balance of overall resources was indecisive, "moral, political, technical, and organizational factors" decided the outcome.

8

Blood, Sweat, and Tears

British Mobilization for World War II

STEPHEN BROADBERRY AND PETER HOWLETT

I

In a total war, more than in any other type of conflict, victory is dependent on the scale of resources that can be mobilized. Here, we analyze the "blood, sweat, and tears" behind British mobilization for World War II.[1] A war economy is presumably one in which the overriding economic imperative is to achieve the war aims of the nation. A *total war* economy suggests an even greater intensity, in that all economic resources are mobilized to that end. However, this should not be taken to mean that all able-bodied people in the economy are in the armed forces or the munitions and related industries. An economy that produces guns but no butter will quickly collapse. The armed forces and the munitions workers need to be fed, clothed, housed, transported from home to work, industry needs to be provided with energy, and so on. Nor can the prewar standard of living of the populace be ignored, as they will expect to maintain some minimum level even during the wartime deprivations, and if the state is to be successful it will need to provide incentives. Therefore, the degree of war mobilization – that is, the level of resources directly devoted to the prosecution of the war – that can be associated with a successful total war economy will differ across economies, reflecting their economic capacity.

Section II examines the level of mobilization in the British economy during the war. It will be shown that, at the wartime peak, just over half of national expenditure was devoted directly to war and that the working population was divided roughly equally between, on the one hand, the

---

1 *Hansard*, 13 May 1940, col. 1502 reports Prime Minister Winston Churchill as saying: "I would say to the House, as I said to those who have joined this Government: 'I have nothing to offer but blood, toil, tears and sweat.'" However, the phrase has been popularly remembered as "blood, sweat, and tears."

armed forces, the munitions industries, and other industries essential to the war effort, and, on the other hand, the less essential industries. Given the level of development and the structure of the British economy (and given the strategic imperatives), this represented a total war economy. The mobilization was achieved primarily through state direction, and the economic scope and role of the state is the subject of Section III. It broadly follows conventional accounts that emphasize the importance of Keynesian macroeconomic management and economic controls. However, the British economy was a market economy, a fact that had to be taken into account by those implementing state directives and which contributed to the success of the wartime economy. Thus, Section IV begins by examining an alternative classical view of resource allocation during wartime before considering the benefits of capabilities developed in a prewar market economy context. Of prime importance among these capabilities were the high level of productivity across all sectors of the economy and the degree of economic flexibility. It will also be argued that market-derived factor specialization lay at the heart of the Allied war effort.

II. THE SCALE OF MOBILIZATION

1. Total War Spending

The extent to which the term "total war" can be justified must depend on the scale of the commitment of resources to the war effort. On this criterion, there is little doubt that Britain during World War II was fighting a total war. Following the Combined Committee on Non-Food Consumption, the data in Table 8.1 divide national expenditure into consumption, war spending, and nonwar investment.[2] Whereas rearmament expenditure accounted for 7.4 percent of national expenditure in 1938, by the peak year of the war effort in 1943, war spending accounted for as much as 55.3 percent of national expenditure. A similar pattern emerges if expenditure is split between private consumption, government consumption, investment, and net exports, with government consumption rising from 13.5 percent in 1938 to a peak of 49.7 percent in 1943, before falling back to 42.2 percent in 1945 and 23.3 percent in 1946.[3]

---

2 Combined Committee on Non-Food Consumption, *The Impact of the War on Civilian Consumption in the United Kingdom, the United States and Canada* (London, 1945).

3 S. N. Broadberry and Peter Howlett, "The United Kingdom: 'Victory at All Costs,'" in Mark Harrison (ed.), *The Economics of World War II: Six Great Powers in International Comparison* (Cambridge, 1998), 47.

Table 8.1. *The Distribution of UK Net National Expenditure, 1938–1944 (% of total)*

	Consumption	War	Nonwar Investment
1938	87.2	7.4	5.4
1939	82.6	15.3	2.1
1940	71.1	43.8	−14.9
1941	62.4	52.7	−15.1
1942	59.0	51.8	−10.8
1943	55.5	55.3	−10.8
1944	56.5	53.4	−9.9

Source: Combined Committee on Non-Food Consumption, *The Impact of the War on Civilian Consumption in the United Kingdom, the United States and Canada* (London: HMSO, 1945), 144.

2. Output of Specific Goods and Services

Britain was a relatively large and rich country in 1938, so that devoting more than half of national expenditure to the war resulted in a formidable war effort.[4] To see what this meant in more concrete terms, it is helpful to examine the output of selected items in Table 8.2, covering agriculture and services as well as industry, since fighting a total war requires more than producing munitions. First, however, note the time path taken by real GDP, the summary measure of domestic output of goods and services. Real GDP rose to a peak in 1943 that was 27 percent above the 1938 level, before falling back during 1944 and 1945.

The main task facing British agriculture was the need to replace lost imports, which had accounted for 70 percent of Britain's prewar food requirements.[5] Between 1939 and 1942, for example, imports of animal feedstuffs fell by 94 percent, imports of butter by 69 percent, sugar by two-thirds, and wheat by a third.[6] Given the need to produce enough calories to sustain the population, resources were diverted from the livestock to the arable sector. The impact on output in the agricultural sector can be seen in Table 8.2. Grain and potato production increased by 81 percent and 96 percent respectively between 1939 and 1943, while meat production fell by 36 percent.

Turning to industry, there was a continuous and significant decline of coal output during the war years from 231 million tons in 1939 to 183 million

4 Mark Harrison, "The Economics of World War II: An Overview," in Harrison (ed.), *The Economics of World War II: Six Great Powers in International Comparison* (Cambridge, 1998), 3.
5 Keith A. Murray, *Agriculture* (London, 1955), 242.
6 Central Statistical Office, *Statistical Digest of the War* (London, 1955), 167.

Table 8.2. *UK Output of Selected Items, 1939–1945*

	1939	1940	1941	1942	1943	1944	1945
Real GDP, 1938 = 100	101.1	111.1	121.2	124.2	127.0	121.9	116.6
Agriculture							
Grains, 000 tons	4,264	5,231	5,942	7,113	7,737	7,445	7,132
Potatoes, 000 tons	4,354	5,375	6,783	8,162	8,537	8,026	8,702
Meat, 000 tons	1,180	1,072	902	772	754	783	812
Industry							
Coal, m tons	231	224	206	205	199	193	183
Iron ore, m tons	14.5	17.7	19.0	19.9	18.5	15.5	14.2
Steel, m tons	13.2	13.0	12.3	12.9	13.0	12.1	11.8
Aluminum, 000 tons	25.0	19.0	22.7	46.8	55.7	35.5	31.9
Machine tools, 000	37.0	62.0	80.9	95.8	76.2	59.1	47.5
Aircraft, units	7,940	15,049	20,094	23,672	26,263	26,461	
Aircraft, m lb	29	59	87	133	185	209	
Warships, 000 tons	76	170	226	234	174	171	
.303 rifles, 000	34	81	79	595	910	547	
Mortars, units	2,822	7,559	21,725	29,162	17,121	19,046	
Cotton yarn, m lb	1,092	1,191	821	733	712	665	597
Footwear, m pairs	132.5			108.2	102.7	99.7	99.8
Construction, £m	442	425	470	425	350	290	290
Electricity, GWh	27,733	29,976	33,577	36,903	38,217	39,649	38,611
Services							
Ship arrivals, units	13,833	8,126	6,362	6,296	6,778	9,297	8,541
Rail passengers, m	1,226	967	1,023	1,218	1,335	1,345	1,372
Rail passengers, m miles	18,993				32,273	32,052	35,248
Rail freight, m tons	288	294	287	295	301	293	266
Rail freight, m ton miles	16,266			23,822	24,358	24,444	22,023

Sources: Central Statistical Office, *Statistical Digest of the War* (London: HMSO and Longmans, 1951), with page references given in parentheses in notes, except where stated otherwise. *Notes:* Real GDP (C. H. Feinstein, *National Income, Expenditure and Output of the United Kingdom, 1855–1965* (Cambridge: Cambridge University Press, 1972: Table 6)); grains are the sum of wheat, barley, and oats harvested (59); potatoes (59); meat is home killed meat (68); coal (B. E. Supple, *The History of the British Coal Industry, Vol. IV, 1913–1946: The Political Economy of Decline* (Oxford: Oxford University Press, 1987: 9)); iron ore (101); steel (British Iron and Steel Federation, *Statistical Year Book for 1946, Part 2: Overseas Countries* (London: BISF: 328–29)); aluminum, virgin (110); machine tools (158); M. M. Postan, *British War Production* (London: HMSO and Longmans, 1952: 207); aircraft (152–53); warships include battleships, aircraft carriers, monitors, cruisers, destroyers, and submarines, measured by displacement tonnage (133); .303 rifles (144); mortars (133); cotton yarn (126); footwear (160); construction, value of gross output (C. M. Kohan, *Works and Buildings* (London: HMSO and Longmans, 1952: 426, 488)); electricity generated (86); shipping arrivals at UK ports (183); railway passenger journeys (189); railway freight traffic (189).

tons in 1945. There were a number of reasons for this decline, including disruption to transport facilities caused by German bombing, the loss of experienced workers to the armed forces, poor industrial relations, the curtailment in the supply of vital materials such as timber and steel, and shortages of mechanical cutting and conveying machinery.[7]

Annual steel-making capacity had reached approximately 13 million tons during the 1930s; this proved sufficient for war needs (apart from additional specialist steel capacity), and steel production fluctuated around this level throughout the war. In particular, this level of production struck a balance between the availability of local ores and the possibility of importing steel from the United States. As Burn notes, if the imported steel had been replaced by the same tonnage of imported iron ore, less steel would have been available in the crucial years.[8] Aluminum was a vital metal for aircraft production, and annual ingot capacity was raised to 31,000 tons in 1939 and increased further to 54,000 tons by 1943.[9] With scrap and imports, the total supply of aluminum reached nearly 300,000 tons by 1943.[10]

The huge expansion of munitions production that was to form the centerpiece of the war effort also required an increase in the production of machine tools, the output of which peaked in 1942 at nearly 100,000, compared with less than 20,000 in 1935.[11] The strain was eased by the import of machine tools from the United States, particularly during the early years of the war, with U.S. imports peaking at more than 33,000 in 1940. The new tools were used to increase munitions output dramatically. To take one important example, whereas in 1938 a mere 2,828 aircraft were produced with an average structure weight of 3,472 lb, by 1941 more than 20,000 aircraft were produced with an average structure weight of 4,342 lb, and by 1944 output had risen to 26,461 aircraft with average weight leaping to 7,880 lb, mainly as a result of heavy bomber production coming on line. Impressive gains in the production of warships, rifles, and mortars can also be seen in Table 8.2.

In the absence of adequate or meaningful price data, the diversity of munitions production makes it difficult to derive a single consistent measure for munitions output. Fortunately, however, the British wartime planners designed an index of total munitions output for the United Kingdom, which

7 Barry Emmanuel Supple, *The History of the British Coal Industry, Vol. IV, 1913–1946: The Political Economy of Decline* (Oxford, 1987), 497–590.
8 Duncan Lyall Burn, *The Steel Industry 1939–1959: A Study in Competition and Planning* (Cambridge, 1961), 10.
9 Joel Hurstfield, *The Control of Raw Materials* (London, 1953), 335–48.
10 *Statistical Digest of the War*, 110.
11 *Statistical Digest of the War*, 158; Michael Moïssey Postan, *British War Production* (London, 1952), 207.

Table 8.3. *Quarterly Index of Total Munitions Output of the UK, 1940–1944 (% of 1939.IV)*

	I	II	III	IV
1939				100
1940			233	249
1941	269	292	307	381
1942	418	535	542	567
1943	591	616	586	628
1944	652	633	547	537

Source: M. Harrison, "A Volume Index of the Total Munitions Output of the United Kingdom, 1939–1944," *Economic History Review*, 43 (1990), 665.

has recently been revised by Harrison.[12] The Harrison index, rebased on the fourth quarter of 1939, is shown in Table 8.3. The index shows that munitions production peaked in the first quarter of 1944, when production was more than six-and-a-half times the level it had been in the last quarter of 1939. Furthermore, as many weapons (particularly aircraft) became heavier and more complex over time, the average quality of munitions almost certainly increased.

Returning to Table 8.2, we can see the collapse in the production of consumer industries such as cotton, footwear, and construction. Although clothing and footwear were still needed for military purposes, civilian demand was severely curtailed through rationing and the introduction of utility specifications.[13] Given the obvious need for the new construction of airfields, camps, training establishments, defense works, storage depots, and other types of military installations, plus the need to make good bomb damage, it may seem surprising that the value of construction did not increase substantially, even in nominal terms, and even fell substantially later in the war.[14] As in the coal industry, there was a loss of experienced labor to the armed forces and a shortage of key materials. Nevertheless, again as in the coal industry, there have also been criticisms of the efforts of managers and workers in the industry.[15] The amount of electricity generated grew rapidly during the early stages of the war as growing industrial demand more than offset any savings from the blackout and exhortations to economize on

12 Harrison, "A Volume Index of the Total Munitions Output of the United Kingdom, 1939–1944," *Economic History Review, 43* (1990), 657–66.
13 Eric Lyde Hargreaves and Margaret M. Gowing, *Civil Industry and Trade* (London, 1952), 424–40.
14 Ian Bowen, "The Control of Building," in Daniel Norman Chester (ed.), *Lessons of the British War Economy* (Cambridge, 1951), 122.
15 Working Party Report, *Building* (London, 1950).

the domestic use of fuel.[16] After industrial demand peaked in 1943, plans to extend capacity were given low priority, and output stagnated.[17]

Dealing finally with services, Table 8.2 provides a number of indicators of shipping and railway traffic, which also made an important contribution to the war effort. Shipping arrivals clearly fell sharply at the beginning of the war as the east coast ports were closed to larger vessels, congestion increased at west coast ports, and ships had to travel in convoy.[18] Shipping arrivals continued to decline until the submarine menace was brought under control from March 1943.[19] By contrast, the utilization of the railways increased substantially during the war. Although the number of passenger journeys did not increase, the average distance traveled rose as service personnel were spread around the country, so that passenger miles increased substantially. Similarly, the increase in rail freight ton miles arose principally from an increase in the average distance of a freight journey rather than from an increase in the tonnage moved, despite zoning arrangements to reduce unnecessary mileage.[20]

III. MACROECONOMIC MANAGEMENT AND MICROECONOMIC CONTROLS

We now turn from the scale of mobilization to the issue of how the mobilization of resources was achieved. This involves a consideration of both financial and real aspects of the resource allocation process. It should be noted that the traditional literature, based on the multivolume official history of the war, is very heavily imbued with a Keynesian view of the world and a strong belief in the superiority of controls over market forces.[21] In section IV we shall consider the more recent literature that has begun to question these assumptions.

1. Fiscal and Monetary Policy

The traditional account usually places Keynes's contribution to the conduct of fiscal and monetary policy close to the center of the story.[22] Keynes

---

16 Leslie Hannah, *Electricity Before Nationalisation: A Study of the Development of the Electricity Supply Industry in Britain to 1948* (London, 1979), 304.

17 Ibid., 307–8.

18 William Keith Hancock and Margaret M. Gowing, *British War Economy* (London, 1949), 248–68.

19 Ibid., 417.   20 Ibid., 480–85.

21 *History of the Second World War, United Kingdom Civil Series* (London, 1949–76).

22 Raymond S. Sayers, *Financial Policy, 1939–45* (London, 1956); Sidney Pollard, *The Development of the British Economy, 1914–1990*, 4th ed. (London, 1992).

developed the idea of an "inflationary gap" to analyze the problem of war finance.[23] He viewed the orthodox "Treasury View" of calculating how much tax revenue would be available on the principle of how much people would be willing to pay as a recipe for inflation. He argued, rather, that the government needed first to calculate national income, so as to assess the war potential of the economy, and then set taxes at the level needed to bring about the necessary transfers from the taxpayers to the government. The extra wartime taxes could be treated as forced savings or deferred pay to be repaid after the war. This had the additional advantage of building up potential purchasing power that could be released in the event of a postwar slump, as well as financing the war effort. To the extent that the government failed to achieve the required levels of taxation or forced savings, there would be an inflationary gap, since the excess of aggregate demand over aggregate supply would bid up prices.

Income tax was the most important source of tax revenue for the state throughout the war, increasing both in terms of its level and its scope. The standard rate of income tax doubled from 25 percent in 1937–38 to 50 percent in 1941–42.[24] More importantly, the proportion of the population paying tax was greatly widened through such measures as the introduction in 1943 of the Pay-As-You-Earn scheme.[25] An important new source of tax revenue was the Excess Profits Tax. This was an attempt to stop wartime profiteering by firms, taxing profits in excess of peacetime levels. Initially set at a rate of 60 percent, it was raised in 1940 to 100 percent.[26] Indirect taxes, especially those on the staples of alcohol and tobacco, were also increased.

A movement was made toward Keynes's forced savings or deferred pay proposal, but the scale of postwar credits was limited and applied only to special cases such as pensioners.[27] The principle of postwar credits was also applied in 1941 to the Excess Profits Tax, which was feared to be adversely affecting incentives. However, it should be noted that in general the Keynesian approach to fiscal policy pays more attention to the effects of taxation on aggregate demand than the effects on incentives, a theme to which we shall return in Section IV. Wartime budgets dealt not only with measures to limit demand-pull inflation, but also with measures to tackle cost-push inflation through cost-of-living subsidies.[28]

---

23 John Maynard Keynes, "How to Pay for the War," *The Times* (1939), reprinted in Donald Edward Moggridge (ed.), *The Collected Writings of John Maynard Keynes, Vol. XXII: Activities 1939–1945, Internal War Finance* (London, 1978), 41–51.

24 Basil Ernest Vyvyan Sabine, *British Budgets in Peace and War, 1932–1945* (London, 1970), 304.

25 Sayers, *Financial Policy*, 112–13.   26 Sabine, *British Budgets*, 158–59, 168–69.

27 George C. Peden, *British Economic and Social Policy* (Dedington, 1985), 133.

28 Sayers, *Financial Policy*, 90.

The conventional Keynesian view assigns only a subsidiary role to monetary policy. Although the Bank Rate was raised from 2 percent to 4 percent on August 24, 1939, it was quickly lowered again to 3 percent on September 28, when it was felt that controls rendered the rate of interest redundant for regulating either domestic demand or the exchange rate. Interest rates then remained low for the duration of the war, which cheapened the cost of financing the large budget deficit and led to the memorable phrase of "A three per cent war," as *The Economist* put it in an article of January 20, 1940.[29] The government chose to finance the large budget deficit through borrowing to avoid inflationary money finance. The aim was to persuade private sector agents to hold government debt, preferably long dated to keep them as illiquid as possible. This was achieved through restricting alternative investment opportunities as well as through expanding the range of government financial instruments.

Alternative investment opportunities were tightly controlled through a Capital Issues Committee and restrictions on bank advances.[30] This left the government free to act as a discriminating monopolist, offering different terms to different classes of investor at the lowest rates necessary to attract each class of funds.[31] This involved Defence Bonds and National Savings Certificates for small investors as well as War Bonds and Exchequer Bonds for institutional investors.[32] In addition, from 1941, Tax Reserve Certificates were offered to firms setting aside funds to meet future tax liabilities.

Any funds not invested in these instruments normally ended up in banks, so it was important that the government developed ways of utilizing banks' liquid reserves.[33] This was done through the introduction of the Treasury Deposit Receipt in addition to the Treasury Bill. The upshot of these changes was a transformation in the balance sheet position of the London clearing banks. On the asset side, commercial advances declined even in nominal terms, while holdings of government paper grew explosively. On the liabilities side, there was a dramatic rise in total deposits, much of it in the form of business deposits.[34]

The monetary consequences of the central government deficit are summarized in Table 8.4. About two-thirds of the deficit was financed by long-term domestic borrowing, with only about one-third financed by short-term floating debt, principally in the form of Treasury Bills and Treasury Deposit Receipts.[35] Only a small fraction of the deficit was financed through

29 Ibid., 159.
30 Ibid., 163–87.
31 Pollard, *Development of the British Economy*, 175.
32 Sayers, *Financial Policy*, 188–218.
33 Pollard, *Development of the British Economy*, 176.
34 Ibid., 176.
35 Sayers, *Financial Policy*, 223.

Table 8.4. *Financing the UK Central Government Deficit, 1938–1945 (£m)*

				Increase in			
	Total Revenue	Total Spending	Current Deficit	Domestic Long Debt	Domestic Short Debt	Money Base	Other Finance
1938	673	781	108	77	−179	18	192
1939	771	1,261	490	72	280	18	120
1940	1,158	3,273	2,115	1,033	517	70	495
1941	1,905	4,727	2,822	1,650	903	109	160
1942	2,314	5,223	2,909	2,100	476	191	142
1943	2,759	5,585	2,826	1,955	1,017	200	−346
1944	2,897	5,569	2,672	1,711	1,081	190	−310
1945	2,806	4,937	2,131	1,885	557	184	−495

Source: Central Statistical Office, *Statistical Digest of the War* (London: HMSO and Longmans, 1951), 202; F. Capie and A. Webber, *A Monetary History of the United Kingdom, 1870–1982, Vol. 1: Data, Sources and Methods* (London: Allen & Unwin, 1985), Table 1.1.

Table 8.5. *Money and Prices in the UK, 1939–1945 (% of 1938)*

	M3	GDP Deflator (Feinstein)	Retail Price Index (Feinstein)	Cost of Living (Ministry of Labor)
1939	99.3	104.4	103.3	101.0
1940	109.2	113.4	117.0	117.8
1941	125.9	123.6	128.8	126.7
1942	142.0	132.5	137.3	127.7
1943	162.4	138.6	141.8	126.7
1944	184.4	146.9	145.1	128.7
1945	208.5	151.3	147.7	129.7

Source: F. Capie and A. Webber, *A Monetary History of the United Kingdom, 1870–1982, Vol. 1: Data, Sources and Methods* (London: Allen & Unwin, 1985), Table 1.3; C. H. Feinstein, *National Income, Expenditure and Output of the United Kingdom, 1855–1965* (Cambridge: Cambridge University Press, 1972), Tables 61, 65; Central Statistical Office, *Statistical Digest of the War* (London: HMSO and Longmans, 1951), 205.

the expansion of the money base. Furthermore, the inflationary consequences of even this small expansion of the money base were muted by the extensive controls exercised over the banking sector, thus limiting the money multiplier effects.

The relationship between money and prices is considered in Table 8.5. Although broad money (M3) approximately doubled over the war period, the price level rose by only about 50 percent, as reflected in Feinstein's

GDP deflator at factor cost and retail price index.[36] It should be noted that the substantially smaller rise in the official Ministry of Labour cost-of-living index reflects the unrepresentativeness of the 1904 working class expenditure weights used in its construction. The excess of money growth over inflation, whichever index of the price level is used, suggests quite a significant role for controls in containing inflation. However, as Capie and Wood note, the role of controls is dwarfed by the role of bond finance.[37] Indeed, their counterfactual calculation indicates that if the war had been financed completely by printing money, the price level would have risen from 100 in 1939 to 1,023,824.3 by 1945. This is just the sort of catastrophic hyperinflation scenario that Keynes's scheme was designed to avoid.[38]

2. Financing the External Deficit

A central issue in most accounts of the mobilization of resources for war in Britain is the external deficit. Although the Treasury initially hoped to meet the import requirements from gold reserves and exports and to this end instituted an export drive, by March 1941 it was clear that this was not feasible.[39] The introduction of lend–lease considerably relaxed the external constraint and allowed a much greater degree of specialization by Britain on war work than would otherwise have been possible.[40]

Despite the massive current account imbalance, the exchange rate was maintained at a fixed parity of £1 = $4.03, about 20 percent below the old gold standard parity, protected by a system of import controls and foreign exchange restrictions.[41] As with so many aspects of the war economy, the price became artificial and attention switched to quantities.

The evolution of the British balance of payments is tracked in Table 8.6. The largest debit item on the current account was imports, accounting for £12.2 billion of the £16.9 billion, with government overseas expenditure (excluding munitions) accounting for the bulk of the rest. With export volumes falling to less than one-third of their prewar level by 1943, current account credits lagged seriously behind debits, creating an accumulated

---

36 Charles Hilliard Feinstein, *National Income, Expenditure and Output of the United Kingdom, 1855–1965* (Cambridge, 1972).
37 Forest Capie and Gail Wood, "The Anatomy of a Wartime Inflation: Britain 1939–1945," in Geofrey T. Mills and Hugh Rockoff (eds.), *The Sinews of War: Essays on the Economic History of World War II* (Ames, IA, 1993), 33.
38 Keynes, "How to Pay for the War."   39 Pollard, *Development of the British Economy*, 177.
40 Roy G. D. Allen, "Mutual Aid between the US and the British Empire, 1941–45," *Journal of the Royal Statistical Society, 109* (1946), 243–71.
41 Pollard, *Development of the British Economy*, 178.

Table 8.6. *UK Balance of Payments, 1939–1945 (£ billion)*

	Current Account			Means of Financing			
	Debits	Credits	Deficit	Net Grants from US	Sale of Investments	Rise in Liabilities	Other Finance
1939 IX–XII	0.3	0.1	0.2	0.0	0.0	0.1	0.1
1940	1.5	0.7	0.8	0.0	0.2	0.2	0.4
1941	1.9	0.8	1.1	0.3	0.3	0.6	−0.1
1942	2.6	0.9	1.7	0.9	0.2	0.5	0.1
1943	3.6	1.5	2.1	1.6	0.2	0.7	−0.4
1944	4.2	1.7	2.5	1.9	0.1	0.7	−0.2
1945	2.8	1.2	1.6	0.7	0.1	0.7	0.1
Total	16.9	6.9	10.0	5.4	1.1	3.5	0.0

Source: R. S. Sayers, *Financial Policy, 1939–45* (London: HMSO and Longmans, 1956), 499.

current account deficit of £10.0 billion over the war period as a whole. The single most important method of finance was grants from the United States under lend-lease, although the deficit was also covered by the sale of investments and the accumulation of substantial liabilities.

3. Microeconomic Controls

Even if the inflationary gap could be closed at the macroeconomic level, there was no guarantee that the consumption of individual goods would be brought smoothly into line with supply.[42] Hence the government also used a barrage of microeconomic measures to ensure that this balance was achieved, including (1) overall central planning to set priorities; (2) rationing to curtail consumer demand; (3) production quotas and the concentration of production in large units in civilian industries; (4) central manpower budgeting to allocate labor across sectors; (5) central allocation of scarce resources such as steel and capital.[43]

Although there were mechanisms of control and planning during World War I and during rearmament, Wiles argues that rational overall planning only really began with World War II.[44] The War Cabinet discussed strategic issues, and overall priorities were fed through a production committee

---

42 William Brian Reddaway, "Rationing," in Daniel Norman Chester (ed.), *Lessons of the British War Economy* (Cambridge, 1951), 182.

43 Peter John Wiles, "Pre-war and War-time Controls," in George David Norman Worswick and Peter H. Ady (eds.), *The British Economy 1945–1950* (Oxford, 1952), 125–58.

44 Ibid., 156–57.

to the supply departments, although the details of the structure changed during the course of the war.[45] At the departmental level, new Ministries of Supply, Home Security, Shipping, Food, Economic Warfare, and Information quickly appeared at the outbreak of war, reflecting the changed priorities of the war economy.[46] In the formulation and coordination of economy policy, the newly established Economic Section of the War Cabinet secretariat and the Central Statistical Office came to play an increasingly important role.[47]

A number of items were rationed from the outbreak of war, and rationing gradually spread to more consumer goods and services.[48] By the spring of 1945, rationing covered about one-half of consumer spending on goods at prewar values and about one-third of consumer spending on goods and services.[49] Initially, rationing operated on a coupon basis, with consumers entitled to fixed amounts of rationed items.[50] From 1941, however, a more flexible points system was introduced, whereby coupon points could be spent on a limited number of goods, thus allowing consumers some scope for substitution in line with preferences.[51] It has been argued that the rationing system operated more effectively in Britain than in other countries. Although some writers see this as reflecting a greater spirit of voluntary compliance in Britain, Mills and Rockoff attribute it mainly to the greater scale of resources devoted to the issue, with a fuller array of controls backed up by both financial and legal resources, ensuring a strict supervision of both production and distribution.[52]

Much civilian production was cut back severely at the beginning of the war, particularly through Limitation of Supplies Orders.[53] In many consumer industries, the state also implemented a temporary wartime concentration of production drive to gain economies of scale and standardization. Figures from the Federation of British Industries suggest that this drive

45 Peter Howlett, "New Light through Old Windows: A New Perspective on the British War Economy," *Journal of Contemporary History*, 28 (1993), 361–79; David Norman Chester, "The Central Machinery for Economic Policy," in David Norman Chester (ed.), *Lessons of the British War Economy* (Cambridge, 1952), 5–33.

46 R. Hopkins, "Introductory Note," in David Norman Chester (ed.), *Lessons of the British War Economy* (Cambridge, 1952), 1–4.

47 Chester, "The Central Machinery for Economic Policy," 14–19.

48 Ina Zweiniger-Bargialowska, *Austerity in Britain: Rationing, Controls and Consumption, 1939–1955* (Oxford, 2000), 9–59.

49 Geofrey T. Mills and Hugh Rockoff, "Compliance with Price Controls in the United States and the United Kingdom During World War II," *Journal of Economic History*, 47 (1987), 209.

50 Hancock and Gowing, *British War Economy*, 446.

51 Ibid., 329–32; Reddaway, "Rationing."

52 Mills and Rockoff, "Compliance with Price Controls."

53 Wiles, "Pre-war and War-time Controls," 151; Hancock and Gowing, *British War Economy*, 117–18.

released 255,900 workers and 61.2 million square feet of capacity for munitions and related industries.[54]

One aspect of the mobilization of labor for the war effort was the need to bring about an overall increase in labor supply by securing increased female participation to replace males recruited into the armed forces. An additional boost to labor input came from the elimination of the mass unemployment of the 1930s. However, in addition to increasing the labor input, it was necessary to reorient civilian labor supply away from group III industries producing nonessential civilian items and into the essential group I industries producing war supplies, while maintaining employment and output in essential group II nonwar industries such as fuel and power. Although during the early stages of the war labor problems appeared mainly in the form of bottlenecks with skilled labor, as time went on the general supply of labor was seen as a constraint. From December 1942, with the first Manpower Budget, the problem of the allocation of labor between the production programs of the different government departments was tackled directly.[55] "Manpower" was the term coined in that bygone age, less gender-conscious than our own, but in wartime the most rapidly growing element was womanpower, as Table 8.7 reveals. The government had wide powers of labor compulsion which it used to control the supply of labor to both the armed forces and industry, although where possible it relied on voluntarism and cooperation.[56]

Other inputs of vital materials and capital were also controlled by the government. For vital materials such as steel, each government order or licensed private order for a product requiring steel carried with it a right to the required amount of steel. This right, known as an "M form," could be cashed at a steelworks. This was administratively complex and led on occasions to "coupon inflation" when too many M forms were chasing too little steel.[57] The Capital Issues Committee controlled all new issues on the capital market, but this is not the same as control over physical investment. Although building and, at times, machine tools were subject to close control, most investment was controlled only indirectly through the controls on labor and materials.[58]

---

54 Peter Howlett, "British Business and the State During the Second World War," in Jun Sakudo and Takao Shiba (eds.), *World War II and the Transformation of Business Systems* (Tokyo, 1994), 144.
55 Hancock and Gowing, *British War Economy*, 446.
56 Edward Austin Gossage Robinson, "The Overall Allocation of Resources," in Daniel Norman Chester (ed.), *Lessons of the British War Economy* (Cambridge, 1951), 50.
57 Wiles, "Pre-war and War-time Controls," 148–49.
58 Ibid., 144.

Table 8.7. *Distribution of the UK Working Population, 1939–45 (mid-June)*

	1939	1940	1941	1942	1943	1944	1945
A. Thousands							
Total	19,750	20,676	21,332	22,056	22,285	22,008	21,649
Male	14,656	15,104	15,222	15,141	15,032	14,901	14,881
Female	5,094	5,572	6,110	6,915	7,253	7,107	6,768
B. Percent of total							
Unemployed	6	3	1	–	–	–	1
Armed forces	2	11	16	19	21	23	24
Civil defence	–	2	2	2	1	1	1
Group I	16	17	20	23	23	23	20
Group II	27	25	26	25	25	25	26
Group III	49	41	36	32	28	28	29

Notes: Group I industries: metals, engineering, vehicles and shipbuilding; chemicals, explosives, paints, oils, etc.

Group II industries: agriculture and fishing; mining and quarrying; national and local government; gas, water, and electricity supply; transport, and shipping.

Group III industries: food, drink, and tobacco; textiles; clothing, boots, and shoes; cement, bricks, pottery, glass, etc.; leather, wood, paper, etc.; other manufactures; building and civil engineering; distributive trades; commerce, banking, insurance, and finance; miscellaneous services.

Source: Central Statistical Office, *Statistical Digest of the War* (London: HMSO and Longmans, 1951), 8.

IV. A ROLE FOR MARKET FORCES?

1. An Alternative Classical View

The analysis so far has reflected the strong Keynesian bias – the emphasis on quantities and the belief in the efficacy of government intervention and controls – of the literature. Although an alternative classical model of the war economy is available, its empirical implementation in the British case has been limited to a general analysis of the twentieth century, rather than a detailed analysis of World War II. Nevertheless, from a classical perspective this may be a strength rather than a weakness, with the stark differences between a war economy and a peacetime economy being overdrawn in the traditional analysis. After all, it is unlikely that the declaration of war suddenly makes a government all-knowing and all-powerful, or leads to the suspension of all pursuit of selfish interests. There may be some virtue, then, in analyzing how we would expect a perfectly competitive market economy to react to war. This can then be used as a benchmark against which to assess the impact of the special measures and controls, rather than simply attributing all change to such measures. This is important because Britain's postwar problems are sometimes seen as stemming from too ready an acceptance of the beneficial effects of government intervention and controls.[59]

Ahmed adapts Barro's model of government spending in a closed economy model to the open economy case and provides an econometric application to the United Kingdom in the twentieth century.[60] There are four key aspects to the model. First, there is a temporary increase in government spending to fight a war. Although this displaces some private spending, the "direct crowding out" effect is less than proportional, since "guns" are not a good substitute for "butter" and people want to go on consuming butter. Hence the level of aggregate demand increases. Second, there is an increase in aggregate supply, as real wages increase to bring forth the required extra labor. In a way, a war acts a bit like a "gold rush," creating a temporary boom. Third, if the increase in aggregate demand exceeds the increase in aggregate supply, there is excess demand, and this can be met by a deterioration in the balance-of-trade deficit. Fourth, it makes no difference to the level of economic activity whether the increased government spending is financed by taxation or borrowing. Under this "Ricardian equivalence" of taxation and bond finance, private spending decisions are unaffected by the form of finance of government spending, since bond finance represents a future tax liability, the present value of which is the same as the taxes that would otherwise have to be raised now.

The model seems to capture the crude features of the British war economy. Overall activity rises, consumption falls but by less than the increase in government spending, and excess demand spills over into a balance-of-payments deficit. Furthermore, the issue of taxes versus bonds in a Ricardian framework simply becomes one of intergenerational transfers and tax smoothing, with a greater reliance on bond financing spreading the burden onto future generations of taxpayers. Doubtless many of the strong assumptions of the model do not hold, particularly with regard to the ubiquity of perfect competition. Nevertheless, it suggests that we should not be too quick to attribute all changes during wartime to the efficacy of regulations and controls.

Few historians are likely to be persuaded that the achievements of the British war economy can be put down to the smooth operation of market forces during the war itself. However, the classical view does remind us

---

59 Correlli Barnett, *The Audit of War: The Illusion and Reality of Britain as a Great Nation* (London, 1986).
60 S. Ahmed, "Temporary and Permanent Government Spending in an Open Economy: Some Evidence for the United Kingdom," *Journal of Monetary Economics, 17* (1986), 197–224; Robert J. Barro, "Are Government Bonds Net Wealth?" *Journal of Political Economy, 82* (1974), 1095–1117; Robert J. Barro, "Output Effects of Government Purchases," *Journal of Political Economy, 89* (1981), 1086–1121.

that before the outbreak of war in 1939, Britain had a long history as a market economy. Clearly, this had to be taken into account by those implementing state controls during wartime. Also, it meant that Britain had the benefit of capabilities developed in a market economy context before the war, including high levels of productivity across all sectors and a high degree of flexibility. We now explore these issues in more detail by comparing Britain with Germany and by considering relations with the United States.

2. Britain and Germany

One important feature of the British economy was its early commercialization and commitment to open markets. In contrast to Germany and much of the rest of Western Europe, Britain remained committed to free trade during the period of the "U.S. grain invasion" from the mid-nineteenth century, and this led to a further decline in the share of the British labor force in agriculture, from an already unusually low level.[61] Taking a strategic view of food supplies during war, it would be natural to think of Britain as particularly vulnerable to economic blockade, and Germany as more secure. And yet, as Olson notes, it was Germany rather than Britain that succumbed to economic blockade during the two world wars.[62]

Olson's explanation for Britain's ability to survive and Germany's tendency to collapse is instructive. He points to the ability of the British agricultural sector to expand output on the stored-up fertility of grasslands brought back into arable use compared with the inability of German agriculture to maintain output at full stretch in the face of wartime disruption. He also stresses the flexibility of the British service sector through administration as well as distribution as the decisive factor.

In fact, careful quantitative examination suggests that Britain's survival owed more to the flexibility of the service sector than the expansion of agricultural output, which was actually quite modest overall in both world wars.[63] Given recent research on international comparisons of labor productivity by sector, we can now see in Table 8.8 that on the eve of World War I, Germany had caught up with Britain in industry, but remained a long

---

61 Nicholas F. R. Crafts, *British Economic Growth during the Industrial Revolution* (Oxford, 1985); Stephen Broadberry, "How Did the United States and Germany Overtake Britain? A Sectoral Analysis of Comparative Productivity Levels, 1870–1990," *The Journal of Economic History* 58 (1998), 375–407.

62 Mancur Olson Jr., *The Economics of the Wartime Shortage: A History of British Food Supplies in the Napoleonic War and in World Wars I and II* (Durham, NC, 1963).

63 Edith H. Whetham, *The Agrarian History of England and Wales, Vol. VIII: 1914–1939* (Cambridge, 1978); Murray, *Agriculture.*

Table 8.8. *Comparative Germany/UK Labor Productivity Levels by Sector, 1911–1935 (UK = 100)*

	1911	1935
Agriculture	67.3	57.2
Industry	122.0	99.1
Services	81.3	85.7
Whole economy	75.5	75.7

Source: Derived from S. N. Broadberry, "How Did the United States and Germany Overtake Britain? A Sectoral Analysis of Comparative Productivity Levels, 1870–1990," *Journal of Economic History*, 58 (1998), 375–407.

way behind in agriculture and services. By protecting agriculture, Germany had retained a relatively "backward" structure with 29.9 percent of the labor force in agriculture in 1935, compared with just 6.8 percent in the United Kingdom. Accordingly, Germany also had a much smaller service sector, which failed to reap economies of specialization, and hence achieved lower productivity than its British counterpart.

We must be careful, then, not to be mesmerized by the success of Germany's rapid industrialization from the mid-nineteenth century on the basis of protectionism, state intervention, and universal banks.[64] Britain's slower, more market-oriented development made for a more flexible economy which was better able to stand the strains of total war.

3. Comparative Advantage and the Allied War Effort

From the perspective of neoclassical economics, development and growth are dependent on free and integrated factor and product markets both nationally and internationally. Indeed, the period before World War I was characterized by economic growth and income convergence underpinned by global factor and product market integration.[65] This gave way in the interwar period to rising autarky, which helped to contribute to the economic, political, and social tensions that would lead to World War II. The war itself, through the disruption it caused to international trade and to the national economies, further weakened the forces of globalization and convergence. Paradoxically, however, at the heart of the Allied war effort (and

---

64 These are the features emphasized in Alexander Gerschenkron, *Economic Backwardness in Historical Perspective* (Cambridge, MA, 1962).
65 Kevin H. O'Rourke and Jeffrey G. Williamson, *Globalization and History: The Evolution of a Nineteenth-Century Atlantic Economy* (Cambridge, MA, 1999).

possibly a defining factor in its success) was a remarkable form of economic integration.

The Heckscher-Ohlin theory of international trade says that economies should trade those goods in which they have an international comparative advantage. Comparative advantage arises from the differences in factor prices across economies and those differences, in turn, reflect their relative supplies of factors of production such as labor and capital. During the war, Britain and the United States applied a variation to Heckscher-Ohlin that also took account of their relative closeness to the theaters of war. Allen has argued that the greater size and productivity of the U.S. economy led it (and Canada) to provide a greater share of munitions, whereas Britain compensated by having a greater mobilization of troops (and of its economy generally).[66] Thus, for example, whereas by D-Day 55 percent of the UK labor force was in the armed forces or in war-related employment, the comparable figure for the United States was 40 percent.[67]

Indeed, the size of the UK armed forces (and those of Australia, New Zealand, and India) exceeded its capacity to equip them and the gap could only be, and indeed was, made up by munitions supplies from North America. The strain of full-scale mobilization on the British economy was such that necessary imports from the United States and Canada also extended to food, consumer goods, and raw materials.[68] It could be argued that because mobilization exceeded capacity, in economic terms the characterization of the British economy as a total war economy is an understatement.

The mechanism by which the United States provided its aid was lend-lease (which began in March 1941). There was also reciprocal aid from Britain to the United States, which again recognized a war-restricted international comparative advantage. To equip American troops in the European and Pacific theaters from the United States would not only have been costly (especially in terms of scarce shipping capacity) but also dangerous, and thus they were supplied with many goods and services locally. Reciprocal aid also extended to the provision of raw materials and foodstuffs to the American economy itself, especially from 1943 and primarily supplied by British colonies.[69]

In monetary terms, the value of lend-lease aid ($27 billion) greatly exceeded that of reciprocal aid ($6 billion). However, relative to the size of the economies the gap was much smaller: reciprocal aid accounted for 4.6 percent of UK national income (3.0 percent of GDP) whereas

66 Allen, "Mutual Aid."
68 Ibid., 247–49.
67 Ibid., 248.
69 Ibid., 254–55, 266–69.

lend–lease aid accounted for 4.1 percent of U.S. national income (3.4 percent of GDP).[70] In the settlement of this mutual aid at the end of the war, the Americans recognized this fact and acknowledged the international division of labor that characterized the Allied war effort by effectively cancelling the notional $21 billion that stood to their credit.[71]

V. CONCLUDING COMMENTS

The British war economy was a success, at least in terms of the overriding objective of achieving victory. Britain overcame early strategic setbacks to mobilize economically without causing internal unrest, managing to raise, equip, and maintain armed forces that would fight on three major fronts: in Asia, in Africa (and later southern Europe), and finally Western Europe. We have analyzed the "blood, sweat, and tears" behind this British mobilization, showing how conventional accounts emphasize the importance of Keynesian macroeconomic management and the microeconomic tools associated with wartime administrative planning. However, we have also argued that attention needs to be given to the market context and market forces. Thus, we have examined an alternative classical view of resource allocation during the war, demonstrated the benefits of capabilities developed in the market context before the war, and shown how comparative advantage lay behind Allied wartime cooperation. The scale of mobilization is probably sufficient to justify the use of the term "total war economy" to describe Britain during World War II. However, the claim is strengthened by the importance of overseas financial aid, dominated by the United States but supplemented by the British dominions and colonies. In a sense, this aid allowed Britain to become "overmobilized," so that we need to think in terms of a Western Allied Economic Market, particularly after the American entry into the war in December 1941. During these years, the war economy was "total" in the additional sense that it eclipsed national boundaries.

70 Ibid., 260.   71 Ibid., 269.

9

The Impact of Compulsory Labor on German Society at War

HANS MOMMSEN

In recent years, after decades of neglect by historians, the topic of compulsory labor has received increasing attention, not only in the international public but also in professional historical research. This interest has been due largely to class-action suits brought by American lawyers and to public debates over the issue of restitution. In the wake of Ulrich Herbert's pioneering work, a series of publications has appeared on the topic.[1] This work has explored the many facets of the problem, particularly the role of German employers. Two major publications have provided an overview of previous research and have placed the topic in broader historical perspective. Herbert's history of compulsory labor in Germany covers developments from the First World War to the present.[2] Mark Spoerer's volume on compulsory labor in the Third Reich presents a systematic description, replete with statistical data, of this phase of the phenomenon.[3]

Although the general problems have now been well explored, a number of issues remain unresolved. One of these relates to compulsory labor in the occupied territories, particularly in Central and Eastern Europe. One difficulty is that statistical data are not available. Another issue concerns the fate of children and adolescents who were brought to Germany along with their parents or who were born in German labor camps. In the early years of the war, pregnant women were usually sent back home, as were sick workers and women who had been raped while doing labor service. Not much is known of their fates. That conditions were terrible in most of the nurseries, where the babies were concentrated and fell victim to epidemics

1 Ulrich Herbert, *Fremdarbeiter: Politik und Praxis des "Ausländer-Einsatzes" in der Kriegswirtschaft des Dritten Reiches* (Berlin, 1985).
2 Ulrich Herbert, *Geschichte der Ausländerpolitik in Deutschland: Säsonarbeiter, Zwangsarbeiter, Gastarbeiter, Flüchtlinge* (Munich, 2001).
3 Mark Spoerer, *Zwangsarbeit unter dem Hakenkreuz: Ausländische Zivilarbeiter, Kriegsgefangene und Häftlinge im Deutschen Reich und im besetzten Europa 1939–1945* (Stuttgart, 2001).

or hunger, became known after the war. The fate of older children remains unclear, and little documentary evidence has come to light. Another issue is the fate of Soviet workers once they returned home in 1945.

Foreign workers had been extensively employed in Germany during World War I. In addition, they continued to play a role in the German economy until the world economic crisis hit in 1929. In the later 1930s, a large influx of labor arrived in Germany from the Netherlands and Belgium as economic rearmament and the buildup of the Wehrmacht resulted in a growing shortage of labor, which the lengthening of the workday for German labor could not alone overcome. The construction of the West Wall in particular burdened available supplies of German labor. The Volkswagenwerk initiated negotiations with the Italian Fascist trade unions, and the German Labor Front concluded an agreement with Dopo Lavoro that provided for the shipment of Italian workers to German industry. This arrangement was successful, but it ended with Italy's entry into the war in 1940, after which only a small number of Italian workers remained in Germany.

After the outbreak of war, a source of additional labor opened up in the neutral countries. In light of the increasing demand for foreign workers, German companies began to recruit workers from countries in southeast Europe as well as from the new Protectorate of Bohemia-Moravia. After the Polish campaign, the German government also dispatched Polish prisoners of war to work in German agriculture as well as in industry. Simultaneously, the Germans were eager to employ Polish civilian workers, at first on a semivoluntary basis. The German government subsequently exerted massive pressure on its local administrators in Poland to meet labor quotas as the process turned into compulsory recruitment and exploitation of the Polish labor market.

Compulsory labor from Poland confronted special conditions from the start. These reflected the racial prejudices of the Nazi party and the SS. Besides harsh regulations that were designed to prevent sexual contact between them and German women and social contacts with the broader German population, Polish workers faced regulations that kept their wages below those of their German counterparts. The so-called *Polensonderabgabe* deprived them of 15 percent of their wages; it also provided that Poles be paid at the lowest wage-levels, and it excluded them from social benefits that were paid to German workers. Moreover, Poles were charged considerably higher prices for their food and lodging.

Ulrich Herbert has demonstrated the fundamental tensions between the Nazis' deployment of foreign forced labor and their hopes of achieving racial purity in Germany. A policy of German autarky would have implied the exclusion of foreign labor. It was hardly a realistic idea, however, for German agriculture and industry alike had relied on foreign labor since the Wilhelmine era. Foreign workers were to be found in increasing numbers not only on the large landed estates of the eastern provinces, but also in the industrial regions of the west. Economic planners in the Third Reich worked nonetheless initially on the assumption that they could reduce or abolish the immigration of foreign labor to Germany. To this end, they regarded the continued presence of foreign workers as a temporary phenomenon and sought to prevent their integration into German society.

Their determination intensified in light of a broader political goal, which was to create a racially homogeneous *Volksgemeinschaft*, by reducing or excluding Jews and other non-German ethnic groups from the Reich. This goal stood at the heart of the Nazi ideological vision, but it was threatened by the recruitment of large groups of foreign workers, particularly from Slavic lands. In the case of Soviet prisoners of war, strong anti-Bolshevik resentments compounded racial prejudices among the Nazi leadership. For this reason, the Nazi government was opposed on principle to deploying Soviet prisoners of war alongside Polish and French prisoners in German industry.

It was symptomatic of this policy, and the ideas that underlay it, that a major proportion of Soviet prisoners of war did not survive the initial months of their captivity because of malnutrition, poor housing, lack of medical treatment, and inhuman treatment in the POW camps behind the front. This was a deliberate strategy, but its radical consequences had not been anticipated. Many German businessmen, who had had positive experiences with Russian prisoners as workers during the First World War, proposed to employ prisoners again in industry as well as agriculture. However, the Nazi leadership, including Hitler himself, rejected this proposal. Only in October 1941 did Paul Pleiger, the head of the Reichsvereinigung Kohle and a leading official in the Hermann-Göring Works, receive permission to employ Russian POWs in mining and other sectors of Albert Speer's enterprise, which was charged with the reconstruction of Greater Berlin as the future capital of the Reich.

To overcome resistance to employing Russian prisoners, which was centered in top party circles and the Reich Main Security Office, Hermann Göring endorsed a set of strict provisions that were calculated to prevent social contact between these prisoners and the German population. This was not a realistic expectation either, for it would have required that foreign workers be employed in separate factories or, at the least, in parts of existing plants that had been isolated from the rest. Soviet workers who were sent into the Reich nevertheless faced a host of discriminatory regulations and deplorable living conditions. They were not permitted nutrition adequate to the working conditions they faced; they were confined to camps that were insulated from the outside world; and violations of rules brought draconian punishment. These regulations reflected Goering's cynicism. They were designed to undercut racist objections among the party chieftains to employing Russian workers in the Reich.

Racist prejudices against Soviet POWs were also fed by Hitler's determination to wage a war of racial annihilation against the Soviet Union. Together, these prejudices, and the policies they spawned, led to the deaths of at least three million Russian prisoners in primitive POW camps or in *Stalags* within the Reich, where starvation, disease, and maltreatment were rampant. The Oberkommando der Wehrmacht (OKW) had anticipated that the Wehrmacht would capture thousands of Soviet soldiers. Initial plans were to keep them in camps near Munsterlager, but the decision to keep them outside the Reich largely defeated this project.

Given the pressures of the Four-Year Plan, however, Hitler changed his mind in October 1941. He now agreed to deploy Soviet POWs in the German economy. He was clearly unaware, though, of the high mortality rates in the POW camps. Because of a typhus epidemic during the winter of 1941–42, the number of Soviet prisoners available for work in the German agricultural and industrial workforce was drastically limited. At the Volkswagen factory, for example, which had been among the first to use Soviet prisoners of war, fewer than eight hundred were available for work after the winter of 1941; attempts by the firm's management to secure additional prisoners brought no results.[4]

One alternative was to use civilian workers from the Soviet Union, the so-called eastern workers (*Ostarbeiter*). This plan had been instituted over the objections of influential party leaders, and over the apprehensions of Hitler, by Paul Pleiger, who pointed out that the conditions Russian prisoners of war faced had critically reduced the available numbers of potential workers and that if other sources of labor were not found, manpower shortages in the mining of bituminous coal in western Germany would soon cripple German industrial output. Although leading German officials agreed to import these civilian workers, they again coupled the campaign with discriminatory regulations that were more severe, although similar in kind, to the regulations imposed on Polish workers. Many companies paid *Ostarbeiter*

---

4 Hans Mommsen and Manfred Geiger, *Das Volkswagenwerk und seine Arbeiter im Dritten Reich* (Munich, 1996).

no wages at all. Elsewhere, their wages were limited to about 40 percent of the lowest levels paid to German workers; and because *Ostarbeiter* were also forced to pay disproportionately high prices for food and shelter, they had little income left to send home to their families.

Nonetheless, a modest improvement registered during the course of the war in the living conditions of the *Ostarbeiter* largely because the supply of East European workers shrank amid the German military setbacks in the east after Stalingrad. The severity of the labor problem registered in the fact that German planning for the offensive at Kursk in July 1943 was geared in part to capture Russian civilians, who were then to be sent to join the compulsory workforce in the Reich. Some of the restrictions on the Soviet workers were eased in 1943, and their rations were raised to the levels of German workers. However, the general deterioration of the food supply in Germany then limited the improvement in their working conditions during the last years of the war.

The system of compulsory labor, which was overseen by Fritz Sauckel, appeared to be successful in a number of respects. Some 26 percent of the German labor force comprised either civilian workers from Western Europe, who worked in Germany under contract, or various categories of forced labor from the east. The argument is plausible that the German war economy would have collapsed as early as 1942 had it not been for the system of forced labor. Virtually no sector of the German economy was not at least partially dependent on it. The presence of these workers relieved pressures on the German workforce and made it possible to limit resort to German female labor before 1944. In this way, the system of compulsory labor also sustained German popular support for Hitler's policies.

Whether this system would be economically efficient in the long term is another question. The general increase in the compulsory workforce took place after the summer of 1941, and it accompanied increases in the output of German armaments that were associated with the name of Albert Speer. The question is apt whether comparable increases could have been achieved by exploiting available reserves of German labor, particularly women. Compulsory labor was costly. It was subject to tremendous turnover, and it required close and constant supervision, which significantly reduced its efficiency – as did malnutrition.

The abominable treatment of Russian prisoners and – after 1943 – Italian military internees, to say nothing of concentration camp inmates or Jews, significantly reduced the productivity of these categories of labor. So did material conditions in the camps and the brutal behavior of German guards and factory police. In these circumstances, the real economic effects of exploiting forced labor were probably negative. In addition, deportations of compulsory labor and the otherwise merciless exploitation of the occupied territories had negative repercussions in these areas as well.

Because most forced laborers were unskilled or semiskilled, their employment made necessary the restructuring of production to minimize the need for skilled workers. Rationalization in the armaments industry was geared primarily to the utilization of unskilled labor. Management emphasized the use of single-purpose machinery (*Einzweckwerkzeugmaschinen*) over more flexible, multipurpose machinery, which could have been better adapted to changing productive needs. The introduction of assembly-line techniques was likewise the consequence of employing unskilled workers, a high percentage of whom were women with no experience in industrial production. These adaptations hardly represented effective modernization of the German industrial plant. Nor should the impact of rationalization be overstated. It failed to reduce production costs significantly, except insofar as wages paid to the *Ostarbeiter* were substantially lower than those of German workers.

As early as 1941, leading German business managers began to look beyond the wartime economy and to lay plans to exploit unskilled foreign labor in the Great German Reich that would emerge from the war. Leading businessmen no longer regarded the work camps and the use of compulsory labor as temporary measures. In anticipation of the postwar situation, the Volkswagen factory built additional housing facilities, which were adapted to the putatively primitive requirements of foreign workers. At the same time, business leaders also pressed for the establishment of Labor Education Camps, in addition to existing detention centers, in the immediate vicinity of German plants.[5]

These Labor Education Camps were designed to complement the system of concentration camps. The initiative for their creation came from employers who were interested in enforcing labor discipline at the plant level but who did not wish to lose recalcitrant workers to the concentration camps. About an eighth of all forced laborers were subjected to the draconian treatment that reigned within the national network of Education Camps. Despite frightening deterrents, some 40,000 *Ostarbeiter* left their workplaces in 1943 in an effort either to escape Germany – a design that was practically hopeless – or to find another workplace. These signs of unrest among the workforce led the Gestapo to view the growing number of forced laborers in Germany as a source of political instability, although

5 Gabriele Lotfi, *KZ der Gestapo: Arbeitserziehungslager im Dritten Reich* (Munich, 2000).

the circumstances made the organization of oppositional networks among foreign workers virtually impossible.

Within the broader framework of the German war economy, the system of compulsory labor had dubious effects. While management quickly overcame its initial hesitancy and accustomed itself to the benefits of the low wage-levels that forced laborers received, the costs of the system were high. They included transportation, the construction of work camps, the feeding and maintaining of inmates, the payment of guards and administrators, and changes made necessary in the organization of production. The bottom line was thus disappointing, even as the conditions of war discouraged deliberations about alternative arrangements.

The mounting pressures on the labor supply also persuaded the regime to employ concentration-camp inmates throughout the economy. Heinrich Himmler had initially hoped to exploit these reserves of manpower to expand the economic empire of the SS and to support the gigantic settlement projects that he was planning in the east. To this end, the population of the concentration camps rose from 110,000 in 1942 to nearly 700,000 in 1945. Hans Pohl, the leader of the SS Office of Economic Administration (*Wirtschafts- und Verwaltungshauptamt*), lobbied for better treatment of the prisoners, reasoning that it would increase their capacity to work. He failed, however, to convince camp commanders to halt the prevailing practice of "annihilation through work," which systematically ruined the health of the inmates.[6]

Himmler's designs to build an extended industrial complex for the SS on the basis of concentration-camp labor foundered on the opposition of Speer, who pressed Himmler to make the prisoners available for work in private companies. Speer's success led to the establishment of myriad satellite concentration camps (*Aussenlager*) near industrial plants and to the systematic exploitation of camp inmates in industrial production. The aluminum foundry at the Volkswagen plant, which began operation in 1941, provided an early precedent. Another reserve of additional labor comprised Jewish workers, but their numbers in Germany never surpassed 50,000.[7] Plans developed in 1941 to employ Jewish workers from the Warthegau in German industry collapsed on Hitler's personal objections. Subsequent attempts by the Gestapo to break up mixed marriages and to deport the Jewish partners for forced labor also met with opposition, and they were dropped when Hitler failed to support the plan.

6 Jan Erik Schulte, *Zwangsarbeit und Vernichtung: Das Wirtschaftsimperium der SS. Oswald Pohl und das SS-Wirtschafts- und Verwaltungshauptamt* (Paderborn, 2001).
7 Herbert, *Geschichte der Ausländerpolitik*, 167–68.

The vision embraced by Himmler and Pohl to build up a reserve of forced labor in support of an economic empire for the SS thus failed to materialize, although several of the SS's industrial projects relied on labor from concentration camps, notably the so-called *Mittelwerke*, the production site for the Fi103 and A4 rockets. This ambitious underground construction project was not confined to the production of rockets, but included myriad other industrial sites. It would have provided space for additional factories as well, and it reflected the plans to build an extended German underground industrial plant in the near future. Its realization required a continuous supply of concentration-camp labor, which was exploited in other sectors as well, such as the air industry.

The Germans planned to use forced labor on an extended scale after the war, and they intended to draw these workers from parts of Eastern Europe whose indigenous populations were, under the guidelines of the General Plan East (*Generalplan Ost*), to be replaced by German settlers. These projects illustrated the inherent long-term contradictions in the aims pursued by the Nazi regime. The system of industrial production by compulsory labor fell apart under the pressure of the war effort, and it could never have functioned under normal conditions. In the meantime, the extensive use of forced labor during the war undermined the regime's primary objective of achieving a racially homogeneous society in Germany.

Party hardliners reacted to the presence of over two million East European laborers in the Reich by tightening the restrictions on these workers and by applying constant pressure on the German population to avoid contact with them. This policy failed, especially in small businesses and on farms but also in factories. Personal relationships did develop. German workers tended to respect the abilities of their Soviet counterparts. When they were provided with adequate rations, in fact, the output of Soviet workers rose to about 90 percent of the Germans'.

As early as 1942, the SD accordingly concluded that popular images of subhuman Russians had to be discarded, insofar as they clashed with the cooperative behavior of a great majority of the *Ostarbeiter*. In the spring of 1943, even Goebbels began a propaganda offensive in an effort to improve the treatment of these guest workers, although his efforts produced only modest results. The Gestapo savagely punished sexual relations between Slavic workers and Germans, but the fact that these relations took place demonstrated that complete social segregation could not, as the party radicals had hoped, be maintained. Nor could more subtle, bureaucratic regulations prevent social contacts between German laborers and the East European workforce.

Few Germans, on the other hand, were prepared to support East European workers openly, given the severity of the Gestapo's sanctions. Protests against the treatment of Soviet POWs and concentration-camp inmates were extremely rare. The German population became accustomed to the presence of East European workers, who were marched publicly from camps to production sites. The experience of Mittelbau–Dora, where an entire region was set aside for concentration-camp labor, provided an extreme example.[8] As in the case of Jews, the general attitude of the German population was characterized by moral indifference and passivity, which could be ascribed at least in part to pressure from the Gestapo.

At the same time, the presence of East European workers in the German workforce affected relations in the factories themselves, insofar as German workers who were exempt from military service functioned there as foremen and supervisors of the foreign workers. These relations of subordination also blocked the development of solidarity between German and Soviet workers. Ulrich Herbert has emphasized that German workers became accustomed to the social inequalities that racism bred, and that these workers remained indifferent to the fate of their foreign counterparts.[9] It is difficult to assess the long-term consequences of systematic discrimination against foreigners, which Nazi propaganda encouraged; but enduring suspicions of foreigners in postwar Germany might well reflect experiences with forced labor during the Second World War. The debate over the German Remembrance Fund, which was set up to provide compensation to former forced laborers, suggests as much, inasmuch as sectors of German industry and commerce – and German public opinion – have proved reluctant to contribute.

Both broad public debate over forced labor in the Third Reich and extensive historical scholarship on the subject, which has now produced a wealth of local case studies, have produced significant changes in the historical picture of the Nazi era. It is now clear that many ordinary Germans profited economically from the exploitation of compulsory labor and that social discrimination against foreign workers was not confined to big business. As a consequence of these findings, a remarkable feeling of collective responsibility has developed, particularly among younger Germans. The Remembrance Fund has not fulfilled all the expectations that historians had placed in it; its arbitrary distinction between "slave labor" and "forced labor" has been a particular disappointment. The fund has nevertheless represented an important response to the illegal and inhumane practices of the

---

8 Jens-Christian Wagner, *Produktion des Todes: Das KZ Mittelbau-Dora* (Göttingen, 2001).
9 Herbert, *Fremdarbeiter*, 357–58.

Nazi regime as well as to the exploitation of deported workers by German industry.

The regime's practices bear on the question of total war. The extensive exploitation of forced workers from the occupied territories and the savage methods used to recruit them were indicative of a new kind of warfare that rejected all responsibility for the fate of indigenous populations, who were deprived of large sectors of their own workforce. Innumerable civilian auxiliaries were pressed into the service of the German army on the eastern front, while a remarkably high percentage of the working population in the occupied territories was compelled to perform compulsory labor in Germany. In this respect at least, the Second World War represented the culmination of total warfare, insofar as it brought to an extreme inhumane practices that had been introduced more tentatively during the First World War.

PART D

Mobilizing Societies

10

Fantasy, Reality, and Modes of Perception in Ludendorff's and Goebbels's Concepts of "Total War"

MARTIN KUTZ

When Germans think of total war, they usually think of Allied strategic bombing and the Russian front after Stalingrad. When they recall the protagonists of total war, they think first of Joseph Goebbels and his notorious speech in the Sport Palace in Berlin on February 18, 1943, and of Erich Ludendorff, whose tract *Total War* appeared in 1935.[1] Ludendorff styled himself as the authoritative leader, the warlord who could draw on his experiences in the First World War for lessons about the total war of the future. Goebbels, on the other hand, regarded himself in the winter of 1942–43 as the great tribune whose role was to exhort and enforce the totalization of war.[2] When he delivered his speech in the Sport Palace, the Second World War had already lasted longer than the period that separated the outbreak of the First World War from the establishment of the third Supreme Command of the Army (Oberst Heeresleitung, or OHL) under Hindenburg and Ludendorff in the summer of 1916. At this point in the conflict, Ludendorff began to undertake what he later understood to be total war, but it was more accurately the most that he could achieve given the political, social, and economic conditions that he faced. In his own eyes, Goebbels's speech represented an attempt to put into practice at last what he himself understood as the need for total war.

Both protagonists participated in a broad political discourse in Germany during the interwar period, which also represented part of a broader European debate over the character and dimensions of a future war.[3] This discussion featured two schools of thought, and they produced two diametrically opposed visions. The best-known and most popularized at the time

---

1 Erich Ludendorff, *Der totale Krieg* (Munich, 1935).
2 *Die Tagebücher von Joseph Goebbels* (ed. Elke Fröhlich, Part II, 15 vols., Munich, 1993), 7: 345.
3 Roger Chickering and Stig Förster, eds., *The Shadows of Total War: Europe, East Asia, and the United States, 1919–1939* (Cambridge, 2003).

was the one that envisaged the total war of the future. Its most prominent representatives were the theorists of strategic airpower.[4] The other school sought the means to prevent just this sort of total war, without abandoning the option of war altogether.[5] Both schools claimed to have discerned the nature of modern warfare, and both insisted that they had drawn the proper lessons from the First World War.

Both were well represented in Germany. The most audible voices were those that advocated total war. Most of these were heard in the years between the installation of the Nazi regime and the outbreak of the Second World War. The advocates of this school comprised retired officers of the First World War and a number of younger, "modern" protagonists, who had a high level of sympathy for the new regime. Along with Ludendorff, these figures were associated with the so-called science of military economics (*Wehrwirtschaftswissenschaft*) in the 1930s, and they included officers of the Wehrmacht who were responsible for armaments and the armaments industry, such as Georg Thomas.

By contrast, the so-called "realists" in civilian offices, like most military officers of the younger generation, paid no heed to the advocates of total war; and they proved more influential. Their views were more attractive to the Nazi leadership, which feared having to wage a total war precisely because the First World War had demonstrated the limits to which the civilian population could be pushed before it collapsed. As Robert Ley, the head of the German Labor Front, put this proposition in November 1936, "There is a limit, and when the level of endurance has been reached, things collapse, just as they did with us on November 9 [1918]."[6]

There was thus a fundamental contradiction among the German theorists of a future war. That the German advocates of total war were ignored even during the buildup for war reflected the fact that the other, "realist" school regarded their ideas as unrealistic and dangerous.

The question is pertinent whether the ideas of those who advocated total war were based on rational analysis of the experiences of the First World War – whether the reality of industrialized war was reflected in their thinking. Even at first glance it is clear that their radicalism was not based on sound analysis. Besides trying to cast political blame for the German defeat

---

4 Giulio Douhet, *Il dominio dell'aria* (Rome, 1921); cf. Richard J. Overy, *The Air War, 1939–1945* (London, 1980), 5–25.
5 J. F. C. Fuller, *The Foundation of the Science of War* (London, 1926); Basil H. Liddell Hart, *The Remaking of Modern Armies* (London, 1927); cf. Jehuda L. Wallach, *Kriegstheorien: Ihre Entwicklung im 19. und 20. Jahrhundert* (Frankfurt, 1972), 217–18, 247–8.
6 Cited in Timothy W. Mason, *Arbeiterklasse und Volksgemeinschaft: Dokumente und Materialien zur deutschen Arbeiterpolitik 1936–1939* (Opladen, 1975), 190.

in the war, their thinking was one-sided, dominated by military modes of thought; it ignored, in shocking fashion, the social and political contexts of war, particularly questions having to do with the comparative military capacities of the belligerents. Their analysis of their own military experience was itself confined and backward-looking. It is thus tempting to argue that illusions and ideological fixations distorted their views.

Neither Ludendorff in the First World War nor Goebbels in the Second was able to organize total war. Both were defeated by systemic obstacles and opposition from rivals who had more political power or more compelling interests. Nonetheless, at least from the German perspective, something approximating total war did eventuate during the Second World War. This unintended development was ultimately due to factors that had acquired a dynamic of their own in the course of an industrial war.

LUDENDORFF'S CONCEPT OF TOTAL WAR

In his 1935 tract, which basically repeated arguments that he had published earlier, Ludendorff gave a turbid picture of war as he tried to justify his own actions during World War I.[7] The most remarkable feature of this picture was that Ludendorff believed that total war would be short.[8] War was to be total in two respects. All available resources of the nation were to be mobilized completely at the beginning of the conflict, and they were to be exploited ruthlessly to the single end of military success. A willingness to run high risks was thus the basic condition of success.

The foundation for this conviction lay in Ludendorff's experience as commander on the eastern front during the campaigns of 1914–15, when he was frustrated by the failure of the High Command to make larger contingents of troops available to him. In these circumstances, he was unable to defeat the Russian armies decisively at the beginning of the war.[9] Ludendorff also recognized that Germany could not win a long war of attrition. Accordingly, a quick decision had to be forced. He based his criticisms of Moltke and Falkenhayn on this premise. He accused the former of lacking the courage to risk it all at the outset; the latter, he charged with squandering troops in battles of attrition.

The radicalization of warfare that Ludendorff envisaged required dictatorial leadership. The frustrations that he had experienced at the head of the

7 Roger Chickering, "Sore Loser: Erich Ludendorff's Total War," in Chickering and Förster, *Shadows of Total War*.
8 Ludendorff, *Totaler Krieg*, 49–50.
9 Ludendorff, *Meine Kriegserinnerungen 1914–1918* (Berlin, 1919), 79–80.

High Command, when he tried to implement the Hindenburg Program, surfaced in this demand. His basic assumption was hence that a warlord inspired by genius should subordinate everything to the army's victory in a radicalized, short, total war.[10] Politics, law, civil society were all to be forged together under military rule. Ludendorff's ideas about the war of the future thus emerged as a series of technocratic reflections on his own experience of the First World War, particularly those aspects of it that he believed had contributed to the German defeat.

Ludendorff's second basic principle of total war emphasized total unity among the leadership, army, and people.[11] This principle, too, reflected his war experiences. In the first place, it represented his reaction to the anxiety of the German elites, who had feared in 1914 that the labor movement would prevent the war by launching a general strike. Second, it represented Ludendorff's reaction to the accelerating deterioration of morale on the home front, which had culminated in the revolution of November 1918. Ludendorff attributed war-weariness and revolution to the clever, effective propaganda of Jews, Socialists, democrats, and ultramontane Catholics, as well as to the superiority of Allied propaganda.[12] Because he believed that total political and moral unity of the populace was the necessary prerequisite of total war, he argued that the First World War had become less total after 1917. He thus wrote about the "de-totalization" of the war after the great industrial strikes began in 1917.

Grave misconceptions about the First World War were evident in these assertions. Ludendorff completely overlooked the basic causes of the decline and collapse of popular morale; these lay in economic deterioration and massive losses sustained at the front.[13] The decline of the standard of living to less than half of its prewar levels eventually broached the limits of popular endurance, particularly among the most disadvantaged parts of the population. Ludendorff's proposal to counteract these realities by means of propaganda testified to a blindness to the facts; so did his belief that enemy propaganda had led to subversion on the home front.

These misconceptions were related to a more general problem. As quartermaster general in the third High Command, where he was effectively the commander-in-chief of the German armies, he was doubtless the

---

10 Ludendorff, *Totaler Krieg*, 114–15.   11 Ibid., 11–28.
12 Ibid., 13, 15.
13 Gerald D. Feldman, *Army, Industry and Labor in Germany, 1914–1918* (Princeton, 1966); cf. Hans-Joachim Bieber, *Gewerkschaften in Krieg und Revolution: Arbeiterbewegung, Industrie, Staat und Militär in Deutschland 1914–1920* (2 vols., Hamburg, 1981).

best-informed authority on everything that bore on the war effort.[14] This circumstance did not, however, make him uniquely able to render an astute analysis of industrialized warfare, even in retrospect. The full context of industrial war, its systemic interdependencies, were not clear to him. Nor was he able to analyze its various individual dimensions or to judge their impact on the whole. He failed to see the significance of differences in the economic and social capacities of the contending powers; and he could not transcend a narrow perspective to deal with the broader challenge of optimizing the performance of both the civilian and war economies.

The bases of a strategy were hence lacking – and so, for that matter, was a strategy. Ludendorff could not conceive of war as a "rational" means to political ends. His vision was organized in Social Darwinist categories; he understood war to be an existential conflict, a struggle for survival among the peoples of the world. War was thus to be prosecuted ruthlessly and radically, for it produced neither victors nor vanquished, only survivors.

Other misconceptions arose from Ludendorff's technocratic military thinking, and they stood in remarkable tension with his ideas about totality. He regarded financial matters, for instance, as the means to create goods: money could produce matériel.[15] He was blind to the lessons demonstrated by the enormous material consumption of the world war – the fact that the problem lay in the commodity side of war production and that the regulation of finances bore instead on the distribution of the war's burdens.

A further misconception lay in Ludendorff's belief that the disruption of domestic political stability, which had resulted largely from shortages of raw materials, fodder, and food, could have been prevented by means of the "just" distribution of goods and by "enlightenment" about the need to restrict consumption.[16] This belief was linked to the conviction that once sufficient supplies of goods that had been scarce during the First World War were secured, the war of the future could be mastered. His conceptions about the economy were basically romantic. He thought that the central obligation of the economy was simply to produce; the prerequisites of production did not much interest him.

Ludendorff's analysis was not even adequate to the First World War, let alone to the total war of the future that he portrayed. But even in his understanding of his own military craft, his powers of insight were limited. He disregarded the lessons of the First World War that fire and matériel were decisive, and that they placed defenders at a massive advantage over attacking

---

14 Martin Kitchen, *The Silent Dictatorship: The Politics of the German High Command under Hindenburg and Ludendorff, 1916–1918* (New York, 1976).

15 Ludendorff, *Totaler Krieg*, 34–6.   16 Ibid., 47.

troops. Instead, he clung to the traditional view that the offensive was the superior mode of combat. Offensive action alone, he thought, could force a decision-at-arms.[17] He coupled this belief with a tactical fixation on infantry firepower.[18] Because he did not contemplate forcing a war of movement, his vision of war remained geared to the battle of attrition. His rejection of motorization was a product of the same fixation. He reasoned that it was too difficult to provide motorized transport for the horses that officers required. In plain terms, even attacks by motorized formations were to be commanded by officers on horseback; officers on foot or in motor vehicles were beyond his powers of comprehension.[19]

Ludendorff's thinking about airpower reflected a remarkable ambivalence between modern and traditional themes.[20] Although not as lucidly or radically as Douhet, Ludendorff believed airpower to be a significant strategic weapon, but he could not foresee using it strategically. He believed that its principal mission would be to create panic among the enemy's civilian populace and thereby to force its military collapse. Behind this vision lurked an understanding of society that was typical among traditional elites throughout Europe – the belief that the "masses" represented an unstructured, undisciplined, incoherent collection of human beings who required the formative power of elites. These elites reasoned further that because they themselves represented a numerically marginal group, there would not be enough of them available to control the popular panic, distraction, and chaos that would result from air attack. Proponents of this thinking had failed even during the First World War to recognize that these same masses displayed enormous discipline and endurance, that their revolt was ultimately due to total overexertion, not to their distraction or want of control. The international discussion of airpower in the interwar period revealed, however, that this misconception was hardly unique to Ludendorff or German commentators.

The general misperception of the *Volk* and the masses led Ludendorff to grotesque fantasies about the causes of the German collapse and its implications for the war of the future. Germany, he thought, had lost the war because sinister forces had destroyed the unity of the German people and had, by means of skilled propaganda, exploited popular hopes and longings, particularly the desire for peace. In his eyes, these forces included "Rome" and German "ultramontanism," neither of which, he reasoned, could abide a German Protestant state. The role of the Pope in trying to arrange a negotiated peace was the subject of particularly vituperative commentary.

---

17 Ibid., 77.   18 Ibid., 64–6.
19 Ibid., 66.   20 Ibid., 87–106.

Ludendorff was no less hateful toward "the Jews." He fully embraced the slanderous assumptions of folkish anti-Semitism. He used the terms "capital" and "Jewish capital" interchangeably, although in this connection at least, he understood "Jewish" to be more a moral than a racial category. Socialism, too, which the German right had long associated with liberalism, Jewry, and democracy, had, in Ludendorff's view, destroyed the unity of the German people during the war, while "freemasons" and "secret sects" had worked in alliance with Germany's enemies to undermine popular support of the war by means of systematic subversion and misinformation.

Ludendorff's final conclusions about the total war of the future rested on this last exercise in "analysis." The solidarity of the German people, he insisted, was the highest goal of politics. The nation was to regard itself as a biologically determined unit in a manner consistent with the "folkish" principles of Social Darwinist racism. This popular realization would only be possible, however, once the nation had liberated itself from all forms of Christianity, which were opposed to the nation in principle, and become educated in accordance with what Ludendorff called a "nationally inherent experience of God," an *arteigenes Gotterleben*. Only in this way could a "healthy national soul" develop.

Reduced to its basics, the total war of the future would be a war of total national unity. The mobilization of all resources would take place at the outset, according to the principle of all or nothing; the war would be an existential, life-and-death struggle conducted without regard for any domestic or external consequences.[21] If this war were lost, the nation would be lost. "In the face of a morally strong nation," he wrote, "the military decision can come alone in victory on the battlefield and in the annihilation of the enemy's own morally steeled armed forces and his morally unified people."[22] The unspoken conclusion was that, despite defeat in World War I, the German nation had remained morally strong; this conclusion was the same as Hitler's at the end of his own career. If the nation were not strong, it deserved to perish.

LUDENDORFF'S FOLLOWERS

The misperceptions and misconceptions of the defeated general reflected a need to justify his own actions during the First World War. Similar or identical beliefs were more remarkable in the next generation of German officers. Younger officers could well have drawn favorable attention to themselves

21 Ibid., 49.   22 Ibid., 106.

by criticizing the leadership during the First World War; one might also have expected them to analyze subsequent military developments without prejudice. But on the subject of total war in the future, a vociferous group of young German officers defied this expectation. Like Ludendorff, they were captivated by a narrow conception of total war, but their hour arrived only under the Nazis – and then in contexts that they themselves had not anticipated.

During the early postwar years, the German military was occupied with civil war in Germany and the consequences of the country's forced disarmament. Only by the mid-1920s had the reconsolidation of the army proceeded to the point where long-range planning could begin. A plan for German rearmament was now developed that provided the blueprint for rebuilding the Wehrmacht after 1933.[23] At the same time, the economic foundations of warfare were studied anew in light of the experiences of the First World War.

A group of German social scientists was commissioned by the Carnegie Endowment to study the economic and social consequences of the war.[24] Their object was to study the origins of the war and hence to help lay the foundations of a durable peace. Given the realities of industrial war, these authors demonstrated that Germany had had no chance of winning. In 1932, Adolf Caspary concluded independently that Germany had been incapable of waging any kind of war.[25] The findings of these authors remained without the intended effect, however, insofar as they conflicted with the objectives of the National Socialist regime. Paradoxically, the significance of their studies lay in the use to which they were put after 1933, when they guided the effort to repair the very weaknesses that they had analyzed and to restore Germany's capacity to wage war.

Because the Versailles Treaty forbade German rearmament, the leadership of the Reichswehr established a cover organization called the Statistical Society. Its purpose was to conduct a survey of all firms in Germany that were of potential use in war production.[26] This organization then became the core of the army leadership's economic staff. "From the first day on, the

23 Carl Dirks and Karl-Heinz Janssen, *Der Krieg der Generäle: Hitler als Werkzeug der Wehrmacht* (Berlin, 1999).

24 Among the most influential were Friedrich Aereboe, *Der Einfluss des Krieges auf die landwirtschaftliche Produktion in Deutschland* (Stuttgart, 1927); August Skalweit, *Die deutsche Kriegsernährungswirtschaft* (Stuttgart, 1927); Otto Goebel, *Deutschlands Rohstoffwirtschaft im Weltkriege* (Stuttgart, 1930).

25 Adolf Caspary, *Wirtschaftsstrategie und Kriegführung: Wirtschaftliche Vorbereitung, Führung und Auswirkung des Krieges im geschichtlichen Abriss* (Berlin, 1932).

26 Georg Thomas, *Geschichte der deutschen Wehr- und Rüstungswirtschaft (1918–1943/45)*, ed. Wolfgang Birkenfeld (Boppard, 1966).

economic staff was animated by the thought that a future war would be a long one, and that armament must comprehend all measures calculated to help endure a long war."[27] In order to popularize this proposition in both the army and the broader public, the office undertook far-reaching activities under its chief, Colonel (later General) Georg Thomas. These included a wide range of publications once German rearmament was announced in 1935. In fact, a glut of literature on "defense science" (*Wehrwissenschaft*) and the "economics of national defense" (*Wehrwirtschaftswissenschaft*) was then published, and its basic purpose was to help prepare for a total war.[28]

The economic staff also founded and promoted the German Society for Defense Policy and Defense Science (*Deutsche Gesellschaft für Wehrpolitik und Wehrwissenschaften*) and, as a section of the same organization, the Working Group on the Economics of Defense (*Arbeitsgemeinschaft Wehrwirtschaft*). Along with Thomas, two officers set the tone: Kurt Hesse and Heinrich Hunke. Hesse, who was one of the most productive propagandists of *Wehrwirtschaft*, edited the "Studies in Research and Training in the Economics of War" (*Schriften zur kriegswirtschaftlichen Forschung und Schulung*).[29] Thomas reported that most of his own work was propagandistic in nature. In the short period before the outbreak of war, he claimed, he had familiarized leaders of the economy, as well as important sections of the civilian administration and the military, with the problems of a modern war economy.[30] He failed to convince them, however, of his own views on the economics of war and defense.[31] He remained a propagandist and admonisher – a Cassandra warning of the grave problems of organizing a war economy. When the regime did decide to begin organizing for total war, Thomas was relieved of his position, and most of his office was thereupon integrated into Albert Speer's ministry.[32]

The principal function of these institutions thus remained propaganda. In their area of real competence, which was the organization of the war economy, they were unsuccessful. Those who advocated total war agreed with the earlier scholars of the First World War that Germany's resources were limited. Hence they, too, emphasized skillful propaganda as the means

---

27 Ibid., 87.
28 Jutta Sywottek, *Mobilmachung für den totalen Krieg: Die propagandistische Vorbereitung der deutschen Bevölkerung auf den zweiten Weltkrieg* (Opladen, 1976); Martin Kutz, "Wirtschafts- und Sozialgeschichte in beiden Weltkriegen: Literaturbericht aus geschichtswissenschaftlicher Sicht und Bibliographie," in Lutz Köllner and Martin Kutz, *Wirtschaft und Gesellschaft in beiden Weltkriegen* (Munich, 1980).
29 Sywotteck, 92–3.   30 Thomas, 89.
31 Ibid., 82.
32 Ibid., 538; cf. Gregor Janssen, *Das Ministerium Speer: Deutschlands Rüstung im Krieg* (Berlin, 1968), 49–55.

to create loyal followers and a willingness to bear sacrifices. In 1936, the journal *Wissen und Wehr* addressed the question of agriculture, the sector of the war economy that had first broken down during the First World War. Given the impossibility of feeding the German people through domestic production alone, the journal formulated the problem in these terms: "How can suitable means of psychological influence be devised to restructure the feeding of our nation, so that Germany becomes autarchic in its food supply? And in what direction must the psychological means be sought to achieve such a necessary restructuring in wartime without injuring the morale of the masses?"[33]

These kinds of considerations had long been on the agenda of the War Ministry's Psychological Laboratory. The trauma of 1918, the decline in morale of the German troops, and the revolution provided the impetus for research in this area. It also governed the thinking not only of military agencies but also of the Nazi leadership until the end of the Second World War.[34]

This trauma was also one of the most important brakes on preparing for total war. Anxieties about overburdening the German people and provoking a second revolution remained a major cautionary and moderating consideration in all discussions of "total mobilization." Here lay one of the reasons for Thomas's failure to persuade others of his vision of total war. He neglected two decisive problems. He overlooked the objective limits of Germany's productive capacities (as did nearly all of Ludendorff's followers), and he thought that total mobilization could itself solve the problem of production. But his concept of total mobilization took no note of the limits on what the population could be expected to bear. His basic criticism of German preparations for war was that armament in breadth, as he put it, was being given priority over armament in depth.[35] This claim gave insufficient credit, however, to enormous investments in the industrial infrastructure that the war made necessary in order to compensate for the weaknesses in the economy. Investments were particularly massive in the chemical sector – in the production of explosives and synthetic rubber as well as in hydrogenation plants – and in the armament plants that were completed after 1942.[36] Thomas overlooked entirely the reorientation of German agriculture to war production, which at least until 1944 prevented

---

33 *Wissen und Wehr*, 3 (1936): 764.   34 Sywottek, 64–72.
35 Georg Thomas, "Tiefe und Breite der Rüstung," *Militärwissenschaftliche Rundschau* 2 (1937): 189–97.
36 Werner Abelshauser, "Germany: Guns, Butter, and Economic Miracles," in Mark Harrison, ed., *The Economics of World War II: Six Great Powers in International Comparison* (Cambridge, 1998), 154–7.

a repeat of the kind of catastrophic hunger that Germany had experienced during the First World War.[37]

Thomas and other authors agreed with Ludendorff that economic exertions would have the desired effect only if accompanied by dictatorship and the total moral solidarity of the nation. Hence these authors, too, accorded propaganda a central place in their calculations.

GOEBBELS AND TOTAL WAR: THE SPEECH AND ITS IMPACT

Goebbels had begun to advocate the radicalization of the German war effort well before 1943. All of his activities in this area came, however, in reaction to military crises. During the crisis of the Russian campaign in the winter of 1941–42, he undertook an initiative in which the term "total war" surfaced. The initiative foundered on the opposition of Göring and Hitler, both of whom at the time feared the implications of radicalizing the war effort.[38]

In the fall of 1942, particularly after the Russian counteroffensive at Stalingrad on November 19, Goebbels took up the need for radicalization in discussions with Speer. After the German failure to relieve the Russian siege of Stalingrad, it became clear to him that the transition to total war was unavoidable. Along with Speer, Walter Funk, Martin Bormann, Heinrich Lammers, and Wilhelm Keitel, he then prepared a directive, which Hitler signed on January 13, 1943.[39] This document reflected the naïve idea that one could achieve a strategic turning point – and ultimately military victory – by raising an additional 500,000–800,000 soldiers. The directive also envisaged a triumvirate to lead this grand effort. To his great disappointment, however, Goebbels himself was not among the triumvirate when its membership was announced on January 18. Two days later, this same body rejected his suggestions about radicalizing the war effort. Two days thereafter, however, Goebbels visited Hitler and emerged with a "complete victory."[40] Hitler had flattered Goebbels, claiming that he needed his propaganda minister as the "motor" of total war and that he had excluded Goebbels from the triumvirate in order to free him from bureaucratic constraints. Goebbels embraced the idea that he was to be the "motor" of the total war effort. And because he reasoned that the whole undertaking would be possible only if the apparatus, which he himself led, maintained the morale of the people,

---

37 Martin Kutz, "Kriegserfahrung und Kriegsvorbereitung: Die agrarwirtschaftliche Vorbereitung des Zweiten Weltkrieges in Deutschland vor dem Hintergrund der Weltkrieg I-Erfahrung," *Zeitschrift für Agrargeschichte und Agrarsoziologie* 32 (1984): 59–82, 135–64.

38 Ralf Georg Reuth, *Goebbels* (Munich and Zurich, 1990), 500.

39 Ibid., 512.   40 *Tagebücher*, 7: 160–72.

Goebbels also insisted that his own operations should be exempt from the control of the triumvirate.[41]

Two weeks later, on February 8, 1942, Hitler revealed what he really thought about total war. In a speech to the Gauleiters in Posen, he declared that the "crisis is not material but psychological." Therefore, the effort would require only shutting down nonessential newspapers and elegant restaurants.[42]

This was the political context in which Goebbels worked. Because Hitler refused to do it, he himself had first to announce the politically devastating German defeat at Stalingrad and then to prevent the collapse of popular morale. He had already spoken out, as Hitler's deputy, on January 30, 1943, in a way that anticipated the total war speech. On the anniversary of the Nazi seizure of power – the day on which the Führer himself normally celebrated both himself and the party – Goebbels made in substance the same points that marked out his speech in the Sport Palace some two weeks later.[43]

Much has been written about this speech and its impact.[44] Here it is appropriate to highlight the features of it that reflected Goebbels's ideas about the character of total war. The resemblance between his views and Ludendorff's was striking, even to the point of language. The banner above the podium at the Sport Palace itself announced a direct debt. Ludendorff had written that total war would be a short war. Goebbels's banner proclaimed: "Total War – The Shortest War." Goebbels certainly knew of Ludendorff's writings on the subject, although his diaries do not reveal a re-reading of these works on the eve of the speech.[45]

Like Ludendorff, Goebbels identified the Jews, specifically "Jewish bolshevism" and "Jewish plutocrats" in England and America, as the enemies of the German nation. Against them, he declared, the German people stood in political and moral solidarity. The Führer, the people, and the army were unified in their resolve. In this way alone could Europe be saved from the

41 Ibid., 177, 298. 42 Ibid., 290–1.
43 The speech is in Helmut Heiber, ed., *Goebbels-Reden 1939–1945* (2 vols., Düsseldorf, 1971–72), 2: 172–209.
44 Willi A. Boelcke, "Goebbels und die Kundgebung in Berliner Sportpalast vom 18. Februar 1943," *Jahrbuch für die Geschichte Mittel- und Ostdeutschlands* 19 (1970): 234–55; Ernest K. Bramsted, *Goebbels und die nationalsozialistische Propaganda 1925–1945* (Frankfurt, 1971); Helmut Heiber, *Joseph Goebbels*, 3rd ed. (Munich, 1988), 299–304; Ludolf Herbst, *Der totale Krieg und die Ordnung der Wirtschaft* (Stuttgart, 1982); Peter Longerich, "Joseph Goebbels und der totale Krieg," *Vierteljahreshefte für Zeitgeschichte* [hereafter VfZG] 35 (1987): 289–314; Günter Moltmann, "Goebbels Rede zum totalen Krieg am 18. Februar 1943," VfZG 12 (1964): 13–45; Ralf Georg Reuth, *Goebbels* (Munich, 1999), 491–524; Marlies G. Steinert, *Hitlers Krieg und die Deutschen* (Düsseldorf, 1970).
45 Cf. *Tagebücher*, I, 3: 322.

"assault from the steppes." Only the German army could accomplish this great task, so it was essential to mobilize all of Germany's might in support of it.

Goebbels portrayed himself in his diary as a demagogue in a good cause.[46] He wished to preserve political solidarity in the wake of Stalingrad. The will to increase the nation's exertions, the exploitation of all reserves of workers, including women, was supposed to make more men available for frontline duty. Exemptions from armed service were hence to be ruthlessly restricted. Goebbels proposed to ride roughshod over institutional and personal resistance and to broaden the realm of improvisation and terror. The end, the totalization of war, justified the means.

In view of the enormous political significance of the speech, it is striking that Goebbels did not mention the economy. He ignored the restructuring of the economy for total war – a fact that was all the more significant in light of the catalogue of other measures that he announced in the speech. For example, enterprises that were devoted to amusement, luxury restaurants, the retail trade in luxury goods, and the nonessential print media were all to be shut down. Even governmental offices were to be combed for men who were fit for frontline duty – a campaign that quickly became known popularly as "clawing after heroes" (*Heldenklau*).

The speech thus displayed the same misconceptions that had characterized the thinking of Ludendorff and his followers about modern industrialized war.[47] Goebbels, too, defined war as a struggle for survival and hence failed to reflect on strategy or political aims. Again, the topos of existential struggle functioned instead as a substitute for strategic thinking, which would have required rational analysis of military realities and would have revealed the futility of Germany's exertions – in fact, the political senselessness of the whole war. The speech – and Goebbels's diary – revealed no awareness of the fact that Germany was involved in a world war, in which the comparative warmaking capacities of the belligerents were the critical factor.

Goebbels believed that ruthless mobilization represented sufficient compensation for Germany's comparative disadvantages; and he understood mobilization to mean increased production of weapons and munitions as well as the "combing out" of civilian manpower for the army. He failed to understand the central interdependencies among economic capacity, social productivity, and political ends.

---

46 Ibid., II, 7: 336.
47 Martin Kutz, *Historische Voraussetzungen und theoretische Grundlagen strategischen Denkens* (Bremen, 2001).

Furthermore, Goebbels was himself regularly bridled in his attempts to realize this vision of radicalization. He had to fight every step of the way. He was given empty promises and bureaucratic positions that lacked authority as real power was distributed elsewhere.[48] Speer increasingly controlled the war economy, and he increased its productivity to an unexpected degree.[49] The vast reserves of female labor were not exploited, however, as Fritz Saukel instead organized millions of forced laborers.[50] The brutality of combat radicalized the army.[51] For Goebbels, there remained only the role of "motor," the propagandist of endurance or – in his own terminology – the tribune of national solidarity among Führer, people, and army.

Goebbels and the other propagandists of total war were systematically frustrated in their efforts to achieve their vision. Nonetheless, the Second World War did in fact become, at least in Germany, a total war. This paradox requires an explanation. In the first place, military developments provoked the radicalization of warfare in Germany; otherwise, defeat was unavoidable. This radicalization was directly related to military crises that threatened the entire war effort, such as the defeat at Stalingrad, the subsequent collapse of the central sector of the eastern front, and the Allied landings in Italy and France.

That the German war economy underwent enormous mobilization and achieved a prodigious increase in production is beyond dispute.[52] This achievement was due less, however, to the kind of mobilization that Ludendorff and Goebbels had envisaged than to the fact that after 1942, increasing numbers of plants were brought into production that had been under construction for years. Construction of a large portion of these plants had in fact begun before the outbreak of war.[53] Between 1936 and 1945, capital investment in war production increased some 75 percent (calculated for German territories as of 1939), while strategic bombing resulted in only a 17 percent loss in industrial capacity over the same period.[54] Even in 1944, though, German industry had not converted to dual-shift production, so industrial capacity remained far from fully exploited.[55] Furthermore, the new

48 Helmut Heiber, *Joseph Goebbels* (Munich, 1988), 263–88.
49 Janssen, *Ministerium Speer.*
50 Ulrich Herbert, *Fremdarbeiter: Politik und Praxis des "Ausländer-Einsatzes" in der Kriegswirtschaft des Dritten Reiches* (Bonn, 1999).
51 Omer Bartov, *Hitler's Army: Soldiers, Nazis and War in the Third Reich* (New York, 1992); Klaus Latzel, *Deutsche Soldaten – nationalsozialistischer Krieg? Kriegserlebnis – Kriegserfahrung 1939–1945* (Paderborn, 1998); Hamburger Institut für Sozialforschung, *Verbrechen der Wehrmacht: Dimensionen des Vernichtungskrieges 1941–1944* (Hamburg, 2002).
52 Abelshauser, "Germany," 124–5; Dietrich Eichholtz, *Geschichte der deutschen Kriegswirtschaft 1939/45* (3 vols., Berlin, 1984–96).
53 Abelshauser, 156.   54 Ibid., 167–8.
55 Ibid., 156.

industrial plants were set up for modern mass production and thus provided the technological means for far greater output than the industrial firms of prewar Germany, most of which were organized along artisanal lines.[56] Increased production was thus but marginally related to the intentions of those who advocated total war.

LEARNING FROM HISTORY

If one compares the German effort during the First and Second World Wars, one discovers fundamental differences. Particularly if one incorporates into the comparison the systematic preparations for war that began in 1934, it is striking how differently the Germans proceeded in many separate sectors.

In the first place, the discussion of tactical and operational innovation began in the 1920s. At the same time, the possibility of employing new technologies was introduced into the planning process.[57] While leading German soldiers continued to see the army of the future as an improved and better-armed version of the army of 1918, other officers, such as Heinz Guderian, were thinking in terms of a new force that would feature armored formations. To a large extent, these officers got their way. Horrible memories of stalemate and great battles of attrition provided the most important impetus to planning for a mobile war in the future. The development of an air force figured large in the attendant modernization of the German armed forces. The principle that the infantry was the "queen of the service-arms" lived on, but the new weapons systems were decisive, as were the new ideas about their operational employment.

The same can be said of efforts to plan for the war economy. In the First World War, the procurement of war-related goods had taken place initially within a liberal market economy, for there had been no peacetime economic preparations whatsoever.[58] Between 1934 and 1939, by contrast, during peacetime rearmament, the regime resorted to control of foreign exchange, while the Four-Year Plan introduced systematic economic preparation for war, which involved rationalization and centralized distribution, while investment was likewise steered to war-related ends.[59] All the preparations were admittedly insufficient for the war that followed, but the investments,

---

56 Ibid., 163.
57 Jehuda L. Wallach, *Das Dogma der Vernichtungsschlacht* (Frankfurt, 1967), 304–50.
58 Lothar Burchardt, *Friedenswirtschaft und Kriegsvorsorge: Deutchlands wirtschaftliche Rüstungsbestrebungen vor 1914* (Boppard, 1968).
59 Eichholz, *Kriegswirtschaft*, 1: 13–63.

most of which yielded results in war production only in the second half of the conflict, made possible the great productive increases that underlay perceptions that Germany was waging a total war.[60]

The British blockade had put intense pressures on Germany's supplies of raw materials during the First World War. In preparation for the Second World War, the regime resolved to draw imports to the greatest extent possible from the "area under the influence of German weapons" in central and southern Europe.[61] In addition, a whole new branch of industry was built up in anticipation of a renewed blockade. Its highlights were the production of synthetic rubber and other artificial materials and the construction of hydrogenation plants to produce fuels and raw materials for the chemical industry.[62]

During the First World War, a completely misconceived policy had destroyed the productive foundations of German agriculture and had exacerbated the effects of the blockade to catastrophic dimensions. After 1934, by contrast, the reorientation of German agriculture toward war began in earnest, and it resulted in a workable system during the war.[63] It provided the basis for feeding the German population adequately until the end of 1944; it also rested however, on the ruthless plundering of the occupied areas, which suffered the kind of hunger in the Second World War that Germans themselves had endured after 1915 during the First World War.[64]

This catalogue of changes could be extended at length. Whether it was a question of using forced foreign labor, systematic terror, or the extermination of the Jews, these measures all reflected in one way or another a process of learning from the experience of the First World War. The recruitment of forced labor had failed during the First World War because of resistance from Belgian workers. The consequence during the Second World War was a policy of using terror to compel laborers to work. Agitation against the Jews during the First World War metamorphosed in the Third Reich first into systematic persecution, then into extermination during the Second World

60 Abelshauser, 146.
61 Heinz-Erich Volkmann, "Die NS-Wirtschaft in Vorbereitung des Krieges," in Wilhelm Deist, et al., *Ursachen und Voraussetzungen der deutschen Kriegspolitik* (Stuttgart, 1979), 177–368; Eckart Teichert, *Autarkie und Grossraumwirtschaft in Deutschland: Aussenwirtschaftspolitische Konzeptionen zwischen Wirtschaftskriese und Zweitem Weltkrieg* (Munich, 1984).
62 Dieter Petzina, *Autarkiepolitik im Dritten Reich: Der nationalsozialistische Vierjahresplan* (Stuttgart, 1968); Wolfgang Birkenfeld, *Der synthetische Treibstoff 1933–1945* (Frankfurt, 1964).
63 Joachim Lehmann, "Die deutsche Landwirtschaft im Krieg," in Eichholtz, 2: 570–644.
64 Christian Gerlach, *Kalkulierte Morde: Die deutsche Wirtschafts- und Vernichtungspolitik in Weissrussland 1941–1944* (Hamburg, 1999); cf. Timothy Patrick Mulligan, *The Politics of Illusion and Empire: German Occupation Policy in the Soviet Union, 1942–1943* (New York, 1988).

War. The process of persecution itself gradually radicalized in the course of the war, culminating in mass killings in a factory-like manner. In all of these cases, reflection on failure during the First World War was decisive in the search for "rational improvements" during the Second. In each case, radicalization was first intellectual, then practical. In no case, however, was the change linked to conscious or systematic preparation for total war.[65] The planning and intellectual experimentation was, as a rule, less radical than the actions undertaken during the war. Radicalization – and rationalization, for that matter – came during the war with little coordination or cohesion; it came instead in reaction to specific events and the specific challenges of war. A coherent plan for the war effort as a whole, to say nothing of a total war, did not exist.

Instead, analysis of the sources of error during the First World War took place autonomously in parts of the military, economic, social, and political sectors. Experts in each sector worked toward improving the wartime performance of their own institutions. There was, however, no comprehensive concept, no war plan, no strategy. The military and the politicians merely planned campaigns and formulated general instructions, such as those that Hitler issued in 1936, when he decreed that Germany must be ready for war within four years.

The discussion of total war in Germany remained talk before 1939. It did not determine the subsequent course of events. Ludendorff's book represented an effort of self-justification for failure during the First World War, although he also attempted to mask this failure. His other aim was to promote political propaganda for folkish-racist Germany. He imagined himself as Germany's warlord during the next war, the head of dictatorially led *Volksgemeinschaft* (a term that did not appear in his tract on total war). Goebbels's vision differed only in its practical goal. He wanted not to rationalize failure, but to prevent it, albeit with misconceived and inadequate means. Otherwise, he and Ludendorff bore a remarkable resemblance.

The practical effects of these discussions of total war lay not in what they intended, but rather in the way they strengthened a general tendency toward loosening the hold of traditional ethical standards on thinking and action, and toward optimizing what was technically feasible. At the same time, the topos of struggle for survival provided a well-tested means to

---

65 For another example, see Claudia Koonz, *Mothers in the Fatherland: Women, the Family, and Nazi Politics* (London, 1988); Birthe Kundrus, *Kriegerfrauen: Familienpolitik und Geschlechterverhältnisse im Ersten und Zweiten Weltkrieg* (Hamburg, 1995); Dörte Winkler, *Frauenarbeit im "Dritten Reich"* (Hamburg, 1977).

lay the emotional groundwork for the radicalization of war and to loosen moral restraints on violence. The ideological premise that war represented a struggle for survival thus released strategic and political actors from the constraints of rational analysis, which would have demonstrated the sense-lessness of this vision of total war and war aims that it prescribed – indeed, the senselessness of the war itself.

11

The Home Front in "Total War"

Women in Germany and Britain in the Second World War

JILL STEPHENSON

In the aftermath of the German VIth Army's defeat at Stalingrad, the Nazi Propaganda Minister, Joseph Goebbels, asked members of an invited audience at the Berlin Sportpalast on February 18, 1943, if, to achieve final victory, they now wanted "total war." The eighth of his ten questions on this theme was: "Do you, and especially you, the women, want the government to ensure that German women, too, devote all their energy to waging the war, by filling jobs wherever possible to free men for action and thus helping their men at the front?"[1] The first implication of this is that, apparently, in the fourth winter of the war, Germany was not pursuing "total war"; the second is that German women were not fully participating in the war effort. By contrast, Britain was the first "civilized nation" to introduce labor conscription for women: "[i]n conscripting women, Britain went further than any other nation . . . far further than Hitler's Germany";[2] "only the Soviet Union outdid Britain in exploiting the potential of female labour."[3] While these orthodoxies have been challenged in recent years, nevertheless the impression has been cherished that British women made far more of a contribution to their home front than did German women. Yet it was in Germany that the theory of total war was most thoroughly developed in the interwar years, as a result of the belief that, in the First World War, a successful German army had been "stabbed in the back" by the home front – specifically, by socialists, Jews, and women – a home front which had collapsed under pressure of shortages of food, in particular, and

I am indebted to Jeremy A. Crang, University of Edinburgh, for reading the conference paper on which this essay is based and offering invaluable insights and advice on points of detail.

1 Wolfgang Michalka (ed.), *Das Dritte Reich, Band 2: Weltmachtanspruch und nationaler Zusammenbruch 1939–1945* (Munich, 1985), 297.
2 Angus Calder, *The People's War. Britain 1939–1945* (London, 1971), 308, 382.
3 Robert Mackay, *The Test of War. Inside Britain 1939–1945* (London, 1999), 77.

which had not been sufficiently mobilized to give the fighting forces the support that they needed.[4]

Total war was conceived of not merely as the rational utilization of all resources, both material and human, for the waging of a successful war. It also involved the ideological mobilization of the population, requiring the commitment, enthusiasm, and sacrifice of the entire nation. Accordingly, total war also – apparently paradoxically – meant that it was legitimate, and at times necessary, to divert some resources away from the purely military and economic spheres in order to ensure that, for example, popular opinion was monitored and official propaganda was geared to combating fears, rumors, and defeatism.[5] As Nazi Germany had the SS's Sicherheitsdienst (Security Service) and several other surveillance organizations, so Britain had Mass Observation, a social survey organization founded in 1937, as well as the Home Intelligence Reports compiled by the Ministry of Information.[6] In both countries, censorship was imposed, the dissemination of news was manipulated, and propaganda was issued; on the whole, however, this was a break with peacetime practice for Britons but a continuation of it for Germans. Other aspects of total war had affected Germans but not Britons in peacetime: for example, in Germany there had been attempts to regiment consumption well before the war as part of the 1936 Four-Year Plan's strategy of autarky. In wartime, this was introduced in Britain and intensified in Germany.[7] In both countries, the modern media of radio and film were used for both propaganda and entertainment purposes. These media could provide escapist entertainment which boosted morale, and they could also

4 Tim Mason, *Social Policy in the Third Reich. The Working Classes and the 'National Community'* (Providence and Oxford, 1993), ch. 1, "The Legacy of 1918 for National Socialism," 19–40; N. P. Howard, "The Social and Political Consequences of the Allied Food Blockade of Germany, 1918–19," *German History*, vol. 11, no. 2 (June 1993): 161–88; Ute Daniel, *Arbeiterfrauen in der Kriegsgesellschaft* (Göttingen, 1989).

5 On "total war," see Peter Longerich, "Joseph Goebbels und der totale Krieg. Ein unbekannte Denkschrift des Propagandaministers vom 18. Juli 1944," *Vierteljahrshefte für Zeitgeschichte*, 35 (1987): 290–92.

6 Marlis G. Steinert, *Hitler's War and the Germans*, ed. and tr. Thomas E. J. De Witt (Athens, OH, 1977), 2, 14–17; Andrew Thorpe, "Britain," in Jeremy Noakes (ed.), *The Civilian in War. The Home Front in Europe, Japan and the USA in World War II* (Exeter, 1992), 16–17; information from Jeremy A. Crang.

7 Nancy R. Reagin, "*Marktordnung* and Autarkic Housekeeping: Housewives and Private Consumption under the Four-Year Plan, 1936–39," *German History*, vol. 19, no. 2 (2001): 162–84; Jill Stephenson, "Propaganda, Autarky and the German Housewife," in David Welch (ed.), *Nazi Propaganda. The Power and the Limitations* (London and Totowa, 1983), 117–42; Kate Lacey, "Driving the Message Home: Nazi Propaganda in the Private Sphere," in Lynn Abrams & Elizabeth Harvey (eds.), *Gender Relations in German History. Power, Agency and Experience from the Sixteenth to the Twentieth Century* (London, 1996), 189–210; Ina Zweiniger-Bargielowska, *Austerity in Britain. Rationing, Controls, and Consumption, 1939–1955* (Oxford, 2000).

vividly relay government-sponsored messages to people, either when they were gathered together in a cinema or else when they were at home. In 1939, there were 9 million licensed radio sets in Britain and 12.5 million in Germany, where 70 percent of households had a radio; few households in Britain were without a radio.[8] As in peacetime, women comprised the majority of daytime listeners, and, accordingly, the Nazi women's organization dispensed advice about recipes over the air, while similarly in Britain *The Kitchen Front* was a daily bulletin "packed with advice on stretching the food rations, tips on 'best buys,' recipes."[9]

Reaching virtually the entire population through modern media was one facet of the "total" nature of this war. It also reflected the extent to which this was the most modern war that could have been fought at the time, with – especially from 1941 – virtually all of the world's most advanced industrial powers as participants. Accordingly, there was an attempt in belligerent countries to mobilize as much of the population as possible for war-related tasks as tens of millions of men were conscripted into the armed forces during the course of the war worldwide. Thus, the balance of the civilian population was altered – even distorted – with the home front consisting disproportionately of women, children, and older men. Building on their experience in the First World War, belligerent countries in the Second World War endeavored to utilize the energies of women in particular for a multiplicity of tasks both on the home front and in support of the fighting front. But only in the Red Army were women involved in direct military combat; some 800,000 women – as about 8 percent of service personnel – had been recruited by the end of 1943, and some of them saw active service at the front, for example as snipers.[10] Even so, in the Soviet Union "women's most immediately vital contribution to the war effort was as labour."[11] And in Germany, last-ditch plans by Bormann in February 1945 to form a "women's battalion" of the Wehrmacht came to nothing.[12] For major participants like Germany and Britain, while women were prohibited

---

8 Calder, *People's War*, 413; Mackay, *Test*, 183–85, 190 n. 27; Kate Lacey, *Feminine Frequencies. Gender, German Radio, and the Public Sphere, 1923–1945* (Ann Arbor, MI, 1996), 102; Z.A.B. Zeman, *Nazi Propaganda* (London, 1964), 51–52, 116; David Welch, *Propaganda and the German Cinema, 1933–1945* (Oxford, 1983), 186–306.

9 Stephenson, "Propaganda, Autarky," 134; Mackay, *Test*, 185.

10 Reina Pennington, "Offensive Women: Women in Combat in the Red Army," in Paul Addison & Angus Calder (eds.), *Time to Kill. The Soldier's Experience of War in the West, 1939–1945* (London, 1997), 249–59.

11 See John Barber's contribution to this volume.

12 Louise Willmot, "The debate on the introduction of an Auxiliary Military Service Law for women in the Third Reich and its consequences, August 1944–April 1945," *German History*, vol. 2 (1985): 10–20.

from firing antiaircraft guns,[13] they might serve as military auxiliaries, for example as aircraft spotters, as drivers or nurses, or on antiaircraft batteries. In Britain, women operated barrage balloons.[14] In these roles, "[t]he most important point about female service was that it freed men for more important tasks, namely combat."[15] Otherwise, as in the USSR, women's most useful function would be to replace conscripted men in civilian roles.

Sometimes this offered women opportunities from which they had previously been excluded, whether by legislation or by custom and discrimination. The governments of both Germany and Britain therefore faced a conundrum: how – and how far – could they involve women in the war effort without compromising prevailing gender roles? The crises in which each of these countries found itself at different points in the war provided the answer: women were to be deployed to meet the country's needs *wherever* necessary, with the single proviso that combat forces remained masculine, because women "could never be more than *ersatz* soldiers."[16] But there was no suggestion from the governments of either Germany or Britain that this was being done as a matter of principle; nor was it intended that the opening of opportunities which had been closed to women should be irreversible.[17] Yet there was a principle involved: in a total war in which the very survival of the nation was at stake, the totality of the population had to be involved in its defense, in however small a way.[18] This was a more explicit demand in the Second World War than in the First, largely because the use of airpower for the extensive bombing of civilian targets put noncombatants in areas far behind the fighting zones potentially in the frontline. It also multiplied the number of essential tasks on the home front: for example, air-raid protection and relief work among the bombed-out required human as well as material resources.[19]

On the face of it, in the era of the Second World War Germany and Britain present many similarities in terms of their socioeconomic structures. In particular, they were two of the most highly industrialized and technologically

---

13 On Germany, I am grateful to Gerhard Weinberg for this information; on Britain, Gerard J. De Groot, "Lipstick on her Nipples, Cordite in her Hair: Sex and Romance among British Servicewomen during the Second World War," in Gerard J. De Groot & Corinna Peniston-Bird, *A Soldier and a Woman. Sexual Integration in the Military* (London, 2000), 116.
14 I am grateful to Gerhard Weinberg for this point.
15 Gerard J. De Groot, "Introduction," in De Groot & Peniston-Bird, *A Soldier*, 16.
16 Gerard J. De Groot, "'I Love the Scent of Cordite in Your Hair': Gender Dynamics in Mixed Anti-Aircraft Batteries during the Second World War," *History*, vol. 82, no. 265 (1997): 92.
17 Thorpe, "Britain," 20; Martin Pugh, *Women and the Women's Movement in Britain, 1914–1959* (London, 1992), 264; Mackay, *Test*, 222.
18 On how this '[military] participation ratio' could affect social structures, see Arthur Marwick, *War and Social Change in the Twentieth Century* (London, 1974), 10, 22–23 n.11, 223.
19 Eleanor Hancock, *National Socialist Leadership and Total War 1941–45* (New York, 1991), 160.

advanced countries in the world, and both geared their wartime industrial production overwhelmingly toward the war effort.[20] Both used technological expertise to produce more accurate lethal weapons and increasingly sophisticated defense, surveillance, and communications equipment. Mainland Britain did not suffer invasion and occupation, and Germany experienced these only in the last few months of the war. But both countries sustained heavy aerial bombardment, and in both, children and also some women were evacuated from urban centers – the main bombing targets – to the safer countryside. Prisoners of war (POWs) were held in both countries for years at a time, and they were often set to work during their captivity, sometimes alongside native civilians, including women. There were shortages, rationing, and a black market in both countries, while citizens experienced the disruption of urban life, in particular, with bombing damaging or entirely destroying houses, schools, businesses, utilities, and transportation systems. In both, some normal social activities were curtailed or even abandoned altogether.[21]

But, beyond the similarities, there were also marked contrasts. Most obviously, the British parliamentary system was distinctively different from the one-party dictatorship established under Hitler from 1933. Second, while the traditional British class system meant that deep divisions persisted within British society, and while nonviolent xenophobia and anti-Semitism were widely regarded as unobjectionable in Britain, there was nothing there to compare with the persecutory racist system that was fully entrenched in Nazi Germany by 1939. Certainly, many in Britain believed that the continuing existence of the British Empire indicated that the "island race" was superior to all others, and the treatment of Britain's colonial subjects was often discriminatory and demeaning. Further, Britain's internment of "enemy aliens" – many of them refugees from Fascism or Nazism – during the war was a crass, if transient, exercise, which one Conservative member of Parliament described as "this bespattered page of our history."[22] Nevertheless, the systematic identification of perceived "racial enemies" within the German population, and their marginalization, persecution, and murder, were unlike anything in British society: that is, within Germany there were groups of native civilians who had transgressed no conventional criminal law but

---

20 Richard Overy, "'Blitzkriegwirtschaft'? Finanzpolitik, Lebensstandard und Arbeitseinsatz in Deutschland 1939–1942," *Vierteljahrshefte für Zeitgeschichte*, 36 (1988): 389–435; Alan S. Milward, *War, Economy and Society 1939–1945* (London, 1987), 58–59.
21 Calder, *People's War*, 74, 423–24; Gerda Szepansky, *'Blitzmädel,' 'Heldenmutter,' 'Kriegerwitwe.' Frauenleben im Zweiten Weltkrieg* (Frankfurt am Main, 1986), 26–27.
22 Calder, *People's War*, 66, 150–53 (quotation on 152), 192–93, 574–77; Mackay, *Test*, 96–101; information from Jeremy A. Crang.

who suffered physical abuse – violence in concentration camps, sterilization, and/or "euthanasia" – as an integral part of government policy.[23] Third, in addition to POWs, civilians from countries occupied by Germany – especially Poland and the USSR – were encouraged, or, more often, co-erced into going to Germany to labor for the German war effort. Fourth, in Germany the agrarian sector remained significant, with 4.4 million women working in agriculture in 1933, many of whom were farmers' wives: in 1939, women accounted for 54.5 percent of the agricultural workforce.[24] By contrast, "the farmwife all but disappeared in England" in the interwar years, with women in agriculture accounting for only 1 or 2 percent of the total female workforce.[25]

These differences and similarities between the two countries did much to determine the conditions their female inhabitants experienced. But, beyond that, it was the course of the war that shaped the contrasts between the wartime experiences of German and British women. At its simplest, from the start – certainly from spring 1940 until into 1942 – Britain was in a state of dire emergency and Germany was seemingly invincible. But from mid-1943, Germany was increasingly in retreat and Britain was growing confident of victory. In addition, Britain endured its worst experience of bombing in 1940–41, with a further serious episode in June 1944, while German cities were bombed, with increasing severity, from 1940 to 1945 and suffered attacks of a far more destructive order, particularly from 1942 to 1945, than those inflicted on Britain. For example, in "Operation Gomorrha," the sustained fire-bombing of Hamburg for ten days in summer 1943, far more bombs were dropped than in the whole of the Blitz on Greater London in 1940–41.[26] The effects of these contrasting fortunes on civilian life and morale are incalculable. British women could harbor cautious optimism, in spite of wartime hardship, from 1943, whereas German women were increasingly disabused of their confidence in German offensive and defensive capabilities as both mortal danger and hardship intensified. As their country was invaded in 1944–45 and bombing raids continued, the plight of large

23 Michael Burleigh & Wolfgang Wippermann, *The Racial State. Germany 1933–1945* (Cambridge, 1991); Marion A. Kaplan, *Between Dignity and Despair. Jewish Life in Nazi Germany* (New York and Oxford, 1998); Wolfgang Benz, *The Holocaust. A Short History* (London, 2000).
24 Gustavo Corni & Horst Gies, *Brot, Butter, Kanonen. Die Ernährungswirtschaft in Deutschland unter der Diktatur Hitlers* (Berlin, 1997), 283; Overy, "'Blitzkriegswirtschaft'?" 428.
25 Anne-Marie Sohn, "Between the Wars in France and England," in Françoise Thébaud (ed.), *A History of Women*, vol. 5: "Toward a Cultural Identity in the Twentieth Century" (Cambridge, MA, and London, 1994), 93, 97. See also Sadie Ward, *War in the Countryside, 1939–1945* (London, 1988), 8–12.
26 Television film, *People's Century*, BBC1, 1995.

numbers of German women – quite apart from the incalculable suffering of targeted victims of the Nazi regime – was desperate.

Within this context of the varying and contrasting fortunes of war, women in both countries found their lives shaped by five features of a total war. First, huge conscript armies meant for many women the absence – temporarily or, potentially, permanently – of male family members who were conscripted into either the armed forces or essential industries. Second, the reciprocal of that was the presence of other men in their vicinity, including native and allied soldiers, POWs and, in Germany, foreign civilian workers. Third, total warfare involved the bombing of civilian targets, necessitating large-scale relief work and evacuation. Fourth, total economic warfare brought shortages, rationing, and a black market. Fifth, the conscription of men required the mobilization of women for the war effort in civilian employment, in work with the armed forces, and in voluntary work. The impact of these factors on women's lives varied within each of the two countries, depending on their personal circumstances. In particular, in Germany official treatment of those who were regarded as "valuable" was very different from the fate of those who were classified as "racial enemies." Nevertheless, there were clear broad similarities and differences in the ways in which British women on the one hand and "valuable" German women on the other were affected by some of these issues. Relationships with foreigners is one example where there were marked differences. But, contrary to much received opinion, there were probably more similarities than differences in the area of mobilization of women for the war effort.

The most obvious difference was that German men were likely to be absent, either fighting at the front or acting as occupation troops, in greater numbers and for rather longer than British men. Casualties reflected this: well over three million German men were killed, while British military deaths amounted to about one-tenth of that.[27] Thus, far more German than British women were left as widows – over one million – or as bereaved mothers, daughters, sisters, girlfriends. To alleviate some aspects of their distress, from November 1941 pregnant fiancées of men lost in battle were permitted to contract a "postmortem marriage" in Germany to legitimize their children. Over and above those whose deaths were reported, the numbers of German servicemen who were either POWs or missing were far greater than those of British servicemen, so that, in the later stages of the war

---

27 Martin Sorge, *The Other Price of Hitler's War* (Westport, CT, 1986), 23; Arthur Marwick, *Britain in the Century of Total War. War, Peace and Social Change 1900–1967* (London, 1968), 259.

and the early peacetime years, large numbers of German women were, for practical purposes, single.[28] While there was particular anxiety among British women whose menfolk were involved in the conflicts in North Africa, in the Middle East or Far East, or in the air war, their numbers were relatively small, and large numbers of British conscripts remained in the tedious safety of training in Britain until mid-1944.[29] With the absence of men from families and households for lengthy periods, unfamiliar responsibilities, both familial and occupational, devolved onto women. This might mean that a wife had to try to run a family business – for example a shop, a service or, particularly in Germany, a small farm – whereas previously she had worked in it under her husband's direction, perhaps on a part-time basis.[30] Women were left to bring up children on their own and, particularly where mothers were working, levels of juvenile delinquency rose.[31] In Germany, members of the dissident youth groups of the "Edelweiss Pirates" were, according to Peukert, more likely than not to come from families where the father was dead.[32]

The separation in wartime of married couples, and also of unmarried sweethearts, imposed pressures on relationships which had previously seemed stable. This was particularly the case when there was an influx of men from other backgrounds and other countries into areas that had been denuded of native men to serve in the forces or in war industry elsewhere. Although there were no foreign occupation forces in mainland Britain at any time and none in Germany until late 1944, there were nevertheless troop movements, and the many native conscripts had to be accommodated in depots or camps within their home country before embarking on a campaign. In Britain, there were also around a half million foreign troops – including French, Dutch, and Poles – for most of the war; by D-Day in June 1944, there were almost a million and a half.[33] Many women found men in uniform a source of interest and diversion – and sometimes also a source of sexual infection. In Britain, rates of sexually transmitted diseases soared in 1941–42, while two-thirds of diseased women in Hamburg in 1942 were

28 Birthe Kundrus, *Kriegerfrauen. Familienpolitik und Geschlechterverhältnisse im Ersten und Zweiten Weltkrieg* (Hamburg, 1995); Elizabeth D. Heineman, *What Difference Does a Husband Make? Women and Marital Status in Nazi and Postwar Germany* (Berkeley and Los Angeles, 1999), 44, 47–48, 51.

29 Jeremy A. Crang, *The British Army and the People's War, 1939–1945* (Manchester, 2000), 2.

30 Calder, *People's War*, 369; Jill Stephenson, "'Emancipation' and Its Problems: War and Society in Württemberg, 1939–1945," *European History Quarterly*, vol. 17, no. 3 (1987): 352–61.

31 Marwick, *Britain in the Century*, 264; cf. Calder, *People's War*, 260; Steinert, *Hitler's War*, 221.

32 Detlev J. K. Peukert, *Inside Nazi Germany. Conformity, Opposition and Racism in Everyday Life*, tr. Richard Deveson (London, 1987), 163.

33 Marwick, *Britain in the Century*, 264; Calder, *People's War*, 355.

reckoned to have been infected by soldiers.[34] In Germany, evacuated urban women pining for the facilities of a town found diversion if an army unit was stationed nearby, and there was considerable official anxiety about the way in which teenage German girls frequented railway stations and other locations where soldiers in transit could be found.[35] Some German soldiers' wives were left as grass widows for months and more at a time, especially in the second half of the war, and, aware of stories about soldiers' infidelity either in Germany or on foreign soil, sought similar comfort for themselves. The authorities became increasingly concerned about this and finally, in 1942, introduced the crime of "insult of soldiers at the front," followed by the denial of family allowances to adulterous wives, and in March 1943 the "postmortem divorce" was introduced to deny the adulterous widow of a fallen soldier her widow's pension.[36]

Both Britain and Germany experienced – at different times – the conspicuous presence of American military personnel. Christabel Bielenberg commented on "the general air of health and well being, of affluence about" an American airman whom she encountered in Germany, and British women were impressed by the GIs' "uniforms of a superior cut and quality . . . their money and endless supply of small luxuries."[37] By the end of the war, the plight of urban German women was particularly acute, with utilities disrupted or destroyed and food barely obtainable. Some formed relationships with Allied – particularly American – soldiers to gain access to illicit rations or luxury goods, like chocolate or nylon stockings, that could either be enjoyed or else used to barter for food. The Americans in Heilbronn district (Württemberg) "soon had their 'lady friends,' particularly among loose women [evacuees] from Duisburg but also among chocolate-hungry Swabians [locals]."[38] In Britain, too, in the midst of wartime shortage, "[w]e were always very suspicious of females who had lovely Jacqmar scarves and nylon stockings. We reckoned they were a bit fast and were hobnobbing [with Americans] a little too freely."[39] But disapproval meant little to "young

---

34 Calder, *People's War*, 361; Heineman, *What Difference*, 54. See also Jeremy Noakes (ed.), *Nazism, 1919–1945*, volume 4: "The Home Front in World War II" (Exeter, 1998), 384–90.

35 Noakes, *Nazism*, 384–90; Jill Stephenson, *Women in Nazi Society* (London, 1975), 66, 68–69; Jill Stephenson, *Women in Nazi Germany* (London, 2001), 47, 102. See also Staatsarchiv Ludwigsburg (StAL), Sicherheitsdienst RFSS-SD-Leitabschnitt Stuttgart, K110, Bü48, SD Lagebericht, September 1, 1941, 43–48.

36 Kundrus, *Kriegerfrauen*, 391–93; Heineman, *What Difference*, 55–56.

37 Paul Fussell, *Wartime. Understanding and Behaviour in the Second World War* (New York and Oxford, 1989), 123; Ward, *War in the Countryside*, 108. See also Alison Owings, *Frauen. German Women Recall the Third Reich* (New Brunswick, NJ, 1994), 209.

38 Hauptstaatsarchiv Stuttgart (HStAS), J170, Bü8, Kreis Heilbronn, Gemeinde Hausen a.d.Z., n.d.

39 Quoted in Ward, *War in the Countryside*, 109.

women who, by lavishing their charms on the visitors, tapped into an apparently limitless source of cosmetics, nylons and chocolates."[40] Yet this conduct – and, perhaps even more, rumors and suspicions of it – could have serious effects on soldiers' morale. Crang shows how "the presence [in Britain] of large numbers of glamorous, well-paid Canadian and American troops created a good deal of anxiety on the part of British soldiers." The British army was so concerned about this that it enlisted welfare workers to try to mediate between estranged spouses before their marriage broke down irretrievably.[41] With the departure of the visitors, there were some "sighs of relief... and some single girls left with babies had cause to regret that they had ever come."[42]

While successful and relatively wealthy newcomers were magnetically attractive to lonely and deprived women, those less favorably placed could also be a source of social and sexual interest. German and Italian POWs in Britain struck up relationships with women who, contrary to official instruction, sometimes provided them with extra rations or other items. There were some sexual liaisons, but these were infrequent; POWs became numerous in Britain only from 1943, and while some were billeted on farming families, most were quite closely regimented, living in camps and subject to a curfew.[43] They were also probably less attractive because so many Allied – and particularly American – servicemen were present. By contrast, in Germany there were large numbers of POWs and foreign civilian workers from autumn 1939, reaching a peak of over seven million in 1944.[44] Many, especially Poles, Russians, and Ukrainians, were set to work in German agriculture, where they lived on family farms and, in the second half of the war, were often the only male workers there. Both the motive – attraction or a pragmatic assessment of the needs of the farm – and the opportunity were much more evident for German women than for British to embark on a sexual liaison with a foreigner in an ostensibly dependent position. But while British "service wives who... 'contemptibly' succumbed to Italian prisoners of war" faced "very intense moral odium,"[45] a German "Aryan" woman with a foreign lover was ritually humiliated and sometimes sent to a concentration camp. Until Hitler ordered a cessation of the practice in 1941, local Nazi Party activists might stage the public shaving of the woman's head

---

40 Mackay, *Test*, 183.
41 J. A. Crang, "The British Soldier on the Home Front: Army Morale Reports, 1940–45," in Addison & Calder, *Time to Kill*, 70–71.
42 Ward, *War in the Countryside*, 111.
43 Calder, *People's War*, 496; Ward, *War in the Countryside*, 111–14.
44 Ulrich Herbert, *Hitler's Foreign Workers* (Cambridge, 1997), 296–98.
45 Calder, *People's War*, 363.

before incarcerating her. Whereas in Britain, fraternization with POWs was an issue chiefly of loyalty and the maintenance of traditional sexual morality, in Germany, the regime's overriding racial priorities demanded Draconian punishment for "pollution of the blood."[46]

Whatever other hardships civilians had to face, the bombing of towns and ports inflicted the greatest terror and upheaval of all, although the Allied invasion of Germany in 1944–45 brought its own horrors, especially in the east. At first, bombing targeted airfields, ports, and industrial areas, but, on both sides, attacks soon concentrated on major conurbations, with the aim of killing and "dehousing" industrial workers, and terrorizing urban populations in order to break their morale and damage the enemy's war effort. For those on the ground, bombing meant terror and disruption. Survivors tried to continue with normal life, perhaps with little sleep for nights on end, as the air-raid sirens summoned them to cold and crowded shelters. In 1940–41, London sustained repeated heavy bombing raids, and towns like Coventry and Plymouth, among others, were severely damaged.[47] Between August 1940 and June 1941, two and a quarter million British people were made homeless by bombing.[48] But the growing superiority of the RAF over the Luftwaffe and, from 1942, the addition of USAF resources enabled the Allies to bomb German cities mercilessly.[49] Whereas in Britain a quarter of a million homes were destroyed in the six years of war, in Hamburg over a quarter of a million homes were demolished in "Operation Gomorrha" alone. By the end of the war, 902,000 Hamburgers had lost all their possessions through bombing, and a further 265,000 had lost part of their property.[50] In both countries, some citizens – in Plymouth and Nuremberg, for example – took to leaving the city at night, to avoid night-time bombing by seeking safety in nearby fields, and returning in the morning.[51]

In any country subjected to aerial bombardment, there were civilian refugees from both bombed-out areas and probable bombing targets. Some left home on their own initiative; others were compulsorily evacuated by government order. In general, urban factory workers were kept at their post,

---

46 Herbert, *Hitler's Foreign Workers*, 75–77.   47 Thorpe, 'Britain,' 22.
48 Jose Harris, "War and Social History: Britain and the Home Front during the Second World War," *Contemporary European History*, vol. 1, part 1 (1992): 22.
49 Sorge, *The Other Price*, 94–109; Roland Müller, *Stuttgart zur Zeit des Nationalsozialismus* (Stuttgart, 1988), 464–79; Neil Gregor, "A *Schicksalsgemeinschaft*? Allied Bombing, Civilian Morale, and Social Dissolution in Nuremberg, 1942–1945," *Historical Journal*, vol. 43, no. 4 (2000): 1051–70.
50 Harris, "War and Social History," 22; Ursula Büttner, *"Gomorrha": Hamburg im Bombenkrieg* (Hamburg, 1993), 26.
51 "People's Century," 1995; Gregor, "A *Schicksalsgemeinschaft*?" 1059–60.

and urban children, especially, were evacuated to the safer countryside. In Britain, one and a half million women and children were evacuated in the first few months after September 3, 1939, and altogether more than four million mothers and children were evacuated during the war.[52] In Germany, in autumn 1939 families were evacuated from the border areas with France, although they were able to return after the fall of France in June 1940.[53] From as early as 1940, there were also German social migrants, women who were wealthy enough to move to south German resorts, which were still safe from bombing and had smart hotels unaffected at first by rationing.[54] Other women who feared the bombing of towns in the north and west migrated to safer rural areas even before mass government-sponsored evacuation began in earnest from 1942, once Allied area bombing began to devastate towns and cities in industrial and port areas. Places like Berlin, Hamburg, and the Ruhr cities were hit hard and repeatedly; as a result, mothers and children, and even teachers and whole school classes, were relocated to rural areas in the south and east. By December 1942, almost a million mothers and children had been evacuated from cities to the countryside, and the numbers would only increase.[55] In all, perhaps ten million German women and children were evacuated by the end of the war.[56]

As the bombing of Germany intensified, wave upon wave of either voluntary or compulsory evacuees descended on remoter rural areas, ultimately creating massive problems as these reception areas became overloaded with incomers. Mothers remaining in towns had to shepherd children and carry babies, first to a shelter and later back to see if their home was still standing. If it was not, they might go to relatives in less vulnerable areas or they might be more or less forcibly evacuated from towns to the countryside.[57] In Britain, smaller numbers than had been expected left the towns as evacuees in 1939–40, and many soon began to drift back home. Calder's view is that the whole scheme was "a failure."[58] But it was also observed that "many evacuees stayed in the countryside for nearly the whole course of the war, often establishing friendly relationships that lasted into peacetime."[59] In Germany,

---

52 Harris, "War and Social History," 22.
53 See, e.g., HStAS, J170, Bü1 (Aalen), Gemeinde Zipplingen.
54 Jill Stephenson, "War and Society in Württemberg, 1939–1945: Beating the System," *German Studies Review*, vol. VIII, no. 1 (1985): 89–105.
55 Earl R. Beck, *Under The Bombs. The German Home Front 1942–1945* (Lexington, KY, 1986), 24–25.
56 Heineman, *What Difference*, 79.
57 E.g., Szepansky, *"Blitzmädel,"* 54–56.
58 Calder, *People's War*, 51–54. See also John Macnicol, "The Evacuation of Schoolchildren," in Harold L. Smith (ed.), *War and Social Change. British Society in the Second World War* (Manchester, 1986), 5–31.
59 Ward, *War in the Countryside*, 106.

too, some evacuees developed a good relationship with their hosts.[60] Yet the experience of evacuation demonstrated in both Britain and Germany the gulf that existed between citizens from contrasting backgrounds – from different classes, different regions, different religions, different socio-economic environments. In Britain, the problems have been attributed to "sluttish, homesick and idle" women evacuees and their snobbish and condescending hosts. Hinton quotes a Women's Voluntary Service (WVS) administrator in Lancashire who referred to evacuees as "people who are a lower type of civilisation."[61] But, as Thorpe observes, "[i]t was as much a clash between rural and urban workers and their lifestyles."[62] The picture was similar in Germany; farming families regarded some of the women migrants and evacuees as greedy and lazy, if not downright promiscuous in addition. The townies, for their part, sometimes despised the simple and stubborn – as they saw it – rural people.[63] From Aalen, it was reported, after the evacuees had left, that "One of the little madams wrote on the school's table: 'We bought everything from the Swabians except their stupidity.'"[64] And sometimes resentful urban evacuees denounced farmers to the Nazi authorities for treating foreign workers better than themselves.[65]

Nevertheless, while urban children often adjusted reasonably well, urban women found the remoteness and tedium of the countryside intolerable, in Britain, "far from the shops and cinema on which they had learned to depend."[66] Similarly, German evacuees from Rastatt (Baden) were horrified to discover that the village of Zipplingen (Württemberg) where they were billeted in autumn 1939 had no café or cinema; they said that they "would rather go back to where the bombs are than live here in a village where nothing ever happens."[67] The rhythms and sounds of the countryside were alien to them, and even women who were less than privileged found the absence of household amenities, like hot water on tap, shocking and intolerable.[68] In both countries, many women drifted back to the towns. This was less dangerous and more feasible in Britain because the Blitz was substantially over by June 1941 and destruction of housing, shops, and other facilities was limited. In German cities, destruction was massive and

60 Szepansky, *"Blitzmädel,"* 67; Gregor, "A *Schicksalgemeinschaft?"* 1060–61.
61 Hinton, "Voluntarism and the Welfare/Warfare State," 287.
62 Thorpe, "Britain," 24.
63 StAL, Bü48, "Betr.: Allgemeine Stimmung und Lage," September 1, 1941, 43–48.
64 HStAS, J170, Bü1 (Aalen), Gemeinde Aalen; see also Noakes, *Nazism*, document 1152, 357.
65 John J. Delaney, "Nazi Racial Policy in the Home and on the Farm," paper given at the German Studies Association conference, Houston, October 2000.
66 Ward, *War in the Countryside*, 89
67 HStAS, J170, Bü1 (Aalen), Gemeinde Zipplingen.
68 Stephenson, "'Emancipation' and Its Problems," 358.

continually increasing. Some civilians were denied the opportunity to leave for safer areas because they were tied to the district where their ration cards were valid. As one Hamburg woman put it in 1943: "No one can now leave Hamburg without permission. . . . You can leave your home area only with the permission of the NSDAP local branch leader. Without his permission, you will not receive a ration card anywhere else."[69]

In Germany, the well-established structure of the NSDAP and its affiliates should have made the organization of voluntary war work and relief work much easier to organize than in Britain, where, at first at least, the organization of the WVS as well as the Auxiliary Territorial Service (ATS) and the Women's Land Army (WLA) were handed over to titled ladies who had private cars to take them around the countryside recruiting helpers, and who also had contacts with friends and acquaintances of similar status. For example, Lady Anne Scott-Montague, daughter of the Marquis of Beaulieu, became the secretary of the Beaulieu branch of the evacuation program.[70] Undoubtedly, it was the persistence of the British class system, and of the prominence of landed aristocrats within it, that allowed self-confident and wealthy women, who had experience of various kinds of charity work before the war, to take over and run projects on behalf of the government. For example, the WVS was launched in June 1938 as the "Women's Voluntary Services for Air Raid Precautions" by Lady Reading. Before 1938 was out, over 32,000 women had enrolled, "mostly recruited initially through a personal network of better-off married women, emanating from Lady Reading's address book."[71] At its wartime peak, the WVS recruited perhaps one million women and remained firmly under the leadership of upper-class ladies, for some of whom "the WVS provided a temporary substitute for Conservative Party politics." In addition to its work among civilians, including evacuation, billeting, and a variety of welfare services, the WVS cooperated with other charitable groups in establishing a network of canteens for soldiers, as an alternative to the forces' own facilities, and its members also gathered information and replied to soldiers' anxious inquiries about the fate of family members and property in bombing raids.[72]

The main relief agency in Germany was the NS-Volkswohlfahrt (NSV: National Socialist People's Welfare), which was an affiliate of the NSDAP

---

69 J. Szodrzynski, "Das Ende der 'Volksgemeinschaft'? Die Hamburger Bevölkerung in der 'Trummergesellschaft' ab 1943," in F. Bajohr & J. Szodrzynski (eds.), *Hamburg in der NS-Zeit. Ergebnisse neuerer Forschung* (Hamburg, 1995), 295–96.

70 Television film, *The World We Lost*, Blakeway Associates for Channel Four, UK, 1999.

71 Gail Braybon & Penny Summerfield, *Out of the Cage* (London, 1987), 152.

72 Hinton, "Voluntarism and the Welfare/Warfare State," 274, 278 (quotation on 274); see also Sue Bruley, *Women in Britain since 1900* (London, 1999), 106; Crang, *British Army*, 93, 101.

and under male leadership. The Nazi women's organization, the NS-Frauenschaft (NSF), boasted that it organized civilian welfare, but in reality much of its work was carried out under the direction of the NSV or the Red Cross. Nevertheless, the NSF helped to organize bomb shelters for expectant mothers. In a Berlin shelter, for example, "there was a delivery room, a midwife and a couple of nurses. About 30 women stayed there" in 1940.[73] The NSF also had the unenviable task of persuading families in rural areas to take in evacuees and to supervise their settling in, to try to ensure that morale was maintained. The "Neighbourhood Aid" section of the NSF's subordinate "mass organization," the Deutsches Frauenwerk (DFW: German Women's Enterprise) – working under the direction of the NSV and mostly staffed by girls of the Nazi Bund Deutscher Mädel (BDM: League of German Girls) – performed various tasks, from cleaning up after bombing raids to darning socks. The BDM also helped to run camps for evacuated children in the *Kinderlandverschickung* program. In the later stages of the war, as male party functionaries were eventually conscripted, the women had some room for initiative. But this was hardly an advantage in a situation where resources, including housing, were completely inadequate to deal with the vast numbers of the dispossessed.[74] As Gregor says of Nuremberg, "[m]obilising aid became progressively harder as the exponentially rising demand stood in increasingly stark contrast to the declining means of responding to it."[75]

While bombing not only damaged housing and industry but also disrupted the provision of supplies of food and other essentials, Germany and Britain each had a further particular reason to be concerned about resources in wartime. In the years 1916–18, there had been acute hunger in German cities as a result of the British naval blockade. Indeed, one of the reasons for the development of the doctrine of total war was to ensure not only that virtually the whole population would be employed in a future war effort, but also that the country would never again be vulnerable in terms of the supply of foodstuffs and essential raw materials. Britain, as an island with a small agricultural sector, was potentially vulnerable to attacks on its supply lines from overseas, especially from German submarines, and this specter materialized in the protracted Battle of the Atlantic. By introducing the rationing of some goods on August 27, 1939, a few days before the Wehrmacht's attack on Poland, and enacting controls on the production and distribution of

73 Szepansky, "*Blitzmädel*," 66.
74 Jill Stephenson, *The Nazi Organisation of Women* (London, 1981), 190, 203; Stephenson, *Women in Nazi Germany*, 103–106, 169–71.
75 Gregor, "A *Schicksalgemeinschaft?*" 1063.

resources, the German government hoped to pace consumption.[76] Britain, too, introduced rationing, on January 8, 1940.[77] In both countries, pregnant and nursing mothers as well as "heavy workers" received special rations; in both, rationing was intended to be equitable, to be seen to be equitable, and to promote a sense of equality of sacrifice, with the important exception that in Germany non-"Aryans" were deliberately and severely disadvantaged: as Kaplan says, "many Jews feared starvation almost as much as they feared the Gestapo." Jewish women's shopping was restricted to an hour or two each day at designated shops; they were obliged to wait until "Aryans" had been served and were forbidden to buy a wide range of goods.[78] The poorer rations decreed for both German non-"Aryans" and foreign workers, along with the plundering of occupied countries, helped to cushion "Aryan," "valuable" Germans against the worst effects of rationing for much of the war.[79]

Both the prevailing division of labor and the increasing number of female-headed households in both countries ensured that the provision of food, clothing, and other essentials was women's responsibility. With rationing and shortages, shopping became a tiring and time-consuming activity as queues proliferated. In Britain, "food queues were described as 'a bigger menace to public morale than several serious German air raids' in February 1941," while in Germany working women, particularly, complained about difficulties in shopping before or after work.[80] Further, in both countries there was widespread suspicion that rationing was not being operated equitably, although in Britain, strategies were adopted to make it more palatable.[81] First, by contrast with Germany, at no time during the war was bread rationed. Second, the "points" system meant that, as Marwick says, "the consumer [was allowed] a certain limited choice among various scarce commodities, a mixed economy writ small."[82] Certainly, Britain had problems, particularly those resulting from the Battle of the Atlantic, but at no time was the Ministry of Food obliged to impose the "largely vegetarian 'siege diet' . . . because livestock farming managed to keep going (albeit on a reduced scale)." Nevertheless, much of the diet – Spam and dried egg, for example – was hardly appetizing: it was no wonder that "HP sauce" was a

76 Stephenson, "Beating the System," 91–93.   77 Marwick, *Britain in the Century*, 271.
78 Kaplan, *Between Dignity and Despair*, 151–52.   79 Stephenson, "Beating the System," 93.
80 Zweiniger-Bargielowska, *Austerity in Britain*, 66; StAL, Bü48, "Betr.: Allgemeine Stimmung und Lage," September 1, 1941, 36–37; H. Focke and U. Reimer, *Alltag unterm Hakenkreuz. Wie die Nazis das Leben der Deutschen veränderten* (Reinbek bei Hamburg, 1979), vol. 1, 182; Stephenson, *Women in Nazi Germany*, 98–100, 172–73.
81 Zweiniger-Bargielowska, *Austerity in Britain*, 70–80; Stephenson, "Beating the System," 93–95.
82 Marwick, *Britain in the Century*, 278–79.

popular additive.[83] In Germany, especially from 1943, as rations were cut repeatedly and shops closed on some days each week, many urban women "had sleepless nights because they did not know what they would put on the table the next day."[84] "War gardens" or, in Britain, allotments helped to eke out rations for the urban population, some of whom even resorted to keeping hens or small (edible) animals in gardens or on balconies.[85]

Even before 1939, German women had become – perhaps wearily – accustomed to government intervention in their conduct as consumers and homemakers. The war's exigencies led to similar concerns and remedies in Britain, with "an avalanche of official propaganda, bolstered by advice in women's magazines" geared to helping women "to economise on foods such as meat, eggs, fats, or sugar and to make the most of plentiful" items.[86] Believing that "the good of the whole state depends on whether women understand how to discharge their household duties, how to budget carefully,"[87] the NSF/DFW had run courses from 1934 on and bombarded women with advice via the media about the thrifty use of available supplies. In wartime, this was intensified, with demonstrations, leaflets, and broadcasts on how to get the best out of food rations, even as they diminished.[88] In Britain, Lord Woolton's Ministry of Food published "Food Facts" in the press and mounted the "Kitchen Front" radio programs and food advice messages in cinemas.[89] This was regarded as doubly important because evacuation had revealed the extent to which many poorer urban women had little idea of how to cook or how to clean and manage a household. As in Germany, where, as Mason observed, there were middle-class "women who felt called upon to bring poor families up to bourgeois standards of self-reliance, thrift and cleanliness," in Britain the WVS's Housewives' Service was regarded as an agent for "enlightenment in working-class neighbourhoods."[90]

While shortages and rationing gave rise to large-scale racketeering in both countries, a small-scale black market also thrived. In Britain, "it operated through widespread infringement of the regulations by producers, distributors, and retailers, ultimately sustained by public demand," and "a

83 Ward, *War in the Countryside*, 60–62.   84 Beck, *Under the Bombs*, 103.
85 Szepansky, *"Blitzmädel,"* 66; Martin Kitchen, *Nazi Germany at War* (London, 1995), 82; Calder, *People's War*, 496.
86 Zweiniger-Bargielowska, *Austerity in Britain*, 109.
87 L. Marawske-Birkner, *Der weibliche Arbeitsdienst* (Leipzig, 1942), 251–53.
88 Reagin, *"Marktordnung* and Autarkic Housekeeping," 162–84; Lacey, "Driving the Message Home," 198–202; Stephenson, "Propaganda, Autarky," 124–38.
89 Ward, *War in the Countryside*, 61–62.
90 Tim Mason, "Women in Germany, 1925–1940. Family, Welfare and Work," *History Workshop Journal* 1 (1976): 101; Hinton, "Voluntarism and the Welfare/Warfare State," 286.

surprising number of people were willing to admit quite freely that they had bought scarce goods through it."[91] In Germany, much of the black market was conducted through barter; women bought up durable commodities – glass jars, detergent, for example – and hoarded them until there was an opportunity to exchange them for scarce food supplies. Sometimes urban women traveled to the countryside to deal directly with food producers. As in Britain, in Germany individual shopkeepers had favored customers who were able to obtain rationed goods "under the counter" without expending ration coupons.[92] It seems clear that in both countries there was a feeling that rationing and other controls did not operate entirely equitably and that, therefore, violation of them in a small way hardly amounted to a crime. In Britain, attempts to control the manufacture and sale of cosmetics were thwarted by ingenious means. For example, with a ban on the production of nail varnish, a new product called "Laddastop" appeared on the market; ostensibly intended to stop ladders in stockings, it "was pink, sold in small bottles, with a brush for application" and – the big giveaway – was "accompanied by a preparation called 'Laddastop remover.'"[93] While ordinary members of the public took what opportunities they could to obtain scarce goods, those supposed to be enforcing the system might also be abusing it. In Britain, police officers were "perhaps no better and no worse than the majority of the population," while in Germany, where Nazi women's organization members monitored shops, "most [NSDAP] members behave no differently from anyone else."[94]

In both Germany and Britain during the Second World War, women's labor would be utilized on the land as well as in factories and in various services that had previously been dominated by men. According to Jose Harris, "the British people were ultimately subject to a greater degree of state-regulation and compulsory mobilisation of physical resources, including both male and female labour, than any other combatant power except the Soviet Union."[95] Certainly, it has been customary to argue that Britain was much more successful than Germany in encouraging or compelling economically inactive women to work for the war effort, and figures are quoted to sustain this argument. For example, the number of working women in Greater Germany was 14,626,000 in May 1939 and 14,897,000 in September 1944; by contrast, in Britain the number of women in paid employment

91 Zweiniger-Bargielowska, *Austerity in Britain*, 152; Calder, *People's War*, 294.
92 Stephenson, "Beating the System," 97–99.
93 Zweiniger-Bargielowska, *Austerity in Britain*, 190.
94 Zweiniger-Bargielowska, *Austerity in Britain*, 156; Stephenson, "Beating the System," 94, 103.
95 Harris, "War and Social History," 17.

was 6,250,000 in 1939 and 7,750,000 in 1943, the peak year of mobilization.[96] Britain introduced compulsion earlier and more comprehensively than did Germany, which is not surprising given that the wartime emergency in Britain was particularly acute in the earlier years, and that Germany had not only POWs as additional labor – as Britain had only later – but also coerced civilian workers from occupied countries, amounting to 5.7 million in 1944, of whom 1.9 million were female.[97] Yet the two countries were starting from different baselines. Partly because of the greater prominence of agriculture in the German economy, proportionately more German than British women were normally economically active, often as "assisting family members," as they were termed in censuses. In addition, by 1939 Germany had achieved full employment and those women who needed or wanted to work could do so. By contrast, in Britain recovery from the Depression had been slower, and significant unemployment among women persisted to the end of the 1930s: even in 1938, only 4,997,000 women were employed.[98] Beyond that, however, Mackay is of the view that "most [British] women doing paid work during the war did not embark on it because of the war."[99]

The conscription of female labor, which with hindsight seems a logical step in a total war, was a controversial matter in both countries. It became necessary because in neither country were there sufficient volunteers. In Britain, "inducements and appeals did not persuade as many as were needed from the pool of potential workers."[100] Yet the British government's initial reservations, fearing popular opposition, proved unfounded – again, doubtless because of Britain's desperate position in 1940. In 1941, the Registration of Employment Order required women aged twenty to thirty to register with the Ministry of Labour, and in 1942 the age range was extended to nineteen to forty. In Germany, the debate about conscription dragged on from the days of success in 1940 until finally, as the VIth Army at Stalingrad was about to surrender, conscription was introduced for women aged seventeen to forty-five (later extended to fifty) on January 27, 1943. In both countries, there were exemptions for those with young children, and there were also many women who were as reluctant to be drafted as they were to volunteer. In Britain, as Smith shows, by August 1941, 500,000 women had been interviewed, but only 87,000 had gone into essential war work. In Germany, according to Winkler, by the end

96 Dörte Winkler, *Frauenarbeit im "Dritten Reich"* (Hamburg, 1977), 201; Penny Summerfield, "Approaches to Women and Social Change in the Second World War," in Brian Brivati & Harriet Jones (eds.), *What Difference Did the War Make?* (London, 1993), 66.

97 Herbert, *Hitler's Foreign Workers*, 296.

98 Penny Summerfield, "The Levelling of Class" in Smith, *War and Social Change*, 186.

99 Mackay, *Test*, 221.   100 Mackay, *Test*, 79.

of June 1943, 3.1 million women had attended an employment office, of
whom 1,235,000 were declared suitable for work. Of these, more than half
(672,000) had household responsibilities which enabled them to work only
part-time.[101] Of those who took up full-time work, "by the end of the year,
half had produced medical excuses."[102] Resistance by government, employers, and male workers in both countries to equal pay for women doubtless reinforced the unwillingness of many women to accept direction into
work.

The legislative framework for conscripting British women certainly
looked more comprehensive than that in Germany, not least with the National Service (no. 2) Act of December 1941, which permitted the drafting
of single British women into work with the armed forces, and the Employment of Women (Control of Engagement) Order in 1942. In April 1943,
women – including childless married women – who had previously been
exempt from conscription were liable to direction into part-time work, resulting in a more than doubling of the number of women part-time workers.
Yet the main target of these orders was the younger woman, probably in her
twenties.[103] This was similar to the position in Germany where – apart from
the conscription of Jewish women under sixty-five for manual labor from
March 1941[104] – it was, as Heineman argues, young women who bore the
brunt of government attempts to increase the female workforce.[105] This was
done partly through conscription into agencies which predated the war. In
1940, for example, 335,972 young women were drafted into a compulsory
year of service (*Pflichtjahr*) in either agriculture or domestic service – the
latter to help mothers of large families or perhaps to release adult women
to run a small business. And from September 1939, seventeen- to twenty-
five year-olds were drafted into the Women's Labor Service (*Arbeitsdienst der
weiblichen Jugend*), whose numbers were raised from 50,000 in April 1940
to 150,000 in December 1943. These young women – who were not included in the employment figures – would perhaps work in agriculture, but,
increasingly, they would be drafted either into civilian clerical work or operating public transport, or, eventually, into work with the armed forces.[106]

---

101 Calder, *People's War*, 309; Harold L. Smith, "The Effect of the War on the Status of Women," in
    Smith, *War and Social Change*, 212–13; Winkler, *Frauenarbeit*, 137.
102 Heineman, *What Difference*, 63; Heinz Boberach (ed.), *Meldungen aus dem Reich* (Munich, 1968),
    146–48.
103 Smith, "The Effect of the War," 215–16.   104 Kaplan, *Between Dignity and Despair*, 173–74.
105 Heineman, *What Difference*, 64.
106 Stephenson, *Women in Nazi Society*, 103–105; Jill Stephenson, "Women's Labor Service in Nazi
    Germany," *Central European History*, vol. XV, no. 3 (1982): 256–63; Jill Stephenson, "Der Arbeits-
    dienst der weiblichen Jugend," in Dagmar Reese (ed.), *Die BDM Generation* (Potsdam, forthcoming).

By contrast, the British Women's Land Army, founded in the First World War and recreated when war seemed imminent, in June 1939, remained a dedicated agricultural workforce.[107]

Maintaining agricultural productivity was a major preoccupation in both countries, but one that was difficult to achieve with the withdrawal of able-bodied male labor. Ward claims that Britain was at a disadvantage compared with Germany because by 1939 Germany was "more than four-fifths self-sufficient in food" whereas "only thirty per cent of the nation's food requirements" were produced by British farmers.[108] Nevertheless, already in the 1930s there were serious labor shortages on Germany's small and often inefficient farms, and the wives of small farmers were often exhausted and prematurely aged even before the stresses of war added immeasurably to their burdens.[109] Germany's own resources may have provided about three-quarters of its basic foodstuffs, but the labor-intensive nature of Germany's farms in the south and west meant that male conscription had a dramatic effect – especially when the requisitioning of farm horses was added to the withdrawal of men. The continuous drain of conscription on Germany's human resources, until "the farms were largely denuded of male labor,"[110] resulted in increasingly acute shortages of food in Germany's towns in the second half of the war, especially in 1944–45 after the European empire whose resources Germany had, pillaged had shrunk to nothing. Foreign workers in agriculture – who numbered 2.7 million, including POWs, in summer 1944[111] – were seen as "saviours in a time of need,"[112] and young women from the *Pflichtjahr* or Labor Service provided assistance that was sometimes welcomed and sometimes regarded as more trouble than it was worth.[113] In comparison, Britain certainly had a labor shortage problem on the land, but it had more farm machinery – like tractors, combine harvesters, self-binders – and horses than many areas of farming in Germany had, as well as relatively small numbers of POWs, of whom there were 37,000 on British farms in summer 1943. In addition, the WLA, which at its peak in summer 1943 had over 87,000 members, managed to overcome initial hostility from

---

107 Braybon & Summerfield, *Out of the Cage*, 152.
108 Ward, *War in the Countryside*, 8.
109 Stephenson, *Women in Nazi Germany*, 67–69, 152–53, 158–59.
110 Thomas Schnabel, *Württemberg zwischen Weimar und Bonn 1928–1945/46* (Stuttgart, 1986), 574.
111 Herbert, *Hitler's Foreign Workers*, 297.
112 Ian Kershaw, *Popular Opinion and Political Dissent in the Third Reich. Bavaria 1933–1945* (Oxford, 1983), 286.
113 Stephenson, *Women in Nazi Germany*, 80–82; Stephenson, "Women's Labor Service," 258–60; J. E. Farquharson, *The Plough and the Swastika. the NSDAP and Agriculture, 1928–1945* (London, 1976), 235.

farmers and make a crucial contribution, with "farmers discover[ing] that Land Girls were a good deal tougher than they had imagined."[114]

In both countries, the governments aimed to bring women into war industry to replace conscripted men, but women – especially, but not only, middle-class women – were most reluctant to work in factories, tending to prefer clerical work, for example. Nevertheless, in Britain there was some success in attracting women into sectors where previously they had not been well represented, like engineering, chemicals, and the metals industries.[115] In Germany, the presence in 1944 of 2.9 million POWs and coerced foreign workers in mining, construction, and the metals and chemicals industries helped to compensate for the loss of conscripted men;[116] nevertheless, the number of women working in producer goods industries doubled between 1939 and 1943, while women in consumer goods industries like textiles increasingly worked on orders for the Wehrmacht.[117] Industrial employers complained about absenteeism or poor productivity on the part of women who had perhaps always been unwilling workers. But if they had had little sleep, if they could not find food because their local shops had been bombed, if their water, gas, and electricity supplies and their transport to work had been disrupted by bombing, it was hardly surprising if they were late for or absent from work – or preoccupied while they were there. This was increasingly the case in Germany, particularly, where it was, indeed, "amazing that the number of employed women remained constant or even rose slightly, right up to the end of the war."[118] In Britain, high rates of absenteeism "sometimes reached worrying proportions, particularly in munitions factories. But much of it was explained by women workers having to shop, to queue, or to look after children."[119] By 1944, British local authorities had provided 1,500 day nurseries, but that still left three-quarters of children under five who had working mothers without childcare provision.[120] In Germany, the picture was much the same, as the government was reluctant to fund "canteens, crèches and other social services" to bring more women into work.[121] Nevertheless, in both countries women were to be found in jobs – like engineering, for example – where they had barely figured before

---

114 Ward, *War in the Countryside*, 16–47 (quotation on 18).
115 Mackay, *Test*, 77.   116 Herbert, *Hitler's Foreign Workers*, 298.
117 Overy, "'Blitzkriegwirtschaft?'" 426–27.
118 Ingrid Schupetta, "Jedes das Ihre – Frauenerwerbstätigkeit und Einsatz von Fremdarbeitern/ arbeiterinnen im Zweiten Weltkrieg," in Frauengruppe Faschismusforschung (ed.), *Mutterkreuz und Arbeitsbuch. Zur Geschichte der Frauen in der Weimarer Republik und im Nationalsozialismus* (Frankfurt am Main, 1981), 297.
119 Thorpe, "Britain," 19; Braybon & Summerfield, *Out of the Cage*, 243–47.
120 Pugh, *Women*, 266.
121 Wolfgang Wippermann, *Umstrittene Vergangenheit. Fakten und Kontroversen zum Nationalsozialismus* (Berlin, 1998), 184.

the war, and there can be little doubt that, in both countries, women made a considerable contribution to the industrial war effort.

Some of those in Britain who aimed to avoid conscription into war industry volunteered for the women's sections of the armed forces, while women conscripted for war service might be directed into them; altogether, a total of almost 500,000 were involved.[122] In June 1938, the First World War Women's Auxiliary Army Corps (WAAC) was revived as the Auxiliary Territorial Service (ATS), at first consisting mainly of soldiers' wives and daughters.[123] At its peak in September 1943, it would have 212,500 members.[124] Middle-class young women, in particular, opted for the WRNS (naval) or WAAF (airforce) women's auxiliaries in preference to the ATS, which was regarded as socially inferior. Otherwise, middle-class women might join the Land Army.[125] After a lengthy campaign, women were officially admitted to the Home Guard in 1943, although some units had informally recruited women members before that.[126] In Germany in 1941–42, with the drain on manpower occasioned by the invasion of the Soviet Union, young women in the Labor Service were drafted into munitions work and auxiliary work with the armed forces, and from autumn 1943, as the military position deteriorated, they were also deployed in air-raid detection work, and then in work on antiaircraft batteries and with radar. By this time, there were 150,000 young women in the Labor Service and its wartime extension, Auxiliary War Service (*Kriegshilfsdienst*). This dwarfed the numbers of the 3,300 girls from the Bund Deutscher Mädel who were trained by the SS in late 1944 for work in signals units.[127] By contrast, toward the end of the war there were 13,000 young women working in air-raid detection and a further 25,000 in antiaircraft work.[128] In the latter case, they might come very close to military action as they operated antiaircraft batteries:

In January 1945 . . . [t]here was a massive British air-raid by low-flying craft. One fired at our gun so that everything was mown down by machine-gun bursts. The NCO took a direct hit. We flew through the air and landed some distance away. My steel helmet fell off my head, the strap broken. I felt blood on my face, coming from my left temple. My thigh was full of splinters from a grenade.[129]

122 Penny Summerfield, "'She Wants a Gun not a Dishcloth!': Gender, Service and Citizenship in Britain in the Second World War," in De Groot & Peniston-Bird, *A Soldier*, 119.
123 Braybon & Summerfield, *Out of the Cage*, 152.
124 Crang, *British Army*, 4.   125 Summerfield, "Approaches to Women," 75.
126 Summerfield, "'She Wants a Gun,'" 120, 124–25, 130.
127 Gerhard Rempel, *Hitler's Children. The Hitler Youth and the SS* (Chapel Hill, NC, 1989), 228–31.
128 Ursula von Gersdorff, *Frauen im Kriegsdienst, 1914–1945* (Stuttgart, 1969), 60–74; Stephenson, "Women's Labor Service," 260–63; "Im Kriegshilfsdienst. Nach dem Bericht von Herta P.," in Szepansky, "*Blitzmädel*," 237–39.
129 "Die Flakhelferin im Café. Über Lisa G.," in Szepansky, "*Blitzmädel*," 47–48.

In Germany, where gender roles are reputed to have been particularly distinct, the desperate circumstances of the last days of the war meant that there were few qualms about having a male NCO directing Labor Service young women on antiaircraft batteries. This contrasted with Britain, where women's "deployment as searchlight operators was curtailed after it was realised that each unit would need one strong male to start the electric generator." The fear was that the press would highlight "'the fact that among these unchaperoned young women lurked a solitary male soldier.'"[130]

It would be wrong to suggest that German women, living under a dictatorship, were either easier to direct or less resistant to government appeals and coercion than women in parliamentary democratic Britain. The ostensible paradox is that, in Britain, where popular opinion had formal influence, through elected representatives and a pluralistic press – even allowing for wartime controls – it seemed easier to implement the conscription of female labor, whereas in Germany, where popular opinion was exhaustively monitored but where it had no formal role, the conscription of women was a much more sensitive issue. More recent research has, however, suggested that German women made a massive contribution to the war effort, and that this has been underestimated. Overy believes that there simply were no more women to be mobilized, particularly once the crises of bombing and evacuation dispersed many from their homes, and Hancock argues that the government overestimated the number of women available for work: "[t]he reservoir of staff they believed existed proved elusive."[131] Equally, in spite of "the Blitz myth ... [of] the countless active, volunteering citizens mobilized by Hitler's bombs,"[132] it has been shown that large numbers of British women managed to escape more than token involvement. For example, Pugh points out that "By 1943, when mobilisation for the war effort reached its peak, there were 7,250,000 women employed in industry, the armed forces and civil defence. . . . However . . . even more (8,770,000 in fact) remained full-time housewives."[133] There was resentment: "Regardless of the direction into war work, the number of officers' wives who managed to avoid this ignominy and follow their husbands around the country was described as a major scandal of the war."[134] Furthermore, as Rendall observes, "the mixture of classes in munitions work so celebrated in propaganda is clearly ... mythical, with no more than 9 percent of munitions

---

130 De Groot, "Lipstick," 116. The quotation is from Frederick Pile, commander of Britain's ground antiaircraft defences.
131 Overy, "'Blitzkriegwirtschaft'?" 430–32; Hancock, *National Socialist Leadership*, 158.
132 Hinton, "Voluntarism and the Welfare/Warfare State," 275–77.
133 Pugh, *Women*, 265.   134 Crang, *British Army*, 67.

workers coming from the upper or middle classes."[135] In both countries, quite apart from the women's attitudes to work, often a husband or father would object to his wife or daughter being conscripted. In Britain, some men opposed "the conscription of our wives and sweethearts who are the very people we are fighting to protect."[136] Some German men argued that, as serving soldiers at the front, their sacrifice was sufficient for their family.[137]

Women in Germany and Britain indisputably had differing experiences in the Second World War. The course of the war was the chief reason for that, with, for example, British women suffering nothing approaching the mass rapes which some two million German women endured, mostly at the hands of Red Army soldiers.[138] But there were broad similarities, with men away from home, perhaps never to return, with shortages and controls, with bombing and evacuation, and with pressure to enter a war-related occupation. The last three of these areas demonstrated that German women had been subjected to quasi-wartime measures even before the war, measures that would continue in wartime, of a kind that would affect British women in wartime also. They also demonstrated that in both countries there was often little sense of *national* solidarity, and that class, region, and environment still deeply divided co-nationals. The "community of fate" in Germany was riven by these divisions, while the binding experience of the "Dunkirk spirit" in Britain was merely ephemeral.[139] Beyond that, the war brought massive change for women in both countries, even if, as De Groot says, in wartime "[t]he message was clear: women might do men's jobs, but they remained women."[140] While large numbers of both men and women longed to return to prewar "normality," for many women either the loss of a male family member or estrangement from one who had been absent for long periods made that impossible. And for those who had had novel – if not necessarily welcome – experiences in wartime, "[t]he possibility of alternative choices would never thereafter completely disappear."[141]

135 Jane Rendall, "Women's History: Beyond the Cage?" *History*, vol. 75, no. 243 (1990): 67.
136 Pugh, *Women*, 273.
137 Gersdorff, *Frauen im Kriegsdienst*, 325, 345–46.
138 Atina Grossmann, *Reforming Sex. The German Movement for Birth Control and Abortion Reform, 1920–1950* (New York and Oxford, 1995), 193; Sorge, *The Other Price*, 117–21.
139 Kershaw, *Popular Opinion*, 281, 373–85; Gregor, 'A *Schicksalgemeinschaft*?' 1070; Marwick, *Britain in the Century*, 296; John Stevenson, "Planner's Moon? The Second World War and the Planning Movement," in Smith, *War and Social Change*, 66–67.
140 De Groot, "'Cordite,'" 92.   141 Mackay, *Test*, 221.

12

Women in the Soviet War Effort, 1941–1945

JOHN BARBER

For none of the other belligerent powers was World War II fought on such a scale of intensity, destruction, and suffering as for the Soviet Union. Its experience, more so than any other nation's, can accurately be described as total war. The massive number of casualties and the devastation resulting from nearly four years of continuous and large-scale warfare, and the exceptional degree of mobilization of its human and material resources, were both unprecedented and unmatched by either its allies or its enemies. So also was the extent and nature of Soviet women's involvement in the war. Russian tradition, Soviet policies, and the desperate character of their country's struggle for survival all contributed to this; but the central fact is that in no society before or since have women been so centrally engaged in their country's war effort as in the USSR between 1941 and 1945. Their contribution to Soviet victory was huge, and so too was its cost. At least seven million Soviet women died premature deaths in World War II, and the lives of many more were ruined or permanently impaired. And their reward when the war was over, with some well-publicized exceptions, was to be largely forgotten.

BEFORE THE WAR

Even before the October Revolution, Russian women had displayed a marked capacity for breaking with gender stereotypes in war. Nadezhda Durova's exploits as a cavalry officer and Vasilisa Kozhina's as a partisan were celebrated in histories of the Napoleonic Wars. Mariya Bochkareva and her women's "battalion of death" were much publicized in World War One,[1] as

---

1 For an analysis of the influence of Russian and Soviet military traditions on the role of women in World War II, see E. S. Seniavskaia, *Psikhologiia voiny v XX veke: istoricheskii opyt Rossii* (Moscow, 1999), 160–68.

was the Provisional Government's formation of women's battalions to prop up the crumbling Russian army in 1917. But it was in the Civil War of 1918–20 that women first enlisted in large numbers, tens of thousands joining the Red Army to defend Soviet power.[2] This was the precedent their successors would follow two decades later.

They would do so at least in part as a result of changes in the position of women in Soviet society in the interwar period. The emancipation of women was seen as a central feature of the transition to socialism by the Bolsheviks. After the Revolution, they encouraged women to participate in politics and public life, sought to increase their employment in the workforce, and promoted the expression and dissemination of radical feminist ideas. Whereas by the beginning of the 1930s the latter had been silenced and the women's department (*zhenotdel*) of the Party Central Committee closed, and in the mid-1930s laws on divorce and abortion were introduced aimed at strengthening the family as a social institution, the drive to attract women to production continued and accelerated. In the Stalinist industrialization drive, they were a major source of new labor. By the end of the decade, two-fifths of the industrial workforce was female, with women employed in many traditionally male occupations in industry, building, and transport. This was held to be equality in practice and figured prominently in Soviet propaganda about the creation of the new socialist society, and with it the new Soviet man and woman. However much driven by the state's economic needs this was, and however ambiguous the Soviet state's general message for women may have been, the continual emphasis on their ability to acquire any skill and perform any role necessary for the construction of socialism was a key component of young women's socialization in the 1930s – they were capable of anything men could do. Partnership, comradeship, and equality with their male counterparts were the norms and values inculcated in the rising generation of Soviet women.

THE OUTBREAK OF WAR

This accounts in part at least for the extraordinary response of Soviet women to the German invasion of the Soviet Union in June 1941. A wave of spontaneous patriotism saw hundreds of thousands of people besieging the recruitment offices of the Red Army, many women among them, demanding to be sent to the front. Few could have had any idea of the brutal realities

---

2 Susanne Conze & Beate Fieseler, "Soviet Women as Comrades-in-Arms," in Robert W. Thurston & Bernd Bonwetsch, eds., *The People's War: Responses to World War II in the Soviet Union* (Urbana, IL, 2000), 214.

of the battlefield, let alone conceived of the possibility that war might last for years, not weeks. Most if not all would have believed Soviet propaganda about the invincibility of the Red Army and the certainty of rapid victory over the enemy.[3] But there is no reason to doubt the genuineness of their response to German invasion. The figures are striking: a quarter of the early volunteers for the Red Army in the Donetsk region were women, a third in the Denepropetrovsk region, half in the Kirovograd region.[4] Many others joined the *narodnoe opolchenie*, the people's militia formed to reinforce the regular troops of the Red Army; or the *istrebitelnye bataliony*, the security units created to deal with enemy agents and deserters; or partisan groups operating in enemy-occupied territory. Although at this point the roles given to women were mainly noncombatant ones, these could involve them being dispatched to the frontline, to immediate risk of injury and death.

EMPLOYMENT

For the government, however, women's most immediately vital contribution to the war effort was as labor. With millions of men mobilized for the Red Army and the workforce cut by many more millions by the loss of territory to the enemy, additional workers were desperately needed, and women were the largest single source available. First voluntarily, through an appeal to patriotism – "Men to the front, women to the factories!" – and then compulsorily, women's labor was mobilized. Under a decree of February 1942, the whole able-bodied urban population not already employed, in training, or solely responsible for young children was made liable to the draft. The resulting influx of women into the workforce meant that they soon comprised the majority of employees and in many factories the overwhelming majority. Women had made up 41 percent of the industrial workforce in early 1940; by October 1942, they constituted 53 percent.[5] In light industry, where women had always predominated, they made up over 80 percent of the workforce. Large numbers of women were also drafted into construction and transport. But it was in heavy industry that their impact was most felt. In 1942, over half of all turbine operators in power stations were women, and over a quarter of coal miners; by the end of the war, two-fifths of Donbas miners were women. Close to the frontline, the female

---

3 For the optimism with which many greeted the outbreak of war, see John Barber, "Popular Reactions in Moscow to the German Invasion of June 22 1941," *Soviet Union/Union Soviétique*, no. 18 (1991), 1–3, 5ff.
4 John Erickson, "Soviet Women at War," in John Garrard & Carol Garrard, eds., *World War 2 and the Soviet People* (Basingstoke, 1993), 59.
5 Mark Harrison, *Soviet Planning in Peace and War, 1938–1945* (Cambridge, 1985), 137.

proportion of the workforce was still higher. At the giant Kirov plant in Leningrad in January 1943, two-thirds of the workers were women; by the following month, 84 percent of all Leningrad industrial workers were.[6] Many were very young, simply girls. With an acute shortage of labor on the one hand, and people's desperate need for the extra rations and income which work provided on the other, managers turned a blind eye to minimum age requirements. Children as young as twelve were to be found working in Soviet factories during the war.

Statistics reflect the change in the position of many women, but they say nothing about the conditions in which they worked. Soviet industry had never been noted for hygiene or labor safety, and in wartime these inevitably deteriorated. Particularly in the eastern regions to which many factories of western Russia had been evacuated, but far from exclusively, working conditions were bad and living conditions dire. At the outbreak of war, the normal working week was extended to fifty-four hours and holidays were abolished. This was a minimum; many worked longer. Large numbers of workers, moreover, had to participate in crash vocational programs aimed at acquiring or improving work skills; in 1942, four-fifths of the workforce were thus occupied. Labor regulations were draconian. Already under legislation of 1938–40, lateness, absenteeism, and quitting jobs without permission were punishable offenses. In December 1941, workers in defense industry, and later those in other key industries, were made subject to military discipline, with breaches punishable by sentences of five to eight years' imprisonment. Thousands of workers found guilty of infringing regulations were sentenced to forced labor in the Gulag. Women figured prominently among them, no doubt as a result for many – particularly new recruits to the workforce – of difficulties in adapting to the harsh environment of wartime employment. The proportion of women among Gulag inmates rose from 8 percent in 1941 to 28 percent by 1945, the total from approximately 150,000 to 400,000.[7] The female proportion of those guarding them also increased, to 31 percent of the administrative staff of Gulag camps and labor colonies by the middle of 1944.[8]

Agriculture meanwhile became an overwhelmingly female sector. Young men virtually vanished from the countryside. Women, who already made up over half the workforce on collective farms at the beginning of the war, were

---

6 John Barber & Mark Harrison, *The Soviet Home Front, 1941–1945* (Basingstoke, 1991), 96–99, 216.

7 Edwin Bacon, *The Gulag at War* (Basingstoke, 1994), 24, 150–51. The increase in the proportion of women among Gulag inmates also reflects the drafting of male prisoners into the Red Army's penal battalions.

8 Ibid., 153.

70 percent of it by 1943 and 80 percent by the end.[9] With much agricultural machinery taken by the military, and with agriculture starved of investment, labor in the countryside reverted to its precollectivization state of being overwhelmingly manual. And with horses also commandeered by the Red Army, their draught power was replaced by human beings, mainly women. It was on this weakened and heavily burdened workforce that the task of feeding the huge numbers in the armed forces and the urban population fell – along with the task of feeding themselves, with the difference that collective farmers had no guaranteed rations, but simply received whatever was available for distribution after deliveries to the state had been made, which could be little or nothing. Essentially, the rural population, made up largely of women, was left to fend for itself.

THE FAMILY

One effect of the substantial increase in female employment was that the "double burden" of paid and domestic work became the norm for Soviet women. To the responsibility of caring for children and dependents – usually alone, with men at the front or drafted elsewhere for war work – was added the strain of long hours of work in conditions often very much harder than in peacetime. For women in evacuation or in cities near the frontline or under siege, life could be a daily struggle for survival. In Leningrad's hungry winter of 1941–42, it was largely women who stood for hours in queues to receive the starvation ration of bread, who improvised food from wallpaper paste and carpenter's glue, bone-meal and bark, cellulose and every possible source, who dragged buckets of water from holes in the canals and rivers back to their freezing apartments, who hauled the dead to the mortuaries and cemeteries. It was often they who could be forced to make decisions of life or death for their own families, to choose whom to feed and whom not. Some in extreme desperation resorted to cannibalism, feeding their families and themselves from the flesh of corpses lying everywhere in the city. In the most terrible cases recorded, women killed one of their children to feed the others and themselves.[10]

For the more fortunate, there was the possibility of receiving extra rations sent by their husbands at the front, particularly if the latter were officers. But this helped only a small minority. More common was the double tragedy of having husbands captured by the enemy. Not only were their fates uncertain

---

9 Harrison (1985), 139.
10 For examples from NKVD archives, see N. A. Lomagin, *V tiskakh goloda* (St. Petersburg, 2000), 169–71, 176–77.

(and the majority of Soviet prisoners of war died in captivity); under the harsh decrees of August 1941 and July 1942 aimed at combating panic and defeatism in the Red Army, the families of men who surrendered, and were therefore considered to have betrayed their country, lost their ration entitlement. For millions of women, however, even this was probably less traumatic than the sheer destruction of their families by war. Such was the slaughter (and, especially in the early months, chaos) at the front that many wives never received notification that their husbands were dead or missing. They lived the rest of their lives in ignorance of their husbands' fate. (And if they were informed of their death or disappearance, the chance of knowing where they had died and were buried was often nonexistent.) In the confusion that frequently accompanied conscription, evacuation, or occupation, husbands and wives, parents and children were separated, losing contact for months, years, often forever. For years, for decades to come, women would stand in public places on Victory Day holding photographs and details of their lost husbands or sons, appealing for information about them; or they would continue the search through newspapers, radio programs, and social organizations. For some the search still goes on.

The war not only imposed great, often terminal, strains on innumerable families; it weakened the family as an institution, albeit temporarily. The number of marriages declined sharply, while the divorce rate remained constant and even rose for marriages of less than a year. The decline in registered marriages may have reflected an increase in temporary relationships typical of wartime, but the basic cause was the sudden fall in the number of men of marriageable age in civilian society. The decline in the birth rate was still more drastic – by nearly three-quarters in Moscow between 1941 and 1943. In starving Leningrad, it was sixty-seven times lower in October 1942 than it had been in January.[11]

The drastic impact of the war on the family eventually spurred the government into action to reverse its effects. A decree of July 1944 created new orders of "heroine-mothers" (for mothers with ten children or more) and "motherhood glory" (for seven to nine children). A progressive scale of grants to mothers was introduced for the third child onward, and special grants were introduced for single mothers. The latter were also given the option of placing their children in state-run children's homes, with the right of reclaiming them at any time. The legal validity of unregistered marriages was withdrawn, divorce was more difficult and expensive, and a tax was

11 Nadezhda Cherepenina, "Hunger and Death," in John Barber & Andrei Dzeniskevich, eds., *Life and Death in Besieged Leningrad* (forthcoming).

leavied on unmarried men and women and on childless couples.[12] As the tide of fortune turned in the Soviet Union's favor, in other words, the state moved to reassert traditional gender roles and norms.

FRONTOVIKI

Nothing so dramatically broke with all preceding traditions of women and warfare as their role in the Soviet armed forces in World War II: 800,000 Soviet women saw military service during the war.[13] When partisans are included, the total number may have been over a million.[14] Given that throughout the war the Soviet Union, in contrast to its allies, was fighting a full-scale war along a frontier stretching hundreds of kilometers, from the Baltic to the Black Sea, the Caucasus and beyond, this meant active service, often at the front itself. Some served in traditional roles – including doctors, nurses, cooks, bakers, and laundry and bathhouse orderlies. A total of 41 percent of all doctors at the front and 43 percent of all surgeons were women.[15] Others performed previously male-dominated functions – as sappers, field engineers, telephonists, radio operators, drivers, mechanics, traffic controllers, as well as interpreters, intelligence personnel, and political officers. All these were essential to the war effort; all were liable to find themselves under fire, to be caught up in fighting, and to suffer casualties.

But thousands upon thousands of women were directly engaged in combat. For some months after the beginning of the war, women in fighting roles were the exception, the result of individual initiatives or of the need for them in specialist roles such as aviators. It was not until early 1942, after millions of Red Army men had perished or been taken prisoner and amid a growing shortage of men to take their place, that a formal decision to admit women volunteers to combat units was taken by the Party Central Committee. A mass recruitment campaign by the Komsomol in spring led to many young women enlisting, including 100,000 in the air defense forces; there would be four more such campaigns over the next two years. By 1943, women would comprise 8 percent of the Soviet armed forces.[16] By 1945, there would be 246,000 women in uniform at the front.[17] They fought in infantry divisions, in hand-to-hand fighting, in artillery and antiaircraft units. They were snipers and machine-gunners, paratroops and partisans. They commanded tank crews and infantry platoons. One fighter regiment and

12 Barber & Harrison (1993), 90–93.   13 Erickson (1993), 50.
14 Conze & Fieseler (2000), 212.   15 Erickson (1993), 61.
16 Conze & Fieseler (2000), 213; Erickson (1993), 62.
17 Richard Overy, *Russia's War* (London, 1997), 241.

three bomber regiments were formed consisting entirely of women, from pilots to mechanics.[18] The leading British historian of the German-Soviet War sums up the military record of Soviet women in World War II:

Theirs is a story of courage, endurance and suffering without parallel in human history. Many of the Red Army's finest soldiers happened to be women, and they won in combat their country's highest decoration – Hero of the Soviet Union – often posthumously.[19]

Their motives varied. Patriotism and the desire to contribute to the war effort in the most direct and active way possible undoubtedly inspired many; and this could be expressed as, in the words of a Volgograd woman, "love for Stalin."[20] But the reminiscences of female veterans often linked their decision with highly personal goals – to avenge their dead husbands, brothers, fathers, sons, lovers, or to find them and join them at the front – which against all odds they sometimes succeeded in doing.

Men's reactions to their presence were, according to a recent study of the psychology of war in Russia, a mixture of admiration, alienation, and guilt.[21] The gulf between conventional images of women and the realities of war produced varied feelings. "If men saw a woman in the front line, their faces changed completely; even a female voice transformed them," recalls one veteran. According to another, "the presence of women in battle ennobled a man, made him braver." On the other hand, a former sniper expresses a common view of the "unwomanly" nature of killing.

When two women crawl out to kill someone with a sniper's rifle in no-man's land – that's 'hunting' ... Though I was a sniper myself ... but after all I'm a man.... I might take such a woman scouting, but not for a wife.[22]

The fact remains that women at the front were exposed to the same terrifying dangers and brutalities as their male comrades, with the additional element of knowing their likely fate at the hands of the enemy in the event of capture.[23] They were also capable of equally violent reactions.

During that battle, when we were attacked by tanks, two men showed cowardice ... The line wavered and men began to run ... The fascists showed our wounded no mercy ... In the morning the entire battalion was drawn up and those

---

18 Ibid.; Albert Axell, *Russia's Heroes* (London, 2001), 59–70.
19 Erickson (1993), 59–60.
20 Quoted from a survey of Volgograd women who had fought at the front. R. Papadopoulos-Killius, "Soviet Women in the Second World War," unpublished paper (Frankfurt, 1993), 2.
21 Seniavskaia (1999), 165.   22 Ibid., 165–66.
23 The Volgograd women veterans, asked what was their predominant feeling at the front, replied fear – fear of death or torture and rape ("for them meaning the same"). Papadopoulos-Killius (1993), 3.

cowards were brought out in front of the men. The sentence was read out: death by firing squad . . . Three men stepped forward, the others held back. I took a sub-machine gun and stepped forward. Everyone else followed when I did that . . . There could be no forgiveness.[24]

Inevitably, relations between men and women at the front often went beyond those of fighting comrades. The expression *pokhodno-polevaia zhena* (field wife) was widely used; and it reflected not only a common attitude in the Red Army toward women, but also a social reality. "As a rule," another veteran recalls, "women at the front soon became officers' lovers. And how could it be otherwise? If a woman were on her own, there would be no end to her being importuned."[25] The intensity and fragility of life at the front no doubt promoted intimate relations there. What was unique about them was their legal status. Marriage at the front was registered without passports, that is, without details of an existing marriage. In a situation where the life expectancy of the men and women involved might well be minimal, the state in effect turned a blind eye to bigamy.

WAR AND WOMEN'S POSITION IN SOVIET SOCIETY

War has often been a vehicle for major social change, but where Soviet women were concerned such change was limited and often negative. Enormous though their role in the war effort was, its actual character was largely unrepresented in Soviet culture and propaganda both at the time and for years afterward.[26] The war as portrayed in the Soviet press was overwhelmingly a male experience; in the accounts published in *Pravda*, women were marginal.[27] Fighting was seen as a male occupation; women's natural role was to support, heal, and comfort. While Soviet wartime propaganda featured women workers, pilots, and partisans, it focused above all on woman's maternal image – as in the best-known of all Soviet war posters, I. M. Toidze's "*Rodina-mat' zovyot!*" ("The motherland summons!").[28] The reluctance to associate women with killing was also reflected in wartime films and poetry.

---

24 S. Alexiyevich, *War's Unwomanly Face* (Moscow, 1988), 110. This book's title well, if perhaps inadvertently, captures the contrasts in social attitudes toward women and war, which are frequently reflected in this book in the reminiscences of the veterans themselves.

25 Ibid.

26 Even today, it has been argued, Soviet women's role as combatants "has not become part of the general history of the war." Conze & Fieseler (2000), 214.

27 Jeffrey Brooks, "*Pravda* Goes to War," in Richard Stites, ed., *Culture and Entertainment in Wartime Russia* (Bloomington, 1995), 21. The main exception to the general role was the women's newspaper *Rabotnitsa.* Conze & Fieseler (2000), 222.

28 Lisa A. Kirschenbaum, "'Our City, Our Hearths, Our Families': Local Loyalties and Private Life in Soviet World War II Propaganda," *Slavic Review* 59, no. 4 (Winter 2000): 825–47.

While the heroism of women such as the partisan Zoya Kosmodemianskaia was celebrated, their essential femininity was emphasized, and the contrast between their gentle nature and the violent acts in which they were involved stressed. As has been argued, "Zoya's death is shown to be all the more tragic because she is not allowed to fulfil her true female destiny . . . to become a wife and mother."[29] Margarita Aliger's poem "Zoya," probably the best known literary work about any Soviet woman in World War II, succeeds in feminizing even the heroine's execution:

> Her slender neck is cut by the merciless noose.
> An unfamiliar power in your thrown-back face,
> Like a woman waiting for her lover,
> Filled with a precious beauty.[30]

As has been noted, it was not accidental that women combatants were absent from the great victory parade in Red Square in May 1945.[31]

The failure of Soviet officialdom to acknowledge women's wartime role, however, pales into insignificance compared with the war's destructive effects on many of them. The combined effects of separation, loss, bereavement, and physical and psychological injury blighted the lives of millions of women. The massive death toll of men, twenty million compared with seven million women, greatly increased the gender imbalance in society, especially among young age groups. As a result, many women were deprived of the possibility of finding partners and raising families, or accepted very unequal relationships for the sake of avoiding loneliness. Some waited for years in hope of being reunited with their partners or resigned themselves to life alone. Those who were reunited with their men could find them broken or scarred by the experience of war. Some remarried, assuming the death of husbands who then reappeared. Millions of women were left to bring up children alone and with little support from the state. Among the most unfortunate were some of those who had been exposed to the greatest danger and violence, those who had served in the armed forces. Even if they were not permanently injured or traumatized by their wartime experiences, they could find readjustment to civilian life extremely difficult. One feature of this was the ostracism or abuse as "field wives" to which female ex-combatants could be exposed for their supposed promiscuity at

---

29 Katherine Hodgson, "Soviet Women's Poetry of World War 2," in Garrards (1993), 80. Zoya's actual fate, though tragic, was far less heroic than portrayed in Soviet accounts; she was betrayed to the Germans by Russian peasants enraged by the actions of partisans implementing the scorched earth strategy. Seniavskaia (1999), 231–32.

30 Cited in Hodgson (1993), 81.   31 Conze & Fieseler (2000), 226.

the front – not least from other women. Some would hide the fact of their military service from their neighbors for years.[32]

The legacy of World War II for Soviet women was not without positive features. In some ways, it reinforced the contrasting revolutionary and traditional images of women which Stalinist policies had reflected in the 1930s: building socialism as men's comrades and equals on the one hand, endowing family and home with their feminine virtues on the other. For all the traumas of the war, it opened new horizons for a large number of women. Many gained skills during the war or were encouraged at its end to enroll in specialist training and higher education that would provide them with the means for advancement and promotion. The massive deficit of men created permanent opportunities for women to make successful careers in previously male-dominated occupations. Through dire necessity Soviet women during the war had to organize their lives independently, to find solutions to the most critical problems. This would stand them in good stead in the hard postwar years, when more than ever the burden of keeping their families going would fall on their shoulders.

In one way or another these were all gains; but the price paid was immense.

32 Alexiyevich (1988), 65.

13

The Spirit of St. Louis

Mobilizing American Politics and Society, 1937–1945

BERND GREINER

> The war will last a hundred years – five years of fighting and ninety-five of winding up the barbed wire.
>
> American doughboys' joke in 1918[1]

Even for a place like the Coliseum, it was an unusual day. A heavy stench of gun smoke lingered over the arena for hours, while hundreds of troops fired their rifles and cannons, exploded mines, launched rockets, were ordered over the top, retreated, dug into foxholes, and tied the enemy down in surprise pincer movements, before at long last the Star Spangled Banner flew in victory. The calendar gave no reason for martial celebration – no anniversary or holiday – nor did the latest news. The war was dragging on. Politicians and military leaders admitted that the worst of the fighting with Germany and Japan was yet to come.

By any standard, November 1943 seemed a strange time to stage a sham battle, and the Los Angeles Coliseum no less a strange location. Nevertheless, the City Council remained determined. Since the early 1940s, billions of defense dollars had flowed into California's shipyards and its nascent high-tech industries. Manpower recruitment for the shipyards, however, was badly behind schedule. Filling the vacancies promised victory in the war and a bright economic future. These goals justified a public-relations spectacle, a multidimensional battle event, live on stage.[2]

The idea of Hollywood's dramatizing war as family entertainment would have been ludicrous only a few years earlier. Since the early 1920s, Americans, probably more than any other people, had denounced war and the military as dangerous to a democracy's political and social health. Even on

---

1 Dixon Wecter, *When Johnny Comes Marching Home* (Cambridge, MA, 1944), 1.
2 Roger W. Lotchin, *Fortress California, 1910–1961: From Warfare to Welfare* (New York, 1992), 133–4.

the eve of the totalitarian onslaught, it looked as if the United States lacked both the will to rearm and the determination to fight. Measured against total government spending, military expenditures fell from 28.3 percent in 1913 to 15.5 percent in 1940. Appropriating 2 percent of the gross national product for defense sustained the world's largest navy, but the army was only the eighteenth largest, and the air force, with its seventeen hundred out-of-date planes, was not even fit for comparison. In 1940, Congress turned down a presidential request for an increase of $500 million to the defense budget. Fiscal limits seemed to be written in stone.

However, the New World did meet the demands of another total war. At its conclusion, contemporaries found a political landscape changed beyond recognition. Instead of demobilization, there was talk about "Permanent Preparedness." Instead of politics as usual, the military rose to levels of power and prestige unprecedented in American history. Instead of condemning "war profiteers," the public enjoyed the profits of war. Even for the United States, the speed and force of this change were puzzling. Within a decade, a legacy of two hundred years of containing military institutions and war production to a bare minimum was abandoned. This transformation remains one of the most intriguing chapters in modern American life.[3]

VOLUNTEERS

In the beginning was the Great Depression, which rendered America's vast productive potential idle. The statistics registered a nightmare. In automobile-manufacturing plants alone, the pride of America's technological achievement, almost 50 percent of capacity lay dormant. Calculations of "lost output" in industry during the 1930s suggested that 35 million homes, 179 million automobiles, and 716,000 schools were not built. The reports from farming areas were frightening. Still home to about 44 percent of the population, the agricultural Southeast and Midwest had not recuperated from the breakdown of world agricultural markets in the mid-1920s when another crisis struck in 1929; then came ecological disaster in the mid-1930s, a drought that left soil in Oklahoma, Arkansas, and Texas literally blowing in the wind. When the rates of unemployment and part-time occupation were

---

3 Richard Overy, *Die Wurzeln des Sieges: Warum die Alliierten den Zweiten Weltkrieg gewannen* (Stuttgart and Munich, 2000), 44–6, 246; David M. Kennedy, *Freedom From Fear: The American People in Depression and War, 1929–1945* (New York, 1999), 386; Paul Koistinen, "Toward a Warfare State: Militarization in America during the Period of the World Wars," in John R. Gillis, ed., *The Militarization of the Western World* (New Brunswick, NJ, and London, 1989), 53, 61; Bernd Greiner, "'The Study of the Distant Past Is Futile': American Reflections on New Military Frontiers," in Roger Chickering and Stig Förster, eds., *The Shadows of Total War: Europe, East Asia, and the United States, 1919–1939* (Cambridge, 2003).

combined, they revealed that almost 50 percent of the nation's workforce was unutilized in the 1930s. Even at the end of the decade, there was no end in sight. The unemployment rate stood at 17 percent in 1939, 15 percent in 1940, as between 8.5 and 9.5 million people were out of work. Even these estimates were conservative, given chronic underreporting in rural areas. In 1940, private domestic investment was 18 percent below the level in 1929, and the gross value of capital plants and equipment was below the 1926 level. Never before in its history had the United States experienced such an ordeal.[4]

The impact of the crisis on American society can hardly be overstated. Until 1929, failure had no part in American mythology. The myth of the frontier had been a saga of conquest and exploiting resources, a promise of everlasting progress. From the late nineteenth century up through the 1920s, the country had thrived and attracted more new immigrants than ever before. Over 20 million people had fled Europe for America. More than 30 percent of Chicago's 2.7 million residents in the 1920s were foreign-born. Even the stock market crash on "Black Tuesday" (October 29, 1929) was played down for months as a temporary aberration as Herbert Hoover, who became a mock presidential hero to later generations, struggled to retain his reputation as the "man who had never known failure." It is hard to imagine a society that was more traditionally optimistic or less prepared for such a change in its fortunes. Yet after 1929 the New World seemed to confront the debris of its dreams. Resignation, apathy, and docility took over, as once abundant energies drained away. Traditional optimism faded.[5]

The 1930s generated a dramatic popular demand for regaining the initiative, revitalizing resources, and reasserting collective drives. Franklin Delano Roosevelt built his political career on his genius for reading this popular demand. On the campaign trail during the 1940 election, he dramatized the economic benefits of military aid to the allies. "You good people here in Boston know of the enormous increase of productive work in your Boston Navy Yard. . . . Citizens of Seattle – you have watched the Boeing plant out there grow."[6] He broadcast similar addresses to southern California, Buffalo, St. Louis, and locations on the eastern seaboard. Building crushing superiority in arms became the great energizer for the nation's wounded soul.

---

4 Harold G. Vatter, *The U.S. Economy in World War II* (New York, 1985), 3, 7, 14, 17; Kennedy, *Freedom*, 87, 167, 213, 617.

5 Kennedy, *Freedom*, 11. See Studs Terkel, *Hard Times: An Oral History of the Great Depression* (New York, 1970); Paul Fussell, *Wartime: Understanding and Behavior in the Second World War* (New York, 1989), 55, 59.

6 Kennedy, *Freedom*, 464.

On January 5, 1942, four weeks after Pearl Harbor, the president took the floor of Congress to call for a breathtaking economic effort. Within two years, he announced, American factories were to pour out 185,000 aircraft, 120,000 tanks, and 55,000 antiaircraft guns. This program was geared primarily to the demands of a two-front war, but Roosevelt took the occasion to signal the end of the Great Depression. Costs were to be no consideration. A couple of hours later, William Knudson, the former automobile executive and now the chairman of the Office of Production Management, followed suit. He lectured a group of leading businessmen on Roosevelt's program and ended the meeting with a simple question: "Who volunteers?"[7]

"Let's volunteer" thereupon became the motto of the American business community. Traditionally hostile to political oversight, business had hit an all-time low in its political relations during the 1930s, thanks in part to congressional allegations of "war profiteering" during the First World War, but primarily because of the regulatory thrust of the New Deal and Roosevelt's crusading populism, which earned him the label "traitor to his class" among the business community. Enmity relaxed once the ambitious reforms of the New Deal had been reduced to insurance programs for the unemployed and elderly. The political warfare between business and the Roosevelt administration was by no means over, however, as war clouds gathered at the end of the decade. Mobilizing for war offered the business community an opportunity for vindication. The price of its voluntary cooperation was to be tax incentives for war-related investment, generous public credits, the end of antitrust lawsuits, and, not least, the awarding of war contracts on a "cost-plus basis" to minimize risks and maximize profits. Roosevelt was in no position to oppose these terms, even had he wished to. "Voluntarism" spelled the end of government-inspired reform of the economy. It put business back in command.[8]

Mobilization for war took on a symbolic life of its own. Orchestrated by the business community, it demonstrated the renewed vitality of American capitalism. It announced the unshackled vigor, power, pragmatism, self-confidence, and other virtues of an idealized America. It provided businessmen the opportunity to recapture their traditional role as the country's pioneering elite. Henry Kaiser and the seventy-eight-year-old Henry Ford took the helm and built their wartime careers on these premises. Kaiser took charge of constructing Liberty Ships, which were launched from mammoth shipyards in Richmond, California, Portland, Oregon, and Vancouver,

---

7 Ibid., 618; Overy, *Wurzeln*, 249.
8 Alan Brinkley, *The End of Reform: New Deal Liberalism in Recession and War* (New York, 1995).

British Columbia. Ford presided over a 900-acre aircraft site southwest of Detroit, where by 1944 a new B-24 left the assembly line every sixty-three minutes. Before the war was over, both Kaiser and Ford had captured the imagination of their countrymen and had become known respectively as "Sir Launchalot" and the creator of the "Grand Canyon of the mechanized world." For the first time, ships and planes became the mass products of America's unique management strategies. An army of new industrial employees, from diverse ethnic backgrounds, adapted to new production techniques and experimental logistics. Under severe pressure and public scrutiny, American capitalism emerged from stagnation. By reinventing itself, it answered the call for a new national commitment.[9]

Business, together with a workforce grateful to follow any trumpet, soon gathered powerful momentum. While both sides had had to be bullied into converting from a consumer economy into military production during the previous war, the whole country was set in motion, literally and almost overnight, in the early 1940s. Some 15 million Americans changed their counties of residence during this war, while 8 million migrated to different states – from south to north, or more frequently from east to west. The combined populations of Washington, Oregon, California, and Nevada grew by about a third, brining an economic boom to the region. California's dockyards hired close to 300,000 workers, its aviation industries about 250,000. By the terms of laws passed by Congress in November 1942, 2 million agricultural workers and over 4 million industrial workers were exempted from the draft. The "new economy" was particularly attractive to young workers – those under thirty years of age – who had little or no vocational skills and had been raised in depressed rural areas, ailing industrial neighborhoods, or in the South, which alone lost 700,000 men and women. Across the great divides of race, class, and gender, the wish to break loose from Depression-era unemployment was so strong that the country did not have to impose the kinds of controls or enforced recruitment found in other belligerent powers. In other words, voluntarism set the stage for a contest abroad rather than a collision between the classes and sexes at home. The war economy therefore was a truly national effort.[10]

---

9 Kennedy, *Freedom*, 650–4; Overy, *Wurzeln*, 89–91, 248, 251–5; Eric Foner, *The Story of American Freedom* (New York and London, 1998), 232–5.

10 Marilynn S. Johnson, *The Second Gold Rush: Oakland and the East Bay in World War II* (Berkeley, 1993), 30–143; Gerald D. Nash, *The American West Transformed: The Impact of the Second World War* (Bloomington, 1985), 23–8, 38–40, 156, 213–14; William Chafe, *The American Woman: Her Changing Political, Economic, and Social Role in the Twentieth Century* (New York, 1972), 135, 140–8, 159–61, 171–3; Leila J. Rupp, "War Is not Healthy for Children and other Living Things: Reflections on the Impact of Total War on Women," in James Titus, ed., *The Home Front and War in the Twentieth*

CRUSADERS

Since Roosevelt's first day in office, the American quest for self-assertion had had a distinctive semantic marker: "Security." In his inauguration speech, the fireside chats, and his annual state-of-the-union messages, the president adoopted "security" and "freedom from fear" as political leitmotifs. These terms reverberated in public debates during the New Deal years. Job security, market security, financial security, life-cycle security, and even the traditional American notion of freedom were redesigned in this spirit. America provided security because it was free, and it would remain free as long as its security was protected. The new language undercut isolationism. Isolationists had thrived on a culture of fear that was embedded in the American political tradition − fear of conspiracy, fear of modernism, fear of the unknown. After a decade of increasingly radical agitation, their pessimistic style of politics had become exhausted. It could indict, but it could not inspire. Inspiration was the New Deal's heart and soul. No matter how serious the setbacks that his programs suffered in Congress or the courts, the president's defiant gospel resonated with the public. "We are going to make a country in which no one is left out."[11] The reasons for Roosevelt's success with this emotional appeal are still a matter of debate. In any case, compared to the record of most of his predecessors, not to mention his successors, his performance was stellar. Even contemporaries who otherwise held different views about Roosevelt agreed that the nation's emotional landscape looked different in the late 1930s. Americans had regained a sense of patriotism and seemed to believe again in their country.[12]

As the threat of war mounted in Europe and Asia, Roosevelt intensified his efforts to educate the American public. After the crises over Austria and Czechoslovakia in 1938, he decided to circumvent the neutrality laws. He began with a strategy "short of war," but during the debate over lend-lease, he moved toward a policy of "risking war." Religious persecution in Europe provided a means to force the issue. After extensive and unusually agitated coverage of the *Reichskristallnacht* in the American press, the president used his State-of-the-Union message in January 1939 to speak out. "There comes a time in the affairs of men," he said, "when they must prepare to defend

---

Century: The American Experience in Comparative Perspective (Colorado Springs, CO, 1984), 156–69; Kennedy, *Freedom*, 634, 748, 768, 775–9.

11 Kennedy, *Freedom*, 378.

12 Ibid., 146, 246–8, 256, 365, 379, 760–1; Foner, *American Freedom*, 237; Edward A. Shils, *The Torment of Secrecy: The Background and Consequences of American Security Policies* (Chicago, 1996), 92–8; George H. Gallup, *The Gallup Poll: Public Opinion 1935–1971*, 3 vols. (New York, 1972), 1: 1–257.

not their homes alone but the tenets of faith and humanity on which their churches, their governments and their very civilization are founded. The defense of religion, of democracy, and of good faith among nations is all the same fight."[13] Religion, the rule of law, and civilization became a rhetorical triangle, which was ideally suited to the emotional resources of a nation built on religious freedom and the promise of a New Jerusalem. It provided in all events the bases for promoting preparedness and mobilization. Albeit with the flexibility that earned him the sobriquet of the "juggler in the White House," Roosevelt stayed the course. As he appealed to other sacred grounds in American history, his message began to sound like a variation of Abraham Lincoln's: "You cannot live in a world half slave and half free." Soon the idea of security took on a different ring. It no longer implied protection from domestic hazards alone, but also safety from foreign threats, a military strategy no less than economic and social reform. Roosevelt was creating a concept of "total policy" that was soon to be popularized under the rubric of "national security." A language of national mobilization was taking shape.[14]

For a while, however, the effort seemed to have exhausted Roosevelt's political capital. He had conveyed the impression of a leader who could walk the devil to the bridge and still outwit him, but powerful isolationist sentiments remained strong in all sectors of American political life. Although they were flawed and open to conflicting readings, public opinion polls suggested that the urban middle class alone was receptive to Roosevelt's arguments. The working class, which was the core of his political coalition, remained as detached and indifferent as lower-class rural voters. To make matters worse, the "Roosevelt recession" of 1938, coupled with setbacks in midterm elections that year and a congressional majority that was still inclined to enact "permanent neutrality" into law, all seemed to paralyze the Democratic Party's faithful. Some commentators wondered if anyone would bother to vote in the presidential election in 1940. As the election approached, even Roosevelt's close friends worried that he might have predicted his own political future years earlier when he had remarked, during a moody session with his inner circle, that "It's a terrible thing to look over your shoulder when you are trying to lead – and find no one there."[15]

---

13 Samuel I. Rosenman, ed., *The Public Papers and Addresses of Franklin D. Roosevelt*, 13 vols. (New York, 1938–50), 2: 1.

14 B. D. Zevin, *Nothing to Fear: The Addresses of Franklin Delano Roosevelt 1932–1945* (Cambridge, MA, 1946), 266–7; Foner, *American Freedom*, 224.

15 Kennedy, *Freedom*, 344, 400–406, 455–7.

Ironically, the Republicans saved the Democratic administration. A new generation had moved into the Republican Party's leadership, eager to build their careers on lessons they had learned during the Great War. For them, America's traditional understanding of national defense needed redefinition. Not only the security of the Western Hemisphere lay in the national interest; so, too, did essential but vulnerable trade routes across the Pacific and Atlantic Oceans. Roosevelt once called this a generation awaiting its "rendezvous with history." Europe's fall from world leadership had opened a host of new, albeit perilous prospects. To design a future in which America could move to these "new frontiers" required preparing for all contingencies. Since the early 1930s, German and Japanese imperialism had made the challenge compelling. While isolationist Republicans like Gerald Nye and George Norris still dominated the Senate floor, the party leadership was preparing a change of course. Stunned by the French surrender to Germany in June 1940, delegates at the Republican convention nominated the internationalist Wendell Willkie as their presidential candidate. Roosevelt encouraged this "interventionist turn" in the party by appointing two Republican elder statesmen, Frank Knox and Henry Stimson, to key positions in his cabinet. These developments removed major political obstacles to mobilization. During the 1940 campaign, a cloak of silence surrounded foreign policy issues, denying critics a nationwide forum in which to air their concerns. Had it not been for this tacit agreement between Willkie and Roosevelt, the Selective Service Act, which provided for early recruitment of able-bodied men for the military, might have failed in Congress. When the isolationist *Chicago Tribune* published a set of contingency war plans, which had been leaked to the editor weeks before Pearl Harbor, it stirred only a bored response. A coalition between the two parties had emerged from the election, providing a bipartisan model for brokering foreign and military policy.[16]

Thus, a new dynamic drove American politics after Pearl Harbor. Captive to their misconceptions about the United States, the Japanese had counted on Washington's unwillingness to fight a long war. Quickly, however, the United States rallied around the call for total war or, as it was formulated in the American idiom, "total victory." This slogan became the currency honored across an otherwise divided political landscape. It not only activated a crusading nationalism among antimilitarists and isolationists, but it also appealed to the insecure and anxious side of American populism, which had embraced conspiracy theories and images of subversive aliens. American

---

16 Frank Freidel, *Franklin D. Roosevelt: A Rendezvous with Destiny* (Boston, 1990), 289–404; David Fromkin, *In the Time of the Americans: FDR, Truman, Eisenhower, Marshall, MacArthur – The Generation that Changed America's Role in the World* (New York, 1995), 181–379.

populists were receptive to calls for total revenge and the obliteration of evil, and they now endorsed a war that many of them had once declared intolerable. Even traditional liberals succumbed to the ideological appeal of "total victory." Many regarded the war as an opportunity to redress the errors of America's diplomacy after the last war. They greeted this second chance to build "one world" around an international organization. The writings of Wendell Willkie and Henry Wallace alike addressed this point. Other liberals joined the campaign because they recognized the threat posed by the Nazis. Liberal periodicals provided ample evidence of this view. All factions agreed with the president about America's new vulnerability. Only total victory promised to eliminate the threat of modern weaponry in the foreseeable future. Curiously, this alliance of perspectives did not stir idealistic passions. Instead, the United States mobilized in a typically businesslike way.[17]

SHAREHOLDERS

Mobilization for total war was a question of networking. It required the art of coordinating economic interests, political programs, and public morale. From this perspective, the United States seemed at first glance to be vulnerable. Compared with European states, it lacked a proper "institutional memory" for managing mobilization. The system that had been built around the War Industries Board during the Great War disappeared after the end of this struggle. Nonetheless, the agency had created a basis for significant advances in the 1920s and 1930s. Under the auspices of the Office of the Assistant Secretary of War (OASW), a tripartite production team was put together that linked executive agencies, the military, and industry. Prior to 1939, the OASW oversaw four different plans for industrial mobilization. Although it was deficient in many respects, this effort helped to bridge the gap between the military and the business community. All major business and trade associations were drawn into its orbit, and some fourteen thousand industrial managers were given the rank of reserve officers as they moved in and out of the program. So as mobilization began again, planning agencies were better prepared than they had been a generation earlier. There is a host of literature on the War Production Board and its affiliated agencies, which oversaw economic mobilization after 1941. And just as plentiful are

---

17 Michael Sherry, *In the Shadow of War: The United States since the 1930s* (New Haven, 1995), 30–5, 41, 57–9, 62, 197; Overy, *Wurzeln*, 141, 146–8, 377; Shils, *Torment*, 118, 133; Koistinen, "Warfare State," 49, 53; Fussell, *Wartime*, 168–73; 177–80; Kennedy, *Freedom*, 619, 630–3; Richard Hofstadter, *The Paranoid Style in American Politics and Other Essays* (Cambridge, MA, 1996), 3–41; Daniel Patrick Moynihan, *Secrecy: The American Experience* (New Haven, 1998), 127–31.

the assessments of the achievements of these agencies. Some authors emphasize the chaotic early years, when a lack of internal coordination wasted enormous material resources and manpower. Other authors charge civilian leaders with favoring big business or the military, and with allowing each to aggrandize its power at public expense and beyond the reach of political control. Still others praise the same record as nuanced power-brokering, the successful negotiation of conflicting interests. Each of these approaches offers valuable insights, but their fixation on state and federal bureaucracies leads them all to ignore a major point.[18]

Beyond the governmental agencies lay a vast variety of yet untapped social networks. Activated in the late 1930s, they were the bases of "grassroots mobilization," of voluntary and often unsolicited engagement in the war effort. The histories of labor unions and African-American organizations are revealing, well-documented cases in point. On the eve of the war, it looked as if the labor and ethnic unrest of the 1930s would continue. In 1940, twenty-five hundred strikes took place, at a cost of 6.7 million labor-days; the next year the number of strikes reached forty-three hundred, the loss of labor-days 23.1 million. Meanwhile, African-American organizations seemed ready to fight against racism both in Europe and on the home front. Within months of Pearl Harbor, however, leading union and civil-rights activists had mobilized their constituencies in an effort to moderate the social costs of war. Black activism converted into "good-conduct campaigns" in support of the patriotic effort. Leading unions joined the race to demonstrate their loyalty with "no-strike pledges," disclaimers of wage increases, and a campaign against militants like the United Mine Workers' John L. Lewis. These efforts all represented an "unmilitaristic militarism." Mobilizing for war represented an opportunity for social and political advancement; mobilization was, in this respect, like a shareholder's investing in the future of a company. Spokesmen for black organizations called for a "New Reconstruction," while union leaders envisaged a "New Unionism" that would bring long-overdue recognition of workers as political and social equals. Similar hopes had been disappointed during the Great War, and proponents of social change encountered setbacks as early as 1942. Disappointments, however, were either brushed aside or deployed as arguments that the cause had to be pushed harder. "This wasn't going to be like the last war," claimed an executive of the United Automobile Workers.

---

18 Paul Koistinen, "The 'Industrial-Military Complex' in Historical Perspective: The Inter-War Years,"
    Journal of American History 56 (1970): 819–39; Koistinen, "Warfare State," 51–62; Overy, *Wurzeln*,
    336.

"Labor was coming up to the quarter-deck just as if it had a right to be there."[19]

Volunteering for the war effort promised social and economic improvement for underprivileged groups around the country. From Idaho to California, the American West had lived economically in the shadow and at the mercy – of the industrial Northeast. Prices of Western raw materials and freight rates were set in New York, Philadelphia, Detroit, and Chicago. Only 5 percent of the western region's gross income came from industrial production, and many observers lamented the West's colonial status. The demand for war production changed everything. Some $70 billion of federal defense contracts headed West. The Bank of America, a private enterprise with headquarters in California, began, at long last, to look after the region's interests. So did the Reconstruction Finance Corporation, which assigned its subsidiaries to provide economic aid to the area. Hundreds of mines and industrial plants began to produce aluminum, iron and steel, magnesium, and other basics in the Rocky Mountain area – in Utah, Nevada, Oregon, Idaho, and Washington. The city of Seattle alone attracted $5.6 billion in defense contracts. California topped them all. It attracted 12 percent of the federal budget earmarked for war-related production, as its industrial output expanded from $2.8 billion in 1939 to $10.1 billion in 1944. Producing raw materials, airplanes, and ships, the country's erstwhile economic hinterland had become a pace-setter.[20]

Federal money encouraged the grass-roots mobilizers. "Never before," stated one Californian, "have there been quite so many people . . . quite so intent on giving a voice to the conviction that we have our foot in the door of an era of dream realization."[21] Economic growth was on everyone's mind. Bankers, union leaders, educators, journalists, city planners, and local businessmen quickly mastered the arts of lobbying and joined forces in a political contest over the federal budget, or, as the mayor of Los Angeles put it, "against the concentration of political interests in the East Coast."[22] Washington, D.C., was receptive to their importunities. Political heavyweights like Harold Ickes, the Secretary of the Interior, Senator Joseph C. O'Mahoney, and many congressmen supported the Western cause, which offered a new opportunity for frustrated New Dealers to realize their vision

19 Brinkley, *End of Reform*, 200–20; Vatter, *Economy in World War II*, 43–5; Nash, *American West Transformed*, 90–103; Harvard Sitkoff, "American Blacks in World War II: Rethinking the Militancy-Watershed Hypothesis," in Titus, *Home Front*, 147–55; Allan M. Winkler, *Home Front U.S.A.: America During World War II* (Arlington Heights, IL, 1986), 16–18; John Morton Blum, V *Was for Victory: Politics and American Culture During World War II* (New York, 1976), 183–9, 196–9, 208–12.
20 Nash, *American West*, 3–8, 17–29, 33, 36.
21 Ibid., 204, 211–12.   22 Lotchin, *Fortress*, 131.

of a decentralized national economy. In the spring of 1945, greater Los
Angeles acquired more defense funds than its workforce could handle. City
planners competed with fantastic designs for urban areas. Compared to the
Reber Plan for the San Francisco Bay Area, Haussmann's reconstruction of
nineteenth-century Paris looked modest. Observers like Wendell Berge, the
deputy Attorney General of the United States, were elated over this new
"frontier," and *Harper's* magazine wrote that the Western quest for industrial
self-determination was about to be realized – as a base for reaching out to the
world's largest market in Asia. "Realization that the dream can be fulfilled
has made the West all but drunk."[23] Hardly a metaphor remained unemployed to describe the return of prosperity and a new "Spirit of St. Louis"
to America.[24]

In 1944, hundreds of towns and cities created citizens' commissions to
ponder the possibilities of postwar economic development. These bodies
included people from all walks of economic, political, and community life.
The richness and breadth of their debates still await their historian. In the
beginning, these debates reflected traditional American concerns about the
proper timing of demobilization. Still, industrial readjustment had to be
implemented quickly if well-organized military interests were to be contained. But calls for reconverting war plants to produce consumer goods
had a curious ring, for they accompanied anxieties lest the region be rele-
gated to its prewar subordination. "San Diego," stated the city's Chamber
of Commerce, "has the alternative of becoming a ghost city after the war,
or retaining its present industries and developing into a great metropolitan
community."[25] In the end, the specter of a "bust economy" loomed much
larger than the dangers of a militarized "boom economy." In all events,
in San Diego, Los Angeles, San Francisco, and countless other Western
towns, the die had been cast by the summer of 1944. These cities called
for maintaining huge naval installations, for greater output of fighter planes,
and for strategic stockpiling to guarantee the prosperity of Western mining.
The West demanded insurance against economic contraction, despite the
foreign policy risks and military ramifications of this course of action. Realizing this vision involved intricate bargaining, particularly because beyond
the aircraft, shipbuilding, and machine-tool sectors, strong industrial interest
groups still favored quick demobilization. Compared with the aftermath of
the First World War, however, the political momentum behind reconversion to peacetime production was weak. The alliance between small business

23 Nash, *American West*, 28, 31–5, 201, 210.
24 Ibid., 28, 31–5, 201, 204, 210–12; Lotchin, *Fortress*, 132–8, 153–5.
25 Lotchin, *Fortress*, 156.

and big navy, between mayors and majors, between unions and Chambers of Commerce had restricted the options before the War Production Board officially ended the reconversion debate in late 1944. The "corporatist network" of defense spending was organized for good.[26]

"Pioneers," "crusaders," and "shareholders" were the protagonists of America's mobilization, and in the process they all became agents of the country's militarization at mid-century. These were not hardboiled militarists, but pragmatic, business-minded civilians, men and women who viewed armament as a necessary evil and who preferred civilian to military values, arbitration to war. By mobilizing for total war, however, they changed history inadvertently. They had not planned to dissolve the lines between American civil society and the military. Yet this dissolution was the major domestic consequence of a war that otherwise could not have been waged, let alone won. Mobilizing for war was an effort to achieve both national organization and social integration. The mock battle at the Los Angeles Coliseum anticipated the dynamics of this process. It revealed the enthusiasm and energy that opened the door to a postwar world of "Permanent Preparedness."[27]

26 Ibid., 136, 142, 146, 151, 157–70; Nash, *American West*, 44–6, 202–12; Koistinen, "Warfare State," 62–4.

27 Michael Geyer, "The Militarization of Europe, 1914–1945," in Gillis, *Militarization*, 70, 80; Peter Karsten, "Militarization and Rationalization in the United States, 1870–1914," ibid., 42–4.

The War Against Noncombatants

14

Partisan War in Belorussia, 1941–1944

HANS-HEINRICH NOLTE

The war between German units and Soviet partisans in the occupied territories of the Soviet Union was fought by both sides with all the means at
their disposal. Both aimed at the destruction of the other, and neither made
a practice of taking prisoners as distinctions between soldiers and civilians
blurred.[1]

The contours of this war are uncontested, but most conclusions have
rested on German sources, primarily the reports of police and army units.[2]
These sources have important limitations. They include few first-hand accounts from German or Soviet perpetrators, whose testimony would have
represented incriminating evidence against themselves. The language of
the German sources is coded. The reports tended to camouflage genocide, whether undertaken against Jews, Gypsies, or Belorussian villagers, in
formalistic language – in terms like "*Aktion,*" "*Sonderbehandlung,*" "*Umsied-
lung,*" and "*Banditen.*" In addition, these sources tend to ignore or understate
the role of collaborators.

---

1 See Rolf-Dieter Müller and Gerd R. Ueberschär, *Hitlers Krieg im Osten 1941–1945: Forschungsbericht*
(Darmstadt, 2000), 321–2, 353–64; Joachim Hoffmann, "Der Krieg aus der Sicht der Sowjetunion,"
in Horst Boog et al., *Das Deutsche Reich und der Zweite Weltkrieg*, 7 vols. (Stuttgart, 1983–2000), 4:
752–7; Jürgen Förster, "Die Sicherung des 'Lebensraums,'" ibid., 1030–62; Bernd Bonwetsch, "Der
'Grosse Vaterländische Krieg,'" in Gottfried Schramm, ed., *Handbuch der Geschichte Russlands*, 3 vols.
(Stuttgart, 1984), 3: 943–7.
2 John A. Armstrong, ed., *Soviet Partisans in World War II* (Madison, 1964), 651–756; Bernd
Bonwetsch, "Die Partisanenbekämpfung und ihre Opfer im Russlandfeldzug," in Wolfgang Wip-
perman and Klaus Meyer, eds., *Gegen das Vergessen: Der Vernichtungskrieg gegen die Sowjetunion
1941–1945* (Frankfurt, 1992), 102–13; Erich Hesse, *Der sowjetische Partisanenkrieg 1941–1944 im
Spiegel deutscher Kampfanweisungen und Befehle* (2d ed., Göttingen and Zürich, 1993); Timm Richter,
"*Herrenmensch*" *und* "*Bandit*" (Münster, 1998); Lutz Klinkhammer, "Der Partisanenkrieg der
Wehrmacht," in Rolf-Dieter Müller and Hans-Erich Volkmann eds., *Die Wehrmacht* (Munich, 1999),
815–36.

Despite a number of extensive published editions, the Russian-language sources have not been much exploited.[3] Soviet historiography tended to ignore questions of human rights, to underplay the role of Jewish partisans, to exaggerate the influence of the party and popular support for it, and to emphasize the heroism and military significance of the partisans.

As a general proposition, the sources of the two sides must be weighed against one another.[4] The crimes committed by the one side registered more frequently in the documents of the other.[5] Soviet sources do make explicit, however, that the families of collaborators were murdered. And German sources reveal that entire villages that were suspected of harboring partisans were burned together with their inhabitants.

Archival material from partisan units in Belorussia sheds important new light on their activities. These documents reveal a surprising degree of bureaucratic organization among the partisans.[6] Each unit kept records with lists of members, supplies, and military engagements. These records belie the conclusion that small partisan units were constantly harassed by the Germans, for they had time to keep extensive files.

The following remarks exploit this archival material, as well as the German records, to address the partisan war in Belorussia. After setting the context, the essay presents case studies from two regions in Belorussia and examines both the development of the partisan movement and the German response. It argues that the methods employed by both sides in this war can be characterized as "total."

THE CONTEXT

The German plans for conquering *Lebensraum* in Soviet territory offered the indigenous peoples no political option but to fight.[7] The invading troops were ordered to treat partisans without mercy and to punish collectively all settlements from which partisans operated. The army was ordered not to

---

3 *Vsenarodnoe partizanskoe dvizhenie v Belorussii v gody Velikoj Otechestvennoj Vojny 1941–1944: Dokumenty i materialy* (hereafter VDPB), 3 vols. (Minsk, 1967–82).

4 On the problems of comparison, see Hans-Heinrich Nolte and Pavel Poljan, "Massenverbrechen in der Sowjetunion und im nationalsozialistischen Deutschland: Zum Vergleich der Diktaturen," in *Zeitschrift für Weltgeschichte* (hereafter ZWG) 2 (2001):125–48.

5 See Hans-Heinrich Nolte, "Weltsystem und Area-Studies: Das Beispiel Russland," ZWG 1 (2000): 75–98.

6 I would like to thank D. Selemenev and M. Redkozubova for their great help at the National Archives of Belorussia, hereafter cited as NARB.

7 Bernhard Chiari, *Alltag hinter der Front: Besatzung, Kollaboration und Widerstand in Weissrussland 1941–1944* (Düsseldorf, 1998); Christian Gerlach, *Kalkulierte Morde: Die deutsche Wirtschafts- und Vernichtungspolitik in Weissrussland 1941 bis 1944* (Hamburg, 1999).

take prisoners of war, and the prosecution of crimes by Germans against inhabitants of the occupied territory was suspended.[8]

The Germans not only anticipated partisan warfare; they welcomed it. In a briefing to his ministers on July 16, 1941, Hitler noted that "the partisan war has its advantages: it opens up the possibility of annihilating all opposition."[9] Later the same month, the army high command intensified the campaign against partisans. It criticized units that had not been vigilant and called for the punishment not only of actual partisan attacks, but also of all attempted opposition. Partisans and their settlements were to be annihilated.[10] These actions were undertaken by the Sicherungsdivisionen of the Wehrmacht, the Sicherheitsdienst of the SS, the German Sicherheitspolizei, and by anti-Bolshevik "Ordnungpolizei" recruited from indigenous groups in the occupied territories.[11]

The Soviet government welcomed partisan war, too, at least in theory, as "peoples' war." Nonetheless, the Soviet Union had made no preparations for this kind of war in 1941, hoping perhaps that the war would be fought in enemy territory, or – more likely – fearing that armed resistance among the peasant masses might eventually turn against the Soviet regime itself.[12] In all events, the partisan war was initiated by committed Communists who exploited the army's orders that every soldier fight to the finish.[13] Hence, soldiers who were not captured by the Germans were given little practical choice but to form or join partisan units.[14]

Already in 1941, Jews from the countryside fled to the woods, aware of the genocide in rural areas committed during the advance of the Wehrmacht. During the summer of 1942, many Jews fled the ghettos, realizing that

---

8 Bundesarchiv Militärarchiv (hereafter BA), RW 4/v. 577; see Hans-Heinrich Nolte, *Der deutsche Überfall auf die Sowjetunion 1941* (Hannover, 1991); Jürgen Förster, "Verbrecherische Befehle," Wolfram Wette and Gerd R. Ueberschär, eds., *Kriegsverbrechen im 20. Jahrhundert* (Darmstadt, 2001), 137–51.

9 Cited in Gerd Ueberschär and Wolfram Wette, eds., *"Unternehmen Barbarossa": Der deutsche Überfall auf die Sowjetunion 1941* (Paderborn, 1984), No. 15, 330–1.

10 Norbert Müller, ed., *Die faschistische Okkupationspolitik in den zeitweilig besetzten Gebieten der Sowjetunion* (Berlin, 1991), No. 24, 169–71.

11 Ibid., No. 40, 193–6.

12 See Hans-Heinrich Nolte, "Stalinism as Total Social War," in Roger Chickering and Stig Förster, eds., *The Shadows of Total War: Europe, East Asia, and the United States, 1919–1939* (Cambridge, 2003).

13 Robert W. Thurston, "Cauldrons of Loyalty and Betrayal: Soviet Soldiers' Behavior 1941 and 1945," in Robert W. Thurston and Bernd Bonwetsch, eds., *The People's War: Responses to World War II in the Soviet Union* (Urbana, IL, 2000), 235–57; Nolte, *Überfall,* 161–2; Heinrich Nolte, *Vom Cannae-Mythos: Tendenzen und Katastrophen* (Göttingen, 1991), 81–4.

14 Vladimir Naumov and Leonid Resin, "Repressionen gegen sowjetische Kriegsgefangene und zivile Repatrianten in der UdSSR 1941 bis 1956," in Klaus-Dieter Müller, Konstantin Nikischkin, and Günther Wagenlehner, eds., *Die Tragödie der Gefangenschaft in Deutschland und der Sowjetunion* (Cologne, 1998), 339.

the towns would not save them either.[15] They then became an important element in the partisan movement. As a member of the German army's command in Minsk noted at the end of 1942, "it is well known that many Jews are fleeing to the bandits. They recognize that they are going to be eliminated sooner or later, so they choose the lesser evil."[16] Jews learned, however, that if they arrived unarmed, the partisans would be reluctant to protect them.

The partisan war in the Soviet Union was governed by no laws or moral considerations. The Germans were determined to exploit the resources of the conquered territories in the interests of the "master race." To this end, they were prepared to murder Jews, Gypsies, and Communists. Even Erich Hesse, whose account of the war tends toward apologetics, concluded of the German effort that "the incapability and unwillingness to take account of the Russian popular psyche and its values is alarming; the [Germans'] willingness to turn their backs on their own traditions of military honor is unexplainable."[17]

On June 29, 1941, the Sovnarkom (Council of Peoples Commissars or government) and TsK (Central Committee) of the Communist Party ordered the army to destroy everything as it retreated to the east. They added that

in the areas taken by the enemy, partisan and diversionary units have to be formed in order to fight against the arms of the enemy, to wage partisan war in all places and at all times in order to destroy bridges, roads, telephone and telegraph poles, and in order to burn down the stores and warehouses. In the occupied areas, unbearable conditions must be created for the enemy and all his collaborators; they must be harassed and destroyed at every step, and all their plans must be disrupted.[18]

In a speech on July 3, Stalin elaborated. He ordered that

partisan units, mounted and on foot, must be formed; diversionary groups must be organized to combat the enemy troops, to foment partisan warfare everywhere, to blow up bridges and roads, damage telephone and telegraph lines, set fire to forests, stores, transports. In the occupied regions conditions must be made unbearable for the enemy and all his accomplices. They must be hounded and annihilated at every step and all their measures frustrated.[19]

This order became part of a general instruction to undertake partisan warfare. It was captured by the Germans in September 1941 and distributed to all military commands.[20]

---

15 Shalom Cholawsky, *The Jews of Belorussia during World War II* (Amsterdam, 1998).
16 BA, RW 30/39, 9.   17 Hesse, *Partisanenkrieg*, 281.
18 VPDB, 1: 50–51.   19 Armstrong, *Soviet Partisans*, 656.
20 Hesse, *Partisanenkrieg*, 287–94.

Meanwhile, the order was given to party departments to form underground organizations and establish an underground press.[21] On July 1, the TsK declared that "in order to exterminate the enemy, do not hesitate to use every possible measure: strangle, strike, burn, and hunt the Fascist monster down. Soon the enemy will feel that the soil is burning beneath his feet."[22] On the same day, Voroshilov and Ponomarenko, the first secretary of the CP(b)B (Communist Party of Belorussia), dispatched the first NKVD group to prepare for work as partisans. On July 6, the Belorussian SovKom (Council of Commissars) and the TSK of the CP(b)B (Central Committee of the Communist Party of Belorussia) ordered the formation of a civil guard (*opolchenie*) and destruction battalions (*iztrebitel'nye bataljony*) in order to support the Red Army from bases in the factories and collective farms, which were instructed to arm themselves, if nothing else was available, with "bottles filled with combustible fluid" (which later became known as Molotov cocktails). In the event a village or town was occupied, these groups were to transform themselves into partisan units.[23]

On June 25, the TsK of the CP(b)B claimed that it had formed 118 partisan groups in Belorussia with 2,644 members.[24] A month later, however, the TsK of the Komsomol of Belorussia criticized the Komsomol leaders of the western, formerly Polish part of the region for abandoning the area without establishing underground networks and combat units. The TsK claimed that in eastern Belorussia, by contrast, all members of the Komsomol had joined destruction battalions and had taken to the woods when their territory was occupied.[25]

Local groups mainly to the east of the old Soviet border reported successes in implementing the measures ordered by the Komsomol and the TsK.[26] On July 16, the Party committee of Vitebsk reported that two partisan units had been founded in its region.[27] On August 16, two additional partisan groups, which counted thirty and fifty-seven members, reported from Starobinsk, near Minsk, about the bridges they had burned down and the German soldiers they had killed. They also reported that the Germans had seized cattle in some villages, while in others the partisans had driven the cattle into the woods as German troops approached. Partisans distributed printed copies of Stalin's speech of July 3 via an underground paper. "The people support the partisans eagerly and help them as much as they can," read

21 VPDB, 1: 52–3. 22 Ibid., 54.
23 Ibid., 55–7. 24 Ibid., 80.
25 Ibid., 77–9. 26 Ibid., 69–70.
27 Ibid.

the report, "but only if they can do so secretly, since the Germans already have shot many people and burned many villages that were connected to the partisans."[28] The group in Zlobinsk, near Gomel, reported on the transformation of a destruction battalion, which the Communists and Soviet *intelligencija* had formed, into a partisan unit. The Germans had encircled a battalion of 150 armed civilians, together with the Red Army's 154th Infantry Division, on August 15. Fifteen men escaped to form a partisan unit. From the peasants they learned that "the Germans rob them and take away everything, and that they collect the Communists, *comsomoltsy*, and the active part of the village, and take them somewhere."[29] In a report from a region along the old Polish border, a woman partisan wrote in August that the partisans lacked weapons and that they had to lie low in the face of German superiority. But after ambushing a German unit, they resolved to become more active and asked for material by airlift.[30]

Partisan warfare developed in several stages. Christian Gerlach, who has written about the German effort, has identified four.[31] The first extended from the summer of 1941 to the spring of 1942. During this period, the Germans hoped that the partisans would not survive the winter. Accordingly, the occupation forces attempted to control them by means of limited actions against Communist cadres and Jews, as well as against people who lacked roots in the villages. From the spring of 1942 until the spring of 1943, the Germans resorted to larger-scale operations, encircling territories held by partisans and murdering the civilian population in them. The Germans' growing need for labor discouraged this policy, however, as the occupiers increasingly conscripted all young people into compulsory labor in the Reich. A third stage began after the spring of 1943, when the Germans began to create "dead zones" from which all inhabitants were evacuated – either to forced labor in Germany or – those unable to work – to special settlements in other districts, where many of them starved to death. The forests were burned down. Finally, in 1944, the Germans resorted to creating so-called *Wehrdörfer*, villages inhabited by collaborators and capable of defending themselves.

Examining the Soviet side, John Armstrong has written of three stages through which the partisan movement developed.[32] From June until December 1941, partisan groups were small and consisted primarily of Communist activists and Soviet soldiers who had escaped capture. The goal of these partisans was to blend into the villages, but they soon took to the

28 Ibid., 110–13.   29 Ibid., 113–17.
30 Ibid., 92–4; cf. Faye Schulman, *Die Schreie meines Volkes in mir* (Munich, 1998), 105–12.
31 Gerlach, *Morde*, 859–1054.   32 Armstrong, *Soviet Partisans*, 21–7.

forests to live as "full-time partisans." From December 1941 until the fall of 1942, the movement grew, particularly in Belorussia, where it was encouraged by the failure of the Germans to take Moscow. Material support for partisan units flowed through "gaps" in the frontlines, which the Germans could not cover, or came by air. The military impact of the partisans did not yet, however, reflect their growing numbers. From the fall of 1942 until the summer of 1944, the Red Army's central command tried to coordinate the operations of partisan groups more effectively against German railways and lines of communication, especially during the destruction of the German central army group in June 1944.

Hannes Heer has suggested that at the beginning of the German occupation, there was a "partisan war without partisans." In many cases, he argues, the Germans invented or imagined partisan activity in order to legitimate their own harsh actions against Soviet civilians.[33] This argument overlooks the large number of Communists and soldiers in the occupied territories – armed groups that had no chance of survival except by fighting. It also disregards the presence of unarmed, but resourceful and brave groups of Jews, who also quickly realized that fighting represented their only chance to survive. Finally, Heer's view does not take into account the fact that the Wehrmacht hoped to break Soviet resistance with very small occupation forces, but that this policy left much of the occupied territories uncontrolled.

Two areas in Belorussia revealed that as early as the summer of 1942 large liberated zones supported extended groups of fighters behind the German lines. These units destroyed German railway lines and even established rural Soviets.

SLONIM

The first case was the region of Slonim, in western Belorussia, which had lain in eastern Poland before 1939.[34] This region was typical of the northern European plain. The soils were largely morainal; villages and towns were found on the better ground, while woods, swamps, small lakes, and fens dominated elsewhere. The region was inhabited by Belorussian peasants, Polish nobles and officials, and Jewish townspeople in the *Shtetl*.

The Germans quickly conquered Slonim in June 1941. The murder of the Jewish population began immediately, as did the formation of partisan

---

33 Hannes Heer, *Tote Zonen: Die deutsche Wehrmacht an der Ostfront* (Hamburg, 1999), 42–60.
34 See Hans-Heinrich Nolte, "Destruction and Resistance: The Jewish Shtetl of Slonim 1941–1944," in Thurston and Bonwetsch, *People's War*, 29–53.

groups among the soldiers who had been cut off behind the German lines.[35] The Soviet side developed an organizational concept for the partisans in Belorussia immediately after the invasion in June 1941.[36] Beginning in July, the regime demanded that the Communist party organize the partisan movement behind the lines. Partisans were obliged to swear "to work a terrible, merciless, and unrelenting revenge upon the enemy for the burning of our cities and villages, for the murder of our children, and for the torture and atrocities committed against our people. Blood for blood! Death for death!"[37]

Near the village of Byten, south of the town of Slonim, Aleksandr V. Fridrik, the president of the rural soviet, and an army political commissar named G. A. Dudko established a partisan movement in the woods in the autumn of 1941. The partisans distributed leaflets throughout the region and undertook their first military operations against the Germans. When Fridrik was killed in action, G. A. Proniagin, a lieutenant in the Red Army, became commander of the unit, which in May 1942 assumed the name "Shhorc-brigade." At this time it numbered a thousand fighters and had the use of three pieces of artillery, ninety-six machine guns, two hundred fifty bicycles, and two trucks.[38] In March 1942, the Jewish resistance in the town Slonim established contact with the partisans; and in the summer a Jewish unit of the brigade was formed. On August 3, 1942, the brigade routed a German garrison in the small town of Kosov, saving the Jewish population; and it liberated the surrounding region, which lay just north of the main German supply route between Brest-Litovsk and Minsk. Ten Germans were taken prisoner. Ten local policemen, who had used their weapons in the action, were shot on the spot, while twenty-seven others, who had not used their weapons, were disarmed and sent home. Another unit that took part in the attack reported that sixty Germans and a hundred fifty collaborating "*politsaj*" were killed.[39] Thousands of civilians, particularly Jews from small neighboring settlements, fled into the reconquered territory (*zavoevannyj rajon*), while the partisans either harvested the grain or requisitioned it from the peasants.

35 A. V. Khackevich and R. R. Kriuchok, *Stanovlenie partizanskogo dvizhenija v Belorussi* (Minsk, 1980); cf. Ralph Mavrogordato and Earl Ziemke, "The Polotsk Lowland," in Armstrong, *Soviet Partisans*, 527–32; Gerhard L. Weinberg, "The Yelnya-Dorogobuzh Area of the Smolensk Oblast," ibid., 401–9.

36 Armstrong, *Soviet Partisans*, 13–14.   37 Ibid., 662.

38 NARB, fond 3178, opis 13, delo 10. list 2; ibid., list 99–115; cf. G. A. Proniagin, *U samoj granice* (Minsk, 1979). The first is published in parts (without reference to the Jewish fighters) in VDPD, 1: 559–62.

39 Ibid., 423.

Only in December 1942 did the Germans respond. In two actions, which bore the names "Hamburg" and "Altona," a special task force under the leadership of the Police and SS chief Curt von Gottberg killed 1,773 partisans and 5,033 civilians.[40] The civilian deaths included 2,784 Jews, 2,295 Belorussians, and 54 Gypsies.[41] The Jewish members of the partisans were not counted separately. The Belorussian casualties were peasants in the liberated territory. The Germans seized the harvest and much of the livestock.

Despite this success, the Germans failed to put the reoccupied territory to use. The settlements had been burned and the peasants killed. It was pointless to defend a useless, empty region, so when the German task force left for another region, the surviving partisans drifted back. In March 1943, an official with the German civil administration informed the general commissioner of Belorussia in Minsk, Wilhelm Kube, that the region of Slonim again contained two large pockets of partisans. "It is remarkable," he reported,

that both regions were cleared some months ago in connection with the von-Gottberg actions, when the peasant population was partly liquidated and partly sent to the Reich. In the same region new bands have now formed. This is in itself proof enough that it is impossible to solve the problem of bandits purely by police actions. I am convinced that the liquidation of a couple of villages not only fails to harm the partisans, but also drives considerable parts of the population into their hands.[42]

The Belorussian peasants were used to bearing heavy burdens, including terror, but they did not understand why the Germans burned their villages. As one woman put it in an interview, the war was a conflict between Stalin and Hitler, "but what did the villages have to do with that? The village had anyway to feed both the Germans and the Russians."[43]

The war between the Germans and the partisans in this region was primarily about controlling territory and its agrarian and forest products. In addition to the laborers whom they sent back to Germany, the occupiers also attempted to enlist indigenous handicrafts and small industry in their war effort. Some shops, for example, constructed small horse-drawn vehicles called *panjewagen* for the Wehrmacht.[44]

40 Gerlach, *Morde*, 899–904.   41 NARB, fond 4683, opis 3, delo 947, 226.

42 NARB, fond 370, opis 1, delo 481, 109.

43 Interview with Nina Radashkevich, now in the Archive of the Gedenkstätte Bergen-Belsen; cf. Hans-Heinrich Nolte, ed., *Häftlinge aus der UdSSR in Bergen-Belsen* (Frankfurt, 2001), 59–60, 154–5.

44 See Ulrich Herbert, *Fremdarbeiter: Politik und Praxis des "Ausländereinsatzes" in der Kriegswirtschaft des Dritten Reiches* (2d ed., Berlin and Bonn, 1986); Pavel Poljan, *Zhertvy dvukh diktatur* (Moscow, 1996); Mark Spoerer, *Zwangsarbeit unter dem Hakenkreuz* (Stuttgart, 2001); Nolte, "Ostarbeiter," in Nolte, *Häftlinge*, 26–37; Pavel Poljan, "Ostarbeiter," ZWG 3 (2002): forthcoming.

In accordance with a command from partisan headquarters "Brest-Litovsk," the Shhorc-brigade relocated to the south, into the Polesie region, where contacts existed to partisan-controlled areas to the east of Bobruisk and Klichev.[45] By now the brigade had abandoned the idea of taking prisoners.[46] The unit derailed trains, ambushed garrisons, and killed Germans. Partisan units assassinated German officials, including Kube and Dr. Ludwig Ehrenleitner, a special district-commissioner.[47] Few German prisoners survived, and many were tortured before being killed.[48] An SS man who was captured near the liberated area of Kosov in September 1942, was burned alive in reprisal for the burning of the Slonim ghetto.[49]

The partisans were particularly savage in their treatment of collaborators, the core of whom were eliminated.[50] Civilian collaborators, real or imagined, were killed, often along with their families.[51] A high percentage of the *politsaj*, the Belorussian police that fought on the German side, were killed, but many were also given the opportunity to change sides.[52] The same was true of village elders and mayors of towns, of whom the partisans kept blacklists.[53]

KLICHEV

The town of Bobruisk was situated 250 kilometers to the east of Slonim and 150 kilometers southeast of Minsk. The wooded terrain extended to the north of Bobruisk toward Mogilev. Some 40 kilometers to the north of Bobruisk lay the small town of Klichev as a gateway to these woods.

The mayor of Klichev, a man named Tikhanovich, was an active collaborator who had organized the local Ordnungsdienst, a detachment of a hundred men who were quartered in the town.[54] The collaborators were unable, however, to defend the countryside against the partisans. In January 1942, the German military police noted a series of incidents. In the village of Krasnyj Bereg, the partisans plundered a granary and distributed grain to the population. In the village of Bazevichi, partisans burned twenty-eight

45 BA, RH 26–203, Kriegstagebuch der 203. Sicherungsdivision, 102.
46 NARB, fond 3500, opis 4, delo 311, list 12.
47 Alexander Dallin, Ralph Mavrogordato, and Wilhelm Moll, "Partisan Psychological Warfare and Popular Attitudes," in Armstrong, *Soviet Partisans*, 220–1.
48 Ibid., 222–3.
49 Fritz Baade Hg., *Unsere Ehre heisst Treue* (Vienna, 1965), 98 (facsimile).
50 Armstrong, *Soviet Partisans*, 40–2.   51 Dallin, "Psychological Warfare," 238–41.
52 Chiari, *Alltag*, 160–94.   53 Ibid., 141–59.
54 BA, RH 26–203, Anlagen zum Kriegstagebuch Mo.3 der 203. Sicherungsdivision, Bericht der Feldkommandatur 581 vom 10. February 1942, 2.

tons of grain and attacked units of the Ordnungsdienst with machine guns as they attempted to put out the fire. Three nights later, a "larger band of partisans" attacked the village again, killed a *starost* (a village elder) and six members of the *Ordnungsdienst*, skinned the mayor alive, and plundered his farm. These attacks on collaborators made it difficult for the Germans to find people to serve as *starosty* or otherwise to cooperate with the occupiers in the villages.[55]

In March 1942, three partisan brigades attacked Klichev with a cannon, howitzer, and three machine guns.[56] After heavy fighting they took the town, killing 120 collaborating policemen. Klichev was then organized as a center of the partisan movement.[57] On April 2, a newly established district Soviet took over power in the town, declaring the entire region liberated from "internal counterrevolution" and "external enemies." Everything was to be undertaken, the Soviet announced, "for the defense of the Fatherland (*rodina*). All were to collect weapons, support the partisans, especially with food, and to help all who suffered from the terror of the German fascists and internal counterrevolution." The regional Communist party and the Soviet decreed the collective sowing of the harvest, but they also distributed plots of land to workers and refugees. Seed and other aid were to be given to the victims of German terror.[58] Each village created a unit for its military defense.[59]

In May, the German military police acknowledged that the region of Klichev was "still completely in the hands of the partisans, who initiate their plundering marches from here." Partisans regularly interrupted the railway from Bobruisk to Minsk.[60] Despite the presence of strong anti-Bolshevik groups in the area, the Germans could not support them in the countryside, nor could they provide relief when Klichev was attacked. By the summer of 1942, the collaborators had been liquidated, and the partisans had organized a line of communication from the woods to the south of Slonim eastward to Bobruisk and beyond.

In June 1942, the regions of Klichev and Berezinsk were likewise reported as liberated, and the road from Mogilev to Bobruisk was closed to German traffic.[61] At the end of the month, however, a counterattack by Germans and collaborators, which was supported from the air, took place against Klichev. The partisans reported a victory against a battalion of "traitors."

55 Ibid., 3–4.   56 VDPD, 1: 608–9.
57 Ibid., 356.   58 Ibid., 165.
59 Ibid., 576.
60 BA, RH 26–203, Bericht der Feldkommandantur 581, May 30, 1942.
61 VDPD, 1: 186.

"One hundred sixty dead remained on the battlefield," they announced, "and much booty was taken." A second enemy battalion was forced to turn back, as Soviet planes brought in armaments and food. On July 20, however, the attackers crossed the river Olsa, which separated Bobrujsk from Klichev, and seized the town. The partisans who had defended it were ordered back into the woods.[62]

The success of the Germans and their local allies was only temporary. The partisans had routed the collaborators of the first hour. Collaborating with the Germans subsequently posed much greater risks, particularly in view of the Germans' own behavior during the recent attacks in the region. As one partisan leaflet claimed, "The Hitlerite cannibals burned the villages, and hundreds of innocent civilians were shot or burned alive. In the village of Uskino a hundred eighty people were exterminated, in the settlements Vjazem and Selets about a hundred, in Bazevich about fifty. The majority were old men, women, and children." The same leaflet urged resistance: "As soon as you have threshed the grain from the new harvest, hide it in the woods, establish stores of food, or the Hitler people will expose our people to starvation. Let us not give a single gram of grain to these Hitler-dogs!"[63] The Party secretary in the region pleaded with Moscow for medical aid.[64]

In the beginning of October 1942, two German infantry divisions encircled the large forested region between the railway from Minsk to Moscow and Mogilev and between the Oslik and Berezina rivers. Two partisan brigades escaped encirclement "without accepting battle," while another escaped after a fight. The German troops thereupon swept the country, "killing like beasts all men in the villages that they conquered." On October 19, however, they left the region for the Stalingrad front. By late October, the plenipotentiary of the Communist Party for the *oblast* (a district mostly bigger than a county) Mogilev reported that Klichev was again functioning as the partisans' operational center.[65]

Christian Gerlach has cautioned against overrating the military significance of Soviet partisan warfare, noting that the partisans were unable to defend the small towns and villages against regular German troops.[66] The point is well taken, and it highlights the fact that the inhabitants of the villages suffered the brunt of the German war against the partisans. But Gerlach in his turn underrates the effects of the German inability to destroy the partisan units. These units avoided pitched battles, retreated into the woods, and returned once German troops had left the area. As the case

62 Ibid., 284.   63 Ibid., 274.
64 Ibid., 325.   65 Ibid., 385–8.
66 Gerlach, *Morde*, 865–8.

of the "Klichev operational center" demonstrated, the German attack did not prevent the center from maintaining ties with the underground in Bobruisk and Mogilev. It continued to distribute a samizdat-style newspaper throughout the region; and it founded three new partisan brigades.[67] The German military police well recognized the growing strength of the partisans in the regions west of Klichev. In November 1942, the German police reported that most of these regions were the "objects of terror" by the "bandits." "The population that is willing to collaborate with us," the report complained, "has concluded that the German army is powerless in the face of robberies and shootings by the bandits."[68] In April 1943, German military intelligence estimated that the whole region as far north as Orsha was entirely in the hands of the partisans. The economy of this region, a report noted, "is completely destroyed."[69]

Klichev offers an example of the early flight of rural Jews to the woods, following the genocide committed there by units of the Wehrmacht and other forces. On August 18, 1941, the 350th Infantry Regiment claimed that the influence of Jews in the region was still significant and should be ended "by the most radical means."[70] In September, genocide in the region extended to all Jewish men in the countryside.[71] On September 24, the 339th Infantry Division passed on a note from a collaborator who reported that the Jews of Klichev and other rural towns to the north of Bobruisk "had fled to the woods . . . to unite with the Communists and partisans who live in the woods."[72] The extent of Jewish participation in the partisan movement around Klichev is not clear yet, though.[73]

It is clear, however, that on the Soviet side of the old Polish border, collaboration with the German occupation forces was strong and active. Numerous battalions of the Belorussian *Ordnungsdienst* operated with the Germans in 1941–42. The Communists of this region first interpreted collaboration as "counterrevolution" and responded by terrorizing those who participated in it.[74] They murdered local supporters – chiefly the *starosty* in villages and mayors in small towns – and they tortured the families of collaborators who had escaped. But the defeat of the collaborators, at least in Klichev, came when the Wehrmacht did not organize continuous support.

---

67 VDPD, 1: 387.
68 BA, RH 26–203, Anlagen zum Kriegstagebuch der 203. Sicherungsdivision, Bericht der Feldkommandantur 550, November 23, 1942, 1.
69 BA, RH 3/V, 149, 20–1.   70 Yad Vashem Archives M.29.FR 209, 294.
71 Ibid., 303, Feldkommandantur 528 of Sicherungsdivision 221, September 5, 2.
72 Ibid., 337.
73 Icchak Arad, ed., *Unichtozhenie evreev SSSR v gody nemeckoj okkupacii* (Jerusalem, 1992), 181, 316.
74 See Nolte, "Stalinism as Total Social War."

THE EVOLUTION OF GERMAN POLICY

At the end of 1942 a German officer reported that it was "completely impossible to call Belorussia a pacified country!"[75] By this time, the character of the Germans' war against the partisans had changed, as they resorted increasingly to collecting labor to send back to the Reich. Inhabitants of the regions who were unable to work were left to starve or survive by their own devices.[76] In October 1942, Göring – in his capacity as head of the Four-Year Plan – ordered that all persons who had had contact with partisans were not to be killed, but sent instead to work in Germany.[77] The greater the German need for labor, the more ruthlessly was this policy implemented in Belorussia after 1942.[78] Wives and other relatives of partisans were sent to "Work-Education Camps" (*Arbeitserziehungslager*) in Germany.[79] Others were dispatched directly to concentration camps.

Drafting the relatives of partisans into forced labor represented a small part of the so-called Sauckel actions, which rounded up labor for German industry and agriculture in the occupied territories. These actions only encouraged young people to join the partisans, who in turn tried to obstruct the Germans' "hunting of men" for forced labor. In this effort, the partisans were largely successful. When Sauckel visited Minsk in July 1943, Kube proposed deporting the entire population of certain partisan-controlled regions to Germany, in order to develop others.[80]

Although Sauckel refused it, this request was a measure of the growing frustration among the German authorities. Several weeks later, Gottberg initiated another of his notorious actions against a region that he considered to be "contaminated with bandits." His orders specified that

All people (men, women, children) are to be moved out. People capable of working are to be seized.... It is inexpedient to let them live near the evacuated territory.... All agricultural goods and livestock are to be seized.... Villages and all other buildings, as well as bridges and that part of the harvest, which cannot be salvaged, are to be destroyed and burned to the ground. To the extent possible, the woods within the territory are also to be burned down.[81]

Despite evidence that these techniques were counterproductive, the office of the general commissioner in Minsk continued, under pressure from Berlin,

---

75 BA, RW 30/39, 9.
76 Christian Gerlach, "Die Rekrutierung von Zwangsarbeitern in den besetzten sowjetischen Gebieten," Wette and Ueberschär, *Kriegsverbrechen*, 193–207.
77 NARB, fond 4683, opis 3, delo 969, S. 82–3. See the chapter by Hans Mommsen, "The Impact of Compulsory Labor on German Society at War," in this volume.
78 Gerlach, *Morde*, 906.
79 NARB, fond 510, opis 1, delo 18, 33–48, 55–8.
80 Gerlach, *Morde*, 464.   81 NARB, fond 38, 100 (sic).

with actions designed to create "dead zones," denuded of their population and even their vegetation, as the Germans recognized, no less than the partisans, the critical significance of the surrounding natural environment to the waging of partisan war.

In May 1943, the office of economic administration for the rear areas controlled by the German army reported that in August 1941, 10 percent of the forested regions had been in the hands of partisans. By October 1942, this estimate had risen to 75 percent, and by April 1943 to 90 percent. The Germans, in other words, could exploit but 10 percent of the forests economically. In addition, 60 percent of the grains, 64 percent of the meats, and 55 percent of the fats produced in Belorussia were controlled by the partisans.[82] Nonetheless, the impact of German policies in Belorussia was devastating. The German campaign aimed at the complete destruction or deportation of the population of the regions controlled by partisans. As the partisan movement grew, this policy extended to ever greater parts of the country. By the time the war ended, 5,454 settlements in Belorussia had been destroyed, 630 of them together with their inhabitants. More than 2.2 million people had been killed – a quarter of the population, including almost 99 percent of the Jews who did not succeed evading the advance of the German armies.[83]

The German attack on the Soviet Union provoked the partisan war. Because the Germans initially planned on employing limited occupation forces, they left large territories without sufficient personnel to support the numerous collaborators. The Wehrmacht anticipated fighting the partisans with a policy of mass terror against civilians. However, the Germans' genocidal policies rendered partisan war a matter of life and death for the large groups of Jews, Communists, Gypsies, and Soviet prisoners of war.

Neither side was bound by legal or moral constraint in this war. The idea of burning the forests as a weapon against the enemy originated with Stalin in July 1941; and it soon became known to the Germans. Prisoners were not taken as a rule by either side. Punishing entire families was not unique to the Germans either; it was an old Soviet practice that had been used during the forced resettlement of the Volga Germans to Siberia and Kazakhstan.

Despite these similarities in the conduct of the war, important differences remained. The Soviet partisans did not set out to murder entire ethnic groups or to destroy whole villages along with their inhabitants. The partisans did

---

82 BA, RH 3/V. 149, 33–4.

83 U. M. Mikhnjuk, *Njamecka-fashyscki genacid na Belarusi* (Minsk, 1995), 31–279; cf. Shmuel Spector, "Jewish Resistance in Small Towns of Eastern Poland," in Norman Davies and Antony Polonsky, eds., *Jews in Eastern Poland and the USSR, 1939–46* (London, 1991), 138–44; R. A. Chernoglazova, ed., *Tragedija evreev Belorussii* (Minsk, 1997); Arad, *Unichtozhenie*, 30; Gerlach *Morde*, 503–774.

not create dead zones. Although they themselves were used to sentences being carried out swiftly, even the NKVD agents were surprised at the speed with which the Germans executed people, including women and children.

Partisan war in the Soviet Union was total on both sides. Both employed unrestricted violence against civilians, but the Germans were more indiscriminate in their practices. They used violence systematically against entire regions. They enslaved captured partisans. And they undertook the wholesale murder of villagers. The partisans' violence against noncombatants was directed against the family members of collaborators, while the Germans attacked entire villages. The German war against the partisans in Belorussia was a total, genocidal war waged in order to conquer a foreign country. The war of the Belorussian partisans was a total war waged in defense of their own country.

15

Allied Bombing and the Destruction of German Cities

RICHARD OVERY

"We have got to kill a lot of Boche before we win this war."
Air Marshal Harris, April 1942[1]

Nothing better fitted the newly defined concept of "total war" after 1918 than the advent of offensive air power. "Total war, made possible by the aeroplane," wrote Bernard Davy, a Fellow of the Royal Aeronautical Society in 1941, "has reversed all the traditional concepts of warfare."[2] The bomber airplane was widely regarded as the fullest expression of the new age of mass war, directed at soldiers as well as civilians, at the enemy armed forces as well as the social and economic fabric that nourished them. When Lord Tedder, Eisenhower's deputy in the invasion of Western Europe, reflected on the nature of war in a series of lectures at Cambridge in 1947, he argued that military operations were now "merely one of the methods" by which a nation imposes its will on another and "not an end in themselves." Air power made possible other forms of warfare: "the political war which aims at weakening morale and authority...; the economic war which aims at starving the enemy war production of its essential materials."[3] Tedder, a senior air force officer himself, arrived at the not unexpected conclusion that air power was the arm peculiarly suited to exert pressure on the political and economic fabric of an enemy state.

Tedder drew on almost a generation of thinking about the nature of modern war after the conflict of 1914–18. The view that modern war was inevitably a contest for national survival, for the defense of whole societies, together with the value systems and institutions that underpinned them, was

1 Royal Air Force Museum (RAFM), London, Harris Papers, H53, Harris to Air Commodore Baker, April 11, 1942.
2 M. J. Bernard Davy, *Air Power and Civilization* (London, 1941), 148.
3 Lord Arthur Tedder, *Air Power in War* (London, 1948), 13–14.

commonplace by 1939. It was an attitude that invited speculation about the staying power of particular political systems or social constructs. The imposition of the national will on an enemy was regarded as a product not of military effectiveness as such, but of the psychological robustness, political aptitude, and economic strength of the national system under attack – and especially under the impact of assault from the air. When American airmen lectured on future war to young officers at the Air Corps Tactical School in the 1930s, they emphasized that the key purpose in war was to undermine "the will of the enemy people" by attacking directly their "sources of resistance" in the economic and social fabric in which they were rooted.[4] In analyzing the ability of a nation to wage war, the "military system" was placed fourth behind the "social, economic and political systems," of which the most important was deemed to be the "social body." If the "social body" could not be sustained, it would bring about "the defeat of the nation."[5]

The emphasis on attacking an enemy society, rather than the armed forces that shielded it, derived from wider concerns about the nature of "modernity." Industrialization came to be regarded as both a strength and a weakness: though it provided the sinews of modern, mechanized warfare, that very fact exposed the industrial system, with its vulnerable network of intricately woven lines of supply and distribution, to potentially fatal interruption. "Civilization has rendered the economic and social life of a nation increasingly vulnerable to attack," explained one senior American airman in a lecture in 1935. "Sound strategy requires that the main blow be struck where the enemy is weakest."[6] The development of great cities produced populations that some sociologists suggested were too rootless, insecure, and psychologically disoriented to withstand the shock of modern war.[7] The mass age brought popular politics, but it also brought societies where the demands of total mobilization might well exceed the willingness of populations to sustain the sacrifices such mobilization might entail. In the report of the British air force annual exercises in 1923, it was assumed that war had now been reduced to "a contest of morale." In such a contest,

---

4 United States Air Force Academy (USAFA), Colorado Springs, Hansell Papers, Ser. III, Box 1, Folder 1, "Fairchild Lecture," December 1, 1964, 8.
5 USAFA, Macdonald Papers, Ser. V, Box 8, Folder 8, "Development of the U.S. Air Forces Philosophy of Air Warfare prior to our entry into World War II," 15.
6 Ibid., 16.
7 J. Konvitz, "Représentations urbaines et bombardements stratégiques, 1914–1945," *Annales* (1989): 826–7.

it was the urban mass, "the crowd," that would prove itself to be "infinitely more susceptible to collapse."[8]

In the event, only Britain and the United States engaged in large-scale independent bombing operations against the urban and industrial centers of their enemy. This fact has presented historians with a paradox. Both Western states claimed the moral high ground during the war by emphasizing the virtues of modern liberal democracies over their politically decadent and militaristic opponents. Yet both states indulged in air campaigns that resulted in the massive loss of civilian life and the destruction of a large fraction of the urban area in Germany and Japan. Some of the explanation for that paradox lies in the uncritical acceptance in the West of the profile of modern war that evolved after 1918; some lies in the particular strategic circumstances both Western states faced in the late 1930s and during the war. The purpose of this essay is not to examine the conduct and impact of the bombing campaign, about which a very great deal has already been written, but to focus on the question of how the two Western states justified and rationalized the relentless bombing of German cities and civilians.

THE ROOTS OF THE BOMBING WAR

It has long been understood that the roots of Anglo-American strategic thinking about bombing stem from the early experience of air warfare in the First World War. In response to German bombing of London in 1916–17 with Zeppelin airships and long-range Gotha bombers, British military and political leaders explored the legitimacy and feasibility of mounting attacks agains urban targets in Germany.[9] From the outset, little distinction was made between attacks on military and industrial targets on the one hand and the morale of enemy civilians on the other. Indeed, the elision made in 1917 between the two types of target – that attacks on economic objectives will ipso facto generate morale crisis in the bombed urban centers – became characteristic of all discussions of bombing strategy in the later period. The inter-allied Air Policy Committee reported to the Supreme War Council in

8 Public Record Office, London (PRO), AIR 9/8, War Office Staff Exercise, address by the Chief of Air Staff, 3; Air Ministry memorandum, "Criticisms offered of COS147," May 17, 1928, 3: "The psychology of the crowd differs enormously from that of a disciplined military force." See also Tami Davis Biddle, "Bombing by the Square Yard: Sir Arthur Harris at War, 1942–1945," *International History Review* 21 (1999): 626–64.
9 On air policy in the First World War, see in particular Neville Jones, *The Origins of Strategic Bombing* (London, 1973); John H. Morrow, *The Great War in the Air: Military Aviation from 1909 to 1921* (Washington, DC, 1993).

January 1918 that the planned bombing campaign would focus on attacking German industrial cities within range until they had been destroyed and the "moral [sic] of workmen is so shaken." A list of twenty-five pages of potential German targets was appended to the report.[10]

During the campaign of 1918, the bombing of industrial targets and civilian morale was routinely regarded as indivisible. In June, the commander of the allied Independent Force of bombers, General Hugh Trenchard, informed the British War Cabinet that the strategic aim of the attacks on Germany was to "pierce into the moral and physical centres of the enemy's being" by conducting systematic attacks on urban areas. "The wholesale bombing of densely populated industrial centres," wrote Trenchard, "would go far to destroy the morale of the operatives."[11] The underlying assumption was that German domestic morale was poor and likely to crack under air attack, a view corroborated by the widespread panic caused by German bombing of London in 1917. It was these earlier attacks that explain why so little thought was given to the legitimacy of otherwise retaliatory operations that were certain to cause high civilian casualties and were deliberately targeted at domestic morale. The absence of German scruple was taken as a sufficient justification to reply in kind, though the British government insisted that attacks were not mere reprisals – indeed, British aircraft had been raiding Germany since early in the war. In the search for an efficient strategy that could be sold to the Allied leadership as a way to end the trench stalemate, airmen chose to emphasize the morale impact of bomb attack and to ignore the issue of whether or not the physical assault of civilian populations was within the rules of war. British politicians glossed over the question by focusing on the apparent efficiency of the new weapon. "This is the beauty of future war," said Lord Fisher in 1919, "No mountains, rivers, protected harbours, no snow-bound Alpine passes are in the business – you just fly over all these things and drop your multiple ton bomb."[12]

Ten years later, in 1928, the British Chiefs of Staff set up an inquiry into the legality of bombing urban areas. Bombing was compared with the effects of naval blockade, where the indirect impact on civilian populations was also potentially severe. The campaigns of the war were carefully examined to decide whether the bombing of industrial cities had exceeded the conventions of modern combat. The conclusion the inquiry arrived at was that attacks on military and economic targets situated in German cities (including the

---

10 PRO AIR 1/463/15/312/137, "Memorandum on Bombing Operations for the Supreme War Council," January 1918, 1–4.
11 PRO AIR 9/8, Chief of the Air Staff, "Review of Air Situation and Strategy," June 27, 1918, 6.
12 RAFM, Harris Papers, H50, cited in Trenchard to Harris, May 20, 1943, 3.

morale of the industrial workforce) were "perfectly legitimate objectives of air attack" and should therefore be regarded as "ordinary acts of war."[13]

AIR STRATEGY AND CIVILIANS IN THE INTERWAR YEARS

During the 1920s, air power theorists postulated the view that wars in the future would be decided by aircraft operating ruthlessly against the densely populated cities and industrial regions of the enemy. This was not a view shared by the other two fighting services, which continued to insist that aircraft ought to be auxiliary to the activity of surface forces on land and sea. It was not a view shared by all air force commanders, many of whom believed that the proper role of air forces was the direct contest with the military power of the enemy. Only in Britain and the United States did air power doctrine come to focus on bombing as the central function of an air force, directed at the economy and popular morale of enemy states. "The bomb is the chief weapon of an air force," ran the Royal Air Force *War Manual* of 1935, "and the principal means by which it may attain its aim in war."[14] The statement on air power doctrine approved by the American War Department in September 1939 included the following: "Air Power is based upon the offensive fire power of the bombardment aeroplane." The strategic function of air forces was to defeat the enemy "by the destruction of his means for waging war or by overcoming his will to resist."[15]

The choice of bombing was not in any sense arbitrary. In both Western states, airmen saw themselves as the self-conscious harbingers of a new form of warfare in which whole societies waged war in a collective national effort. The waging of "total war," or wars "of national attrition," as Trenchard called them, exposed the enemy society to legitimate attack.[16] "War being national," announced one senior RAF officer in notes for a lecture given in 1936, "therefore involves industrial mobilisation. No longer possible to draw a definite line between combatant and non-combatant."[17] Later in the war, the Commander-in-Chief of Bomber Command, Air Marshal Arthur Harris, used this same argument to explain why it was necessary to attack workers' housing in Germany: "It is clear that any civilian who produces more than enough to maintain himself is making a positive contribution to

---

13 PRO AIR 9/8, Chiefs of Staff paper, "The War Object of an Air Force," May 22, 1928, 2.

14 PRO AIR 9/39, "Air Policy and Strategy," lecture by Air Vice-Marshal Barrett, March 23, 1936, 1.

15 National Archives, Washington, DC (NARS), RG 165/888–103, memorandum from Marshall to General Watson, October 10, 1939.

16 PRO AIR 9/8, Chief of the Air Staff, "Review of Air Situation and Strategy," June 27, 1918, 2.

17 PRO AIR 9/39, Barrett lecture, 5–6.

the German war effort and is therefore a proper though not necessarily a worthwhile object of attack."[18] In a lecture on "The Aim in War" given at the American Air Corps Tactical School (ACTS) on the 1936–37 course, the war against civilians was defined as the central aim:

Where is the will to resist centered?... It is centered in the mass of the people.... they represent the mainspring of every national machine. Hence, the ultimate aim of all military operations is to destroy the will of those people at home.... The Air Force is at liberty to proceed directly to the accomplishment of the ultimate aim in war: overthrow of the enemy will to resist through destruction of those vital elements upon which modern social life is dependent.

The deliberate destruction of the civil fabric was nothing less than "*a new means of waging war.*"[19]

In the Royal Air Force, the idea that the moral impact of bombing outweighed the material effects of attacks on economic targets was enshrined in all doctrinal thinking from the early 1920s when Trenchard first suggested an unproven, and unprovable, ratio of 20:1 between the two types of effect. The RAF *War Manual*, published in 1935, explicitly accepted the Trenchard doctrine:

Moral effect – Although the bombardment of suitable objectives should result in considerable material damage and loss, the most important and far-reaching effect of air bombardment is its moral effect.... The moral effect of bombing is always severe and usually cumulative, proportionately greater effect being obtained by continuous bombing especially of the enemy's vital centres.[20]

When the RAF began operational planning in 1938 before the Munich crisis, it was recognized that attacks on German "vital centres" – in this case the industry of the Ruhr valley – were "bound to cause heavy loss of civilian life."[21]

British air leaders assumed that under conditions of total war the enemy's vital centers were to be found in the industrial economy, transport system, and industrial workforce that sustained the fighting fronts. The RAF *War Manual* described what would not be called a strategy to "degrade" the enemy's ability to make war by destroying "organised systems of production, supply, communications and transport." Total war made the national structure "delicate." "Such systems," continued the Manual, "have their nerve

18 RAFM, Harris Papers, H47, Harris to Air Ministry, March 7, 1944.
19 Emphasis in original. USAFA, Macdonald Papers, Ser. V, Box 8, Folder 8, "Development of the United States Air Force Philosophy of Air Warfare prior to our entry into World War II," 25.
20 NARS, RG 18/223, Box 1, Royal Air Force *War Manual*, Part I, May 1935, 57.
21 PRO AIR 8/251, "Short Note of Action of the Air Force at the Outset," n.d. [September 1939], 3.

centres, main arteries, heart and brain. If they are exposed to air attack, the continued interruption, delay and disorganisation of the activities of those vital centres by sustained air bombardment will usually be the most effective contribution which can be made by air power."[22] This damage was not regarded as necessarily decisive in itself: the object was so to demoralize the population or alarm the enemy government that the will to continue resistance would be extinguished. Anything that contributed to achieving the aim of breaking the "national effort" of the enemy was regarded as strategically worthwhile, except for deliberate and indiscriminate attacks on the enemy civilian population, which, as one British airman bluntly put it, did not "comply with the principle of concentration."[23]

This conception of warfare was shared by airmen in the United States. The 1926 Manual of Combined Air Tactics placed even greater emphasis on the psychological effects of bombing than the RAF:

The objective is selected with a view to undermining the enemy's morale. This end may be accomplished at the beginning of hostilities by using the air force to attack the enemy's interior. Such employment of air forces is a method of imposing will by terrorizing the whole population of a belligerent country while conserving life and property to the greatest extent. It is a means of imposing will with the least possible loss by heavily striking vital points rather than gradually wearing down an enemy by exhaustion.[24]

During the 1930s, a small group of senior air officers based on the Air Corps Tactical School elaborated a sophisticated defense of the idea of independent bombing against the enemy's heartland in the face of widespread criticism from the ground army.

Like the British, American air power theorists rooted their conception of how an air force should be used in discussions about the changed character of warfare in an era of advanced, heavily industrialized states. In another ACTS lecture, under the heading "An Inquiry into the Subject 'War,'" Major Harold George presented his class with the argument that modern industrial systems were peculiarly vulnerable in an age of total war. Rather than attack the enemy's armed forces, modern war was concerned only with breaking the enemy nation's "will to resist" by any means regarded as feasible. For George, this meant an air campaign against the enemy's economic structure rather than his armed forces: "It appears that nations are susceptible to defeat by the interruption of this economic web. It is possible

22 NARS, RG 18/233, Box 1, Royal Air Force *War Manual*, 57.
23 PRO AIR 9/39, Barrett lecture, 9.
24 PRO AIR 9/8, "Notes on a memorandum by the Chief of the Imperial General Staff" by Group Captain Foster, 1–2.

that the moral collapse brought about by the breaking of this closely knit web will be sufficient."[25] These assumptions about the character of war underpinned not only American air strategy in the Second World War, but the conduct of the Cold War that followed. In a lecture given in 1939 by Major-General "Hap" Arnold, commander of the Air Corps, on the subject "Can We Be Bombed," he warned his audience that "every man, woman and child" was now in the frontline if, or when, an enemy chose to attack the industrial and urban complexes that sustained American economic potential. Arnold was in no doubt that the United States was vulnerable to bombing because her vital targets could be easily located and destroyed by enemy aircraft. He advocated a powerful air striking force to deter the potential enemy or to ensure a devastating second strike should American cities come under air attack.[26]

By the time war broke out in 1939, airmen in the two Western states were intellectually predisposed to see modern war as "total war," blurring entirely the distinction between military and civilian and legitimizing the planned attack on enemy economic structures and popular morale. These views were reinforced by beliefs about the vulnerability of modern economic systems to air attack and the unwillingness of urban populations to tolerate high levels of disruption. They were necessarily couched in abstract or metaphorical language about systems or the social "body." Indeed, biological metaphors were commonly used in describing targets – nerve centers, heart, brain, arteries, and so on – while paradoxically ignoring the many thousands of real bodies that bombing would destroy. Harris regularly used the metaphor of insect extermination (attack the source, not the isolated wasp or mosquito), a metaphorical device that was widely exploited during the war in many other contexts.[27] The willingness to detach the language of air power theory from the reality of bomb attack by deliberate abstraction, to render it in some sense metaphorically, is one explanation for the almost complete absence of any discussion about civilian casualties in the theoretical writing of the 1930s.

Both air forces also adopted the contemporary obsession with "rationalization" or "national efficiency" to justify attacking the enemy economy and society. First, air power was presented as a means of avoiding the heavy

25 Library of Congress, Washington, DC (LOC), Andrews Papers, Box 11, Lecture at the ACTS by Maj. Harold George, "An Inquiry into the Subject 'War,'" 17.
26 USAFA, Hansell Papers, Ser. III, Box 1, Folder 2, lecture by Maj.-Gen. H. H. Arnold, "Can We Be Bombed?" 6a, 9a.
27 Edmund P. Russell III, "'Speaking of Annihilation': Mobilizing for War Against Human and Insect Enemies, 1914–1945," *Journal of American History* (1996): 1505–29.

manpower losses of the First World War. In a lecture in 1933, the American
Major Donald Wilson explained that the air force supplied the only nationally efficient form of warfare. While "the ground forces operate through a
tedious, time-consuming series of raids, battles and campaigns, normally
requiring great expenditures of lives, efforts and resources," the air force
was able to bring pressure to bear on the enemy will-to-resist "immediately
upon the outbreak of war." This capacity matched the demands of modern
democratic states to wage war with "maximum efficiency"; air power, in
Wilson's view, offered a means of warfare that might bring victory "with the
least expenditure of lives, time, money and material."[28] In the RAF, both
Trenchard and Harris argued that bombing was a shortcut to victory that
would avoid the loss of life of the First World War and maximize Britain's
offensive power. The idea of air power as an expression of national efficiency
was an extension of the argument about war and modernity and gave a spu-
riously scientific foundation to strategies that endorsed massive collateral
damage in the nation under attack.

Nevertheless, it would be wrong to infer that Western air forces were
free in the 1930s to unleash bombing campaigns at will with the onset of
hostilities. British and American air forces were designed primarily to be
deterrent forces whose existence would carry sufficient and serious threat of
retaliation to prevent an enemy state from contemplating air attacks on the
home front. RAF Bomber Command was built up as a striking force in the
1930s to be able to hit an enemy with enough initial impact to compel him
to abstain from bombing or to suspend his own bomb attacks once started.[29]
However, interpretations of the "enemy" made it appear virtually inevitable
that all-out bombing warfare would set in early in any war between the
major powers. The British Chiefs of Staff recorded their belief in 1938 that
in war Germany would be "ruthless and indiscriminate" in the way it waged
war.[30] The elaborate air raid precautions undertaken in Britain in 1938–
39 exemplified the widespread official (and popular) belief that war with
Germany would bring immediate air attack and the almost certain use of
poison gas. The exaggerated publicity given in newspapers and newsreels to
the destruction of the Spanish town of Guernica by German aircraft during
the Spanish Civil War only served to reinforce the assumptions about total
war and the necessity to oppose like with like.

28 USAFA, Macdonald Papers, Ser. V, Box 8, Folder 8, "Development of the United States Air Force
   Philosophy of Air Warfare prior to our entry into World War II," 8–9.
29 R. J. Overy, "Air Power and the Origins of Deterrence Theory Before 1939," *Journal of Strategic
   Studies* 15 (1992): 73–101.
30 PRO AIR 14/381, Director of Plans, Air Ministry, to Bomber Command, April 1938, 1.

The demonization of the potential enemy not only affirmed theories about the changed character of warfare but also permitted liberal states to contemplate waging the same kind of war without serious moral scruple on the grounds that they had to ensure their national survival at all costs. Indeed, the British response in the First World War to German bombing of London was undertaken on the basis that moral concerns about attacking civilians could be suspended once the enemy was deemed to have crossed a particular moral threshold, and that attitude was enshrined in air force perceptions of what was permissible in war thereafter. In the discussions surrounding Bomber Command operations before the Munich crisis and during the months leading up to the outbreak of war in 1939, attacks on Germany were expected to be endorsed by the government only following German air attacks on civilians. Once such attacks had occurred, the RAF was, in the words of a planning document from January 1940, "freed from all humanitarian considerations."[31]

In the United States, the same arguments circulated. The Air Corps commander in 1932, General Frank Andrews, suggested that in the event of attacks on American civilians, like should be met with like. Later commanders seem to have had little sense that any prior justification was needed beyond the functional requirement to wage war as efficiently as possible. Most significantly, Roosevelt himself, despite his efforts in the 1930s to secure international agreement to outlaw the bombing of civilians, came to accept that against a ruthless enemy only ruthlessness would prevail:

Against naked force the only possible defense is naked force. The aggressor makes the rules for such a war; the defenders have no alternative but matching destruction with destruction, slaughter with greater slaughter.[32]

Roosevelt was so incensed by the decision to allow Germany to occupy the Sudeten German areas of Czechoslovakia in 1938 that he famously informed his cabinet the day following the Munich agreement that Germany might have been constrained by relentless bombing attacks directed from neighboring states.[33] Michael Sherry has demonstrated that by the time America found itself at war in December 1941, Roosevelt was, according to his confidant Harry Hopkins, "a believer in bombing as the only means of gaining a victory." Moreover, he privately believed that German morale

---

31 PRO AIR 9/422, Air Ministry (Plans) to Chief of Air Staff, "Appreciation of the Attack of Germany by Night, Plan W.A.8," January 1940.
32 Jeffery S. Underwood, *The Winds of Democracy: The Influence of Air Power on the Roosevelt Administration, 1933–1941* (College Station, TX, 1991), 170. Roosevelt's views were read out by Senator Lyndon B. Johnson to a Young Democrats' Convention.
33 Harold L. Ickes, *The Secret Diary of Harold L. Ickes*, 2 vols. (London, 1955), II 469.

would crack only if every town and city in Germany were subjected to bomb attack.[34]

BOMBING GERMAN CITIES, 1940–1945

When war broke out in September 1939, the official position of the British government was to avoid any air attack that carried the risk of civilian casualties. The British prime minister, Neville Chamberlain, refused to allow Bomber Command to do more than drop leaflets over Germany. The RAF chafed at the bit. After years of assuming that the onset of major hostilities would see a mutual assault by bomber fleets, the self-denying ordinance imposed severe restrictions on British air strategy. A few days after the outbreak of war, Bomber Command's director of plans called for immediate action against Germany while it was fighting Poland. The concluding paragraphs were significant in the light of the subsequent offensive:

It is of the utmost importance that, *when* we do initiate air action on a serious scale, we must be allowed to do so *in the most effective way and against those objectives which we consider will have the greatest effect in injuring Germany, unhampered by the inevitable fact that there is bound to be incidental loss, and possibly heavy loss of civilian life.* [emphasis in original][35]

Bomber Command waited for Germany to take the initiative, but their planning during the "phoney war" made it clear that they expected to carry the air war directly to the German home front when permission was finally given. In September 1939, the deputy director of plans in the Air Ministry warned against any attempt by the politicians to water down a retaliatory strike "with a view to avoiding those targets which lie in the most populated areas."[36] Bomber Command shared the widespread opinion that Hitler's Germany was "politically rotten, weak in finance" and hence more vulnerable to air assault than Britain. At a meeting of the War Cabinet in October 1939 to discuss air policy, it was agreed that any air attacks by Germany that threatened to have decisive results (undefined) should be met by air attacks that held out the prospect of decisive results against Germany. The Ruhr was proposed as just such a target because it "contained

---

34 Michael S. Sherry, *The Rise of American Air Power: The Creation of Armageddon* (New Haven, 1987), 95–8. See also Conrad C. Crane, *Bombs, Cities and Civilians: American Airpower Strategy in World War II* (Lawrence, KS, 1993), 32–3.
35 PRO AIR 14/194, Bomber Command, "Note on the question of relaxing the bombardment instructions," September 7, 1939, 8.
36 PRO AIR 9/96, Deputy Director of Plans, Air Ministry, "Summary of Plans for action by the Air Striking Force," September 17, 1939, 2.

a population which might be expected to crack under intensive air attack." It was noted that such attacks would only be permitted once Germany had killed a lot of civilians.[37]

This Germany obligingly did in Warsaw and, later, Rotterdam. The day following the attack on the Dutch port, on May 15, 1940, Winston Churchill, appointed prime minister only five days before but a longtime enthusiast for air power, finally gave Bomber Command permission to begin attacks on the German home front. Like Roosevelt, Churchill placed uncritical faith in the effects of bombing until the poor accuracy and feeble impact of the early attacks was made evident to him later in the war. After defeat in France, Churchill saw bombing as the only strategic option left for Britain, and in an often-quoted letter to his close companion Lord Beaverbrook in June 1940 he suggested, "there is one thing that will bring . . . [Hitler] down, and that is an absolutely devastating, exterminating attack by very heavy bombers from this country upon the Nazi homeland."[38] This conviction hardened during the German air campaign against British cities during the winter of 1940–41, which the British regarded as precisely the kind of unrestricted terror attack they had anticipated so extensively in the 1930s. Any remaining qualms about causing German civilian casualties disappeared during the Blitz. Churchill pushed the War Cabinet to accept the possibility of using poison gas against German cities if there was any evidence that German forces had used gas first. The Chief of the Air Staff prepared operational plans either to drop Britain's meager supply of gas bombs in four days of intensive attack on German cities or to mix gas and high explosive bombs together for a campaign of two weeks.[39]

It is significant that both Churchill and Roosevelt shed any regard for the civilian population to be subjected to attack. Without their political support for bombing, the campaigns might well have been cut back in favor of more direct assistance to surface forces. Moreover, both Roosevelt and Churchill accepted without demur that attacks against the German homeland were justifiable operations in the context of a war for survival. Thus, when the RAF and the American Army Air Forces came to frame

---

37 PRO AIR 14/194, Bomber Command, "Note on the question of relaxing the bombardment instructions," September 7, 1939, 6; AIR 8/277, War Cabinet, minutes of meeting, October 13–14, 1939, 1.

38 Winston S. Churchill, *The Second World War*, 6 vols. (London, 1948–54), II 567.

39 PRO PREM 3 88/3, War Cabinet paper from Chiefs of Staff, "Plans for Employment of Gas from the Air in Retaliation for its use against us by the enemy," October 8, 1940; letter from Portal to Churchill, February 13, 1941. Portal preferred the idea of mixing gas with high explosives: "This will make the enemy lose his protective clothing and will thus greatly hamper him while the HE will damage his vehicles, equipment, petrol and stores besides inflicting casualties."

policy for the campaign against Germany, they were able to do so free from any political restrictions or moral considerations. The priority for both air forces was strategic efficiency, which meant in effect the self-interested pursuit of strategies that might maximize the contribution of air power to victory.

The consequence was the development of strategies to undermine German war production and popular morale by the systematic destruction of German industries, infrastructure, and urban areas. This strategic conception was entirely consistent with Anglo-American views on bombing as far back as 1918. Bomber Command began operations against Germany in the summer of 1940 under orders to attack military and military-economic targets, but the impossibility of hitting targets with existing technology moved the Air Ministry to endorse in the summer of 1941 more indiscriminate attacks against German civilian morale and finally, a week before the appointment of Harris as Commander-in-Chief, to endorse a campaign of city bombing designed to undermine "the morale of the enemy civil population" while reducing the supply of a range of essential industrial products and armaments.[40] The Ministry of Economic Warfare drew up a list of one hundred German industrial cities whose destruction was deemed sufficient to erode Germany's ability to wage war.[41]

Harris was appointed Commander-in-Chief of Bomber Command on February 14, 1942. He did not initiate the strategy of so-called area bombing and was not attracted to the idea of morale as a target in its own right. He interpreted the campaign as a means to degrade German economic and military power through attacks on industrial areas and the industrial workforce, until a point was reached where the military re-entry to Europe would be a mere mopping-up operation. His force began the systematic attack of the "100 industrial cities" (they were crossed off the MEW list as they were attacked). This was not all that Bomber Command did: the majority of operations were in support of naval or land strategy or against specific target systems (oil, the submarine industry, etc.). Harris, it is well known, regretted the fragmentation of effort. His views on the bombing of German cities were formed in the 1930s, a product of the search for national efficiency. He believed that in modern war the chief source of enemy resistance had to be identified and attacked remorselessly in order to avoid another trench stalemate. He found that source in German

40 Charles Webster and Noble Frankland, *The Strategic Air Offensive Against Germany*, 4 vols. (London, 1961), IV 143–5.
41 RAFM, Harris Papers, Misc. Box A, Folder 4, Ministry of Economic Warfare, "100 German Cities," n.d. [1943].

industrial areas. "Attacks on cities like any other act of war are intolerable unless they are strategically justified. But they are strategically justified in so far as they tend to shorten the war and to preserve the lives of Allied soldiers."[42]

In the course of 1943, Harris was given the opportunity to define more closely his justification for the systematic attack on German cities in a lengthy correspondence with the Air Ministry. The arguments are worth examining closely. In October 1943, Harris reacted with his characteristic robustness to the Air Ministry propaganda on bombing, which in his view misrepresented what his Command was actually doing by suggesting that it was engaged in pinpoint bombing of particular factories. Harris rejected this profile in favor of candid acceptance that his force aimed at "the obliteration of German cities and their inhabitants." The "fundamental purpose" of attacks lay in the destruction of German economic and social resources. He advised the Air Ministry to present Bomber Command strategy in the following terms:

(a) The aim of the Combined Bomber Offensive [agreed at the Casablanca Conference in January 1943], and the part which Bomber Command is required to play in it, . . . is the destruction of German cities, the killing of German workers and the disruption of civilized community life throughout Germany.

(b) It should be emphasised that the destruction of houses, public utilities, transport and lives; the creation of a refugee problem on an unprecedented scale; and the breakdown of morale both at home and at the battle fronts by fear of extended and intensified bombing, are accepted and intended aims of bombing policy. They are not by-products of attempts to hit factories.[43]

This was too candid for the Air Ministry. Harris was told that devastation should not be presented to the public as an end in itself, "but the inevitable accompaniment of an all-out attack on the enemy's means and capacity to wage war."[44] Harris later replied that to him the distinction seemed "merely academic," as it well might to any reader.

Harris used his reply to explain in greater detail why he regarded the destruction of industrial cities as strategically justifiable. "The German economic system," wrote Harris, "which I am instructed by my directive to destroy, *includes* workers, houses and public utilities, and it is therefore meaningless to claim that the wiping out of German cities is 'not an end in itself' . . . the cities of Germany including their working population, houses

---

42 RAFM, Harris Papers, H9 letter from Harris to Air Marshal Bottomley, March 28, 1945, 3.
43 RAFM, Harris Papers, H47, letter from Harris to Sir Arthur Street, Air Ministry, October 25, 1943, 3.
44 RAFM, Harris Papers, H47, letter from Street to Harris, December 19, 1943, 2.

and pubic utilities are literally the heart of Germany's 'war potential.' That is why they are being deliberately attacked." Harris rejected the view that British public opinion would not accept bald statements of intent simply to appease "the sentimental and humanitarian scruples of a negligible minority."[45]

The Air Ministry had been less circumspect about German opinion. In a leaflet thoughtfully entitled "Why We Bomb You," written in the Air Ministry in 1942 but signed by Harris, the German population was informed: "*We are bombing you and your cities, one by one, and ever more terribly, in order to make it impossible for you to go on with the war*" [emphasis in original]. To make it clear that bombing was not simply random or vindictive, the Air Ministry provided the following justification, which says much about why the British persisted with city-bombing:

> Obviously we prefer to hit your factories, shipyards, and railways. It damages your Government's war machine most. But nearly all these targets are in the midst of the houses of those of you who work in them. . . . Therefore we hit your houses – and you – when we bomb them. We regret the necessity for this. But this regret will never stop us; you showed the world how to do it.[46]

A second pamphlet, issued a year later, dismissed the idea that bombing operations were terror attacks directed solely at popular morale ("We leave terror attacks to Goering"). Bombing was presented as a strategy of national attrition, "systematically, thoroughly and completely destroying [Germany's] industrial centres" in order to make it "impossible for Germany to continue the war."[47]

The policy of the U.S. Army Air Forces was, like that of the RAF, rooted in the theoretical discussions of the 1930s. When American airmen were asked to draft an air force plan late in the summer of 1941 to support a long-term procurement program for aircraft, they assumed without question that they should plan to attack the German economy and infrastructure systematically. The "basic concept" of what became designated AWPD-1 was described by General Hayward Hansell, one of its authors, as the "application of air power for the breakdown of the industrial and economic structure of Germany." This they hoped to achieve by attacks on specific target systems supporting the war effort and the "livelihood of the German people" until German morale appeared to crack when "area bombing of

45 RAFM, Harris Papers, H47, letter from Harris to Street, December 23, 1943, 2–3.

46 RAFM, Harris Papers, H51, letter from Harris to Air Marshal Richard Peck, enclosing draft of leaflet, "Why We Bomb You: a message from the Commander-in-Chief of the British Bombers to the German People," July 22, 1942.

47 RAFM, Harris Papers, H51, letter from Peck to Harris, enclosing draft of leaflet, December 21, 1943.

civil concentrations may be effective."[48] The distinction between British and American bombing policy has often been prone to exaggeration. American airmen believed that it was more efficient to attack by day with heavily defended bombers, but they shared the underlying assumption that degrading German industry and civilian resource would lead to military and morale collapse. When General Arnold produced a paper in September 1942 critical of American failure to concentrate air forces sufficiently on the campaign against Germany, he described the American plan in the following words:

> That plan calls for the maximum possible air effort [,] British and American[,] directed against German military and industrial objectives, with a view of destroying their productive capacity, causing vital deficiency in her airpower, causing confusion and chaos in transportation systems, breaking down the morale of the civilians, and thereby destroying her will to fight.[49]

Four months later, Arnold was among those lobbying vigorously at the Casablanca Conference for air power to be given a central role in Allied strategy. Churchill and Roosevelt both accepted the need for a pooling of the air effort. The result was the Combined Bombing Offensive, whose stated object was "the progressive destruction and dislocation of the German military, industrial and economic system, and the undermining of the morale of the German people to the point where their capacity for armed resistance is fatally weakened."[50]

American airmen were less candid than Harris about the fact that bombing killed workers (and nonworkers), even when specific industrial or military installations were designated for attack. This stemmed partly from the belief that American opinion could more readily be made to support the bombing campaign if the overt destruction of housing and civilian facilities were overlooked (though when a Bomber Command exhibition of damage to German cities was sent to Washington in the early months of 1943, the British Embassy reported great enthusiasm among American officials and politicians invited to view it, including the vice president – "completely sold on the necessity of bombing Germany" – and, in February 1943, the president himself).[51] The second argument for "precision

---

48 Haywood S. Hansell, *The Strategic Air War Against Germany and Japan* (Washington, DC, 1986), 34.
49 RAFM, Harris Papers, H77, memorandum by General Arnold, "Plans for Operations against the Enemy," September 3, 1942, 1–2.
50 Webster and Frankland, *Strategic Air Offensive*, IV 273–83.
51 RAFM, Harris Papers, cypher message, air attache Washington to Air Ministry, January 11, 1943; cypher telegram from air attache, February 20, 1943. On divisions in American opinion on bombing, see Crane, *Bombs, Cities and Civilians*, 31–41.

attacks" was military efficiency: "Day bombing is point bombing, effective in destroying factories and other key targets," as General Ira Eaker submitted at Casablanca.[52] However, commanders in the American bombing force in Britain knew that accuracy was very difficult to obtain under battle conditions, or in poor weather, or against German decoy measures – and all from a great height. Operational research showed before the end of the war what had already been demonstrated in British inquiries conducted in 1941 and 1942: accuracy within 1,000 feet of the aiming point was poor and under adverse conditions almost nonexistent (only 5.4 percent on smoke-screened targets). In reality, American bombing was spread widely over the urban areas in which the chosen factories were located. This technically unavoidable outcome pushed American forces toward more direct area bombing from the autumn of 1943, particularly in poor weather. "Blind bombing" research in January 1944 confirmed that only 5 percent of crews bombed within five miles of the stated target. During 1944, a much larger tonnage was dropped through blind bombing than visual, and further operational research indicated that a more or less constant rate of no more than 5 percent of bombs fell within 1,000 feet of the aiming point.[53]

In practice, both air forces caused widespread and random urban destruction and loss of civilian life. As the war went on and the technical difficulty, and high loss rates, of hitting accurate targets persisted, American air forces found themselves ordered to fly operations little different from those of Bomber Command. During the last nine months of the war, the assault on German cities reached a climax, culminating in the notorious bombing of Dresden by both British and American air forces in February 1945 in support of the Soviet offensive in eastern Germany. This cooperation proved too much even for Churchill, who warned Bomber Command to avoid attacks "simply for the sake of increasing the terror."[54] Harris responded at once to the criticism by explaining why cities continued to be attacked when Germany was self-evidently close to defeat. Dresden itself he described (wrongly) as "a mass of munitions works, an intact government centre, and a key transportion point to the east" whose destruction was ordered by SHAEF, not by the British and American bomber commanders.[55]

Harris, however, saw Churchill's rebuke as a more general criticism of bombing. He justified the destruction of cities on the basis that it had "fatally

52 W. Hays Park, "'Precision' and 'Area' Bombing: Who Did Which, and When?" *Journal of Strategic Studies* 18 (1995): 146.
53 Ibid., 147–58.
54 RAFM, Harris Papers, H98, letter from Bottomley to Harris, March 24, 1945.
55 RAFM, letter from Harris to Bottomley, March 29, 1945, 1.

weakened the German war effort" to the extent that Allied forces could "advance into the heart of Germany with negligible casualties." Rather than cease city attacks, Harris argued that "The nearer Germany is to collapse the less capable she is of re-organising to meet disasters of this kind." The air forces should "make a special effort to eliminate the few cities which still remain more or less serviceable." Harris ended by suggesting that what had been done to German cities should be visited on Japanese. "Japan remains," he wrote. "Are we going to bomb their cities flat – as in Germany – and give the Armies a walk over – as in France and Germany – or are we going to bomb only their outlying factories and subsequently invade at the cost of 3 to 6 million casualties?"[56] Since no order was given to suspend city attacks, the Allied air forces continued the campaign up to the end of April 1945. When the bombing of Japan began in earnest the following month, whole cities were targeted on the grounds that the war industry was so dispersed in the urban area as to make pinpoint bombing uneconomical. Like the RAF, the U.S. Army Air Forces moved from attacks on specified target systems to the destruction of industrial cities, with massive social dislocation and loss of life. The waging of total war had its own inexorable logic. Three months later, two atomic bombs were detonated on Japan without regard for the consequences for the civil populations.

FROM TOTAL WAR TO COLD WAR

In 1919 and again in 1945, the Western states gave some thought to putting German airmen on trial for violations of the laws of war when civilian populations were subject to bombing. In both instances, the plans were dropped for fear that Allied bombing might find itself under scrutiny as well.[57] There was always an element of ambiguity in Anglo-American prosecution of unrestricted air warfare, which is why both countries' propaganda continually emphasized the military or war-related character of the targets under attack. The apparent moral equivalence between German attacks on British cities and Western attacks on Germany was glossed over by the argument that Germany began the policy of bombing civilians and had in that sense unilaterally suspended the usual laws of war to its own detriment. More commonly, the argument for bombing Germany derived from assumptions about the moral character of total war inspired by a vulgarized Darwinism

---

56 Ibid., 2–3. On the American reaction, see Crane, *Bombs, Cities and Civilians*, 117. Arnold reminded critics of the operation, "We must not get soft. War must be destructive and to a certain extent inhuman and ruthless."
57 PRO AIR 9/8.

in which the struggle of nature was transposed onto the struggle between nations. In both Britain and the United States, wars of national survival were regarded as different in character from other forms of warfare, for they permitted the states under threat to use any means, however ruthless or indiscriminate, to defeat an enemy deemed a priori to be fighting just such a war. This mind-set helped to shape air strategy in particular, since only aircraft were capable of immediately exerting direct and serious pressure on the national structure of the enemy.

The view that the nature of the enemy and the threat he posed justified the waging of war as an absolute struggle, entire people against entire people, system against system, was sustained on into the confrontation with the Soviet Union after 1945. In 1964, Hayward Hansell, who had helped to draft AWPD-1 in 1941, was invited to give the Fairchild Lecture at the Maxwell Air Force base in Alabama. He used the occasion to demonstrate the very large changes that had taken place in the character of air warfare with the advent of nuclear weapons, where war might be won or lost in an afternoon. Nevertheless, the basic premise remained the same: the Soviet Union now took the place vacated by Hitler's Germany as a profound threat to the Western way of life and a ruthless "totalitarian" opponent. Instead of bombing the enemy will to resist, Hansell substituted the need to develop a credible threat of nuclear destruction. Faced with the implacable menace of communist imperialism, Hansell suggested, the United States had "no choice but full scale war if necessary," fully in the knowledge that America's "civil population faces mass extermination." Hansell favored the ability to strike back massively at Soviet or Chinese populations if the United States faced a serious menace to its national existence.[58] During the high point of the Cold War, leaders on both sides had to contemplate the destruction of their major cities and civilian deaths in the tens of millions. This Cold War confrontation was the apotheosis of the discourse on total war and air power first generated in the 1920s and mobilized with such devastating effects between 1939 and 1945.

58 USAFA, Hansell Papers, Ser. III., Box 1, Folder 1, "Fairchild Lecture," December 1, 1964, 18–24.

16

"Accidental Judgments, Casual Slaughters"

Hiroshima, Nagasaki, and Total War

ROBERT L. MESSER

My purpose here is to discuss the advent of the atomic bomb as part of a process that, if not a master narrative leading inevitably to total war, has taken us to the brink and allowed us to see into the abyss of the unthinkable, our self-destruction by means of our own invention. That invention is not only nuclear weapons. It is also the concept of total war.

As has been observed elsewhere in this collection of essays, total war as an abstract theoretical concept may never have happened in history.[1] But in my opinion World War II comes close enough to that fearful reality. It was in many respects history's most total war. That first truly global conflict mobilized economies and populations of the world on a scale and to a degree that, if not total, was unprecedented in history. The Allied war aims were the unconditional surrender and total subjugation of the Axis powers. Hitler's goals were imperial, ideological, and genocidal. In theory, Japan's slogan "Asia for Asians" and the promise of a Greater East Asian Co-Prosperity Sphere might have appealed to anticolonial nationalists. In practice, Japan's brutal conquest of native Asian populations – including the enslavement of Koreans, the use of chemical and biological warfare in China, the slaughter of Chinese civilians, the torture and starvation of prisoners – characterized a total war mentality restricted only by available means. In the end, that extremist mentality revealed itself in Japan's irrational inability to accept defeat in the face of horrific losses as total war was brought home to its people in the form of naval blockade, massive conventional bombing, and finally, nuclear weapons.

In addition to the goals and policies of the warring powers, the technology of World War II contributed greatly to its totality. The range and lethality of

---

1 See for example Stig Förster's discussion of developments leading in the direction of total war from 1861 to 1945 in his essay, "Das Zeitalter des totalen Krieges, 1861–1945: Konzeptionelle Überlegungen für einen historischen Strukturvergleich" in *Mittelweg* 36, 8, no. 6 (1999): 12–29.

the weapons mass produced by industrialized societies pushed the death toll to nearly sixty million, the vast majority of whom were civilians, often far from the frontlines. The development of nuclear weapons was only the war's final, virtually last minute, technological innovation. Strategic bombers, jet aircraft, rockets, and the perfection of tactics such as the creation of a "firestorm" in urban centers were all products of the military necessity to win at virtually any cost. Although not part of the military battlefield, the gas chambers and crematoria of Hitler's death camps industrialized murder and came to epitomize the evil against which the "Good War" was waged.[2] The indiscriminate nature of many of these weapons and tactics lowered the moral threshold by obliterating the distinction between combatants and noncombatants. If World War II was not a total war, it was not for lack of trying. It was total enough to provide an instructive example of what total war can be and what it means to history.

Unlike other modern wars, World War II killed more civilians than uniformed combatants, and it killed them not just accidentally, not only incidentally as "collateral damage." It at times killed them deliberately either as subhuman undesirables worthy of mass extermination or as legitimate military targets of the devastatingly lethal new technology that did not discriminate between noncombatants of all ages and the enemy armed forces. By the end of World War II, civilian factory workers, their families, neighbors, the entire population of cities large and small, those living near and sometimes not so near military targets such as railroad lines, or bridges, had become legitimate targets and thus victims of total war.

This essay focuses on one aspect of that near total war, the atomic bombings of Hiroshima and Nagasaki. The atomic bombings cannot be understood outside the context of World War II as a total war. The war changed the world. It also changed the way people think about war and morality. In the years following World War II, full-scale nuclear war came to be considered unthinkable. At the end of World War II, what had just five years before seemed unthinkable, beyond the limits of any standard of humanity, morality, or rationality, had become not only acceptable, but a necessary, beneficial course of action.

This altered state of mind is illustrated by two conversations. The first is the famous exchange between Pablo Picasso and a German officer who

---

2 Those who point out that, with the exception of Japan's deadly but militarily ineffective attempts to use it in China, poison gas was not used extensively in World War II ignore the fact that Zyklon B and other such chemical agents killed millions of unresisting prisoners of Hitler's racial war. Gas was not used in battle because of its unpredictability, limited effectiveness, and the possibility of retaliation. Deterrence, not morality, limited chemical and biological warfare in World War II.

had come to the artist's studio in occupied Paris to conduct an inventory of his "degenerate" art. Seeing a photograph of *Guernica*, Picasso's scathing condemnation of the bombing of the Basque city, the German asked: "Did you do this?" Picasso replied: "No, you did."[3] Although the Germans, by virtue of their ruthless employment of aerial bombing and other terroristic methods, might be winning militarily, Picasso and others who opposed them occupied the moral high ground. In 1940, bombing cities crowded with innocent, defenseless civilians was barbaric, cowardly, immoral. That moral standard soon fell victim to a combination of military necessity and technological innovation.

In 1995, on the fiftieth anniversary of the atomic bombings, the second conversation took place during an interview for a television documentary commemorating the event. The person being interviewed was McGeorge Bundy, who as a young man had served as an aide to Secretary of War Henry Stimson, one of a handful of presidential advisers who participated in the atomic bomb decision. Bundy had gone on to serve as National Security Advisor to Presidents John F. Kennedy and Lyndon Johnson. After retiring from public life, Bundy became a well-known authority on the history of decision-making in the nuclear age. As an expert witness Bundy served a dual role as someone whose scholarly credentials were backed by real world experience.

When the interviewer began his question by referring to "the myth of Hiroshima and Nagasaki as military targets," the always gentlemanly Bundy abruptly cut him off and with barely restrained irritation challenged the questioner's premise. Bundy pointed out that under the wartime doctrine of strategic bombing, Hiroshima and Nagasaki in fact were legitimate military targets "in the same way that New York is a military target today."[4] As someone who came of age during World War II and who had advised the president during the Cuban missile crisis, Bundy could not accept the idea that the first atomic target cities were any different from those cities such as New York or Moscow targeted as part of Cold War nuclear strategy. Bundy's assertion of the altered meaning of what is a military target reflects how World War II and nuclear weapons mounted on long-range delivery systems changed the world we live in.

The element linking these two conversations is the idea of legitimacy, not just the legality, but the morality of bombing cities and of the inevitable

---

3 The most authoritative version of this much-repeated story is that of Simone Signoret, who heard it the following day as Picasso proudly related it to his friends. Simone Signoret, *La Nostalgie n'est plus ce qu'elle etait* (Paris, 1976), 58.

4 Bundy interview, "Hiroshima: Why the Bomb was Dropped," ABC Television, July 27, 1995.

result, the indiscriminate killing of everyone who happens to live in them. At most, a few hundred inhabitants of Guernica died as a result of the German dive-bombings in 1937. Four years later, thousands more died in the blitz of London and in other British cities from bombs, jet-powered V-1 buzz bombs, and the ultimate conventional strategic weapon for which there was no defense or even warning, the V-2 rocket. By the last year of the war, what has been called "the killing year," tens of thousands of noncombatants had already been killed in cities such as Hamburg, site of history's first "firestorm." As the war dragged on to its bloody conclusion, cities such as Dresden and Tokyo joined the list of victims of total war on civilian populations.

On the ground, the fighting grew more desperate. This was especially true in the Pacific where the fighting, often to the last man, produced fewer and fewer prisoners and gave rise to Japanese *kamikaze* tactics. These suicidal gestures of defiance were largely futile but nonetheless deadly, and they reinforced the idea that nothing short of total annihilation would end the fanatical Japanese resistance. The war in the Pacific had by the summer of 1945 become a "war without mercy." The horrendous casualties suffered by both sides in the battles for Iwo Jima and Okinawa made the prospect of invading the Japanese home islands, a task far more formidable and costly than the invasion of France the year before, almost unthinkable. But that was the job of military planners such as Chief of Staff General George Marshall. Those plans included using virtually any means, including tactical nuclear weapons and poison gas, of reducing Allied losses.[5] In such a context, the atomic bomb seemed a godsend, a deliverance from an infinitely more costly prolongation of the war. Little wonder that even years later American combat veterans who were spared the burden of ending the war by invading Japan could say: "Thank God for the atomic bomb."[6]

At the time, the vast majority of Americans and supporters of the Allied cause throughout the world shared that sense of relief in hearing the news

5 Barton J. Bernstein, "Eclipsed by Hiroshima and Nagasaki: Early Thinking about Tactical Nuclear Weapons," *International Security* 15 (Spring 1991): 149–73. Marc Gallicchio, "After Nagasaki: General Marshall's Plan for Tactical Nuclear Weapons in Japan," *Prologue* 23 (Winter 1991): 204–21. Both Bernstein and Gallicchio see Marshall's plan for the possible use of nuclear weapons in support of the invasion as evidence that American officials were unsure that the war would end prior to the final assault on the home islands. For Marshall, such contingencies were part of his job. He also was a strong advocate for the use of poison gas against Japanese defenses. Unlike tactical nuclear weapons, stockpiles of poison gas were on hand. However, Truman, Stimson, Byrnes, and others involved in the atomic bomb decision had other priorities and perspectives. See my reply [with Gar Alperovitz] to Bernstein in "Marshall, Truman and the Decision to Use the Bomb," *International Security* 16 (Winter 1991–92): 204–21.
6 Paul Fussell, *Thank God for the Atomic Bomb and Other Essays* (New York, 1988), 13–44.

of the atomic bombings, especially when it was coupled with the news just a few days later that Japan had surrendered and the war was at last over. It seemed obvious that the miraculous new bomb had won the war and saved the world from a much greater carnage.

But not everyone celebrated the advent of nuclear weapons as the absolute weapon in the age of total war. A few dissenters wondered if the atomic bombings were necessary. Some even doubted their morality. Many of these doubters were those who had objected to the practice of area, obliteration, or terror bombing of civilians with conventional weapons. In a debate that would echo over the years and surface again fifty years later in the controversy over the Smithsonian Institution's display of the Hiroshima atomic bomber *Enola Gay*, the reasons for using atomic weapons against Japanese cities and the meaning and morality of that decision were pondered even in the still radioactive rubble of Hiroshima. What follows is a detailed examination of how that decision was made by the one man who had the power to alter the course of history.

In the aftermath of the atomic bombings of Hiroshima and Nagasaki, Father John Siemes, a German Jesuit priest who had witnessed first hand the horrors of the world's first nuclear weapons, set forth in his report to the Vatican the views of his fellow Jesuit missionaries as they tried to make sense out of an event that more than fifty years later the world still struggles to comprehend. As Germans living in wartime Japan, their views provide a somewhat more detached perspective of the meaning and morality of the use of nuclear weapons in the context of "total war." But even though they were of the same nationality and brothers in a Roman Catholic religious order, Siemes and his colleagues differed about how to interpret the atomic bomb as a weapon of war. Indeed, their differences mirror the debate that still surrounds Hiroshima in history.

Some of us consider the bomb in the same category as poison gas and were against its use on a civilian population. Others were of the opinion that in total war, as carried on in Japan, there was no difference between civilians and soldiers and that the bomb itself was an effective force, tending to end the bloodshed, warning Japan to surrender and thus to avoid total destruction.

Having described the division of opinion among his brethren about the atomic bomb, and its military and moral justification, Father Siemes, a professor of modern philosophy at Tokyo's Catholic University, went on to reflect on the broader issue of the ethics of total war.

It seems logical to me that he who supports total war in principle cannot complain of a war against civilians. The crux of the matter is whether total war in its present form is justifiable, even when it serves a just purpose. Does it have material and spiritual evil as its consequences which far exceed whatever good might result?

The good Father succinctly posed the ethical question of proportionality; can even a good end justify such a means as "total war in its present form"? Had the incredible, unheard of destructive power of modern technology combined with the concept of total war itself become a "spiritual evil"? In his report to the Vatican, Father Siemes doesn't presume to have the answer. Instead, he ends with a question: "When will our moralists give us a clear answer to this question?"[7]

Just weeks before Father Siemes made his plea for moral clarity about the bomb, President Harry Truman sat at a desk in the outskirts of the ruined city of Berlin and penned his thoughts on war, technology, morality, and the advent of nuclear weapons.

I hope for some sort of peace. But I fear that machines are ahead of morals by some centuries and when morals catch up perhaps there will no reason for any of it. I hope not. But we are only termites on a planet, and maybe when we bore too deeply into the planet there'll [be] a reckoning – who knows?[8]

Such ruminations on "machines," or modern technology, and morals came after the new president had toured in an open car the rubble-strewn streets of the once proud German capital. That same afternoon, Truman had received the top secret message telling him that the enormously expensive gamble started by his predecessor Franklin Roosevelt had paid off in a way that stunned even its scientist creators. The test denotation of the world's first fission atomic bomb in the desert of New Mexico exceeded all expectations. Truman didn't get a full report for a few more days, but he was, in the words of his Secretary of War Henry Stimson, immediately "pepped up" by the newfound power of what Truman referred to alternately at the time as

---

7 Quoted in John Hersey, *Hiroshima* (New York, 1985), 89–90. Father Siemes's full report is reprinted in Yale University's Avalon Project website: http://www.yale.edu/lawweb/Avalon/abomb/.

8 Truman's longhand notes, July 16, 1945, President's Secretary File, Ross File, Harry S. Truman Library. Hereafter cited as Truman Diary and HSTL. These spontaneous, fascinating, revealing, and sometimes confusing private reflections were first discovered in late 1979. They are reprinted in Robert Ferrell, *Off the Record: The Private Papers of Harry S. Truman* (New York, 1980). For a more detailed analysis of them and Truman's personal correspondence that reportedly had been destroyed and then reappeared after his wife's death in 1983, see Robert L. Messer, "New Evidence on Truman's Decision," *Bulletin of the Atomic Scientists* 41(August 1985): 50–56.

both "the most terrible thing ever discovered" and the "greatest thing in history."[9]

It is clear from Truman's own private writings at the time, some of which did not surface in the archives until the 1980s, and the observations of those closest to him, also recorded at the time, that Truman, while awed by what the Manhattan Project scientists had wrought, had no hesitation and no moral qualms about using the entire atomic arsenal as quickly as possible against Japanese cities and without any explicit warning.[10] In the years following his decision, Truman repeatedly and consistently held that to him, the bomb "was just another piece of artillery"; just a bigger bomb among all the other tens of thousands of bombs that already had rained from the skies over cities such as Hamburg, Dresden, and Tokyo. For Truman and those around him at the time, the question was not whether to use or why use the bomb, but why not? The plain truth is that for the American leaders in the summer of 1945 there were no compelling or even good reasons for not using atomic weapons as fast and as fully as possible. Looking back on the event, Hiroshima seems more a beginning of the nuclear age. But history is lived forward. Hiroshima was the logical culmination of the Allied strategic bombing campaign and the altered moral context of total war.[11]

However logical, even inevitable Hiroshima may have been, that same archival record shows that Truman at the time was uninformed or misinformed about aspects of the weapon that he wielded so readily and indiscriminately. For example, he did not ask, nor was he told, about the horrendous and long-term effects of atomic radiation. He and his top advisers were ignorant of this qualitative difference in nuclear versus conventional weapons. As survivors of the atomic bombs continued to die in the weeks and months after the war, some of those same advisers at first dismissed such stories of a mysterious debilitating "atomic bomb sickness" as the work of Japanese propaganda and privately wondered if Japanese blood might be

---

9 Diary entry July 18 and 19, 1945, Henry L. Stimson Papers, Yale University Library. Hereafter cited as Stimson Diary. Truman Diary, July 25, 1945. Potsdam Log, August 6, 1945, 50, Book Collection, HSTL.

10 The rather cumbersome phrase "recorded at the time" is necessary here because soon after the fact Stimson, Truman, and other key figures in the decision-making process began constructing their own version of history. Thus, primary sources such as diaries, letters, and minutes created without the advantage of hindsight or altered perspectives on the event are crucial to reconstructing what and how Truman and his advisers thought at the time. On this point see Barton J. Bernstein, "Seizing the Contested Terrain of Early Nuclear History: Stimson, Conant and Their Allies Explain the Decision to Use the Atomic Bomb," *Diplomatic History* 17 (Winter 1993): 35–72.

11 Michael Sherry, *The Rise of American Air Power: The Creation of Armageddon* (New Haven, 1987), 316–30; Ronald Schaffer, *Wings of Judgment: American Bombing in World War II* (New York, 1985), 128–48.

different.[12] The experts who might have advised policy-makers about the known effects of radiation apparently assumed that anyone exposed to lethal levels of radiation from the bomb would be killed outright by the blast and heat. In fact, in 1945 no one knew or really could know the full effects of gamma radiation and the residual radiation or atomic fallout produced by nuclear weapons.

Truman later claimed that he had been told at the time of his decision that the population of Hiroshima was about 60,000 and that the bomb would kill an estimated 20,000 Japanese.[13] The actual size of the city and death toll at Hiroshima were nearly six times those estimates. Planners assumed that the Japanese air defense would have sounded the alarm and most if not all of the population of the target cities would seek refuge in bomb shelters. However, in contrast to the hundreds of similar bombers that had ranged over more than sixty Japanese cities in the preceding months, the B-29 bombers that made up the atomic bombing missions were so few that the warning sirens around Hiroshima sounded the "all clear" signal minutes before the atomic fire ball burst over streets crowded with morning rush hour traffic, including groups of school children who had been excused from their studies to volunteer in creating fire breaks in anticipation of conventional incendiary bombing. Instead there was in Hiroshima and Nagasaki what survivors referred to as "the unforgettable fire."

The president was deliberately not told about the minority of atomic scientists who at the last minute attempted to petition against use of the bomb on civilian populations without warning. Pointing out that an "early unannounced" attack would sacrifice America's moral leadership in the eyes of the rest of the world, prejudice any attempt to establish international control of this new technology, and precipitate a postwar nuclear arms race, these "dovish" scientists favored a warning shot in the form of a bloodless demonstration on some uninhabited target witnessed by international, including Japanese, observers. In sum, they argued that the atomic bomb be treated as part of long-range international relations rather than in terms of what they called "military expediency." Secretary of War Henry Stimson made certain that what was called the Franck Report's dissent against indiscriminate use of the new weapon never reached Truman's desk. Stimson later defended his action by pointing out that the scientists advising the Interim Committee, who in turn advised the president on how best to use the bomb, all

---

12 Memorandum of telephone conversation, General Leslie Groves and Lt. Col. Rea, August 25, 1945. Reprinted in Michael B. Stoff, Jonathan F. Fanton, and R. Hal Williams, *The Manhattan Project: A Documentary Introduction to the Atomic Age* (New York, 1991), 258–62.

13 Messer, "New Evidence," 51.

concurred that such a warning shot would not be the most effective use of the precious few bombs available and that the best use for "maximum psychological impact" upon the Japanese leadership was "direct military use," without warning, against industrial targets surrounded by civilian housing.[14]

Truman did precisely what the Interim Committee recommended. No president, however strong or imperial, is a totally free agent. He must rely upon the information available to him and on the advice of those he trusts. In retrospect, the military head of the Manhattan Project, General Leslie Groves, likened Truman to "a little boy on a toboggan," with little control over the course of history.[15] But such a caricature is misleading. As the famous sign on his desk put it, the buck stopped with the president. Thus, what Truman knew and did not know at the time is crucial to understanding the relation between the atomic bombings of Hiroshima and Nagasaki and total war.

It is true that in his first weeks as Roosevelt's successor Truman was insecure and unsure of his ability to handle the job, especially in matters of international relations. On matters relating to the atomic bomb, he relied heavily on Secretary of War Henry Stimson. On foreign affairs in general, no one at that time had more influence than Truman's handpicked Secretary of State, James Byrnes. At certain key moments leading to the atomic bombings, Stimson and Byrnes had significant impact on how the decision was made and carried out. But both Stimson and Byrnes recognized that their influence extended only so far as they were able to gain Truman's assent and cooperation. Only the president could have altered the course of history had he chosen to do so.

Certainly Stimson and Byrnes weren't the only advisers Truman trusted and relied upon at this time. On a personal level, Truman admired General George Marshall and valued his military judgment. But it is clear from the record that Marshall's influence did not extend to political or diplomatic issues. His primary responsibility at this time was planning for the invasion of Japan. By the summer of 1945, the necessity of such a full-scale invasion was receding as intelligence intercepts brought news of Japanese peace feelers, Japan's situation became more and more hopeless, and American leaders anticipated both the Soviet entry into the war as promised at the Yalta conference and the successful completion of the atomic bomb project. Invasion

14 Arthur Compton to Secretary of War, June 12, 1945 and Memorandum on the Political and Social Problems from Members of the Metallurgical Laboratory of the University of Chicago, June 11, 1945 [Franck Committee Report]. Scientific Advisory Panel to the Interim Committee, Recommendations on the Immediate Use of Nuclear Weapons, June 16, 1945. Reprinted in *Manhattan Project*, 138–50.

15 Groves's view of Truman is quoted in *New York Times Magazine* (August 1, 1965): 9.

planning continued, but its priority was lowered by the rising prospect that the twin blows of Soviet entry and/or the still untested atomic bomb would convince Japan's leaders to accept the reality of defeat. Even if the Japanese imperial hierarchy refused to bow to the inevitable, Truman and his advisers hoped that a peace faction or what they referred to as a "submerged class" within Japan would force the issue before the actual invasion.[16]

As they prepared for the end of the war and planned for the peace to follow, Truman and his advisers looked increasingly to the American monopoly on atomic weapons to solve not only military but political and diplomatic problems. When in June Marshall supported inviting Soviet observers to the atomic test detonation in New Mexico, Byrnes promptly vetoed the idea on grounds that revealing the existence of the bomb before its use would raise political problems in dealing with Stalin at the upcoming Big Three summit conference. Marshall deferred to Byrnes, who was not only Secretary of State–designate but also Truman's personal representative to the committee charged with advising the president on how best to use the new weapon.[17] For Truman, that weapon promised not only to win the war but to provide him with the "winning weapon" in shaping the peace to follow.

Unlike Franklin Roosevelt, Truman was a combat veteran. He was proud of his service as a captain of artillery on the western front in World War I. He had personally witnessed the effects of poison gas on Allied troops.[18] As a civilian on the home front during World War II, he was well aware of the contribution Allied bombing made to winning the war both in Europe and the Pacific. Like most Americans, he had an exaggerated appreciation of the accuracy and efficacy of what was referred to as "precision bombing" and the presumed ability of American technology, such as the famed Norden bombsight, to discriminate between legitimate military targets and areas inhabited by innocent noncombatants.

Such wartime perspectives about what was a legitimate military target are perhaps the best explanation for what otherwise seems Truman's incomprehensible observation in the diary he kept at the time about how the atomic bombs were to be used. "I have told the Sec. of War, Mr. Stimson, to use it [the atomic bomb] so that military objectives and soldiers and sailors are the target and not women and children. . . . He and I are in accord. The target

---

16 Arnold Offner, *Another Such Victory: President Truman and the Cold War, 1945–1953* (Stanford, 2002), 67.

17 Stimson Diary, May 31, 1945, Notes on the Interim Committee Meeting, May 31, 1945, reprinted in Martin J. Sherwin, *A World Destroyed: The Atomic Bomb and the Grand Alliance* (New York, 1975), 295–304.

18 Alonzo Hamby, *Man of the People: A Life of Harry S. Truman* (New York, 1995), 68.

will be a purely military one."[19] The aiming point at Hiroshima was a bridge in the middle of the city. The bomb detonated directly above the parade ground of the Home Army's Pioneer Regiment. Nagasaki was an important port and industrial center. But more than 90 percent of those killed by the atomic bombs were civilians, not soldiers and sailors. Under the doctrine of total war, bridges, ports, industrial areas of cities, and civilian housing had become military targets. But they were hardly what Truman called "purely military"; women and children were inevitably part of so-called collateral damage. The confusion arises from the fact that during the war Americans did not accept or even recognize their complicity in indiscriminate "terror" or "obliteration" bombing aimed at civilian populations.[20] Truman apparently was no exception.

In the same diary entry, written on the day he gave the order to use all available atomic bombs as soon as they could be made ready, Truman recorded his explanation of why certain cities were to be atomic bombed and others spared. "Even if the Japs are savages, ruthless, merciless and fanatic, we as the leader of the world for the common welfare cannot drop this terrible weapon on the old capital [Kyoto] or the new [Tokyo]." In fact, Tokyo was not on the list of atomic bomb target cities because it had been devastated by the massive "firestorm" incendiary raid five months before. The target committee limited its choices to so-called "virgin" cities that deliberately had been spared conventional bomb damage. At one point, Stimson had expressed his concern to Truman that unless some cities were declared off-limits, the American conventional bombing campaign might well leave no suitable targets for demonstrating the power of atomic weapons. He also warned against the appearance of outdoing Hitler in committing atrocities. In reply, Truman reportedly laughed and said that he understood.[21]

As for Kyoto, the old imperial capital, Stimson struck it from the target list – over objections from the military – not for humanitarian considerations, but because, as he put it at the time, such a "wanton act" of destroying a sacred historic and religious center could fan anti-American sentiment in postwar Japan and "might make it impossible during the long post war period to reconcile the Japanese to us rather than to the Russians." As Stimson put it at the time, Truman was "particularly empathic" in agreeing that the choice of the target for the bomb must not conflict with American

19 Truman Diary, July 25, 1945.
20 On this point see George Hopkins, "Bombing and the American Conscience During World War II," *Historian* (May 1966): 451–73; and Schaffer, *Wings of Judgment*, chapters 2, 8, 9. Race as a factor in the Japanese-American conflict is treated in John Dower, *War Without Mercy: Race and Power in the Pacific War* (New York, 1986).
21 Stimson Memorandum of a talk with the President, June 6, 1945, *Manhattan Project*, 131.

postwar policy in Asia which included a Japan sympathetic to the United States "in case there should be any aggression by Russia in Manchuria."[22]

The revisionist contention that the atomic bombings of Hiroshima and Nagasaki were the first shot in the Cold War rather than the last shot in the hot war with Japan has been at the center of the long-running debate over why the atomic bombs were dropped on Hiroshima and Nagasaki.[23] Contrary to Truman's subsequent denials, evidence of a Cold War motive for the atomic bombings is there, not just in the form of circumstantial or indirect evidence, not just from hindsight, but in the contemporary documentary record. Indeed, some of it is in Truman's very legible handwriting.

Almost literally to his dying day in late 1972, Truman vehemently denied ever having based any part of his atomic bomb decision on considerations of containing or intimidating the Russians. He always contended that the only reason he used the bomb was to save lives that would have been lost in the planned invasion of the Japanese home islands. How many American and Japanese would have been killed or wounded in the invasion need not concern us here.[24] Whatever that counterfactual or hypothetical number may have been, the American people, had they been given a choice, would have preferred using the bomb to any prolongation of the war. Indeed, not long after the fact some 23 percent of Americans in a nationwide poll expressed regret that more atomic bombs had not been used before Japan had a chance to surrender.[25] For most Americans, shortening the war even

---

22 Ibid; Stimson Diary, July 24, 1945.

23 The revisionist case, based largely on circumstantial evidence, was first put forth in P. M. S. Blackett, *Fear War and the Bomb: Military and Political Consequences of Atomic Energy* (New York, 1948). The most recent and thorough statement of this argument is Gar Alperovitz, *The Decision to Use the Atomic Bomb and the Architecture of an American Myth* (New York, 1995).

24 The numbers game about how many Americans would have died in an invasion that never happened began soon after the war, when Stimson published his influential defense of the bombings as a net life saver. Stimson set the casualty total at one million. Henry L. Stimson, "The Decision to Use the Atomic Bomb," *Harpers Magazine* 194 (February 1947): 97–107. Truman in his memoirs used a total of one-half million American "lives" saved; not casualties, which includes wounded and missing and which would be 3 to 4 times the total lives lost. Such a casualty figure is greater than the total number of Americans in the invasion force. Harry S. Truman, *Memoirs: Year of Decisions* (Garden City, NY, 1955), 417. For a convincing refutation of the Stimson/Truman version of history, see Rufus E. Miles, Jr., "Hiroshima: The Strange Myth of a Half Million Lives Saved," *International Security* 10 (Fall 1985): 121–40. In his detailed study of the invasion planning, John Skates concludes that Truman and Stimson's subsequent inflated casualty figures were "without basis" in the contemporary documentary record. John Skates, *The Invasion of Japan: The Alternative to the Bomb* (New York, 1994), 244.

25 Unlike other "approve or disapprove" polling questions, the wording of this poll asked the respondents to choose among five descriptions of how "you feel about our use of the atomic bomb." A majority (53.5 percent) endorsed using the two bombs against cities "just as we did," 14 percent favored a warning demonstration prior to use on cities, and 5 percent opposed any use of atomic weapons. The remaining percent replied "don't know." Fortune survey, *Fortune* 32 (December 1945): 305.

by days would have been justification enough in 1945. The postwar myth of the bomb having saved 500,000 American lives was and remains a powerful argument justifying the 200,000 Japanese killed by the atomic bombs. It is a myth that Americans, particularly those of the World War II "Greatest Generation," cling to as an integral part of the "Good War."

But at the time, the war itself, most particularly the virtually universal acceptance by 1945 of the doctrine of total war, justified using the bomb. The effect on postwar policy, especially regarding expansion of Stalin's truly evil empire, was a bonus, a reinforcing factor that added to the momentum of the bomb decision.[26]

But is important to note that had there been no Soviet Union, no Stalin, no threat of communist expansion in 1945, Hiroshima and perhaps Nagasaki probably still would have been atomic bombed. Even without the bonus of containing Stalin's role in postwar Asia, other factors rendered Truman's decision all but unavoidable. Not the least of these was the refusal or inability of the Japanese leadership to end the paralysis that inflicted them in their attempts to find an acceptable, honorable end to the war.[27] Even after the twin blows of the atomic bombings and the Soviet declaration of war, when he was asked if the war would continue if the Americans rejected the condition of preserving the imperial household and national polity [*kokutai*], Hirohito replied, "of course."[28]

As Leon Sigal has shown, bureaucratic politics on both sides blocked alternative courses of action.[29] The Japanese leaders couldn't bring themselves to deal directly or realistically with the Americans. Truman and those around him saw the atomic bomb as a solution to a range of problems and concerns. Not using the bomb was simply not an option.

For an analysis of opinion on the bomb, see Michael Yavenditti, "The American People and the Use of Atomic Bombs on Japan: The 1940s," *Historian* 36 (February 1974): 224–47.

26 This "post revisionist" multicausal explanation of the reasons for the atomic bombings has been the consensus of expert opinion since the 1980s, although the popular myths endure in works such as David McCullough, *Truman* (New York, 1992), 437. A discussion of scholarly opinion about the bomb decision is J. Samuel Walker, "The Decision to Use the Bomb: A Historiographical Update," *Diplomatic History* 19 (Spring 1995). For a succinct, balanced discussion of the bomb decision, see J. Samuel Walker, *Prompt and Utter Destruction: Truman and the Use of the Atomic Bombs Against Japan* (Chapel Hill, NC, 1997).

27 Japan's agonizing seven-month struggle to find a formula for "peace with honor" is expertly treated in Herbert P. Bix, *Hirohito and the Making of Modern Japan* (New York, 2000), 487–530. See also Barton J. Bernstein, "Understanding the Atomic Bomb and the Japanese Surrender: Missed Opportunities, Little Near Disasters, and Modern Memory," *Diplomatic History* 19 (Spring 1995): 230–34; and Sadao Asada, "The Shock of the Atomic Bomb and Japan's Decision to Surrender – A Reconsideration," *Pacific Historical Review* 67 (1998): 477–512.

28 Bix, *Hirohito*, 519.

29 Leon Sigal, *Fighting to the Finish: The Politics of War Termination in the United States and Japan, 1945* (Ithaca, 1988).

Many in the American decision-making bureaucracy wanted to demonstrate the bomb's power to end the war for their own reasons. Some of the arguments for using the bombs before the Japanese surrendered seem incredibly petty or banal. Among them is the widespread concern that if the bomb was not ready in time to justify its blind-funded cost overruns, Congress would hold everyone involved responsible, from the president on down. As one War Department staff member put it: "If the [bomb] project succeeds, there won't be any investigation. If it doesn't they won't investigate anything else."[30] Although he would never have admitted it perhaps even to himself, Truman's wartime role as budgetary watchdog on the Senate's "Truman Committee" must have brought home to him the necessity to justify the unprecedented expense of the bomb project. Not to use the bomb as soon as possible would have been an unforgivable waste of time, lives, and money.

This does not mean that Cold War or anti-Soviet considerations were irrelevant to how the bomb decision was made and particularly to how and when the bombs were used. The documentary record clearly shows that Truman and his closest advisers had concluded that, in light of the successful testing of the bomb, the Russians were no longer needed to defeat Japan. This was a dramatic reversal of opinion and policy produced by the fact of having a workable bomb of known power. As Secretary of State Byrnes put it at the time, the goal at that point was to end the war quickly with the bomb before the Russians "could get in so much on the kill."[31]

On the opening day of the Potsdam conference, after a private meeting with Stalin, Truman recorded his belief that once the Soviet Union declared war on Japan the war would end, without an invasion and without the atomic bomb having been used. As he put it: "Fini Japs when that [Soviet entry] comes about."[32] Any doubt about what Truman meant by "Fini Japs" is dispelled by his explanation to his wife in a letter written the following day. In it, he celebrates having secured Stalin's promise to join the war against Japan by mid-August, and makes clear what this meant in shortening the war before the dreaded invasion: "I say we'll end the war a year sooner now, and think of the kids who won't be killed. That is the important thing."[33] It

---

30 Leslie R. Groves, *Now It Can Be Told* (New York, 1962), 70, 360. Groves in particular insisted that "two bombs" be used in order to justify the cost of the Plutonium project that fueled the Nagasaki bomb. Ibid., 298. For the rush to use the bomb for public relations reasons, see Stanley Goldberg, "Racing to the Finish," in Kai Bird and Lawrence Lifschultz, eds., *The Shadow of Hiroshima* (Stony Creek, 1998), 119–29.

31 Walter Brown Diary, July 23, 1945; WB's Book, James F. Byrnes Papers, Clemson University Library.

32 Truman Diary, July 17, 1945.

33 Harry Truman to Bess Truman, July 18, 1945. Reprinted in Robert Ferrell, *Dear Bess: The Letters From Harry to Bess Truman, 1910–1959* (New York, 1983), 519.

seems indisputable that at that moment Truman believed, rightly or wrongly, that Soviet entry would end the war a year earlier than would be the case without Soviet participation, saving the lives of American "kids" who would otherwise die in the invasion.

But as the reports from the New Mexico test site reached him in Potsdam, Truman's perspective on how the war would end changed. Nowhere is that transformation more clear than in his diary entry recorded on the evening of the same day he had written his wife about Soviet entry shortening the war. After a private lunch with Churchill, during which they discussed the successful atomic test, Truman wrote: "[I] Believe Japs will fold up before Russia comes in. I am sure they will when Manhattan [the atomic bomb] appears over their homeland."[34]

To bring about that desired optimal conclusion of the war – Japan's surrender without significant Soviet participation – Truman used the means at his disposal, the world's total atomic arsenal. In effect, he waged total atomic war. In his first public announcement of the Hiroshima bombing, he called the city of 360,000 people a "military base." The script was written for him well in advance of its delivery. Certainly he knew that such a description was inaccurate and misleading. But under the doctrine of total war, cities were considered military targets. By the end of World War II and in the ensuing nuclear age of MAD, or mutually assured destruction, "kids," women, and children, would be among the targeted enemy populations. Some philosophers and theologians would declare such warfare, even in intent, immoral. In the immediate aftermath of Hiroshima and Nagasaki, Truman himself seems to have had some second thoughts about what he had done. The day after the destruction of Nagasaki, he told his cabinet that he had ordered a halt to any other atomic bombings in part because the thought of wiping out another 100,000 people was just too horrible and that he did not like the thought of, as he put it, killing "all those kids."[35] Some weeks later, as relations with the Soviet Union deteriorated, an aide tried to console the beleaguered president by noting that if all else failed, at least Truman had the atomic bomb. Truman replied that the atomic bomb was not a military weapon, that it kills women and children and thus could never be used again.[36]

---

34 Truman Diary, July 18, 1945.
35 John Morton Blum, *The Price of Vision: The Diary of Henry Wallace, 1942–1946* (Boston, 1973), 474. In fact, Truman did not issue such an order. A factual treatment of the third atomic bomb and the end of the war is in Barton Bernstein, "The Perils and Politics of Surrender: Ending the War with Japan and Avoiding the Third Atomic Bomb," *Pacific Historical Review* (February 1977): 1–27.
36 Diary entry October 5, 1945, Harold Smith Papers, HSTL.

And yet this was the same man who immediately after the war publicly declared the atomic bomb America's "sacred trust," a God-given power too precious to share with the lawless world until such time when there were guarantees against its misuse. Under Truman, America would rely on its atomic monopoly as its "winning weapon" in the Cold War.

Four years after Hiroshima, Stalin's scientists gave him the equivalent of America's sacred trust. In the wake of the public revelation of the Soviet atomic bomb, Truman met with his advisers about the prospects of creating the "Super" or H-bomb, a thousand times more powerful than those used against Japan. The meeting lasted seven minutes. Truman asked one question: "Can the Russians do it?" Informed that such a possibility existed, Truman gave the go-ahead to launch the effort to build the first H-bomb. A few days before Dwight Eisenhower was elected to succeed Truman as president, the United States detonated the first fusion explosion with the power of more than 500 Hiroshima atomic bombs.[37]

In the ensuing years of the Cold War, what Winston Churchill called the "balance of terror" helped to keep the Cold War cold. It is perhaps no consolation to the 20 million people who died in "limited wars" during what historian John Gaddis has called the "Long Peace" that no nuclear war, no total war on a global scale has been fought since 1945. But wars such as those in Korea, Vietnam, and Afghanistan were total to those who suffered the consequences of modern "conventional" nonnuclear weapons. Also total was the ideological fanaticism that produced the genocidal killing fields of Cambodia and the ethnic cleansing in the Balkans.

Harry Truman died the day after Christmas 1972 in the midst of Richard Nixon's "Christmas bombing" campaign that dropped the destructive equivalent of two Hiroshima-type atomic bombs on North Vietnam. It can be argued that Nixon's massive use of American airpower helped bring about the signing of the Vietnam peace accords. Whether that end to America's longest war was good or honorable can also be debated.

The destruction of Hiroshima and Nagasaki may have helped hasten the end of history's most destructive war and the last global total war. To many, the horrors of that war helped to justify the lesser evil of the atomic bombings. But even at the distance of more than a half century, we are still left with no clear answer to Father Siemes's question about the morality of killing some innocent people in order to save the lives of others. In 1945, Truman was faced with such a choice. The historical record shows that for

---

37 McGeorge Bundy, *Danger and Survival: Choices About the Bomb in the First Fifty Years* (New York, 1988), 213; Richard Rhodes, *Dark Sun: The Making of the Hydrogen Bomb* (New York, 1995), 407.

him it was really a nondecision, the answer to which was implicit in the context of the question. Bombs had been used and were being used daily to win the war. The new atomic weapon was a bomb; an exponentially bigger bomb, one 2,000 times more powerful than any ever used in war, but still a bomb. Under the "doctrine" of total war bombing civilians was acceptable, legitimate, a regrettable but unavoidable product of the fact that "machines were ahead of morals." Even though immediately after the fact he would privately admit that it was horrible to think about killing "all those kids," he always maintained publicly that he had no choice.

But even Truman may have had second thoughts. The title of this essay "accidental judgments, casual slaughters" is taken from Horatio's oration in the final scene of *Hamlet*, the final lines of which were underlined twice by then former President Truman in a book on the atomic bomb decision in his personal library.[38] It reads as follows:

Let me speak to the yet unknowing world
How these things came about.
So shall you hear of carnal, bloody, and unnatural acts,
Of accidental judgments, casual slaughters,
Of deaths put on by cunning and forced cause,
And, in this upshot, purposes mistook
Fall'n on the inventors' heads. . . .
But let this same be presently perform'd,
Even while men's minds are wild; lest more mischance,
On plots and errors, happen.

Whether these lines have any significance regarding Truman's thoughts about the atomic bombings of Hiroshima and Nagasaki, I will leave to the reader's judgment. My purpose here is not to judge Truman nor to weigh the rights and wrongs of the atomic bombings. It is rather to discuss the connection between total war as developed during World War II and the simultaneous development of the world's first nuclear weapons. If there is a lesson to be drawn from this intersection of the concept of total war and the absolute weapon, the modern versions of which are capable of destroying not just cities but civilization, it should be summed up in the phrase: "Never again."

38 Gregg Herken, *The Winning Weapon: The Atomic Bomb in the Cold War, 1945–1950* (New York, 1981), p. 21; Merle Miller, *Plain Speaking: An Oral Biography of Harry S. Truman* (New York, 1973), 248.

PART F

Criminal War

17

Sexual Violence and Its Prosecution by Courts Martial of the Wehrmacht

BIRGIT BECK

"Warfare with and against civilians is one of the hallmarks of total war," writes Stig Förster.[1] Despite continuing disagreements among historians over which wars can be characterized as "total," there is consensus on the factors that define the concept. The primary markers seem to be the extent and intensity of warfare, the adoption of limitless war aims, the abolition of restraints posed by morality or law, and the systematic mobilization of all available economic, social, and political resources for the war effort. These features of total war entail the "calculated erasure of the bounds between combatant and noncombatant," the transformation of civilians into principal victims of military violence.[2] Although the losses during the global conflict from 1939 to 1945 cannot be calculated with any precision, civilian casualties far exceeded military losses. In the Soviet Union, two-thirds of all the losses were civilian.[3]

Despite the importance of civilian casualties in total war, little research has been done on one of the problem's central aspects: gender-specific crimes, particularly sexual assaults on girls and women.[4] Wartime rape has remained a taboo for historians. Susan Brownmiller's pioneering work on sexual crimes in wartime was first published in 1975, but her work has found few successors.[5] It has taken the public outcry over the mass rapes of

1 Stig Förster, "Das Zeitalter des totalen Kriegs, 1861–1945: Konzeptionelle Überlegungen für einen historischen Strukturvergleich," *Mittelweg* 36, 8, no. 6 (1999), 17.
2 Roger Chickering, "Total War: The Use and Abuse of a Concept," in Manfred F. Boemeke, Roger Chickering, and Stig Förster, eds., *Anticipating Total War: The German and American Experiences, 1871–1914* (Cambridge, 1999), 26.
3 Gerhard L. Weinberg, *A World At Arms: A Global History of World War II* (Cambridge, 1994), 894. See also Eric Hobsbawm, *The Age of Extremes: A History of the World, 1914–1991* (New York, 1996), 43.
4 Kelly Dawn Askin, *War Crimes Against Women: Prosecution in International War Crimes Tribunals* (The Hague, 1997), xvi.
5 Susan Brownmiller, *Against Our Will: Men, Women and Rape*, 5th ed. (London, 1991).

Bosnian women during the Yugoslavian civil war to renew scholarly interest in sexually related war crimes.[6]

The topic of wartime rape has surfaced briefly in connection with recent scholarly debates over total war. In his analysis of guerrilla warfare in the West during the American Civil War, Michael Fellman emphasized the prominence of rape, as well as the fact that one particular group of women fell victim to such assaults. Regular soldiers on both sides of this conflict, as well as Confederate guerrillas, shared a set of cultural values that included the protection of women and their families. Consequently, white women were spared rape and murder. According to Fellman, a special "code of honor" applied to members of white society, but not to those who were defined by race as "others" or subhuman. Because of this code, Union soldiers and Confederate guerrillas often beat, raped, and murdered black and Indian women.[7] The link between racism and sexual violence was also transparent during World War II and other conflicts. Many American soldiers in the Vietnam war, for example, held racist attitudes, which justified or encouraged atrocities against Vietnamese civilians.[8]

In the debate over the "totality" of the First World War, John Horne and Alan Kramer have analyzed German atrocities against enemy civilians during the invasion of Belgium and France. They have found that "Rapes occurred fairly widely, although in numbers that are difficult to ascertain."[9] Here the two authors raise an enormous problem that the historian faces in studying wartime rape. In most cases, statistics or hard evidence of any kind are lacking. The rapes of 1914 became notorious as journalists and

---

6 Alexandra Stiglmayer, ed., *Massenvergewaltigung: Krieg gegen die Frauen* (Freiburg/Br., 1993); Norma von Ragenfeld-Feldman, "The Victimization of Women: Rape and the Reporting of Rape in Bosnia-Herzegovina, 1992–1993," *Dialog: Internationale Zeitschrift für Kunst und Wissenschaft* 6, no. 21 (1997), 3–26.

7 Michael Fellman, "At the Nihilist Edge: Reflections on Guerrilla Warfare during the American Civil War," in Stig Förster and Jörg Nagler, eds., *On the Road to Total War: The American Civil War and the German Wars of Unification, 1861–1871* (Cambridge, 1997), 527–33.

8 Joanna Bourke, *An Intimate History of Killing: Face-to-Face Killing in Twentieth-Century Warfare* (London, 2000), 204–8; Michael Hochgeschwender, " 'Mired in Stalemate': Zur Geschichte vietnamesischer und amerikanischer Kinder und Jugendlicher im Vietnamkrieg (1964–1975)," Dittmar Dahlmann, ed., *Kinder und Jugendliche in Krieg und Revolution: Vom Dreissigjährigen Krieg bis zu den Kindersoldaten Afrikas* (Paderborn, 2000), 187, 190–93.

9 John Horne and Alan Kramer, "War Between Soldiers and Enemy Civilians, 1914–1915," in Roger Chickering and Stig Förster, eds., *Great War, Total War: Combat and Mobilization on the Western Front, 1914–1918* (Cambridge, 2000), 157.

government officials attempted to exploit the fates of individual women for propaganda purposes in wooing the neutral states.[10] The role of sexual violence as a tool of wartime propaganda thus represents another problem with which the historian must deal.

Sexual assault has historically been an important dimension of the conflict between soldiers and enemy civilians. The Second World War is a case in point. Sexual violence in this war is associated primarily with the atrocities committed by the Wehrmacht, the Red Army's behavior at the end of the war, the Japanese "Rape of Nanking," and the Japanese army's system of forced prostitution.[11]

The Japanese record is well documented. The history of sexual assaults by members of the German army and the Waffen SS remains, by contrast, virtually unwritten. Two contradictory – and undocumented – views have governed the sparse historiography on the subject. One view, which relies on memoirs and other accounts by German veterans, does not regard sexual violence as a serious problem during World War II. German soldiers, so the argument runs, would have been severely punished, if not sentenced to death, for such crimes. Since few soldiers were punished, few assaults took place.[12] Susan Brownmiller offers a different analysis:

The point I want to make here is that as rape is the quintessential act by which a male demonstrates to a female that she is conquered – vanquished – by his superior strength and power, it was perfectly logical within the framework of fascism that rape would be employed by the German soldier as he strove to prove himself a worthy Superman. In fact, it would have been highly *illogical* if rape were not in the German soldier's kit bag of weapons. Rape for the Germans, and to a similar extent for the Japanese, played a serious and logical role in the achievement of what they saw as their ultimate objective: the total humiliation and destruction of "inferior peoples" and the establishment of their own master race.[13]

Brownmiller and others who share her view base their conclusions primarily on reports that were presented at the International Military Tribunal

10 Ruth Harris, "The 'Child of the Barbarian': Rape, Race and Nationalism in France during the First World War," *Past and Present* 141 (1993): 170–206.

11 Helke Sander and Barbara Johr, eds., *BeFreier und Befreite: Krieg, Vergewaltigungen, Kinder* (Frankfurt am Main, 1995); Norman M. Naimark, *The Russians in Germany: A History of the Soviet Zone of Occupation, 1945–1949* (Cambridge, MA, 1995), 69–140; Iris Chang, *The Rape of Nanking: The Forgotten Holocaust of World War II* (New York, 1997); Yuki Tanaka, *Hidden Horrors: Japanese War Crimes in World War II* (Boulder, CO, 1996), 79–109; George Hicks, *The Comfort Women: Japan's Brutal Regime of Enforced Prostitution in the Second World War* (New York, 1995).

12 Hermann Graml, "Die Wehrmacht im Dritten Reich," *Vierteljahrshefte für Zeitgeschichte* 45 (1997): 373.

13 Brownmiller, *Against Our Will*, 49. Emphasis in the original.

at Nuremberg after the war.[14] French and the Soviet prosecutors submitted evidence of rape, forced prostitution, and sexual mutilation.[15] These reports were not entirely reliable, however, for they often did not distinguish between regular soldiers and members of the SS, referring instead simply to "fascist German soldiers." Furthermore, the reports were based on testimonies from witnesses, not victims. Nevertheless, this sketchy evidence suggests that sexual violence was a serious problem during World War II. Given the two contradictory views of this subject described here, the question arises: did the Wehrmacht indeed use – or at least tolerate – rape as an element of warfare to terrorize the enemy civilian population, or did it try to prohibit or punish sexual violence? As important as it is to attend to the experiences of the victims, to answer this question we need to examine how the armed forces themselves dealt with sexual violence.

This essay accordingly presents a short examination of the nature and practice of German military justice in connection with sexual crimes in the occupied territories during the Second World War.[16] It will focus on the question whether the ideology of total warfare comprehended sexual crimes.

RAPE AS A CRIME UNDER MILITARY LAW

More than 17 million men served in the Wehrmacht during World War II.[17] We do not know, however, how many of them became involved in the system of military justice. Some 1,300 German courts martial handled 3 million criminal cases, many of which involved multiple defendants. The majority of these cases concerned members of the Wehrmacht, while the rest involved prisoners of war and civilians in the occupied countries.[18] The main purpose of military justice was to safeguard order among the troops and to uphold the so-called *Manneszucht*, or military discipline. *Manneszucht* was the highest commandment of military life, as one noted legal authority

---

14 Christine Eifler, "Nachkrieg und weibliche Verletzbarkeit: Zur Rolle von Kriegen für die Konstruktion von Geschlecht," in Christine Eifler and Ruth Seifert, eds., *Soziale Konstruktionen – Militär und Geschlechterverhältnis* (Münster, 1999), 162.

15 *Der Prozess gegen die Hauptkriegsverbrecher vor dem Internationalen Militärgerichtshof, Nürnberg, 14. November 1945 – 1. Oktober 1946*, 42 vols. (Nürnberg, 1947–49) (hereafter IMT), 6: 445–8; 7: 499–503.

16 See Birgit Beck, "Rape: The Military Trials of Sexual Crimes Committed by Soldiers in the Wehrmacht, 1939–1944," in Karen Hagemann and Stefanie Schüler-Springorum, eds., *Home/Front: The Military, War and Gender in Twentieth-Century Germany* (Oxford, 2002), 255–73.

17 Rüdiger Overmans, *Deutsche militärische Verluste im Zweiten Weltkrieg* (Munich, 1999), 215. Another million men were in the Waffen SS.

18 Manfred Messerschmidt and Fritz Wüllner, *Die Wehrmachtjustiz im Dienste des Nationalsozialismus* (Baden-Baden, 1987), 49–50.

commented before the war.[19] The lessons of the First World War – the memory of the growing ranks of deserters and the naval mutiny in the fall of 1918 – figured large in this thinking. In August 1938, the National Socialist regime accordingly introduced the Military Code of Criminal Procedure (*Kriegsstrafverfahrensordnung*, KStVO) and the Special Military Penal Code (*Kriegssonderstrafrechtsverordnung*, KSSVO), which were designed to ensure the rapid and severe punishment of indiscipline.[20] Convicted soldiers were not, however, to serve their sentences away from the battlefront. As German losses mounted and the need for manpower rose, the army established additional penal institutions, beyond the regular system of military prisons in the Reich, to keep convicted men at the front.[21] These included frontline military prisons (*Feldstrafgefangenenlager*), field detachments for convicts (*Feldstrafgefangenenabteilungen*), and probationary battalions (*Bewährungsbataillone*). Service in these units was dangerous and their casualty rates extremely high.

The majority of soldiers who appeared before courts martial were charged with desertion, subversion of the military (*Wehrkraftzersetzung*), absence without leave, disobedience, or theft. Desertion and subversion were regarded as particularly serious offenses insofar as they threatened discipline among the troops. These crimes were thus prosecuted relentlessly; and they occasioned most of the death sentences that were imposed by German courts martial during the Second World War.[22]

As was the case in most military codes in the west, rape was also legally prohibited in the Wehrmacht.[23] The military criminal code held members of the Wehrmacht punishable by courts martial if they committed crimes that were covered by the civilian criminal code (*Reichsstrafgesetzbuch*, RStGB), including "crimes and offences against morality" – a category that comprehended rape, sexual coercion, and sexual relations with minors. The civilian criminal code also prescribed sentences from six months to life. For soldiers, serving time in a penitentiary was particularly degrading, for it included dismissal from the army, the loss of all pay, and hence heavy

19 Erich Schwinge, "Manneszucht, Ehre und Kameradschaft als Auslegungsrichtpunkte im Militärstrafrecht," *Zeitschrift für Wehrrecht* 2 (1937/38): 29.
20 *Reichsgesetzblatt* (hereafter RGBl) 1 (1939): 1455–7 (KSSVO); 1457–76 (KStVO).
21 Hans-Peter Klausch, " 'Erziehungsmänner' und 'Wehrunwürdige': Die Sonder-und Bewährungseinheiten der Wehrmacht," in Norbert Haase and Gerhard Paul, eds., *Die anderen Soldaten: Wehrkraftzersetzung, Gehorsamsverweigerung und Fahnenflucht im Zweiten Weltkrieg* (Frankfurt am Main, 1995), 66–82.
22 Steven R. Welch, " 'Harsh but Just'? German Military Justice in the Second World War: A Comparative Study of the Court-Martialling of German and US Deserters," *German History* 17 (1999): 380; cf. Messerschmidt and Wüllner, *Wehrmachtjustiz*, 90–168.
23 Askin, *War Crimes*, 19–48.

consequences for the soldier's family. In September 1941, an amendment to the military criminal code enabled judges to punish sex offenders with death, should such a sentence be deemed necessary "to protect the national community (*Volksgemeinschaft*)."[24] This language referred primarily to cases that involved German and other "Aryan" women.

The law was seldom enforced if the victim belonged to the enemy population in France or the Soviet Union, for these cases did not directly affect the interests of the *Volksgemeinschaft*.[25] In a majority of cases in which a court martial sentenced the perpetrator of a sex crime to death, it did so because the soldier had used a weapon or committed rape in connection with another serious offense.[26] In these cases, the courts invoked the "Decree against Violent Criminals" (*Verordnung gegen Gewaltverbrecher*).[27] This decree prescribed the death penalty for crimes such as rape or robbery when the perpetrator was armed with a dangerous weapon. In cases where a soldier had killed his victim after raping her, the military courts also imposed the death penalty. To this extent, the commonly held view that the German army sentenced soldiers to death for sexually assaulting women in the occupied territories had some basis in fact, but the courts martial usually acted in this manner only in special circumstances.

The Wehrmacht's criminal statistics from 1939 to 1944 (*Wehrmachtkriminalstatistik*) reveal, however, that rape was infrequently prosecuted. More than 5,300 military personnel were charged with sexual crimes: more than 4,000 were in the army, the rest in the navy or air force. The number of convictions peaked in the third quarter of 1940 after the defeat of France. Following the attack on the Soviet Union, the number of convictions declined until 1943, when it rose slightly.[28] Despite their many errors, irregularities, and gaps, these statistics reflect the handling of prosecutions for sexual offenses in the several theaters of the war.[29] However, the figures reveal only the prosecutions of such offenses and provide no evidence about the number of rapes that went unreported or untried.

---

24 *Strafrecht der deutschen Wehrmacht*, 7th ed. (Munich, 1944), 1, § 3; 103, §§ 176–8; RGBl, 1 (1941): 549–50.

25 Bundesarchiv/Zentralnachweisstelle Kornelimünster (hereafter BA-ZNS), Gericht der 9. Pz. Div./ 54: 27–9, Feldurteil, 27 June 1944.

26 BA-ZNS, Gericht der 21. Pz. Div. /275: 58–69, Feldurteil, 1 October 1943.

27 RGBl. 1 (1939: 2378), "Verordnung gegen Gewaltverbrecher. Vom 5. Dezember 1939," § 1, "Gewalttaten mit der Waffe."

28 Otto Hennicke, "Auszüge aus der Wehrmachtkriminalstatistik," *Zeitschrift für Militärgeschichte* 5 (1966): 452, 454.

29 Wüllner, *NS-Militärjustiz*, 265–329.

RAPE AND MILITARY PROSECUTION IN FRANCE

During the war in France as well as after the armistice of June 22, 1940, rapes of French women and girls became a problem for German military courts. There was a broad variety of incidents. In many cases, sexual crimes occurred when German soldiers stayed in one place for an extended period time and came in contact with the French civilian population. It is not possible to generalize about either the perpetrators or the victims. Young, unmarried soldiers as well as older soldiers with families and years of military experience committed sex crimes; the majority of the perpetrators belonged to the enlisted ranks. The victims were not only the youthful, unmarried, and attractive young women portrayed in literary works and movies that deal with wartime rape. The victims ranged from six-year-old girls to sixty-seven-year-old women, unmarried women, married women, and mothers.[30] In many cases, French women reported the assaults to the local police, who then informed the German military police or local military headquarters. These reports were then pursued.

During a court martial, the French victim would be interrogated as intensively as the accused soldier or, in the case of gang rapes, soldiers. As was common in peacetime trials for sexual assault, the victim, her lifestyle, and particularly her moral character came under thorough scrutiny. German military police questioned the victim's neighbors and the local police about the woman in question. The Wehrmacht could usually count on their cooperation, for younger women, unmarried women without children, and especially the wives of French prisoners of war were widely suspected of living "loose" lives, and they were watched by neighbors, relatives, and colleagues.[31] Military judges gave particular attention to determining whether the victim had "provoked" the sexual assault or might be falsely accusing an innocent German soldier. Giving false testimony could have serious consequences.[32] The way German male judges treated female victims of sexual assault in these courts martial bore resemblance to patterns at such trials both before and afterward, but the fact that French women were regarded as members of the enemy population made them the objects of additional mistrust.[33]

---

30 BA-ZNS, Gericht der 106. Inf. Div./287; BA-ZNS, Gericht der 211. Inf. Div./350.

31 Hélène Eck, "Die Französinnen unter dem Vichy-Regime: Frauen in der Katastrophe – Bürgerinnen dank der Katastrophe?" in Georges Duby and Michelle Perrot, eds., *Geschichte der Frauen*, 5 vols. (Frankfurt am Main, 1997), 5: 237.

32 BA-ZNS, Ostbestand S 300, Gericht der 52. Inf. Div.; Gericht Chef d. Mil. Verw. Bez. C.

33 Tanja Hommen, *Sittlichkeitsverbrechen: Sexuelle Gewalt im Kaiserreich* (Frankfurt am Main, 1999), 126–33.

Although the military courts attached great importance to examining the details of each case, the sex crime itself, the victim, and the traumatic effects were not the decisive issues in determining the verdict or penalty. Instead, the courts were primarily concerned lest these crimes have negative long-term consequences for military discipline and the Wehrmacht's role as an occupying power. At the beginning of the occupation, most of the French civilian population was impressed by the Wehrmacht's discipline and correct behavior.[34] Harsh punishment of German soldiers who were guilty of sexual assault was calculated to prevent the spread of anti-German sentiment. A few days after the armistice, the commander of the 4th German Army, Günther von Kluge, called for severe punishment in cases of rape. He described some rapes that had been brought to his attention as "atrocious" (*bestialisch*) and emphasized that they could endanger the "reputation of the Wehrmacht."[35] Whenever German military judges feared for the army's reputation among the French population, they imposed severe sentences.[36]

These instances notwithstanding, the High Command of the German Army (*Oberkommando des Heeres*, OKH) did not regard rape as a serious crime. On July 5, 1940, a few days after Kluge's pronouncement, the Commander-in-Chief of the Army, Walther von Brauchitsch, informed the commanders of the German armies about how courts martial were to deal with rapists. He explained that he strongly condemned rape, but that "during the operations and occupation, soldiers must cope with circumstances that differ considerably from those at home"; therefore, he counseled, "straying *once* from the path of moral decency" should not be punished as severely as it would be "under normal circumstances."[37] Making contact with French women was the order of the day during the occupation, although the OKH tried to regulate these contacts, principally because it feared the spread of sexually transmitted diseases. In another order, which was distributed in 1940 to most of the military commanders, Brauchitsch observed that since German soldiers would remain in the occupied areas for an extended time, the problem of sexuality had to be addressed. Soldiers had to do their jobs under circumstances that could cause "sexual tensions," he reasoned (as did

34 Nicole Ann Dombrowski, "Surviving the German Invasion of France: Women's Stories of the Exodus of 1940," in Dombrowski, ed., *Women and War in the Twentieth Century: Enlisted with or without Consent* (New York, 1999), 122, 125–6, 130–3; Rita Thalmann, *Gleichschaltung in Frankreich 1940–1944* (Hamburg, 1999), 67.
35 Bundesarchiv-Militärarchiv Freiburg (hereafter BA-MA), RH 26-12/274, Bl. 602, Der Oberbefehlshaber der 4. Armee, 27 June 1940.
36 BA-ZNS, S 226, Gericht der 251. Inf. Div., Feldurteil, 4 June 1940, Bl. 14.; BA-ZNS, S 208, Gericht der 1. Pz. Div., Feldurteil, 21 June 1940.
37 BA ZNS, RH 15aG/8, Disziplin und Rechtspflege, ObdH GenQu (III). GenStdH, Nr. 16098/40, 5 July 1940. Emphasis in the original.

many courts martial when they imposed lenient sentences). A general pro-
hibition of sexual contact between soldiers and women in the occupied
areas would not solve the problem, he noted, but would only increase the
number of rapes and homosexual relationships. The solution was for the
Wehrmacht to establish more brothels under medical supervision.[38]

The subject of military brothels extends beyond the framework of this
essay, but it bears mention that this aspect of daily military life in France
provided further evidence of the Wehrmacht's view of soldiers' sexuality.
A well-organized, bureaucratically supervised system of military brothels
operated in France and elsewhere in an effort to prevent homosexual relationships and venereal disease.[39] The German armed forces in France not
only took over brothels that were already in existence, but they also forced
French women from internment camps to become prostitutes in the military
brothels. Records from similar brothels on the eastern front are missing, but
evidence suggests that women in Poland and the Soviet Union were likewise
forced into prostitution.[40] The German brothel system was an institutionalized form of the broader phenomenon of sexual violence.

Despite Brauchitsch's instructions in the summer of 1940, German military courts meted out harsh punishments in some cases of sexual assault on
French women. Sentences ranged up to ten years' imprisonment and dismissal from military service.[41] Good conduct and a positive evaluation from
a soldier's superior officer could, however, bring about a lighter sentence. In
keeping with provisions of the civilian criminal code, judges also reduced
sentences when the perpetrator could prove that he was drunk and thus
acted with diminished responsibility when he committed the rape. Many
trials thus witnessed accused soldiers denouncing the consequences of alcohol consumption, for judges were known to be receptive to this explanation
for criminal behavior.[42]

Nevertheless, verdicts in France gave the impression that German military
courts dealt severely with rapists whenever their actions endangered the
interests and goals of the Wehrmacht as an occupying power. Although
military utility guided the prosecution of sexual crimes, the way in which

38 BA-MA, RH 53-7/v. 233a/167, "Anlage 1 zu ObdH Nr. 8840/41, GenQu GenStdH," 31 July
    1940.
39 See for example BA-MA, H 20/825, Abschr. OKH, GenStdH, GenQu Nr. 11244/40 geh., "Pros-
    titution und Bordellwesen in Belgien und im besetzten Gebiet Frankreichs," 29 July 1940; Insa
    Meinen, *Wehrmacht und Prostitution im besetzten Frankreich* (Bremen, 2002).
40 Meinen, *Wehrmacht*, 131–85; Franz Seidler, *Prostitution, Homosexualität, Selbstverstümmelung: Probleme
    der deutschen Sanitätsführung 1939–1945* (Neckargemünd, 1977), 135–92.
41 BA-ZNS, S 294, Gericht des Kommandanten des Armeegebietes 590, Feldurteil, 11 July 1940.
42 BA-ZNS, Gericht der 96. Inf. Div./77; BA-ZNS, RH 26-6 G/1, "Ersatz-Strafliste des Gerichts der
    6. Inf. Div./, Nr. 254.

the majority of French victims were treated by the German military courts showed that some, though not all, of the defeated population had the right to judicial redress when German soldiers committed sexual crimes.[43] This situation changed radically once the German armed forces launched an ideological war against the Soviet people.

RAPE AND MILITARY PROSECUTION ON THE EASTERN FRONT

The Wehrmacht and the SS gave indications of the kind of war they intended to wage against the Red Army and the Soviet people well before the invasion began on June 22, 1941. Hitler and some of his military commanders had early made plans for a state of emergency in which the stipulations of international and martial law were to be suspended in the interests of a "war of extermination" and the implementation of the "General Plan for the East" (*Generalplan Ost*). In this respect, the war against Poland represented a dress rehearsal. The Wehrmacht, the special operation teams (*Einsatzgruppen*), and the SS began the mass killing of Jews, political opponents, and the Polish intelligentsia. After the victory over France, the German leadership began to train soldiers to be "determined and aggressive" fighters in a National Socialist spirit, and inundated them with propaganda against "Jewish Bolshevism."[44] At the command level, the bases for criminal warfare were also laid out in frightening detail in the so-called criminal orders. In addition to the commissar order, which prescribed the shooting of captured Soviet political commissars, the notorious Barbarossa Decree of May 13, 1941, regulated the activities of German courts martial in the east.[45] In accordance with this decree, no criminal offenses committed by German soldiers against Soviet civilians were to be punished unless military discipline or the security of the troops required it. The decree also categorized "serious actions that are caused by a lack of sexual restraint" as punishable offenses.[46] The term "lack of sexual restraint" was hardly explicit, however. It allowed immense freedom of action and placed responsibility for deciding whether to prosecute in the hands of officers. The decision thus depended on an officer's knowledge of the soldier's behavior

43 Ahlrich Meyer, *Die deutsche Besatzung in Frankreich 1940–1944: Widerstandsbekämpfung und Judenverfolgung* (Darmstadt, 2000).

44 Jürgen Förster, "Motivation and Indoctrination in the Wehrmacht, 1933–1945," in Paul Addison and Angus Calder, eds., *Time to Kill: The Soldier's Experience of War in the West, 1939–1945* (London, 1997), 269–70.

45 Helmut Krausnick, "Kommissarbefehl und 'Gerichtsbarkeitserlass Barbarossa' in neuer Sicht," *Vierteljahrshefte für Zeitgeschichte* 25 (1977): 682–738.

46 IMT, 34: 249–55, "Erlass über die Ausübung der Kriegsgerichtsbarkeit im Gebiet 'Barbarossa' und über besondere Massnahmen der Truppe," May 13, 1941.

toward Soviet civilians, the hold of National Socialist ideology on the officer's thinking about the war, and the frontline military situation at the time.[47]

A variety of sources – official reports, soldiers' letters home, commanders' complaints about their troops' aggressive behavior toward Russian civilians – make clear that the military's criminal statistics do not give an accurate picture of the extent of individual soldiers' crimes against civilians on the eastern front. Looting and sexual violence against civilians occurred commonly, but incidents were prosecuted only when commanders felt that soldiers had breached military discipline.[48] While moral views or feelings of decency might have led to prosecution in some cases, the courts intervened in most only when they feared that rapes might endanger the discipline and cohesion of the troops. According to Omer Bartov, on the eastern front,

> the troops were rarely punished for unauthorized crimes against the enemy, both because of their commanders' underlying sympathy with such actions, and because they constituted a convenient safety valve for venting the men's anger and frustration caused by the rigid discipline demanded from the men and by the increasingly heavy cost and hopelessness of the war.[49]

On both the eastern and western fronts, military law served primarily to maintain discipline among the troops; the protection of military interests, not what had been done to the women, was the decisive factor. Nonetheless, some soldiers on the eastern front were punished with lighter sentences than in France. The reason lay in the Nazi theory of race.

SEXUAL VIOLENCE AND RACISM

The policies of German occupation differed in the various theaters of war. These differences were due to political, economic, strategic, and other military considerations, but particularly to ideological factors. The verdicts of German military courts in cases of sexual crimes reflect the influence of ideology. Soldiers who were convicted of rape in the western theater were punished more harshly than their counterparts in the Soviet Union, many of whom escaped with light sentences of one or two years' imprisonment. The expansion of the war and the Wehrmacht's personnel needs admittedly

---

47 Jürgen Förster, "Das Unternehmen 'Barbarossa' als Eroberungs- und Vernichtungskrieg," in Horst Boog, et al., *Das Deutsche Reich und der Zweite Weltkrieg*, 7 vols. (Stuttgart, 1979–2000), 4: 430–3.

48 Klaus Latzel, *Deutsche Soldaten – nationalsozialistischer Krieg? Kriegserlebnis – Kriegserfahrung 1939–1945* (Paderborn, 1998), 143–5; Christian Gerlach, *Kalkulierte Morde: Die deutsche Wirtschafts- und Vernichtungspolitik in Weissrussland 1941–1944*, 2d ed. (Hamburg, 2000), 253–65.

49 Omer Bartov, *Hitler's Army: Soldiers, Nazis, and War in the Third Reich* (New York, 1991), 61.

were often mitigating factors, but the reasons given by the courts martial for their verdicts revealed the central place of racism in their thinking. Soldiers who had committed sex crimes on the eastern front could expect light sentences whenever judges cited the supposed racial traits of the assaulted women.

The way in which misogyny and racism compounded one another was well illustrated in a case from 1941. A lance-corporal in the 7th Panzer Division appeared before a court martial in August to answer to charges of "coercion to commit sexual offence." In sentencing him to an eight-month term in jail (*Gefängnis*), the judge made his views clear:

The accused must be punished under § 176 clause 1 of German law for the crime of sexual assault. The court martial has, however, refrained from imposing a term in prison [*Zuchthaus*] on account of mitigating circumstances, also taking into consideration the fact that the accused is in other respects a decent soldier, who has confessed to his crime and fulfilled his duty in action, both here and on the western front, to complete satisfaction. A further extenuating circumstance, which must be taken into consideration, is the fact that the severe punishment set out in § 176 of German law is justified by the German conception of the sexual honor of German women, but that such severe punishment cannot be applied when – as in the present case – the injured party belongs to a people for whom the concept of woman's sexual honor has more or less entirely disappeared. The decisive consideration for imposing the punishment was first and foremost the serious violation of discipline of which the accused is guilty, by virtue of his committing this crime, and the serious damage to the reputation of the German Wehrmacht that resulted from his crime.[50]

The significance of this judgment and its reference to the old-fashioned term "sexual honor" (*Geschlechtsehre*) was transparent: for the Wehrmacht, rape was not always rape.[51]

The rape of a Soviet woman was not regarded as a serious crime because, according to the National Socialist ideology, the Soviet people had no concept of women's sexual integrity.[52] Racism and Social Darwinism constituted the ideological bases for dehumanizing the enemy population; and this dehumanization informed the trials in which cases of sexual violence

---

50 The judge's ruling makes reference to the important distinction between a *Gefängnis* and a *Zuchthaus*: imprisonment in a *Zuchthaus* was likely to be harsher and considered more shameful than in a *Gefängnis*. A soldier sentenced to imprisonment in a *Zuchthaus* was also expelled from the army. BA-ZNS, S 269, Gericht der 7. Pz. Div., Feldurteil, 19 August 1941, 22–3.

51 Ute Frevert, "*Mann und Weib, und Weib und Mann": Geschlechter-Differenzen in der Moderne* (Munich, 1995), 187–212; Hommen, *Sittlichkeitsverbrechen*, 48–53.

52 Gisela Bock, "Frauen und Geschlechterbeziehungen in der nationalsozialistischen Rassenpolitik," in Theresa Wobbe, ed., *Nach Osten: Verdeckte Spuren nationalsozialistischer Verbrechen* (Frankfurt am Main, 1992), 126–30.

were heard.[53] On few occasions was testimony heard from the raped women or members of their families. In some cases, the instability of the front, the advance or retreat of the German forces, made it impossible for the courts to examine victims or witnesses. However, few of the victims dared testify against a member of the occupying forces. Many cases of sexual violence were reported instead by German soldiers who had witnessed them or by Wehrmacht interpreters who had learned of them from Soviet civilians.[54] The most important reason for the victims' silence, however, was the general belief that German soldiers were not supposed to be found guilty of rape on the basis of "false" testimonies from members of "inferior peoples." The Barbarossa Decree had itself made clear that testimony from enemy civilians in trials against members of the Wehrmacht was to be handled with extreme caution and skepticism.[55]

In light of this ideology, the question arises why sexual violence on the eastern front was prosecuted at all. The answer is that the Wehrmacht had to cope with a conflict that it had itself encouraged at the beginning of the war against the Soviet Union. German forces were fighting a "war of extermination" with all available means against an entire population, including women and children. At the same time, however, commanders struggled to prevent the increasing brutalization of their troops, insofar as pillage, murder, and rape could threaten German military interests. In hopes of moderating the effects of the Barbarossa Decree, some commanders enacted new guidelines on military discipline.[56] In November 1941, the commander of the 11th Army, Erich von Manstein, called for restraint with respect to women and demanded aggressive action against German soldiers' "running wild [*Verwilderung*] and lack of discipline [*Undiszipliniertheit*]."[57] The tension between the war's ideological basis and far-flung aims, on the one hand, and the need for discipline at the front, on the other, made "total" control of the soldiers impossible. In some cases, soldiers who had committed acts of sexual violence were harshly punished because the courts feared such crimes might increase local support for the partisan movement.[58] In cases where the accused had a criminal record or was characterized by his superior as a bad soldier, the sentence could also be harsh. The verdicts in some cases suggest, however, that sexual violence was often not seen as a serious breach

53 See Rolf-Dieter Müller and Gerd R. Ueberschär, *Hitlers Krieg im Osten 1941–1945: Ein Forschungsbericht* (Darmstadt, 2000), 272–303.
54 BA-ZNS, S 243, Gericht der 7. Pz. Div., Feldurteil, 27 August 1941.
55 IMT, 34: 254.   56 Förster, "Unternehmen 'Barbarossa,'" 432–5.
57 IMT, 34: 129–32, Armeeoberkommando 11, Abt. Ic/AO Nr. 2379/41 geh., 20 November 1941.
58 BA-ZNS, S 334, Gericht der 339. Inf. Div., Feldurteil, 28 April 1942.

of military discipline. Judges belittled the significance of sexual assault on grounds of the racial inferiority of the victims. They also expressed understanding for the soldiers' "sexual needs." In one case, a private who had injured a Russian woman and then tried to rape her was sentenced to eight months' imprisonment. The judge cited mitigating factors, including the soldier's good military behavior and his lack of opportunity to satisfy his "sexual urges in the local occupied area, which would inevitably result in sexual tensions."[59]

The judge's obliging reaction in cases like this stood in glaring contrast to the savage punishments that were imposed on soldiers who were found guilty of military theft, self-mutilation, or desertion. These offenses threatened the *Volksgemeinschaft* as well as the combat capabilities of the Wehrmacht; thus, they often carried the death sentence.[60] In these cases, judges tended to give free reign to the ideological precepts of National Socialism and applied the law inexorably, with no heed for extenuating circumstances.

The instances of rape that were brought to trial represent but the tip of the iceberg. Unreported cases were certainly much more numerous. In any event, military commanders and courts martial alike judged sex crimes in light of prevailing military interests and political aims. After the war against France, the High Command of the Army tried to instruct courts martial about how to punish sex crimes. Harsh sentences were the exception, not the rule. Despite these instructions, some rapists were punished harshly in France, while in the east the Barbarossa Decree spared many soldiers who had committed sexual violence from facing trial. If they did face trial, many could count on sympathetic judges to apply the law in a way that reflected the regime's ideology. In the eyes of these judges, the victims belonged to an "inferior race," and the perpetrators had to struggle with "sexual tensions" that were aggravated by difficult circumstances at the front. Rapes accordingly were defined as behavior lapses, the consequence of sexual abstinence during the war, but excusable when committed against racially inferior women. This judicial attitude hardly represented a warning to other soldiers, nor was it so intended. In this fashion, military judges, who had internalized the racist ideals of National Socialism, themselves undermined the law as they underscored the criminal nature of the German war on the eastern front. Total warfare against the Soviet Union aimed at both the destruction of the enemy military forces and the subjugation of the civilian population. Rape represented part of this subjugation. Soldiers were

59 BA-ZNS, S 352, Gericht der Feldkommandantur 190, Feldurteil, 28 November 1942, 14.
60 Messerschmidt and Wüllner, *Wehrmachtjustiz*, 169–71.

court martialed for it only when commanders and judges believed that sexual violence might threaten military discipline or subvert political objectives. Sexual crimes were tolerated more on the eastern than on the western front. The limits imposed on warfare against women reflected military calculations, not the principles of morality or humanity. The fact that some rapists were punished on the eastern front suggests, however, that the German military command did not order sexual assaults on enemy civilians. In Europe and elsewhere, sexual crimes nonetheless represented a crucial dimension of the Second World War, and they demonstrated the extent to which civilians had become principal targets of violence.

18

Ideologies of Difference and the Turn to Atrocity

Japan's War on China

LOUISE YOUNG

[W]e must show that each time a head is cut off or an eye put out in Vietnam and in France they accept the fact, each time a little girl is raped and in France they accept the fact, each time a Madagascan is tortured and in France they accept the fact, civilization acquires another dead weight, a universal regression takes place, a gangrene sets in, a center of infection begins to spread; and that at the end of all these treaties that have been violated, all these lies that have been propagated, all these punitive expeditions that have been tolerated, all these prisoners who have been tied up and "interrogated," all these patriots who have been tortured, at the end of all the racial pride that has been encouraged, all the boastfulness that has been displayed, a poison has been instilled into the veins of Europe and, slowly but surely, the continent proceeds toward *savagery*.

Aime Cesaire, *Discourse on Colonialism*

The central argument of this essay is that ideologies of difference and hate crimes are produced from and enacted within a variety of social contexts. The context of total war harnessed these to the full instrumentality of the total war state, meaning that mechanisms of social and spiritual mobilization rendered entire populations complicit in acts of racial violence committed by the state. Moreover, under regimes of total warfare, the total war state repressed dissent and refusal. This provided the conditions of possibility for atrocities on a colossal scale such as the Final Solution and the Nanking Massacre, or the fire and atomic bombing of Japanese cities. Although conditions of total war make war crimes more egregious and allow them to expand to an enormous and horrifying scale, a critical genealogy of the atrocities of World War II brings us to other moments and different contexts. These include the development of racial ideologies as integral to the nation-state form as well as the process of colonialism-imperialism; tactics and justifications of colonial warfare; ideologies of colonial mission and policies of colonial developmentalism; and the connections between escalating violence in the empire and increasing brutality at home.

This essay looks at Japanese atrocities against Chinese populations during the Asia-Pacific War that lasted from 1931 to 1945.[1] Though China had been the object of Japanese imperialism since the 1880s, and two imperial wars had been fought with, over, and in China (Sino-Japanese War of 1894–95, Russo-Japanese War 1904–5), mass killings of civilians were not a conspicuous feature of this history before 1931. A key question, therefore, is: how do we account for the turn to atrocity in China during the Asia-Pacific War? I answer this question by tracing the genealogy of atrocity to four contexts of the China-Japan relationship. The first looks at the development of a discourse on China as the Other of Japan within the contexts of the project of nation-building and imperialism. The second analyzes the turn to a new China policy in 1931. When a Japanese invasion triggered a guerrilla war of resistance, counter-insurgency both ennobled and enabled a new kind of violence against civilians. Third, I look at the vision of a new order in Asia that emerged as the central ideological justification of the occupation of China and war against America and Britain. Claiming to speak for a unity of Chinese and Japanese nationalist aspirations, architects of the New Order tried to silence an autonomous voice of Chinese nationalism and uncouple it from the military resistance to Japan. Finally, I examine the relationship between atrocities toward Chinese civilians and the escalating violence toward internal categories of Others. I conclude by trying to tease out the specific characteristics of atrocities in moments of total warfare. What makes atrocities of total war distinct from other categories of what we call "hate crimes"? Acts of violence that are connected with ideologies of difference.

NATION, EMPIRE, AND THE DISCOURSE ON CHINA

The nineteenth- and twentieth-century discourse on China is particularly complex, not the least because of the ways it sought to reframe Japan's historical relationship with the Asian continent. Long before there was a "Japan," early state formations on the Japanese archipelago bolstered particular forms of power and social organization by importing the model of Chinese civilization. This implied borrowing forms and norms relating to everything from the written language and the arts, to political organization and religion. Later, after Japan's first encounter with European missionaries

---

1 This essay draws on research presented in Louise Young, *Japan's Total Empire: Manchuria and the Culture of Wartime Imperialism* (Berkeley, 1998).

and merchants in the sixteenth century, a form of centralized state emerged under the Tokugawa dynasty, expelled the European foreigners, and limited interaction with the world market to the single port city of Nagasaki. During the Tokugawa period, nativist discourse began to rethink the China connection and devalue [depreciate] the cultural debt by distinguishing a native aesthetics and political form from continental culture. In the late nineteenth century, after Japan's second "opening to the West," social and political elites revised the view of China once again, reevaluating both the earlier wave of Sinification as well as the Tokugawa nativist refiguration of the Chinese impress.

One of the triggers for this reappraisal of China was the specter of China's defeat and humiliation in the opium wars of the mid-nineteenth century. This demonstration of European military might as well as China's manifest inability to withstand the foreign threat energized reformers and critics of the Tokugawa regime, touching off a debate over whether to end seclusion and enter into cultural and material exchange with Europe so that Japan would not suffer the fate of China. For a time, of course, Japan did suffer China's fate; American gunboats forced Japan's "opening" in 1853, and the Tokugawa regime was compelled to sign unequal treaties just as the Chinese emperor had, bringing Japan into a world market and an interstate system on highly disadvantageous terms.

The social and political dislocations engendered by the irruption of global capitalism into what had been a largely self-contained market ignited the movement to overthrow the Tokugawa regime. The oligarchy of former samurai rebels that ran the new government undertook to build the territorially bounded nation-state called Japan through the selective adaptation of institutions and ideologies from the group of foreign powers they came to call "the West." The project of creating institutions to build the nation and create a putatively homogeneous community of Japanese subjects invented categories of Japanese and non-Japanese as two sides of the same coin. The unifying appeals of Japanese nationalism thus relied on the images of a Chinese and Western Other against which the Japanese subject was culturally defined, socially formed, and politically mobilized. While the project of Japanese nation-building figured the West as external threat, model, and rival, China became the foil for a national narrative of successful Western-style modernization. To this end nationalist ideologues contrasted an ancient and decrepit China with Japan's youth and vigor, China's political torpor and disorganization with Japan's bureaucratic efficiency and centralized control, Japan's capacity for progress with China's inability to reform. Such binarisms racialized the meanings of "China" and "Japan" and recast their relationship from one between literati cultures to one between nations.

Earlier views of China as a source of knowledge ("Chinese learning") were eclipsed by the idea of China as a people defined by cultural essences and racial capacities.

As Japan turned to empire-building as part of its modern project, this discourse on China was imported into a developing ideology of imperialism. In the last decades of the nineteenth century, China represented Japan's first imperial rival.[2] As the two governments competed to control the Korean court politics, Chinese and Japanese merchants struggled with one another to gain entry into the Korean market. Tensions in both spheres led to the outbreak of war with China in 1894–95. Japan's victory reconstituted the view of China once again: the imperial rival transmogrified into an object of empire, as the terms of peace rewarded Japan with an unequal treaty and Japan joined the club of foreign powers in China. Ten years later, victory in the Russo-Japanese War augmented Japan's position in China with the transfer of the Russian sphere of influence in South Manchuria as part of the terms of peace.

The informal nature of Japan's empire in China meant that the expansion of Japanese interests relied on using a combination of threat and bribery to extract ever more concessions from local Chinese leadership. Equally important, such negotiations were never simply between Japan and China, but were embroiled in the multilateral intricacies of China diplomacy. The diplomacy of imperialism turned, in China, on a complex interplay between Chinese domestic politics and European rivalries, punctuated in the early twentieth century by American and Japanese entries onto the imperialist playing field, the Russian and Chinese revolutions, and World War I. Imperialist pressures heightened the political crisis, leading in part to the overthrow of the Qing Dynasty in 1911 and the subsequent descent into civil war. Although Japan, like other foreign imperialists, took advantage of this political chaos to advance its position in China, the tables were turned in the 1920s, when the Chinese Nationalist Party and the Chinese Communist Party organized a nationalist movement to unify the country and expel the imperialists. The strength and discipline of the Right's Recovery Movement caught the foreign powers off guard and ruptured the imperialist unity; now, instead of the imperialists playing divide and rule with a fragmented China, China played divide and rule with a fragmented imperialist coalition.

This history changed the meaning of China as Other. An ideology of difference created in advance of Japanese imperialism in China and

2 For a fuller discussion of Japanese imperialism in China, see Young, *Japan's Total Empire*, 21–54.

developed as part of the nation-state form now became reshaped and reconstituted within the framework of informal empire. Within the leaseholds of Manchuria and the treaty ports south of the Great Wall, a host of imperial agents – garrison forces, a network of consulates, the South Manchurian Railway, and the Governor-General of Kwantung Leased Territory; bankers, traders, and manufacturers; scholars and artists, spies and criminals – all contributed to transforming the Japanese image of China. The ideology of imperialism that emerged authorized military and political intervention in China in a language that fused received Confucian categories with newly embraced Social Darwinist conceptions of international relations. Replacing China as the head of a Confucian family of nations, Japan had the prerogative to guide younger Asian brothers down the path it had itself so recently trod – toward Western-style modernization, civilization, and enlightenment. In an international order where the "strong devour the weak," Japanese concluded they could either join the West as a guest at the table or be served up with China and Korea as part of the feast. Such narratives of imperial mission figured China in terms of what it lacked: an ancient civilization missing the internal capacity to modernize and crying out for Japan to export the programmatic of the Meiji Restoration and oversee China's progress into the modern age. Although the new epistemology of China was shot through with the tensions and contradictions characteristic of all imperial ideologies, its unifying appeal was to Japan's mission to bring Asian-style modernity to a backward and crippled China.

GUERRILLA WAR AND THE TURN TO ATROCITY

The turn, in 1931, to a new mode of empire-building on the continent changed the meanings of "China" once again. Violence against civilians had accompanied the colonial occupations of Taiwan and Korea, but had not been a conspicuous part of Japan's early expansion into China.[3] Yet after 1931, systematic mass murder became one of the techniques of occupation. What were the conditions that produced this turn to atrocity? How did the new vision of "China" enable acts of unspeakable cruelty and inhumanity toward Chinese populations?

Though Japanese atrocities in China are most famously associated with the Rape of Nanking in 1937, Japan's new propensity for violence against civilians was demonstrated in the early phases of the war during the Manchurian

3 See discussion of violence against Taiwanese aborigines and Korean peasants in Saburo Ienaga, *The Pacific War 1931–1945*, tr. Frank Baldwin (New York, 1978), 7–9.

Incident of 1931–33. It was then that the tactical uses of atrocity as a military strategy as well as the ideological justification for new forms of violence against civilians both emerged as central elements in the new China policy. During the occupation of Northeast China in the early 1930s, campaigns against the forces of Nationalist-allied warlord Zhang Xueliang and against other regional military leaders provided the context for the deployment of a range of new military strategies, strategies that were expanded and systematized in later campaigns. Moreover, media coverage of military action and government propaganda justifying the new policy reshaped the image of China and the Chinese. Part of this reshaping involved the naturalization of violence, making the killing of civilians seem unexceptional, the logical outcome of the conditions of war in China. The ideology of difference, in short, became an ideology of atrocity. Both the new strategies of warfare as well as their official and unofficial representations made atrocity against civilians all but inevitable; the first such incident occurred in the context of the Manchurian Incident.

During what became known as the Pingdingshan or Fushun massacre, in September 1932 Japanese soldiers torched and bombed a number of villages near the industrial city of Fushun, bayoneting and machine-gunning village residents and killing some 3,000 men, women, and children. The assaults were made in retaliation for the anti-Japanese actions of a Chinese militia known as the Red Spears, who had fired on Japanese soldiers as they passed through one village and later had attacked the Japanese garrison in Fushun. The Red Spears were not from the area, but had merely passed through the villages in order to carry out the raid on Fushun. Yet in tracking the rebels as they fled back through the villages, Japanese soldiers assumed all who were in the vicinity either to be members of the militia or their confederates and punished them by burning homes and summary execution.[4]

This was not a case of Japanese soldiers running amuck, but of a deliberately planned and meticulously executed slaughter. Such assaults on civilians became a generalized feature of war in China because of the nature of the Japanese occupation. While some of the military engagements between Chinese and Japanese forces were characterized by formal encounters between massed formations (especially battles over the major cities after 1937), much of the fighting took the form of a guerrilla war where a fragmented enemy used guerrilla tactics to harass Japanese troops. The high proportion of irregular troops constituted both a strength and weakness of

4 Rana Mitter, *The Manchurian Myth* (Berkeley, 2000), 112–15.

the Chinese army. Though short on the discipline and training required for pitched battle, the capacity to quickly break into smaller independent units, to mobilize and demobilize quickly, and to melt into the civilian population all gave Chinese troops key advantages of mobility and flexibility. Moreover, Chinese military resistance depended heavily on the relationship with rural villages, relying on local supplies for food and shelter from districts through which they traveled. Chinese troops hid in the villages; they escaped through and into them. Significantly, the Japanese army also requisitioned supplies from local sources and relied on villagers for intelligence on the movements of the Chinese troops. Civilians thus became a strategic element in and target of military operations on both sides. Japanese designed operations both to co-opt their allegiance and to cut off contact with the resistance. To this end, the army systematically used violence as the means to set examples and terrorize the civilian population into cooperation with the Japanese war effort. From the standpoint of the military strategist, atrocities became a tactic of counterinsurgency, rendered an unfortunate necessity by conditions of guerrilla warfare.

In Manchuria, Japanese counterinsurgency campaigns were coded under the rubrics of "bandit-pacification" and "peace preservation." In the face of the Japanese invasion that began in 1931, the army of regional warlord Zhang Xueliang adopted a policy of nonresistance. Under the advice of Jiang Jieshi [Chiang Kai-shek], head of the Guomindang central government to which Zhang Xueliang declared allegiance in 1928, Zhang's troops responded to Japanese aggression with voluntary disarmament, while Guomindang diplomats appealed to the League of Nations for diplomatic intervention in the Sino-Japanese dispute. Although Zhang's troops laid down their arms in the face of the Japanese advance, pockets of military resistance remained. In places, breakaway units of Zhang's forces carried out unauthorized actions against Japan; elsewhere, allied warlord militias refused to go along with the Guomindang's nonresistance policy. In the lexicon of the Japanese media and government reports, all of this was categorized as a form of "banditry," and became the central justification for continuing to wage war against an enemy that refused to fight back.

Barely days into the first operations in Manchuria, the Japanese army inaugurated a massive publicity campaign, eventually publishing some 123 pamphlets between 1931 and 1937 that detailed the army's claim that Japan was conducting a war of self-defense in Manchuria. Early pamphlets in the series asserted that Zhang Xueliang, while giving lip service to "nonresistance," was in fact engaging in "machinations" to foment resistance against the Japanese and "pitch Manchuria into a state of unrest" by dispatching soldiers in civilian clothes and instigating bandits to action against Japan.[5] The army made the case that all anti-Japanese action was a form of banditry coordinated by Zhang Xueliang. One pamphlet characterized the process of Zhang's voluntary disarmament as a typical Chinese military "retreat," in which the Chinese army disperses and goes to ground, continuing to pose a danger to public security. Instead of remaining ordered and disciplined upon defeat, the pamphlet explained, Chinese militias "scatter to the four winds. Once they scatter Chinese soldiers soon turn to banditry as they always have in the past."[6] These soldiers-turned-bandits, the pamphlet continued, engaged in "looting and violence" and other "atrocities" against "Japanese subjects and Japanese rights and interests throughout Manchuria," "disturbing the peace and menacing the [Japanese-owned South Manchurian] railway zone."[7]

Two points about the army's account of the Manchurian Incident deserve note here. First, the pamphlets willfully misrepresented nonresistance as an undisciplined retreat. Second, they depicted Chinese soldiers as lawless and violent, describing them engaged in criminal acts and atrocities against Japanese civilians. Such characterizations were carefully calculated to magnify the "bandit" threat in order to justify expanding operations against an enemy that had already surrendered. Having recoded the enemy as bandits, the army invoked a new strategic mandate to "preserve the peace" through military action aimed to "wipe out," "pacify," or "suppress" banditry.[8] Thus, tales told through the army's publicity campaign inverted the roles of victim and aggressor and transformed an unprovoked [unilateral] invasion into a righteous war of self-defense. In the process, pamphlets instructed the home population on the necessity to match fire with fire and answer the lawlessness of Chinese banditry with harsh and merciless reprisals. The ennobling of atrocity had begun.[9]

Picking up on the army's narrative, accounts of the Manchurian Incident in popular magazines reinforced the identification of the Chinese soldier with banditry. An article in *Boy's Club* on "The Chinese Soldier in Manchuria" explained that "bandit soldiers" were "just like flies, no sooner do you drive them off but they come right back out again." Worse still were "soldiers out of uniform," "nuisances" who disguised themselves as civilians

5 Rikugunshō, *Manshū fuan no jissō* [The Truth about Unrest in Manchuria] (Rikugunshō, 1931), 1, 9.
6 Rikugunshō, *Mantetsu fuzokuchi gai shutsudō butai hikiage no fukanō naru yuen ni tsuite* [Why It Is Impossible to Withdraw Troops Back within the Railway Zone] (Rikugunshō, 1931), 3.
7 Ibid., 2–3; Rikugunshō, *Chō Gakuryō Kinshū seiken no tai Nichi kōsen junbi ni tsuite* [Zhang Xueliang's Jinzhou Government Prepares for War Against Japan] (Rikugunshō, 1931), 92.
8 Rikugunshō, *Mantetsu fuzokuchi gai shutsudō*, 20.
9 For more extensive analysis of Japanese Army pamphlets, see Young, *Japan's Total Empire*, 140–49.

and sneaked about causing trouble. "Because the Chinese Army loses if it fights in an open and sportsmanlike manner, it uses this cowardly method to harass the Japanese Army."[10] Like army pamphlets, mass media accounts of the Manchurian Incident turned Zhang's voluntary surrender into a cowardly disinclination to "fight openly," and identified a Chinese penchant for sneak attacks. These accounts made two moves that shifted the moral ground upon which the army's claims could rest. First, they condemned tactics of guerrilla resistance as an illegitimate mode of warfare, and second, they blurred the line between soldier and civilian, pointing to the difficulty in distinguishing between the two. Such representations of Chinese prepared people for military action against civilians and gave moral cover for the new counterinsurgency tactics the army was developing against guerrilla resistance in China.

Popular representations of the occupation also reinforced army justifications of "self-defense" by erasing China's nonresistance policy from their story lines. Incessant boasting about the "200,000 Chinese against 10,000 Japanese" made it seem as if Zhang's 200,000 troops were actually fighting Japan. Transforming these figures into an index of China's martial deficiency, popular magazines gave rise to a sense that each Japanese soldier was worth twenty of the enemy's.[11] As major military targets such as Fengtian and Jilin were occupied virtually without bloodshed, magazines like *Boy's Club* characterized voluntary withdrawal, voluntary disarmament, and other forms of nonresistance as cowardly and disorganized retreats. Accounts of the Manchurian Incident invariably showed Chinese soldiers in the act of "bolting," "escaping," "running off," "hiding," or in the favored figure of speech: "fleeing pell-mell like scattering spider babies."[12] In another story, an eyewitness registers his surprise to see Chinese "officers creep out from under the floor" when the Japanese army "set fire to the Chinese barracks to smoke-out hiding enemy soldiers."[13] While the point of such stories was to highlight the cowardice of Chinese soldiers and officers, they also suggested that tactics such as torching the barracks of an enemy who voluntarily surrendered were legitimate and moral.

The question of civilians was one given extensive coverage in popular magazines during the Manchurian Incident. While soldiers were often quoted declaring their commitment to protect innocent civilians from

---

10 Imamura Kakichi, "Manshū no Shinahei," *Shōnen kurabu* (February 1932), 76–77.
11 Ibid., 75.
12 Suzuki Gyōsui, "Teki no shōkō ressha o kōgeki suru waga hikōki," *Shōnen kurabu* (February 1932).
13 Takinaka Takeo, "Shōnenkan no mite kita Manshū senchi no hanashi: tetchō kara," *Shōnen kurabu* (February 1932), 109.

the depredations of evil and corrupt warlords, such characterizations of
the civilian as innocent victim in need of Japanese protection were coun-
tered by another, more ominous narrative. As one roundtable discussion
among Manchurian Incident veterans revealed to the population at home,
all Chinese civilians were potential enemies. "Even though we are told not
to kill civilians, you just cannot tell them apart," confessed one soldier.
Added another, "You wouldn't believe the number of Chinese who are really soldiers. You can basically consider anyone on the street in Manchuria
a plainclothes soldier. They say in Jinzhou alone there were more than
300,000 of them." Under these circumstances, the soldiers explained, they
had developed a simple technique for telling friend from foe: "When you see
someone coming you put your gun on them. If they cry or run away, they
are good people. If they put their hands up, you know they are soldiers in
urban dress." But as one personal anecdote demonstrated, you could never
be too careful.

Everybody thinks that only men are plainclothes soldiers. But there are women,
kids . . . all kinds . . . Once a young woman of twenty-two or twenty-three came
up to me looking very friendly. There in front of her house stood a crippled old
grandmother, again smiling in a friendly way; naturally I thought they were good
people. But then I had a bad feeling about one of them and I shouted out a
warning. The old woman ran hobbling off. I strip-searched the girl . . . she couldn't
understand me so I gestured with my hands . . . Underneath her clothes she was
wearing two pairs of panties. Hidden inside, sure enough, there was a pistol. I did
not want to kill her but she tried to hit me with the gun and that was why she died.
She said something abusive before she died. Afterwards I felt sorry for her but at
the time I knew that if I did not handle it right I would have been done for. I was
provoked.[14]

Such words revealed the intensity of the fear and mistrust that Japanese
directed at Chinese in occupied Manchuria. The anecdote recounted the
story of an atrocity: the murder of a Chinese woman. It communicated to
the home front the bullying and terrorization of the civilian population that
was standard operating procedure during the occupation; Chinese life was
held cheap. The matter-of-fact retelling of this story in a popular magazine
showed that to the soldiers, the editors, and probably the audience, the
murder was unexceptional. In this way, the brutality of imperialism made its
practitioners brutal – both the soldiers who actually wielded the bayonets
and the cultural consumers who took part vicariously in the violence.

Although the army was careful to censor newspaper reports of the Fushun
Massacre in 1932 as it would later reports of the Nanjing Massacre, this did

---

14 "Jissen ni sanka shita gunjin no zadankai," *Ie no hikari* (July 1932), 50–51.

not mean that depiction of routine and systematic violence against civilians was absent from the mass media. Even setting aside the question of what information about Nanking managed to pass through the many holes in the state's censorship apparatus in 1937, the more pertinent question is why so few were inclined to follow up the inevitable and disturbing rumors trickling back home via the foreign press or returning soldiers and support personnel. Why did so many Japanese turn a blind eye to violence against civilians in China? Part of the answer surely lay in the fatalism toward atrocity nourished by the publicity of the Manchurian Incident. By the end of the first phase of the Asia-Pacific War, the home population had already been persuaded of the necessity and inevitability of atrocities, already barbarized by their army's barbarity.

THE NATIONALISM QUESTION

Responding to the challenge of the anti-imperialist movement of the 1920s, Japan's new China policy sought to overcome nationalism militarily, on one hand, and, on the other, to co-opt it by claiming a unity with China against the West. Sinking unprecedented military, social, and economic resources into the pursuit of this vision, Japan declared that it would save China from the depredations of a Western imperialism that imperiled the autonomy of Asia and from its own internal weakness and inability to recognize the justice of Japan's cause. Through a succession of labels – Monroe Doctrine for Asia, New Order in East Asia, East Asian Community, Co-Prosperity Sphere in Greater East Asia – the vision of a Japanese-led economic and security bloc that included at first, Japan, its colonies, and Manchuria; later China in total; and finally Southeast Asia as well, emerged as the central ideological justification for the Asia-Pacific War.

Two critical claims about Chinese nationalism lay at the heart of the regional bloc idea. First, Japanese spokesmen for the bloc asserted a unity of Chinese and Japanese nationalist aspirations. Second, architects of the New Order tried to silence an autonomous voice of Chinese nationalism and uncouple it from the military resistance to Japan. In the name of saving China from the West and from itself, Japan carried out a war of staggering violence against the Chinese, a war in which hundreds of thousands of Chinese civilians were slaughtered in the name of Asian brotherhood. Just as accounts of guerrilla war produced fatalism and willful blindness to war crimes against civilians, a tin ear for the voice of Chinese nationalist aspirations allowed Japanese to believe they were fighting the good fight in Asia and fueled the rage against Chinese who refused to join the cause.

In attempting to appropriate the Chinese nationalist cause, architects of the New Order tapped into an ideological reservoir that had long justified imperial action in China. What Japanese regarded as China's great shortcomings – incapacity for military self-strengthening and economic development, inability to create modern educational and political institutions, failure to organize a state and unify the nation – authorized a Japanese civilizing mission to bring China into the modern world. While Western imperialists justified their actions by invoking a civilizing mission composed of pseudoscientific racism and the imperatives of Christian evangelism, in Japan a "yellow-man's burden" called on right-minded Japanese to participate in what promised to be a historic transformation on the continent, as Japan became the architect of Asian revolution. While disdain for China's capacity to modernize suffused New Order thinking, paradoxically, a sense of Japan's own lack and frustrations with deadlocked domestic reform programs also fueled ambitions in Asia. For the countless radicals of both left and right who flocked to the continent in the 1930s, the New Order represented an opportunity to trigger a revolution that would transform both China and Japan. In the name of doing good, radical idealists of all political stripes threw their lot in with the army and its program of using the military as the instrument of progress in China. In the process, they helped turn atrocity into a tool of Japan's civilizing mission in Asia.

Japan's program for nation-building in the puppet state of Manchukuo was shot through with such fantasies of orchestrating nationalist revolution on the continent. Soon after Manchukuo's foundation, Japanese created the mass political organization known as the Concordia Society (*Kyōwakai*) to serve as the vehicle for connecting the Chinese masses to their new state. Under the official slogans "Racial Harmony" (*Minzoku kyōwa*) and "Harmony of the Five Races" (*gozoku kyōwa*), the Concordia Society declared its determination to end the anti-Japanese movement on one hand, and Japanese racial prejudice on the other. To overcome mutual hostility the Concordia Society vowed to create a "multiracial polity in which Chinese, Manchus, Mongolians, Koreans, and Japanese" would "cooperate as equal citizens in a self-governing unit." This new political structure would permit "Chinese and Japanese to mix harmoniously in a single society where human beings loved one another" and which would bring to reality the "ideal of coexistence and co-prosperity."[15]

Whether or not the Chinese elite was taken in by this rhetoric, the stated political goals of the Concordia Society appealed strongly to progressive

15 Matsuzawa Tetsunari, "Manshū jihen to 'minzoku kyōwa' undo," *Kokusai seiji* 43, no. 1 (1970), 97.

Japanese intellectuals. Japan's China hands who were sympathetic to Chinese nationalist aspirations had faced a difficult choice when the Chinese nationalist movement began to focus its energies against Japanese imperialism – would they betray Chinese aspirations or their own national loyalties? Rejecting the principle of racial self-determination, the formula of a multiracial state resolved their dilemma, constructing an alternative to the two-sided struggle between Japanese imperialism and Chinese nationalism. As one prominent intellectual insisted, Japanese were "by no means the only race who were the founders or even the essential constituents of the new state"; "of course Chinese were involved as were all other races."[16] This was a comforting fiction, abetting the delusion that Manchukuo had ended Sino-Japanese conflict in the Northeast. Herein lay one of the central appeals of the Concordia Society and the doctrine of "racial harmony": it allowed progressive Japanese intellectuals to believe that they could be patriots and friends of the Chinese people at the same time.

Concurrent with pronouncements trumpeting the construction of a new pan-Asian nation in Northeast China, a variety of news stories began to circulate that excised the nationalist character of the military resistance to Japan. The discursive erasing of Chinese nationalism from the picture was accomplished by offering an alternative account of the anti-Japanese resistance that imputed a base set of motives to resistance fighters, identifying Chinese soldiers with corruption and venality and depicting them as utterly divorced from the Chinese masses.

Ignoring the boycott movements against Japanese goods, strikes in Japanese factories, and student demonstrations as clear manifestations of a militant and disciplined Chinese nationalist movement, Japanese chose to view China as a disorganized state without a sense of nation. In an argument that was put forward by Japanese diplomats at the League of Nations in 1932 and widely reported at home, the defense against Chinese accusations of an illegal invasion of Chinese territory in turn called China an international outlaw and denied its status as a nation-state in the international system. Pointing out that China had "for more than ten years been in a state of civil war, in a condition of complete chaos and incredible anarchy," Japanese diplomats announced that "the Japanese Government do not and cannot consider that China is an 'organized people' within the meaning of the Covenant of the League of Nations."[17] Charging China with coordinating "campaigns for the unilateral denunciation of

---

16 Yamamoto Hideo, ed., *"Manshū hyōron" kindai: sōmokuji* (Fuji shuppan, 1982), 14, 32–33.
17 Westel W. Willoughby, *The Sino–Japanese Controversy and the League of Nations* (1935; reprint, New York, 1968), 243–45.

treaties . . . anti-foreign agitation . . . and systematic violation of undertakings solemnly entered into," Japanese diplomats depicted China as a bandit nation and drew a sharp and invidious contrast with Japan, model member of the international community.[18] "Our history during the past sixty years is, I think, a guarantee of our good faith; is that history of no worth beside China's history, the history of creating disturbances and bringing about catastrophes in the Far East?"[19]

Accounts of the reaction of the Chinese "masses" to Japanese military action in Manchuria likewise rendered the nationalist movement invisible, portraying peasants and workers as both ignorant of the broader issues at stake and indifferent to the fate of the Northeast. Popular Japanese travel writer Gotō Asatarō frequently commented on the absence of national feeling among the Chinese. "Chinese coolies," wrote Gotō in 1932, "are happy to build sandbags for the Japanese Army because they can get money for it. The next day they sit atop the sandbags, drinking sorghum wine and watching their own soldiers being destroyed by the Japanese, saying, 'Wow, look at that!' "[20]

Another source of evidence marshaled to support China's putative absence of nationalism were stories of the easy corruptibility of warlords and their militias, generalized to a racial characteristic that explained the alleged lack of loyalty to the nationalist cause. An image constructed in the course of the teens and twenties, the stereotype of venality reflected as much on the Japanese inclination toward corruption as it did on the putative dishonesty of the Chinese. Bribing their way through a string of warlord allies, Japanese agents in China sold their patronage for the biggest concession and sold out their erstwhile clients when a better offer came along. Perceived, ironically, as an indication of Chinese venality and absence of national feeling, the actions of Japan's China hands became the basis for claims that Chinese lacked the capacity for loyalty to anything beyond their own financial interest. The mercenary theme was given wide play in 1931–33. An article on "ordinary crimes of bribery and betrayal" illustrated the character of the Chinese soldiers with a drawing of two Chinese warlords, one with a giant "money" magnet pulling the army off the other warlord's weaker magnet. The accompanying text read, "Civil wars occur often in China but it is rare for these conflicts to be resolved by a decisive military victory. Rather, victory is decided through one side purchasing the betrayal of the enemy with money . . . According to Japan's code of war it is shameful to allow yourself

18 Ibid., 214–16.   19 Ibid., 215–16, 489.
20 Gotō Asatarō, "Shina no heitai," *Kingu* (April 1932), 53.

to be bought off by the enemy," but Chinese change sides "the minute they are handed some money."[21]

In the same way that Chiang Kai-shek's policy of nonresistance to Japanese military action was erased from the stories Japanese heard about the Manchurian Incident, the story of the intimate connection between the anti-Japanese movement and the rising tide of Chinese nationalism was not told within Japan. Instead, state pronouncements and mass media accounts alike stressed the absence of national feeling and the lack of a unified state in China. This story of military resistance to Japan that discounted Chinese nationalism occupied a central position in the ideological scaffolding of the Asia-Pacific War. As wartime ideology represented the question of Asian modernity, China's deficiency authorized Japan to see for China, to speak for China, to act for China. Resistance to Japan's program was interpreted over and again as a sign of insincerity, ineptitude, incomprehension. With such an object, the failure of civilized persuasion made brute force necessary. In a war that was justified in terms of emancipating Asia from Western domination and that embraced the mission of renovating China, Japan, and Asia, Japan could brook no compromise, could accept nothing less than total compliance. Although these appeals proved quite effective at mobilizing a wide range of Japanese behind the war effort in China, they fed the tendency to grossly underestimate China's capacity to resist and made it almost impossible for people to grasp the impossibility of overcoming Chinese nationalism militarily. As the string of Japanese victories in China's coastal cities simply pushed the fight out into the countryside and strengthened the resolve and unity of nationalist resistance, Japan's response was always to call up more soldiers, to order a new bombing raid, to plan a new campaign. Blinded to the signs, the Japanese Army embarked upon battles like the Shanghai campaign utterly unprepared for the ferocity of street fighting they would encounter. Undersupplied and overconfident, the battle-weary veterans of Shanghai were quickly dispatched to Nanjing, where they unleashed their murderous rage on Chinese civilians in an orgy of violence.

BRINGING BRUTALITY BACK HOME

In the escalation of violence that characterized the turn to total war in China in the 1930s, new lines were blurred between civilian and soldier, between the war without and the war within. Just as new tactics of warfare were obliterating the distinction between civilian and soldier in a field of

---

21 Shimonaga Kenji, "Shinahei Mandan," *Kōdan kurabu* (May 1933), 84.

battle that now encompassed the social totality of the enemy, new tactics of mobilization were erasing the very same line at home. Japan's experience makes clear that the barbarity and brutality of total war was not something that simply happened "over there." Far from it, the turn to atrocity in China reverberated back into the social space of the nation, where marginal peoples, internal others, and finally the social body as a whole became the targets of state violence. As Aime Cesaire brilliantly observed about the Final Solution: "that it is barbarism, but the supreme barbarism, the crowing barbarism that sums up all the daily barbarisms; that it is Nazism, yes, but that before they were its victims, they were its accomplices; that they tolerated that Nazism before it was inflicted on them, that they absolved it, shut their eyes to it, legitimized it, because, until then, it had been applied only to non-European peoples."[22] Because barbaric violence barbarized the perpetrators, the experience of brutalizing colonial Others intensified a propensity for violence that turned inexorably against the Self.

For Japan, this observation brings us back to the first phase of the Asia-Pacific War, where we can locate the beginnings of atrocity's inward turn. To whip up popular support for the campaigns in Manchuria, the state, the media, and the culture industries glorified and aestheticized death, turning self-sacrifice and self-directed violence into the measure of personal and national virtue. In the process, they brought brutality back home. The fatalism toward killing civilians as a "necessary evil" of guerrilla war translated into a ready acceptance of civilian sacrifice at home and indifference toward battlefield casualties. The cheapening of Chinese life became a cheapening of all life. The whittling away of ethical limits against violence toward the Chinese Other eroded moral qualms about violence in general. Socialization for brutality stoked aggression toward marginalized groups at home and made atrocities against internal scapegoats all but inevitable.

The new moral economy of violence emerged in the context of the war fever of the early 1930s. From the flood of films, theater productions, cartoons, and stories dramatizing the bloodshed in China, a succession of new national heroes issued forth. Kawai Pictures sensationalized the battlefield death of Captain Kuramoto (posthumously promoted to major) in *The Big-Hearted Commander Captain Kuramoto*, while Tōkatsu Films memorialized his bravery in *Ah! Major Kuramoto and the Blood-Stained Flag*.[23] The story of Private Yamada, captured by the Chinese during a reconnaissance mission and later rescued by a Korean interpreter, was made into the movie *Scout*

22 Aime Cesaire, *Discourse on Colonialism*, tr. Joan Pinkham (New York, 1972), 14.
23 "Sensō eiga," *Eiga to engei* (April 1932).

of North Manchuria, the play *The Occupation of Qiqihar*, and recorded on the Victor label as the minstrel chant "Private Yamada and Mr. Tei."[24] All seven Japanese movie companies produced versions of the sensational suicide of Major Kuga Noboru, who was apotheosized by Shinkō as *The Perfect Soldier*, by Kawai as *The Yamato Spirit*, and by Tōkatsu as an *Embodiment of the Way of the Warrior*.[25] Injured and left behind when the Japanese force withdrew after the first failed assault on Shanghai, Kuga was taken prisoner by the Chinese. After he was released, he returned to the battlefield where he had fallen. He then shot himself to expiate the shame of capture. Announcing Kuga's suicide on April 1, 1932, Army Minister Araki Sadao praised Kuga's martial spirit: "Soldiers of the Imperial Army go to the battlefield to win or to die. Choosing the course of death, Major Kuga displayed the highest military spirit. We will treat him as a battlefield casualty, honoring him as if he died in battle."[26] Even the death of an Osaka Mainichi newspaper reporter in the course of covering the front became the stuff of heroic drama. Nikkatsu Pictures' *The Blood-Stained Pen* glorified the daring and zeal of the reporter when he rushed off behind enemy lines to pursue a scoop. Describing his martyrdom, *Screen and Stage* wrote that he was struck down by an "enemy of unparalleled violence."[27]

The most sensational of the martyred heroes to emerge from the early phase of the war in China were the "three human bombs" – the soldiers who were blown up in the line of duty during the assault on Shanghai in early 1932. The army publicized the three deaths as a conscious act of suicide, claiming the young men had sacrificed themselves to explode a section of wire fence impeding the army's advance. Various rumors circulated at the time contradicting the army's account. Some said the three had died because their commanding officer cut the fuse too short or because he had given them the wrong type of fuse; others suggested that the men attempted to abandon the mission but their commander ordered them to follow through. And it was quietly pointed out that something was amiss with the official report because three other soldiers accompanied the mission and were able to return unharmed.[28] However, this soon became immaterial because the "three human bombs" boom in the mass media gave popular authority to the army's version of the event.

24 *Eiga to engei* (January 1932), 22; *Eiga to engei* (February 1932), 44; *Rekōdo* (February 1932), 74.
25 *Eiga to engei* (May 1932), 16; "Gunji eiga," *Eiga to engei* (June 1932).
26 On media sensationalism of Kuga's suicide, see Eguchi Keiichi, *Jūgonen sensō no kaimaku*, vol. 4 of *Shōwa no rekishi* (Shōgakkan, 1988), 150. For Araki's statement, see ibid., 157–58.
27 "Sensō eiga," *Eiga to engei* (April 1932).
28 Eguchi, *Jūgonen sensō no kaimaku*, 144–45, 154–57.

Throughout March, "three human bombs" productions swept the entertainment world. The *Screen and Stage* reported "Tokyo's theaters, including all the major houses . . . are filled with 'three human bombs' plays. The story has been dramatized in every form, from *shinpa* [new school] to *kyūgeki* [classical drama]." No fewer than six movie versions were produced in March alone, and at vaudeville reviews, the chorus line kicked their heels to the "Three Human Bombs Song."[29] Record companies brought out a string of "human bombs" songs, which were multiplying due to song contests in newspapers and magazines. Entrepreneurs from the dead men's home towns even began to sell "three human bombs' sake" and "three human bombs bean paste candy," and an Osaka department store dining room showed questionable taste in offering a "three human bombs" dinner special: radish strips cut to simulate the explosives tube and butterburs representing the "human bombs."[30] As the war effort consumed bodies of Japanese soldiers, the population at home consumed their stories. By the time it became available as restaurant food, cultural commodification had leached all sense of grief or horror – or indeed the reality of death – from the grisly story of the three young soldiers. Commodified violence naturalized the loss of life and transformed the body count from a source of sorrow to a matter of pride.

Although self-sacrifice had been linked with patriotism during earlier wars, the narratives of heroism that circulated during the early 1930s redefined the concept of sacrifice. In the new formulation, sacrifice meant the embrace of death. Accounts of the battlefield showed an extraordinary preoccupation with death. Death provided the dramatic center of the stories, and patriotic heroism was defined by martyrdom through death – preferably by suicide. The case of Regimental Commander Koga Dentaro provided what became the classic narrative. As part of the "mopping-up" operations following the occupation of Jinzhou in early January 1932, Koga's cavalry regiment had occupied the walled city of Jinxi, southwest of Jinzhou. After a large "bandit" force attempted to retake Jinxi in early January 1932, Koga determined, against orders, that he would mount his own attack. Impatient for action, he was unwilling to stand guard over the city and wait passively for reinforcements. Leaving a platoon of some 21 men at Jinxi to guard the flag, Koga took the remaining 130 men with him to attack a force of over 1,000. Although Koga's forces soon found themselves in desperate difficulties, upon hearing that the flag-guarding platoon was in danger, Koga split his forces again, taking half to rescue the flag and leaving the rest to

---

29 *Eiga to Engei* (April 1932), frontispiece, 18.   30 Eguchi, *Jūgonen sensō no kaimaku*, 157.

"hold off the enemy." In the end this reckless course of action accomplished nothing and cost the regiment virtually all its officers, leaving Koga and eleven others dead and nineteen wounded.[31] Yet Koga became one of the most celebrated heroes of the Manchurian Incident. His story was the subject of a *naniwabushi* chant on the Polidor label, of Tōkatsu and Shinkō movies, and was staged by the famous Tokyo Kokuza Theater.[32] Told and retold countless times in every popular entertainment medium, the Koga narrative glorified his actions as the archetype of military heroism.

In an illustrated version published in the magazine *Boy's Club*, "Ah! The Imperial Flag Is in Danger," the suicidal attack on the "bandit army" (which had multiplied into a force of 5,000) was depicted as an act of courage and daring. Without mentioning Koga's insubordination, *Boy's Club* narrated Koga's actions as a series of glorious last stands at Jinxi. At each stage another band of Japanese soldiers – cut off from their comrades and hopelessly outnumbered – fought to the death to protect the flag. While the story exalted sacrifice for the nation (in the symbol of the flag), it did so by celebrating individual acts of heroism. In sequence each of these last stands grew more dramatic and heroic. They were, in effect, a kind of competition: the reader moved up the tournament ranks, finally witnessing Koga's triumph – the most glorious act of heroism.[33]

Like other stories of the Manchurian Incident, Koga's story conveyed the message that sacrifice through death was the only path to virtue. Rendered with images like "crimson-stained snow" and the "glittering face of death," or by the traditional metaphor of a "fallen cherry blossom," death in these stories was transformed into a symbol of poignant beauty. The *Boy's Club* version of the Koga story departed from this convention and described Koga's final moments under the caption, "The Command that was Vomited with Blood." This decidedly unbeauteous yet arresting image of Koga's dying visage left the reader with a brutally powerful visual impression. Koga's last moments saw him hit and fallen, only to raise himself on his sword point to issue the forward order.

The Commander looked so bad that the others stood blankly for a moment. Then suddenly, he was lurching up from between the bodies and they could hear his voice drying out mightily:
"Save the flag! Forward, forward!"

---

31 Ibid., 135.
32 *Rekōdo* (May 1932), 82; *Eiga to engei* (March 1932), 26; "Sensō eiga," *Eiga to engei* (April 1932); *Eiga to engei* (May 1932), 16.
33 Kume Gen'ichi, "Sōretsu senwa: Aa gunki ayaushi," *Shōnen kurabu* (March 1933), 144–55.

As he cried out blood spurted from his mouth and he slid to the ground. But again he pulled himself up on his sword point and forced out a raspy cry, "Forward, forward . . ."

He continued thus three or four times more, falling and rising, rising and falling, till finally, face down on the grass, he moved no more.[34]

Sacrifice in the line of duty provided both the dramatic climax and aesthetic heart of Koga's story. Distinguished by his suicidal act of bravery, Koga became a hero at the very moment of his death.

By the end of the decade, this new vocabulary of sacrifice became a stock element of wartime propaganda. As war spread and mobilization intensified, the state elevated the ideology of sacrifice into a pseudoreligious and transcendental aesthetic. The aestheticization of death reached a new level in 1943, when the government introduced the phrase *gyokusai* or "shattered jewel" to describe the beauty and purity of collective suicide. The term was deployed to glorify suicide attack units such as the *kamikaze* and to eulogize the military units on the Aleutians, Saipan, and elsewhere who chose suicide over surrender. Government propagandists incorporated the "shattered jewel" metaphor into the slogan *ichioku gyokusai* – "the shattering of the hundred million like a beautiful jewel" – to promote the sacrifice of the social body as whole. Under the ennobling rhetoric of sacrifice, the state cannibalized its population for the war effort. In Okinawa and Manchuria, the Japanese Army sanctioned the forced suicides of tens of thousands of civilian men, women, and children, and in many instances, carried out the slaughter itself. In the face of certain defeat, military leaders chose "death over dishonor," allowing city after city to go to the torch of American bombs. To prepare for the coming invasion of the home islands, government leaders drew up plans for a glorious last stand by the home-front equivalent of the *kamikaze* fighters. In this feckless and pathetic vision, civilians were to be placed on the frontlines to face machine guns and cannon with bamboo spears. The terrible violence of Nanjing had come home.[35]

---

34 Ibid., 152–54.

35 On *gyokusai*, see John Dower, *War without Mercy: Race and Power in the Pacific War* (New York, 1986), 231–33. On Manchurian settlers, see Young, *Japan's Total Empire*, 405–11. On forced suicides of Okinawans, see Norma Field, *In the Realm of a Dying Emperor* (New York, 1991), 56–67. For other examples of brutality at home, see Saburo Ienaga, *The Pacific War 1931–1945*, especially chapter 9: "The Horrors of War," 181–202, and Haruko Taya Cook and Theodore F. Cook, *Japan at War: An Oral History* (New York, 1992), Part IV, "Lost Battles," and Part V, "One Hundred Million Die Together," 259–400. On the bamboo spear defense, see Thomans R. H. Havens, *Valley of Darkness: The Japanese People and World War Two* (Lanham, MD, 1986, 1978), 188–91.

CONCLUSION

Atrocity is surely one of the most disturbing and daunting subjects in modern history. Here, I have connected the atrocities of the Asia–Pacific War to the history of colonialism-imperialism in China, both the instrumentalities of colonialism and the ideologies that authorized them. My argument suggests that atrocities were neither specific to the context of total war itself, nor generated out of some peculiarity of Japanese culture. Rather, the causes of atrocity may be located in the commonalities and commensurabilities of modern world history: the interstate system and the nation-state form which serve to globally produce and circulate racial and national ideologies, new tactics of warfare that erase the line between civilian and soldier, and especially the processes and procedures of colonialism-imperialism that ennoble and enable racialized violence. In this sense, Japanese atrocities in China must be placed within a larger history that includes the Amritsar Massacre in British India, the white terror of the Ku Klux Klan in the American South, and the "red rubber days" of the Belgian Congo. As these and countless other examples of recent mass violence show, atrocity constituted a central element in maintaining social hierarchies within colonial empires and nation-states.

Although the problem of atrocity transcends total war, it was only in the context of a total war that certain forms of atrocity took place. Despite claims to the contrary, violence on the scale of a Nanjing massacre could not be the work of a rogue unit, nor could it be carried out in secret or kept from public view. Unlimited in scale, sustained in duration, systemic in instrumentality, the mass atrocities of World War II required the full authority of a state that had assumed extensive "emergency" powers, and the full complicity of a public mobilized for the war effort. In the name of total war, the state spared no efforts to defend the instrumental use of atrocity, and people found themselves willing to transgress continually receding ethical limits on violence.

19

On the Road to Total Retribution?

The International Debate on the Punishment of War Crimes, 1872–1945

DANIEL MARC SEGESSER

How can one prevent brutal manifestations of righteous anger among an overexcited population when a whole nation mobilizes in defense of homes? How can one ensure that the sentiments of law or humanity prevail?[1]

These words were written in 1870 by Gustave Moynier, the first president of the Comité international de secours aux militaires blessés in a treatise on the recently negotiated Geneva Convention for the Amelioration of the Condition of the Wounded in Armies in the Field. At that time Moynier was convinced "that generally speaking the Convention will be observed in the future and that precautions taken to obtain this result will not prove to have been in vain."[2] The Franco-Prussian War, which broke out shortly thereafter, left him anxious, however, about the power of "a purely moral sanction to ease unleashed passions."[3] In January 1872, he accordingly launched a campaign to establish an international tribunal to adjudicate violations of the Convention.

Moynier thus became the first to propose that the problem of war crimes be regulated at the international level.[4] He was not, however, the first who sought to develop positive legal guidelines to prosecute violations of the laws of war.[5] The eminent American jurist, Francis Lieber, had, at the

---

1 Gustave Moynier, *Étude sur la Convention de Genève* (Paris, 1870), 303.
2 Ibid., 304.
3 Gustave Moynier, "Note sur la création d' une institution judiciaire internationale propre à prévenir et à réprimer les Infractions à la Convention de Genève," *Bulletin international des Sociétés de secours aux militaires blessés* 11 (1872): 122–23.
4 Throughout this essay the term war crimes is used generically rather than technically. See Gerry J. Simpson, "War Crimes: A Critical Introduction," in Timothy L. H. McCormack and Gerry Simpson, eds., *The Law of War Crimes: National and International Approaches* (The Hague, 1997), 1–30.
5 On the laws of war and their development in general, see Geoffrey Best, *Humanity in Warfare: The Modern History of the International Law of Armed Conflict* (London, 1980); and Michael Howard, George J. Andreopoulos, and Mark R. Shulman, eds., *The Laws of War: Constraints on Warfare in the Western World* (New Haven, 1994).

behest of Abraham Lincoln, proposed during the American Civil War to punish "crimes punishable by all penal codes such as arson, murder, maiming, assaults . . . and rape, if committed by an American soldier in a hostile country against its inhabitants."[6] Unlike Moynier, who proposed an international tribunal, Lieber had preferred to work through national legislation and courts because he believed that an international tribunal would be neither desirable nor efficient.[7] Other jurists such as Conrad von Holtzendorff, Gustave Rolin-Jaequemyns, and Achille Morin agreed with Moynier that an international tribunal to judge violations of the Geneva Convention would be a step in the right direction; they wondered, however, whether such an institution would be accepted by the states concerned, and criticized some of the details of Moynier's proposal.[8]

Moynier recognized the pertinence of these objections and concluded that additional legal groundwork had to be laid before an international tribunal would be feasible. Accordingly, in 1873 he became one of the founding members of the *Institut de droit international*, whose goal was "to promote the development of international law" and "to become the organ of the civilized word's legal conscience."[9] Moynier continued to press for punishing violations not only of the Geneva Convention, but also of the laws of war in general. However, he dropped his demand for an international tribunal and called instead on governments to address violations of the Geneva Convention and the laws of war in their own penal codes.[10] With the support of eminent jurists, such as Johann Caspar Bluntschli, Jacobus Catharinus Cornelis den Beer Poortugael, and Fjodor Martens, Moynier persuaded the *Institut de droit international* to include a clause in its manual on the laws of land war, the so-called Oxford Manual, stipulating that "offenders against the laws of war are liable to the punishments specified in the penal law."[11] Moynier also continued to press for an international legal agreement that would not only compel governments to adapt their

6 Dietrich Schindler and Jiří Toman, eds., *The Laws of Armed Conflict: A Collection of Conventions, Resolutions and Other Documents* (Geneva, 1981), 10.
7 Gustave Rolin-Jaequemyns, "Note sur le projet de M. Moynier, relatif à l'etablissement d' une institution judiciaire internationale, protectrice de la Convention, avec lettres de MM. Lieber, Ach. Morin, de Holtzendorff et Westlake," *Revue de droit international et de législation comparée* 4 (1872): 330–32.
8 Ibid., 332–44.
9 "Status votés par la conférence juridique internationale de Gand, le 10 Septembre 1873," *Annuaire de l'institut de droit international* (hereafter AIDI) 1 (1877): 1.
10 Gustave Moynier, "Rapport sur la réglementation des lois et coutumes de la guerre," AIDI 3/4 (1880): 312–20; Moynier, "Rapport sur la réglementation des lois et coutumes de la guerre," AIDI 5 (1882): 149–56; Moynier, *Considérations sur la sanction pénale à donner à la Convention de Genève* (Lausanne, 1893).
11 *The Laws of War on Land: Manual Published by the Institute of International Law 9 September 1880 [Oxford Manual]*, Art. 84: text given in "Les lois de la guerre sur terre," AIDI 5 (1882): 173; Schindler and Toman, *Laws of Armed Conflict*, 47.

penal codes to the Geneva Convention, but also to create an international commission to investigate violations of the Convention.[12]

Moynier's ideas met with opposition both within the community of international jurists and outside. Particularly in Germany, military officers were unwilling to accept rules that limited their ability to use force in any way they thought necessary. Many jurists were likewise unwilling to limit the existing concept of national sovereignty.[13] The discussion of the laws of war at the Hague Peace Conferences in 1899 and 1907 thus brought no significant advance. The deliberations elaborated upon ideas already laid out in the Declaration of Brussels concerning the Laws and Customs of War of 1874 and in the Oxford Manual of 1880. The question of penal sanctions was not discussed, nor was it included in the Hague Conventions on the Laws and Customs of War on Land of 1899 or 1907. Participants at both Hague conferences agreed that sovereign states were responsible for dealing with their own perpetrators.[14]

Only the revised Geneva Convention of 1906 laid down binding international guidelines, calling for legislation to prevent the misuse of the Red Cross emblem and to prevent "individual acts of robbery and ill treatment of the sick and wounded of the armies."[15] These articles represented the sum of the practical results that Moynier and others had achieved in their efforts to impose a regime of penal sanctions to constrain the passions of (total) war.

It was in the context of the Hague Conventions that, in 1906, the term "war crime" was used for the first time. The well-known international jurist Lassa Oppenheim used it to denote a phenomenon that had hitherto been described variously as *animadversio in hostes, infractions aux règles du droit international*, "crimes against the captor's army or people," or "offences against the customs of war." Oppenheim defined war crimes as "such hostile or other acts of soldiers or other individuals as may be punished by the enemy on capture of the offenders."[16] The term has been widely used since

---

12 Gustave Moynier and Edouard Engelhart, De la Sanction Pénale à donner à la Convention de Genève, AIDI 14 (1895): 17–31, 170–87.

13 Emilio Brusa, "Di una sanzione penale alla convenzione ginevrina per i ferriti in guerra," *Atti della R. Accademia delle Scienze di Torino*, 31 (1895): 326–45; Manfred Messerschmidt, "Völkerrecht und 'Kriegsnotwendigkeit' in der deutschen militärischen Tradition seit den Einigungskriegen," *German Studies Review* 6 (1983): 237–43.

14 Jost Dülffer, "Regeln im Krieg? Kriegsverbrechen und die Haager Friedenskonferenzen," in Wolfram Wette and Gerd R. Ueberschär, eds., *Kriegsverbrechen im 20. Jahrhundert* (Darmstadt, 2001), 40–42.

15 Schindler and Toman, *Laws of Armed Conflict*, 239.

16 Lassa Oppenheim, *War and Neutrality* (London, 1906), 263; cf. Jens-Peter Zander, "Das Verbrechen im Kriege – Ein völkerrechtlicher Begriff: Ein Beitrag zur Problematik des Kriegsverbrechens" (Diss. Jur., Julius-Maximilians Universität, Würzburg, 1969), 21.

Oppenheim's initial discussion, but scholars and legal experts have yet to agree on a definition.[17]

THE BALKAN WARS, THE FIRST WORLD WAR, AND THE INTERWAR PERIOD

In response to reports of violations of the laws of war during the Balkan Wars, the Carnegie Endowment for International Peace set up an international commission of inquiry. It was chaired by the Frenchman Baron d'Estournelles de Constant and included many authorities on international law, among them Walther Schücking, Josef Redlich, Paul Milioukov, and Francis W. Hirst. The commission concluded in 1914 that all combatants had violated the rules governing land warfare; it also proposed that a permanent international commission of inquiry be established to issue public reports on the conduct of belligerent armies in future wars.[18] The commission's proposals were to receive little attention, however, as a result of the outbreak of war in 1914. Theodore S. Woolsey, one of the few to comment upon them, noted only that the belief "that an investigating committee can humanize war by reports upon past savagery or criticism of present brutality, involves a childlike credulity."[19]

The First World War quickly demonstrated that public scrutiny alone would not prevent violations of the laws of war. The German violation of Belgian neutrality and reports of German atrocities on Belgian soil provoked outrage in the west as well as public demands that the responsible parties, including the Kaiser, be punished.[20] It was a sign of the changing character of warfare in the new century that even in countries as far away as Australia[21] public outrage became a tool of propaganda, a means to fortify morale on the home front. The question of how to deal with

17 Simpson, "War Crimes," 3; Mario Geuenich, "Die Erweiterung des Begriffs des Kriegsverbrechens durch das Erste Zusatzprotokoll zu den Genfer Abkommen von 1949" (Diss. Jur., Köln, 1985), 5–9; Yoram Dinstein, "The Distinction between War Crimes and Crimes against Peace," in Yoram Dinstein and Mara Tabory, eds., *War Crimes in International Law* (Den Haag, 1996), 3–4.
18 Carnegie Endowment for International Peace, *Report of the International Commission to Inquire into the Causes and Conduct of the Balkan Wars* (Washington, DC, 1914).
19 Theodore S. Woolsey, review of Carnegie Endowment, *Report of the International Commission*, AJIL 9 (1915): 281.
20 James F. Willis, *Prologue to Nuremberg: The Politics and Diplomacy of Punishing War Criminals of the First World War* (Westport, CT, 1982), 8–12; John Horne and Alan Kramer, *German Atrocities, 1914: A History of Denial* (New Haven, 2001), 227–61.
21 Judith Smart, "'Poor Little Belgium' and Australian Popular Support for the War 1914–1915," *War & Society* 12 (1994), 27–46; Daniel Marc Segesser, *Empire und Totaler Krieg: Australien 1905–1918* (Paderborn, 2002), 333–34.

perpetrators remained open, however. In 1915, in connection with the massacre of Armenians, the Allied governments warned the Ottoman leadership that they would "hold personally responsible [for] these crimes all members of the Ottoman government and those of their agents who are implicated in such massacres."[22] The Allies could not agree, however, until 1919 to declare war crimes punishable. But the issue was clearly on the international agenda, not least due to the "totality" of the wars between 1912 and 1918.[23]

By the end of the war, most of the Allied governments had concluded that punishing war crimes should be addressed at the peace conference. Early in 1919, they created an official commission to inquire into responsibility for the outbreak of the war and violations of the laws of war, as well as with drafting a proposal for a tribunal to try these offenses.[24] The commission's report, submitted in March, represented a compromise between the majority of the commission and the two American delegates, Robert Lansing and James Brown Scott. The contentious issues were whether aggressive war was itself a punishable offense and whether an international tribunal or national tribunals should have jurisdiction. Ultimately, the commission called for punishment of the Kaiser and others who had been responsible for the war, as well as for an international tribunal. Supported by the Japanese delegates, the American members of the commission submitted their own views in a minority report.[25]

The two reports then came before the Council of Four, where political considerations were paramount. The product of the Council's debates was Article 227 of the Versailles treaty, which arraigned the Kaiser "for a supreme offence against international morality and the sanctity of treaties" and called for a special tribunal – political rather than legal in character – "to try the accused, thereby assuring him the guarantees essential to the right of defense."[26] The treaty also provided that offenders against the laws and customs of war were to be tried before national military tribunals or, in cases where offenses bore on the interests of more than one country, mixed

---

22 William G. Sharp to William J. Bryan, 28 May 1915, *Foreign Relations of the United States* (Washington, DC, 1928), 83: 981.

23 Willis, *Prologue*, 23–64.

24 United Nations War Crimes Commission, *History of the United Nations War Crimes Commission and the Development of the Laws of War* (London, 1948), 32.

25 Commission on the Responsibility of the Authors of War and the Enforcement of Penalties, "Report to the Preliminary Peace Conference," AJIL 14 (1920), 95–154; Walter Schwengler, *Völkerrecht, Versailler Vertrag und Auslieferungsfrage: Die Strafverfolgung wegen Kriegsverbrechen als Problem des Friedensschlusses 1919/20* (Stuttgart, 1982), 90–106; Willis, *Prologue*, 68–77.

26 Willis, *Prologue*, 177.

tribunals. Article 228 of the treaty compelled the German government to extradite for trial all persons whom the Allied governments charged with war crimes. Excepting only the case of the Kaiser, the proposal for an international criminal tribunal did not prevail.[27]

The Germans followed these discussions with intense interest. The new republican government opposed the idea of trying the leaders of the old monarchy for war crimes, and it could count on broad public support. Leading German scholars, including specialists in international law like Walther Schücking, Albrecht Mendelssohn-Bartholdy, and Hans Wehberg argued, as did Max Weber, that Germany had not been the only party responsible for the World War. Legal scholars who, like Alfred Verdross, agreed in principle that persons guilty of war crimes could be charged under national and international law kept a low profile.[28] The Allies, however, rejected all changes in the final draft of the treaty, which the German government subsequently signed under protest.

When the first list of over 800 alleged war criminals arrived, the German government declared that extradition would be impossible. In the end, the Allies, who feared weakening the republican government, accepted a German counterproposal to hold trials before the Reich's Supreme Court in Leipzig.[29] Of the individuals named on a shortened list of forty-five alleged offenders, only twelve defendants stood trial. Few were found guilty; and they were given light sentences. In view of these developments, the Allied governments lost faith in additional trials in Germany and informed the German government that they would again demand extradition of German war criminals. No Allied government did in fact do so, however, and only in France were trials of selected war criminals conducted in absentia.[30]

Although interest waned in punishing war crimes, the debate on the subject continued within the international legal community. The Council of the League of Nations appointed a committee to draft a statute for a Permanent Court of International Justice. In this context, the Belgian Minister of State, Baron Descamps, argued that, because International Law recognized the existence of a category of international crimes, it was necessary to create some sort of international criminal court in order to avoid problems with the creation of institutions ex post facto. The League did not, however, take

---

27 Schwengler, *Völkerrecht*, 106–16; Willis, *Prologue*, 177.
28 Schwengler, *Völkerrecht*, 125–232; Alfred Verdross, *Die völkerrechtswidrige Kriegshandlung und der Strafanspruch der Staaten* (Berlin, 1920).
29 Willis, *Prologue*, 113–25; Schwengler, *Völkerrecht*, 322–43.
30 Willis, *Prologue*, 139–47.

up the committee's proposal. Lord Phillimore, one of the leading British specialists in the field, summarized the disappointment:

At the close of the meeting of the Committee of Jurists summoned to prepare the project for the Permanent Court of International Justice . . . three Resolutions or Voeux were appended Resolutions which by reason of the character of their proposers and the unanimity of acceptance by the Committee, would seem to deserve more consideration than has been accorded to them at present by the members of the Council or by the members of the Assembly [of the League of Nations].[31]

The International Law Association also discussed the feasibility of an international criminal court in three consecutive meetings between 1922 and 1926. In 1926, it resolved that "if the rule of law is to be established in the family of nations, it can only be satisfactorily established by the cooperation of all nations expressed through an International Court."[32] Other organizations, such as the Inter-Parliamentary Union and the *Association internationale de droit pénal*, joined the call for an international criminal court. But the proposal drew many scholarly critics, too. James Leslie Brierly, Chichele Professor for International Law and Diplomacy at Oxford, spoke for them when he remarked that

the notion that war crimes can be banished from war or even appreciably reduced by an institution of a criminal court is probably a delusion . . . and even if this were not so, an international court to deal with war crimes after a war is over would still be undesirable, because the supreme need then is to calm the passions which the war has raised and to work for the prevention of another.[33]

National courts, he insisted, were preferable to an international tribunal. They were both more convenient and appropriate for trying war criminals. Neither German jurists nor the international peace movement did take a great interest in any kind of tribunal, for their principal interest lay in preventing another war.

They had a lot of company. The First World War gave rise to a popular movement in favor of outlawing war. One of the men involved in this movement was Quincy Wright, a young professor at the University of Chicago and a member of the board of editors of the renowned *American Journal of*

31 Lord Walter George Phillimore, "An International Criminal Court and the Resolutions of the Committee of Jurists," *British Yearbook of International Law* (hereafter BYIL) 3 (1922–23): 79.
32 Benjamin B. Ferencz, *An International Criminal Court: A Step toward World Peace – A Documentary History and Analysis* (London, 1980), 256. See also William Latey, "The International Law Conference," *Law Journal* 62 (1926): 106–7; and Timothy H. L. McCormack, "From Sun Tzu to Sixth Committee: The Evolution of an International Criminal Law Regime," in McCormack and Simpson, *Law of War Crimes*, 52–53.
33 James Leslie Brierly, "Do We Need an International Criminal Court?" BYIL 8 (1927): 87.

International Law. In 1924, he proposed that scholars devise a set of legal standards to determine responsibility for wars and define justifiable acts of self-defense; he also called for the establishment of international agencies to enforce these standards.[34] In the belief that international law could resolve the question of aggression, he concluded that the use of force by a state was legitimate only when it involved

(1) instant and overwhelming necessity for defence of territory or citizens, (2) redress for properly validated legal claims, (3) prevention of flagrant violations of international law, (4) fulfillment of privileges expressively given by treaty, and (5) enforcement of law within the state's own jurisdiction.[35]

Public Opinion and international institutions for settling international disputes were, he believed, the most effective means to prevent war.[36] Wright was accordingly less skeptical than many other legal scholars about the Kellog-Briand Pact. "Many treaties have no specific sanctions," Wright wrote, "but in so far as they create obligations under international law those obligations are covered by the sanctions of all international law."[37]

THE INTERNATIONAL DEBATE ON WAR CRIMES DURING THE SECOND WORLD WAR

With the onset of war in 1939, both sides were aware of the normative power of the Kellog-Briand Pact, and each accused the other of being the aggressor.[38] The issue of war crimes was not yet on anyone's agenda, however. Even though German barbarities in Poland quickly became known, the Polish government in exile waited several months to ask the French and the British governments to condemn them, to threaten punishment of the perpetrators, and to demand compensation for damages that had resulted from German violations of international law. Officials in the British Foreign Office were skeptical. Some questioned the veracity of reports of war crimes that had been received from Polish and Czech sources. Nevertheless, the Foreign Office agreed in principle to a formal joint Anglo-French-Polish protest against the action of the German government. This

34 Quincy Wright, "Changes in the Conception of War," *American Journal of International Law* (hereafter AJIL) 18 (1924): 767.
35 Quincy Wright, "The Outlawry of War," AJIL 19 (1925): 94; Wright, "The Concept of Aggression in International Law," AJIL 29 (1935): 373–95.
36 Quincy Wright, "The Interpretation of Multilateral Treaties," AJIL 23 (1929): 94–107.
37 Quincy Wright, "The Meaning of the Pact of Paris," AJIL 27 (1933): 41.
38 Axel Freiherr von Freytagh-Loringhoven, *Kriegsausbruch und Kriegsschuld 1939* (Essen, 1940), reviewed by Gustav Adolf Walz, *Zeitschrift für Völkerrecht* 24 (1941): 267–69; Walther Hofer, *Die Entfesselung des Zweiten Weltkrieges: Darstellung und Dokumente* (2d ed., Düsseldorf, 1984), 383–94, 404–8.

document reaffirmed "the responsibility of Germany for these crimes and [the Allies'] determination to right the wrongs . . . inflicted on the Polish people."[39]

Although the Foreign Office wished to encourage the Polish people to hold out, it argued – confidentially of course – that the British government should not address German war crimes in detail, lest German propaganda claim that the British objective was to destroy the German people. The fact that the Germans had taken British soldiers and airmen as prisoners of war during the western campaign and in Norway affected the British attitude on war crimes.[40] The British (and later the American) position on this issue was therefore the product of complex negotiations among groups and agencies within and outside government – a fact that was often not appreciated by governments-in-exile or, later, the Soviet Union.[41]

In May 1940, Ernst Joseph Cohn, a German professor of civil law who had emigrated to Great Britain after his dismissal by the Nazis in 1933, presented his ideas on "The Problem of War Crimes Today" to the Grotius Society. He examined various ideas that were then circulating about punishing war crimes, which he defined as "violations of the international law, both written and unwritten, regarding land, sea and air warfare."[42] Against criticism that trials for such crimes would be subject to popular passions, Cohn pleaded for "an open trial ending in the due punishment of the accused person or in his acquittal if he cannot be found guilty." "Absence of sanction," he argued, "is nothing but a direct incitement to the repetition of violations of law."[43] War crimes in the strict sense would thus have to be punished at the end of the war, but because no international criminal court had yet been created, he concluded that trials should take place in the victim countries' national courts on the bases of their individual penal codes. The role of international law in this process would be confined to deciding the question "whether an act . . . is excluded from punishment because it was an act of lawful warfare."[44] Cohn rejected the proposal of the German jurist Helmuth von Weber that the national courts of the country of the accused should hold such trials.[45] He was also opposed to the inclusion of violations of international obligations – such as unleashing an aggressive

---

39 Arieh J. Kochavi, *Prelude to Nuremberg: Allied War Crimes Policy and the Question of Punishment* (Chapel Hill, 1998), 9.

40 Kochavi, *Prelude*, 44–45.   41 Ibid., 27–137.

42 Ernst Joseph Cohn, "The Problem of War Crimes To-day," *Transactions of the Grotius Society* 26 (1941): 125.

43 Ibid., 131.   44 Ibid., 143.

45 Helmuth von Weber, *Internationale Strafgerichtsbarkeit*, Völkerrechtsfragen 40. Heft (Berlin, 1934), 128–29; see comment by Cohn, "Problem of War Crimes," 136–37.

war in contravention to the Kellogg-Briand Pact – into the category of
war crimes because this proposal was "too far from practical politics and
constitutes therefore an unnecessary burden for the whole plan."[46]

Not everyone agreed. Other scholars argued that international laws were
already in place to serve as the basis of criminal proceedings. In October
1942, the London International Assembly resolved that because the League
of Nations had declared in 1927 that "aggression was an international crime
and that the [Kellogg-Briand] Pact of Paris condemned recourse to war for
the solution of international controversies . . . the Axis Powers had violated
both the resolution and the Pact of Paris, to which they were both parties."[47]
Bohuslav Ecer concluded from this resolution that not only the aggressor
states as such, but also their rulers and military leaders were personally
responsible for the "gigantic chain of crimes which compose this war and
which are punishable under the criminal laws of the countries affected,
the penalty according to all these laws [being] death."[48] Hans Kelsen, an
Austrian professor of international law who was in exile in the United
States, and Albert Levy from University of Chicago also favored punishing
the authors of war.[49] Kelsen insisted that the category of punishable crimes
included "violations of international law committed by having resorted to
war in disregard of general or particular international law, or by having
provoked war" and "breaches of the rules of international law regulating the
conduct of war."[50] Kelsen believed that these were crimes in a strict sense,
while violations of the more abstract principles of humanity represented
breaches only of norms of morality, for which no legal responsibility could
be established.[51] Marcel de Baer, a Belgian scholar, also concluded that the
authors of the war should be tried on the basis of the Kellogg-Briand Pact,
but only if the Allied countries incorporated the pertinent rules into their
national penal codes.[52] Other experts argued against trying aggressors under
international law, contending that the effort would only confuse the much
clearer issue of liability for atrocities committed during the war.[53]

46 Cohn, "Problem of War Crimes," 141.
47 United Nations War Crimes Commission, *History*, 100.
48 Ibid., 101.
49 Hans Kelsen, *Peace through Law* (Chapel Hill, NC, 1944), 71–75; Albert Levy, "The Law and Procedure of War Crimes Trials," *American Political Science Review* (hereafter APSR) 37 (1943): 1067–68.
50 Hans Kelsen, "Collective and Individual Responsibility in International Law with Particular Regard
   to the Punishment of War Criminals," *California Law Review* 31 (1943): 530–31.
51 Kelsen, "Collective and Individual Responsibility," 531–32.
52 Marcel de Baer, "No Peace for War Criminals," *Free World* 7 (1944): 131–35.
53 Sheldon Glueck, *War Criminals: Their Prosecution and Punishment* (New York, 1944), 37–38. See also
   William B. Simons, "The Jurisdictional Bases of the International Military Tribunal at Nuremberg,"
   in George Ginsburgs and Vladimir N. Kudriavtsev, eds., *The Nuremberg Trial and International Law*
   (Dordrecht, 1990), 45–50.

Several other questions were also at issue. The most central remained how war crimes were to be defined and who should have the jurisdiction to punish them. George A. Finch, the secretary of the American Society of International Law, raised the question whether the very concept of war crimes might have changed in light of the new scale of warfare. Although war crimes had occurred in the past, the expansion of the present war to global dimensions, the obliteration of the distinction between combatants and noncombatants, and the determination of the Axis forces to exterminate or reduce conquered populations to permanent subjection had resulted in an "orgy of inhuman brutalities on scale unprecedented in previous wars."[54] Finch nonetheless argued that only those persons who had violated existing laws and customs of war should be punished and, moreover, that ample norms and precedents existed in international conventions, the common laws of war, and in the manuals of war of the belligerents. For him, it was clear that everything had to be done to avoid a repetition of the Leipzig Trials. Finch did not specify which crimes ought to be tried at the end of the war; he did not think, however, that it was advisable to punish the authors of war because he thought such an offense political rather than criminal. Given his frequent references to the Hague and Geneva Conventions, it seems obvious that he was mainly concerned with violations of this part of international law, but that he was open to discuss further aspects of the problem if necessary.[55]

Sheldon Glueck, professor of criminology at Harvard, also geared his discussion of war crimes to the new dimensions of war. "Considering the Nazi conception of 'total war,'" he wrote,

we may legitimately define war criminals as persons – regardless of military or po-litical rank – who, in connection with the military, political, economic or industrial preparation for or waging of war, have, in their official capacity, committed acts contrary to (a) the laws and customs of legitimate warfare or (b) the principles of criminal law, generally observed in civilized States; or who have incited, ordered, procured, counseled or conspired in the commission of such acts; or, having knowl-edge that such acts were about to be committed, and possessing the duty and power to prevent them, have failed to do so.[56]

Glueck did not include aggressive war in this definition, because he did not believe that the Kellogg-Briand Pact offered an adequate legal basis. On the other hand, he argued, those who were responsible for the mass slaughter of innocents in concentration camps and crimes against the Jews

---

54 George A. Finch, "Retribution for War Crimes," AJIL 37 (1943): 81.
55 Ibid., 81–88.   56 Glueck, *War Criminals*, 37.

and other civilians should not be permitted to escape the judgment of law. These crimes he included under the rubric of war crime, "since they were committed in preparation for or during the progress of a war upon helpless civilians in the clutches of ruthless military and political officials; and the miscreants could efficiently be tried for them by the same tribunals that will deal with violations of the laws and customs of warfare."[57]

Other scholars developed the same theme. Manfred Lachs, an eminent jurist from the University of Krakow who was in British exile, contended that war crimes included any act of violence that was committed in connection with a war that was contrary to the codified international laws of warfare, or in violation of customary law or general principles accepted by civilized nations.[58] Georg Lelewer, an exiled Austrian specialist on military law, wrote likewise that war crimes comprehended "those in committing which the perpetrator takes advantage of the impression of defenselessness and deprivation of rights which the presence of hostile forces exercises on the person attacked."[59] Vaclav Benes, the nephew of the exiled president of Czechoslovakia, argued with specific respect to German atrocities at Lidice that "the methods of warfare forbidden by the Hague Conventions only cover to a small extent what world public opinion today regards as war crimes."[60] The definition of war crimes therefore extended well beyond the precepts of positive international law, such as those laid out in the Hague Conventions. The definition comprised, in addition to war crimes traditionally defined, all grave crimes against an allied state, whether committed during preparation for war, the waging of war, or occupation or domination of enemy territory.[61] Professor Aaron Naumovitch Trainin from Moscow followed the same line of reasoning and accused the German government of inhumanity, extermination, and plunder of cultural treasures. He added that the economic leaders of the Axis powers were also guilty of war crimes because "with their funds, factories and guns they support and maintain the system of governmental banditry."[62] Other Soviet jurists made similar claims about the guilt of German economic elites; jurists in the West, where

---

57 Ibid., 45, 56–62.
58 Manfred Lachs, *War Crimes: An Attempt to Define the Issues* (London, 1945), 100–101.
59 Georg Lelewer, "The Definition of War Crimes," *Central European Observer* (hereafter CEO) 21 (1944): 116.
60 Vaclav Benes, "The Question of the Definition of War Crimes," CEO 20 (1943): 282.
61 Benes, "Question," 283; cf. Benes, "The Punishment of War Criminals," *Spirit of Czechoslovakia* 5 (1944): 23.
62 A. Farrin, "The Responsibility for Nazi Crimes," CEO 20 (1943): 282; cf. Aaron Naumovich Trainin, *Hitlerite Responsibility under Criminal Law* (London, 1944).

political theory emphasized the distinction between state and economy, were skeptical toward these arguments.[63]

In light of the growing range of potential war crimes and the disagreements among legal experts, many observers argued that the Allied powers should hold an international conference to set the parameters for postwar prosecution of war crimes.[64] Such a conference was not held during the war, and the issue of war crimes was only resolved in London at the beginning of August 1945. War crimes proper and the waging of aggressive war were made into two separate categories, while the other, broader crimes that many experts had defined as war crimes during the war were subsumed under the heading of crimes against humanity.[65]

The problem of jurisdiction over war criminals was another contested issue. Many legal scholars continued to advocate an international criminal court that would not only resolve conflicting claims of jurisdiction, but would also represent a major step toward institutionalizing an international legal system. Albert Levy, for example, called for an international criminal court "in order to give proof of the fact that the United Nations have been fighting this global conflict to vindicate the principles of the General Pact for the Renunciation of War."[66] The idea of an international criminal court was also supported by Sheldon Glueck, who argued that only such a court would be able to resolve the technical difficulties that would come up if national tribunals would judge war criminals,[67] and, to a more limited extent, by Georg Schwarzenberger.[68] Many Soviet legal experts also supported the idea.[69] But, as before the war, legal opinion was divided on whether an international criminal court should be established. Some opposed the idea of war crimes trials altogether, preferring what Georg Schwarzenberger called a quietist approach; advocates of this approach believed that trials would only prolong "the bitterness of war into a time when both sides should be re-knitting broken ties of friendship rather than brooding over

---

63 Richard Overy, *Interrogations: The Nazi Elite in Allied Hands, 1945* (Harmondsworth, 2001), 38–41.
64 Charles Cheney Hyde, "Punishment of War Criminals," *Proceedings of the American Society of International Law* 37 (1943): 46; Clyde Eagleton, "Punishment of War Criminals by the United Nations," AJIL 37 (1943): 499; Benes, "Question," 283.
65 Dinstein and Tabory, *War Crimes*, 379–81.   66 Levy, "Law and Procedure," 1076.
67 Sheldon Glueck, "By What Tribunal Shall War Offenders be Tried?" *Harvard Law Review* 56 (1943): 1059–89.
68 Georg Schwarzenberger, "War Crimes and the Problem of an International Criminal Court," *Czechoslovak Yearbook of International Law* 1 (1942): 85–87.
69 George Ginsburgs, *Moscow's Road to Nuremberg: The Soviet Background to the Trial* (The Hague, 1996), 71–83.

the past."[70] Citing the precedent of Reconstruction after the American Civil War, Charles Arnold Anderson of Iowa State College claimed that war crimes trials would be detrimental to reestablishing stability after the war.[71] Others continued to argue that offenses against the laws and customs of war should be tried by national courts as violations of national penal norms. In 1943, George Manner argued:

For the present . . . solutions to the problem of retribution for war crimes, other than national postwar trials or post-armistice proceedings in enemy municipal courts, either rest on the uncertain precedent established by the treaties of peace of 1919–1920 or constitute propositions *de lege ferenda* which are as much outside the province of law as is the decision to exact such retribution in enemy tribunals after actual hostilities have ceased.[72]

The Norwegian writer Sigrid Undset also argued that war criminals ought to be tried in national courts, while Georg Lelewer argued for the creation of special tribunals to be set up in each of the Allied states.[73] Aaron Naumovitch Trainin, by contrast, claimed that "there is no necessity for a special investigation and judicial procedure for the determination and judgment of the monstrous misdeeds which they have committed. The fate of Hitler and his clique can be settled by political verdict of the victorious democratic states."[74]

The question of superior orders also remained an issue. The *British Manual of Military Law* and the United States *Rules of Land Warfare* both provided that "individuals of the armed forces will not be punished for . . . offenses in case they were committed under orders or sanction of their government or commanders."[75] George Manner and Clyde Eagleton therefore argued that the courts that judged war criminals at the end of the war would have to accept a defendant's plea that he had acted under superior orders.[76] Kelsen agreed.[77] But other eminent legal experts argued that superior orders were not accepted per se as a legitimate defense in continental European law, nor

---

70 Schwarzenberger, "War Crimes," 81–82; Schwarzenberger himself was critical of the quietist approach.
71 Charles Arnold Anderson, "The Utility of the Proposed Trial and Punishment of Enemy Leaders," APSR 37 (1943): 1081–1100.
72 George Manner, "The Legal Nature and Punishment of Criminal Acts of Violence Contrary to the Laws of War," AJIL 37 (1943): 434–35.
73 Sigrid Undset, "War Criminals and the Future," *Free World* 6 (1943): 490–91; Georg Lelewer, "Punishment of War Criminals," CEO 20 (1943): 283.
74 Trainin, *Hitlerite Responsibility*, 93; Ginsburgs, *Moscow's Road*, 81.
75 Glueck, *War Criminals*, 140.
76 Manner, "Legal Nature," 417–18; Eagleton, "Punishment of War Criminals," 497.
77 Kelsen, "Collective and Individual Responsibility," 556–58.

had they been earlier in the United States or Great Britain.[78] Others, among them Schwarzenberger and Sheldon Glueck, claimed that military law did not reduce the soldier to an automaton and that he owed obedience only to lawful orders.[79]

Most scholars agreed that the fundamental legal principle that there could be no violation of laws that did not exist at the time the alleged offenses were committed, would not constitute an obstacle to war crimes trials. Even George Manner, who recognized the legitimacy of only national courts, argued that "the principle *nullum crimen, nulla poena sine lege* does not necessarily apply to acts prohibited by established rules of warfare but not made crimes by the offender's national regulations."[80] Schwarzenberger argued that the principle *nullum crimen, nulla poena sine lege* would not stand in the way of trials because the German barbarities were contrary even to the criminal law of the Third Reich.[81] Albert Levy pointed out that "a community has inherently the right to punish its members who seek to destroy it."[82] Hector Munro claimed that "the chief difficulties of the infant science of International Criminal Law are not legal, but political. Given the political will, coupled with a readiness to apply the law impartially, there is no real reason to fear that the strict method of justice [. . .] will lead to the escape of criminals, or prove less effective than the dark road of indiscriminate lawless reprisal."[83]

Hersh Lauterpacht observed that total war had introduced elements of uncertainty and complexity into many rules. An impartial tribunal would hold many acts of warfare to be violations of international law, even though these acts had been controversial or excluded from prosecution before courts of individual belligerent countries. Modern warfare required the general mobilization of society, Lauterbach noted, blurring the fundamental distinction between combatants and noncombatants. Questions about the legitimacy of aerial bombardment of civilian centers had to be addressed, but he doubted whether tribunals charged with punishing war criminals were the proper forums for resolving these questions. Guilty states could not escape the

---

78 Alexander N. Sack, "Punishment of War Criminals and the Defence of Superior Orders," *Law Quarterly Review* 60 (1944): 63–66; Mitchell Franklin, "Sources of International Law relating to Sanctions against War Criminals," *Journal of Criminal Law and Criminology* (hereafter JCLC) 36 (1945): 161–64.

79 Georg Schwarzenberger, *International Law and Totalitarian Lawlessness* (London, 1943), 62–64; Sheldon Glueck, "Punishing the War Criminals," *New Republic* 109 (1943): 708–9; Glueck, *War Criminals*, 140–58; Hersh Lauterpacht, "The Law of Nations and the Punishment of War Crimes," BYIL 21 (1944): 69–74; Lelewer, "Punishment," 284.

80 Manner, "Legal Nature," 419.   81 Schwarzenberger, *International Law*, 78–79.

82 Levy, "Law and Procedure," 1069.

83 Hector Munro, "War Crimes and Criminals," *New Commonwealth* 8, 10 (1943): 226.

obligations of compensation that the Hague Convention envisaged, nor could legal ambiguities shield clearly criminal acts, such as the bombardment of Rotterdam.[84] Lauterpacht's intention was probably to defend the operations of the British and American air forces from charges that they, too, had committed war crimes. This problem had earlier surfaced in the *British Yearbook of International Law*, where James M. Spaight, a renowned specialist, wrote about the legitimate objectives of air warfare. He contended that the fact that millions of civilians were employed in armament factories had robbed "the great cities of a belligerent country of the virtual immunity which once they could claim. They have become an integrated part of the whole war-machine. They are part of the war. They do not stand aside."[85] A similar claim could be made for the use of the atomic bomb.[86]

THE EXPERTS AND THE DIPLOMATS

After the fall of France, the British government paid little attention to the issue of war crimes or stories of German atrocities in occupied Europe. Occasional announcements that the Germans would be held accountable for their acts were calculated to encourage resistance movements in occupied Europe and to calm fears among governments-in-exile. These statements did not, however, signal any firm intentions. Despite increasing evidence of atrocities against civilians, the German invasion of the Soviet Union did not much alter this situation.[87] The British Foreign Office at first again regarded information about atrocities with suspicion. In October 1942, however, given increasing pressure from public opinion and President Roosevelt, the British government issued a condemnation of atrocities in occupied Europe.[88] It refused, however, to endorse officially a common declaration that the governments-in-exile had published in January 1942 which insisted "the guilty parties should not evade punishment."[89] The governments-in-exile then intensified their pressure on the war crimes issue.[90] Their

---

84 Lauterpacht, "Law of Nations," 74–75.
85 James M. Spaight, "Legitimate Objectives in Air Warfare," BYIL 21 (1944): 162.
86 Ellery C. Stowell, "The Laws of War and the Atomic Bomb," AJIL 39 (1945): 784–88.
87 See Jürgen Förster, "Das Unternehmen 'Barbarossa' als Eroberungs-und Vernichtungskrieg," in Horst Boog et al., *Das Deutsche Reich und der Zweite Weltkrieg*, 7 vols. (Stuttgart, 1979–2000), 4: 413–47; Förster, "Verbrecherische Befehle," Wette and Ueberschär, *Kriegsverbrechen*, 137–51; Messerschmidt, "Völkerrecht," 244–69.
88 Kochavi, *Prelude*, 9–15.
89 "The Inter-Allied Conference, January 13, 1942," *Bulletin of International News* (hereafter BIN) 19 (1942): 52.
90 "The Allied Peoples and Retribution," CEO 19 (1942): 21, 23–24; "German Crimes in Poland," CEO 19 (1942): 202; Jaroslav Stransky, "The Inter-Allied Conference on War Crimes and the Problem of Retribution," *New Commonwealth Quarterly* 7, No. 4 (1942): 250–57.

influence on the governments of Britain, the United States, and the Soviet Union remained limited, but unofficial bodies and scholars began to take up the issue. The first was the International Commission for Penal Reconstruction and Development, which was composed of prominent jurists from Britain and occupied countries. The studies of this body, as well as those of the London International Assembly, were later to be of great value to the United Nations War Crimes Commission.[91]

Aware of the fact that neither the Polish nor the Czechoslovak government could be mollified, Churchill and Roosevelt discussed the issue of war crimes in the summer of 1942. They agreed in principle to set up an international commission to investigate alleged atrocities and to report to the Allies. The British Cabinet itself created a committee on War Crimes, which was headed by the Lord Chancellor, Lord Simon. Under pressure from the governments-in-exile, this committee proposed the creation of a United Nations Commission for the Investigation of War Crimes. After more than a year of additional negotiations, which were complicated by the question of the Soviet Union's role, the commission, renamed the United Nations War Crimes Commission, was officially established in October 1943. Fourteen Allied nations, but not the Soviet Union, participated in the commission. Its mandate was to collect and assess all available evidence with a view to establishing the responsibility of the those individuals guilty of war crimes and thereby to limit the number of people to be tried at the end of the war. But as no precise terms were ever defined, the commission felt free to deliberate on further aspects of the war crimes issue.[92] In November 1943, the foreign ministers of the Big Three issued the so-called Moscow Declaration on atrocities, which specified that those responsible for war crimes would be tried in the countries where these crimes had been committed, while criminals whose offenses had no particular geographical location were to be punished by joint decision of the Allies. This vague formula concealed disagreements among the Big Three about whether aggressive war was to be regarded as a war crime.[93] The declaration represented an attempt to decide nothing while appearing resolute in prosecution of the war.

Discussions among the experts continued as well. The United Nations War Crimes Commission took its mandate seriously. It also tried to deal with matters outside its mandate. The two leading figures were the British and the American delegates, Sir Cecil Hurst and Herbert C. Pell. They

91 United Nations War Crimes Commission, *History*, 94–104.
92 Kochavi, *Prelude*, 27–62; United Nations War Crimes Commission, *History*, 118–34.
93 "Moscow Conference," BIN 20 (1943): 997; United Nations War Crimes Commission, *History*, 107–8; cf. Ginsburgs, *Moscow's Road*, 51–52; Kochavi, *Prelude*, 97–100.

established the principle that the commission was the only official Allied body on questions of war crimes. Lengthy discussions took place, particularly about whether aggressive war should be considered a war crime. The delegates from Czechoslovakia, Australia, China, New Zealand, Poland, and Yugoslavia all argued that it should. The British and American delegates, however, preferred to leave the issue undecided, and their position prevailed.[94]

Discussions also focused on the question whether summary trials and punishment of war criminals might be preferable to formal tribunals. Churchill and Stalin both favored summary trials, although they differed over details of procedure and the numbers of persons who should be treated in this way. The Americans were divided. Secretary of the Treasury Henry Morgenthau was sympathetic to the idea of summary trials, while Secretary of War Henry Stimson opposed it. After the American press began to argue that summary trials would encourage the Germans to fight to the bitter end, the idea was dropped, not least because Stalin – probably for considerations of propaganda – suddenly reversed himself in favor of tribunals for the major war criminals.[95] The views of the experts certainly also played a role, for most opposed summary trials.[96] In April 1945, Churchill also gave up the idea and agreed to formal tribunals for the major war criminals.

Further discussions took place about crimes that had not traditionally been defined as war crimes, but that the new character of warfare had made urgent. Probably with the encouragement of the World Jewish Congress, although without the support of the American government, Pell took up this issue in the War Crimes Commission, where a majority refused to consider it. Only toward the end of the war did the British, French, and American governments agree to an expanded definition of war crimes.[97]

At a conference in London in August 1945, delegates from Britain, France, the Soviet Union, and the United States finally agreed to both the terms of the indictments and the charter of the international tribunal that was to try the major war criminals. This agreement provided that indictments should comprehend crimes against peace, war crimes proper, and

---

94 Ibid., 92–100.
95 Bradley F. Smith, *The American Road to Nuremberg: The Documentary Record, 1944–1945* (Stanford, 1982), 27–33; Kochavi, *Prelude,* 63–91; Overy, *Interrogations,* 8–10.
96 Glueck, "Punishing War Criminals," 708; Glueck, *War Criminals,* 78; P. F. Gault, "Prosecution of War Criminals," JCLC 36 (1945): 180–81; [Marcel de Baer], "The Treatment of War Crimes and Crimes Incidental to the War," BIN 22 (1945): 202; Hyde, "Punishment of War Criminals," 39–44. Charles Warren and George A. Finch argued in favor of summary executions, in order to save the purity of law. See their comments on Hyde, PASIL 37 (1943): 51–53, 56–58.
97 Kochavi, *Prelude,* 143–71.

crimes against humanity.[98] These three categories included most of the crimes that legal scholars and other observers had categorized as punishable during the war; and they have since been subsumed broadly under the heading of war crimes.[99] At the same time the indictments were extended to German economic and financial leaders.[100]

The trial of the major war criminals was held in Nuremberg between November 1945 and September 1946. It was followed by further trials in courts of the occupying powers. Following the principles of the Moscow Declaration, additional trials were held in the liberated countries. Nuremberg and its East-Asian counterpart in Tokyo have since become the point of departure for the development of international penal law. The end of the Cold War and the atrocities committed in the wars in Yugoslavia and Rwanda have brought the first international trials for war crimes since then. In 1998, the Charter of Rome created the International Criminal Court that many commentators had favored during the Second World War.[101]

Many legal historians have focused on Nuremberg as the turning point, because it had finally become possible to judge violations of the laws of war on the international level.[102] I believe, however, that the impact of what has been called the Age of Total War has been underestimated. The American Civil War and the Franco-German War had brought about the first code for the punishment of war crimes and the first proposal for an international criminal court. The ensuing debates, most notably at the Hague Conferences, brought meager results, but the issue of punishing war crimes remained on the agenda. The First World War, which some regard as the first total war,[103] compelled politicians and legal experts to engage in serious public discussion, and it culminated in at least a gesture toward the idea

---

98 Ibid., 213–30; Simons, "Jurisdictional Bases," 41–45; Dinstein and Tabory, *War Crimes*, 382–91.

99 Gerhard Hoffmann, *Strafrechtliche Verantwortung im Völkerrecht: Zum gegenwärtigen Stand des völkerrechtlichen Strafrechts* (Frankfurt am Main, 1962), 61–66; Geuenich, Erweiterung des Begriffs des Kriegsverbrechens, 5–9; Simpson, "War Crimes," 3.

100 Overy, *Interrogations*, 38–41.

101 Jean-Paul Bazelaire and Thierry Cretin, *La justice pénale internationale* (Paris, 2000), 51–114; Madeleine Vouilloz, "La Cour pénale internationale," *Aktuelle Juristische Praxis* 9 (2000): 821–38; Bronwyn Worswick, "Enforcement of International Humanitarian Law," *Australian Defence Force Journal* 137 (1999): 47–55.

102 Reinhard Merkel, "Das Recht des Nürnberger Prozesses: Gültiges, Fragwürdiges, Überholtes," in Nürnberger Menschenrechtszentrum, ed., *Von Nürnberg nach Den Haag: Menschenrechtsverbrechen vor Gericht. Zur Aktualität des Nürnberger Prozesses* (Hamburg, 1996), 68–92; Roger S. Clark, "Nuremberg and Tokyo in Contemporary Perspective," in McCormack and Simpson, *Law of War Crimes*, 171–187; Bazelaire and Cretain, *Justice pénale internationale*, 5–27.

103 Roger Chickering, "World War I and the Theory of Total War: Reflections on the British and German Cases 1914–1915," in Roger Chickering and Stig Förster, eds., *Great War, Total War: Combat and Mobilization on the Western Front, 1914–1918* (Cambridge, 2000), 35; Hans Herzfeld, *Der Erste Weltkrieg* (Nördlingen, 1968), 184; Segesser, *Empire*, 522–30.

of bringing war criminals to justice, although the results did not match the high expectations. Discussion of the issues continued in the interwar period. During the Second World War, it became clear to legal scholars and leading sectors of public opinion that war crimes had to be punished: the war had seen atrocities committed against both civilians and military personnel on an unprecedented scale.[104] Popular calls for retribution and justice were now amplified to the point that political leaders, many of whom had been reluctant to accept the principle during the Second World War, agreed that war criminals would have to be punished. Virtually up to the end of the war, however, it was not clear whether retribution would take the form of summary execution or trials by way of organized justice. Total retribution in the form of a summary execution of up to 50,000 men could not be put into practice. The call for a judicial trial of war criminals, which had become louder and louder since the wars of the mid-nineteenth century, led to a limitation of how total retribution could be enforced because most legal experts involved demanded that justice be done, but only through the channels of an organized judicial trial.

104 Peter Calvocoressi, Guy Wint, and John Pritchard, *Total War: The Causes and Courses of the Second World War*, 2 vols. (London, 1989).

20

Total War

Some Concluding Reflections

MICHAEL HOWARD

The concept of "total war" we owe to Karl von Clausewitz, although he never used that word. The word he used was "absolute."[1] For him it was a philosophical rather than a military expression, and he coined it to clarify a problem arising out of his own experience. Writing as he did in the 1820s, he wondered why the Napoleonic campaigns that had occupied his military career between 1806 and 1815 – swift, brutal, decisive – had differed so greatly from the "cabinet wars" of the eighteenth century on whose lessons he had been brought up. What had changed? Logically, all wars should be "absolute": there was no reason in the abstract why they should end short of the complete overthrow of one side or the other. In practice, they seldom or never were; at least, not within the rather narrow slice of European history that he took as his database. For him the problem was, not why and when did wars become "absolute" or "total," but why and when did they not? It was in his search for an answer that he coined the two ideas with which his name is most generally associated: that of "friction," which distinguished war in practice from "war on paper," and that of war as "political intercourse with the addition of other means."[2] The first imposed the internal, the second the external constraints that determined the nature of war in the real world.

This essay touches upon topics and questions addressed in the present volume and its four predecessors: Stig Förster and Jörg Nagler, eds., *On the Road to Total War: The American Civil War and the German Wars of Unification, 1861–1871* (Cambridge and Washington, DC, 1997); Manfred F. Boemeke, Roger Chickering, and Stig Förster, eds., *Anticipating Total War: The German and American Experiences, 1871–1914* (Cambridge and Washington, DC, 1999); Roger Chickering and Stig Förster, eds., *Great War, Total War: Combat and Mobilization on the Western Front, 1914–1918* (Cambridge and Washington, DC, 2000); and Roger Chickering and Stig Förster, eds., *The Shadows of Total War: Europe, East Asia, and the United States, 1919–1939* (Cambridge and Washington, DC, 2003).

1 Carl von Clausewitz, *On War* (Princeton, NJ, 1976), p. 579.
2 Ibid., pp. 119, 87.

Clausewitz wrote at a time when the European "system of states" was at its zenith. Older nonstate actors, in particular the Roman Catholic Church and the Holy Roman Empire, had lost their authority if not disappeared altogether. New ones, the transnational political movements launched by the French Revolution, were only beginning to make an appearance. Governments still held a monopoly of armed force within their territory and of legitimacy in their mutual relations. But with the French Revolution a new and disturbing element had made its appearance – "the People" – a force distinct from government and not necessarily under its control. For Clausewitz, as for all soldiers of his generation, "the People" was a force of ambiguous value. Without the support of the French people, Napoleon could never have engendered the military power to conquer Europe; but as the revolutionary wars had shown, unless popular passions were controlled by governments, there could be neither domestic peace nor international order. Their force had been successfully restrained after 1815, but once they had been released there could be no guarantee that it could not be unleashed again, with unforeseeable consequences. It was largely this fear of "the People" that kept the peace among the European Powers for half a century after 1815, and it was largely the democratization of European states thereafter, and the democratic nature of the United States of America, that transformed the nature of war in the second half of the century.

One of the most effective constraints on war in eighteenth-century Europe had been the aristocratic monopoly of "bearing arms." This had the effect not only of ensuring that war as an institution never died out so long as the continent was governed by a ruling class that regarded fighting as its primary function, but also of keeping it within the limits of a transnational game whose boundaries were well known and generally respected. Between armies, or at least between their officer-classes, the conduct of war was limited by carefully crafted considerations of "honor," which had not entirely disappeared even in the First World War. Those limits, it must be said, were concerned with the way the military treated one another rather than their behavior toward any civilians who were unfortunate enough to get in their way. It is significant that the first formal efforts to control war, the Geneva Convention of 1864 and the Hague Conventions of 1899 and 1907, were primarily concerned with the welfare of the military themselves; their treatment as wounded or prisoners of war, and the nature of the weapons with which they fought one another. Noncombatants who found themselves caught up in military activities had to take their chances, and if they were suspected of participating in them, those chances were slim. This applied particularly to the wars of colonization or conquest fought against non-European peoples in both hemispheres, where non-European peoples fought total wars, *faute de mieux*, for their survival, and the occupying armies – not excepting those of the United States in dealing with their own native "Indians" – responded accordingly.

Clausewitz himself lived to see the advent of "The People in Arms" in the form, not only of the French *levée en masse* and Carnot's revolutionary armies, but of European reaction to French occupation, not least in his own Prussia. He wrote mainly of its operational significance – the differing virtues of volunteer as against regular armies, and the effectiveness of guerrilla warfare. But he recognized also that the impact of popular participation on the conduct of war was not just operational but basic. "The passions of the people," as he termed it, was one of the three elements, together with military expertise and political control, that constituted war.[3]

For those "passions" made war a very serious matter indeed. As Tolstoy's Prince Andrew put it on the eve of the battle of Borodino in *War and Peace*: "They talk to us of the rules of war, of chivalry and flags of truce, of mercy to the unfortunate, and so on. It's all rubbish. . . . If there was none of this magnanimity in war, we should go to war only when it was worth going to certain death, as now. . . . War is not courtesy, but the most horrible thing in life; and we ought to understand that, and not play at war. We ought to accept this terrible necessity sternly and seriously."[4]

The people, in short, as distinct from the aristocracy, could be mobilized and persuaded to fight only over matters of life and death; the survival of their own communities, the preservation or creation of their "nations." War indeed made them aware of themselves as nations, distinct from and potentially hostile to other nations. The American Civil War and the Franco-Prussian War of 1870 both involved the birth of a Nation, though that of the Confederacy was aborted and that of the German Empire was the result rather than the cause of the war, a device by Bismarck to muzzle the liberal nationalism that threatened the stability of Europe.[5]

Both victories created national myths that were to cement the social and political cohesion of the two new industrial powers and created in each a populist militarism that was to mold their political cultures. Each began as a "limited" conflict fought between uniformed armed forces under commanders trained in the conservative school of Jomini. They were to spiral down toward savage duels of revenge between peoples – the "escalation" of

---

3 Ibid., p. 89.
4 Leo Tolstoy, *War and Peace*, Book X, Chap. XXV.
5 See the essays collected in Stig Förster and Jörg Nagler, eds., *On the Road to Total War: The American Civil War and the German Wars of Unification, 1861–1871* (Cambridge and Washington, DC, 1997).

which Clausewitz had warned. Helmut von Moltke was rightly praised after 1870 for his brilliant conduct of a "limited" war that was believed to be decisive and taken as the model for all future *Kriegsfuhrung*. But he himself was more conscious of how indecisive that war had been, and was concerned rather with the lessons to be learned from the messy "People's War" in France that spluttered on during the four months that followed the Battle of Sedan rather than with the brisk four-week campaign that preceded it. It was the former, he feared, that would provide the pattern for future war in Europe. As he warned in his last great speech to the Reichstag in May 1890, "The era of Cabinet Wars lies behind us. We now have to face that of the *Volkskrieg*, and one with such unforeseeable consequences that any reasonable government will find it very hard to undertake. Gentlemen, it may be a seven years war, it may be a thirty years war – and woe to him who sets Europe on fire, who first throws the match into the powder keg!"[6]

If the growth of democracy created a tendency to total war, the growth of industry created an increasing capacity for it. Industrialization made things possible that would have been inconceivable to Clausewitz and his contemporaries. First, railroads and the telegraph enabled states to mobilize, transport, and maintain in the field armies numbering millions. The distinction between army and "people" disappeared: the army itself became quite literally "the Nation in Arms," and the longer the war lasted the more this became the case.

And wars were now likely to last a long time. As Jean de Bloch had foreseen at the end of the nineteenth century,[7] the development of rifled firearms, especially artillery firing high-explosive ammunition, with the huge range at which they could now be used, made battles both prolonged and indecisive; and the longer they lasted, the greater was the strain placed on society as a whole. The Russo-Japanese war of 1904–5 proved that this did not make war "impossible," as de Bloch's disciples had hoped, but it made it an ordeal that would test, perhaps to destruction, a nation's "fitness to survive" and its claim to the status of a Great Power in the coming century. Japan clearly passed that test, as was observed with some apprehension, especially in the United States.

Thus, traditional "operational strategy," the destruction of enemy armies on the battlefield (*Vernichtungsstrategie*), was gradually eclipsed by *Ermattungsstrategie*, the erosion of the enemy's capacity to keep his army in the field at all. Clausewitz had emphasized the importance of discerning the

---

6 *Der Weltkrieg 1914–1918, Kriegsrustung und Kriegswirtschaft Vol 1 Anlage* (Berlin, 1930), p. 43.
7 *The Future of War* (London, 1898). (English abstract by W. T. Stead of Russian original edition.)

Schwerpunkt, the "center of gravity" against which all military effort should be directed; but he assumed, while admitting that there might be alternatives, that this would normally be the enemy army.[8] But in a war between Peoples in Arms the ultimate objective was the morale of the enemy people; and such a conflict would be as near a total war as one was likely to get.

It took some time for this to sink in. It should have been evident after the American Civil War that Ulysses S. Grant, with the campaign of deliberate attrition that he fought in 1864–65, should be the model commander for the future, not Stonewall Jackson or Robert E. Lee with their tactically brilliant but operationally sterile victories. But it was the campaigns of the latter that the British Army studied when it began to prepare for continental warfare at the beginning of the twentieth century. The French still studied the campaigns of Napoleon, those miracles of operational strategy, and the Germans the lightning victories of von Moltke in 1866 and the summer of 1870. The possibility of a prolonged war was not ignored by the German General Staff – von Schlieffen had famously warned against campaigns costing billions of marks and involving millions of men – but it was one so alarming that in 1914 they made no effort to prepare for it but instead relied on a successful *Vernichtungsstrategie*, based on the aspirations if not the plans of von Schlieffen himself, to avoid it. They failed. The following year both they and their adversaries fell back on a strategy of attrition by land, sea, and ultimately air; directed not against the enemy armed forces but the morale of the enemy people: total war in intention, if not yet in fact or in name.

In land warfare, it was the Chief of the German General Staff, Erich von Falkenhayn, who, with his Verdun campaign of 1916, first saw that the battlefield could be used quite deliberately as a tool to demoralize rather than to disarm the enemy; to destroy the morale of their people through the losses inflicted on their armies. Themselves unable to devise any operational means to solve the deadlock on the western front, the Allies followed suit, counting such success as they achieved on the Somme and in Flanders in terms of the casualties they inflicted rather than any territory they gained. Simultaneously at sea, Germany escalated the mutual blockade, in which the British had taken the initiative and retained the upper hand, by abandoning the traditional constraints of cruiser warfare that crippled their capacity to use the only weapon that gave them an advantage – the submarine. By 1916, both sides had torn down the barriers that had preserved the rights of neutrals and noncombatants and openly accepted the ruin and starvation of

8 Clausewitz, *On War*, p. 595.

enemy civilians as a necessary concomitant of victory. As for the air, developing technology enabled aircraft to destroy targets at ever deeper distances behind the battlefield; but their inaccuracy inevitably resulted in "collateral damage" that rapidly became accepted as a legitimate contribution to the demoralization of the enemy. The result was a mutual demonization that was taken to justify any measures of retaliation, however extreme.

By the end of World War I, the internal and external constraints on total war had thus been critically weakened. Internally, deadlock on the battlefield had forced the belligerents to broaden their objectives to include the whole social and economic structure that supported the enemy armed forces. Although aircraft could still inflict only marginal damage against "strategic" targets, their performance was encouraging enough for their protagonists to foresee the day when they would be the decisive weapon and render surface warfare unnecessary. Insofar as war had become "total," it was the result of naval warfare – mutual blockade. Even so, as a result of effective countermeasures on both sides, it took longer to take effect than anyone had ever expected. As Adam Smith had observed a century earlier, "there is a great deal of ruin in a Nation."

More important was the erosion of external constraints, the political objectives of the belligerents. Initially, at least, these were quite moderate. The nations of Europe did not go to war in 1914 to destroy one another's existence as states, much less annihilate their populations. Their immediate objectives were defensive. Even where their ultimate aims were more ambitious, as were those of Imperial Germany, they were still limited, like those in previous European wars, to changing the balance of power within a stable system of states. But the war carried within it its own dynamic. Each side came to see in the other an "evil" to be destroyed. The rulers of Germany had their own agendas of expansion, but the German people as a whole believed themselves to be heroes defending a unique cultural heritage against the devious, cunning, and decadent foes made familiar to them through Wagnerian myth. Their adversaries, especially the British, believed they were fighting to destroy a brutal and militaristic adversary who had torn up the laws of nations and could be tamed only by a "regime change." As for the United States, its objectives – or rather, those of President Wilson – were even more extreme. America did not go to war, as had its associates (whom Wilson refused to recognize as "allies") to tame German ambitions and redraw the European balance of power, but to reshape the entire world order and make it "safe for democracy." This was as "total" an objective as had yet appeared in modern warfare, and one that could be achieved only by the complete overthrow of its enemies.

External political constraints on the conduct of the war were thus diminishing as fast as internal ones, but limits still remained. These were largely cultural: a combination of the transnational codes of honor among the military themselves inherited from a feudal past; the ecumenical traditions of the Christian churches; and the concern for individual and universal rights established by the Enlightenment. The Geneva and Hague Conventions were still observed to a remarkable degree. The Red Cross Society was generally treated with respect and given a *droit de regarde* over the treatment of prisoners of war. When such constraints ceased to apply, as happened on the eastern front all too often, it was more often through force of circumstances and inefficiency than deliberate breach. But again, these limitations still applied mainly to the armed forces. The way in which the Germans treated civilians in the territories they overran was a different matter, whether in Belgium or the *Ostland*, the Baltic provinces of the Russian Empire, where a sense of racial superiority powerfully affected their attitude and pointed the way to an even grimmer future. Yet it could still be said that in the *Ostland* the German occupiers behaved no worse than had the British in many parts of their Empire, not to mention the Americans in cleansing their continent from its indigenous inhabitants. In colonial conquest, total measures to subjugate if not exterminate the natives had long been taken for granted by European democracies.

After 1918, military specialists sought a philosopher's stone that might bring them victory without attrition. One was strategic air bombardment, whose exponents, especially Giulio Douhet,[9] maintained that the rapid demoralization of the civilian population through air attack, by making attrition unnecessary, would be a humane form of "total war." Another was the combination of tanks, mobile infantry, and tactical airpower that became known as *Blitzkrieg*. Both disappointed their protagonists. Air defenses and civilian morale proved tougher than expected. *Blitzkrieg* certainly made possible the conquest of an unprepared Western Europe and produced total victory with limited means, but it proved ineffective against adversaries who, like the Russians, could trade time for space, or who, like the British, still commanded the seas. More far sighted was the nightmare vision of Erich Ludendorff. For him, "total war" was a description, not of a particular kind of war but of a permanent and inevitable relationship between the great powers of the world in which peace provided only brief intervals for recuperation and all the activities of the state were directed under military control either to fighting or preparing for war.

9 Giulio Douhet, *The Command of the Air* (New York, 1942).

We might dismiss Ludendorff's vision of total war, like Clausewitz's concept of absolute war, as an unachievable abstract model, if it had not been put into practice by Josef Stalin. The Soviet Union was in a state of near-total mobilization from the beginning of the first Five-Year Plan in 1927. But for that it might well have been defeated in the Second World War. No other state could match it. Great Britain had made far-reaching plans for total mobilization on paper, and thanks to the victory of the Royal Air Force in 1940 and the Royal Navy's command of the seas was granted a breathing space to put them into effect. The United States had even more time, but, in any case, the enormous strength of its economy (and the entrepreneurial skills of its people) made total mobilization unnecessary. As for the Germans, total mobilization had always been part of the Nazi ideology but had not been implemented before war broke out – partly because Hitler was reluctant to subject the German population to the hardships from which they had only recently escaped, partly because the success of his operational strategy in the early years of the war made it seem unnecessary, and partly because of the administrative inefficiency of his regime. Only by 1943 did it become clear that the operational skills of the German Army could provide no shortcut to victory, and that only the *Totalkrieg* that Goebbels demanded of the German people in his Sportpalast speech of February 18, 1943, would enable them to prevail in the global conflict into which they had been precipitated.

Total victory, in short, demanded total mobilization, in the Second World War as in the First. But skillful operational strategy could secure the kind of initial advantages that the Germans gained in both wars and the Japanese in the Second. Indeed, if Hitler had limited his objectives to the unfinished business of the First World War and established a peaceful German hegemony over Western Europe, it is at least arguable that the Second could have been kept limited to that theater and the British brought to accept defeat. But the total nature of his war aims, the establishment of a *Reich* dominating Euroasia governed by a master-race, not to mention the ruthless methods he used to achieve it, meant that the war against his principal adversary, the Soviet Union, was "total" from the very beginning: a struggle for mutual annihilation, restrained by none of the cultural limitations that still applied in the European theaters, limited only by the physical capacity of the occupation forces to destroy property and massacre people.

As for the United States, it was not in its nature to fight anything less than total war. Its wars were seen not as a continuation of policy by other means, but as crusades against evil adversaries who had to be destroyed so that a new world might arise on their ashes. The Second World War was fought not against the Germans, from whom so many Americans were descended, but against *Nazis* who could be easily demonized with very little distortion of the truth. Their other adversaries, the Japanese, could be even more easily dehumanized, and the campaigns in the Pacific took on all the characteristics of a race war. In any case, it was no more possible for the United States to fight a limited war than it would be for an elephant. Everything it did was on a gigantic scale. Once it acquired the capacity to destroy German and Japanese cities, whether by conventional or, ultimately, nuclear means, it was almost inconceivable that the United States would not do so. Whatever the military necessity or ethical justification for using the first nuclear weapons, American public opinion would have found it hard to understand or forgive its government if it had not. The Americans were not only prepared, in their own argot, "to do whatever it takes" to overthrow their enemies, but were quite capable of doing it. America's wars may not have been total so far as the American people were concerned, but they were for its enemies.

But for the past half century the Americans, like the rest of the world, have lived under the shadow, if not of total war, then of total destruction. It may be doubted whether "war" is the correct word to describe either the threat of mutual annihilation that prevailed during the "Cold War" or more recent terrorist threats perhaps better regarded as monstrous crimes. Certainly neither falls into the same category as the total wars of attrition waged by mobilized peoples in the first half of the twentieth century, or even the "wars of liberation" (again, total on the one side, limited on the other) by colonial peoples against European empires in the second. In both the Cold War and the War against Terror, popular participation has been minimal. "The people" have been hostages rather than participants in conflicts conducted by small expert elites, planning and acting in profoundest secrecy.

Globalization has eroded if not destroyed the Grotian "system of states" that provided the framework for Clausewitzian concepts of strategy. It is a moot question, whether these conflicts can be described and analyzed within the categories used in this work. Certainly it would require another volume to do so.

Index

Abyssinia, 21–22, 64. *See also* Ethiopia
Africa, 60
agriculture
    productivity, Great Britain, 227
    Soviet women, 236
Air Corps Tactical School, 278
Air Policy Committee, 279
airpower, 9, 12, 381
    Great Britain and United States, 281,
        283. *See also* Arnold, Hap; Hansell,
        Hayward
    Lord Tedder, 277
    Ludendorff and total war, 194
    national efficiency, 285, 289,
        293
Aliger, Margarita's "Zoya," 242
allied shipbuilding, 78
Aly, Götz, 66
American military personnel, 215
Andrews, Frank, 286
anti-sedition Decree
    (*Kriegssondertrafrechtsverordnung*),
        92–93
anti-Semitism. *See* Jews
Arbeitsdienst der weiblichen Jugend
    (Women's Labor Service, WLA),
        226, 227
Armenian Massacre, 20, 61–62, 359.
    See also Council of Four; *Forty Days
    of Musa Dagh*
Armstrong, John, 266
Army Air Force, 110

Arnold, Hap, 121, 284, 292
(*S.S.*) *Athenia*, 37, 74
Atlantic, Battle of the, 72, 73
atomic bomb, 29, 51, 132, 304, 310
Auschwitz, 66
Auxiliary Territorial Service, 220,
    229

Baedeker raids, 43
balance of terror, 312
Baltic states, 37
Barbarossa Decree, 329, 330
Barbarossa (operation), 46, 65, 90,
    98–99
Barro's model of government spending,
    172
Bartov, Omer, 46, 327
Beck, Ludwig, 89
Beightler, Robert, 112
Benes, Vaclav, 366
Bernstein, Michael Andre, 5
Bielenberg, Christabel, 215
Bierly, James Leslie, 361
Bismarck, sinking of, 74
Black Tuesday, 247
Blackbourn, David, 62
Blamey, Thomas, 48
Blitzkrieg, 89–90, 97, 381
Bloch, Jean de, 378
Blomberg, Werner von, 92
Bochkareva, Mariya, 233
Bomber Command, 43, 287, 290–291

CPSIA information can be obtained at www.ICGtesting.com
Printed in the USA
LVOW06s0130220813

348936LV00002B/100/P